ESSAYS

THE WHITNEY PAPERS

literaru Essays=brief and long

by

Charles E Miller

Note for Librarians: A cataloguing record for this book is available from Library
and Archives Canada at www.collectionscanada.ca/amicus/index-e.html

Printed in Victoria, BC, Canada.

ISBN: 978-1-4269-2107-0 (sc)

*Our mission is to efficiently provide the world's finest, most comprehensive book publishing
service, enabling every author to experience success. To find out how to publish your book, your
way, and have it available worldwide, visit us online at www.trafford.com*

Trafford rev. 10/12/2009

 www.trafford.com

North America & international
toll-free: 1 888 232 4444 (USA & Canada)
phone: 250 383 6864 ♦ fax: 812 355 4082

CONTENTS

BRIEF DISCOURSES

EDITORIALS

GODDESS, WITCH OR MORTAL?

Thomas Hardy's Eustacia

When villager and furze-cutter Timothy Fairway clasps Susan Nonsuch and whirls her round among the remaining embers of their Rainbarrow pyre, like ancestral particpants in ancient *"Drudical rites and Saxon ceremonies,"* their oblations of shrill cries and men's laughter work a kind of witchery in the night. With this and other sensous tributes to the dark and gloomy Egdon Heath, as the November celebration of Guy Fawkes Day, the action of Hardy's novel opens in the mysterious and foreboding mood of tragedy.

In **The Return of the Native** he describes the voluptuous, strong-willed Eustacia Vye as a goddess of fate and myth, "the raw material of divinity," she who lives in the heath's vast wilderness, frustrated and anguished. Her hope of escape is her Rubicon to destiny, a flight from oblivion into the ideal dream world of Paris through her improvident marriage, later on, to diamond merchant Clym Yeobright from the Parisian salons. She says,

> *"We are together now, and sit is unknown how long we shall be so; the unknown always fills my mind withs terrible possibilities,* even *when I may reasonably expect to be cheerful."*

Her divinity does not come from supernatural power, although village folk--Susan and her children, Christian Cantle and Sam suspect her of possessing occultic powers. She exhibits the aloof aspect of a goddess, but that is her basic alienation from life, except for the village dances. Her intimate capacity to suffer belongs to human-like gods of antiquity.

Divinity that is pagan, obsessive, transmutable touches, the intelligence and emotions of the beautiful Eustacia, *"who should have done well with little preparation,"* Hardy writes.

> *"She had the passions and instincts which make a model goddess, that is, those which make not quite a model woman...."*

She had pagan eyes, full of *"nocturnal mysteres,"* Hardy speculates. Perhaps her divinity was *"the gift of heaven,"* he writes.

Eustacia Vye hates her exile. she is the daughter of a village bandmaster who drank himself to death, she whose maiden name is not Vye, she who has come to live at Blooms-End on the heath with her ship's-captain grandfather Vye, feeling *"like one vanished; but here she was forced to abide."* Mrs. Yeobright disdains her parentage, calls her a seductress, and reinforces sEustacia's cross and shame of adself-indulgence.

As a would-be goddess she yearns for a smotal, any mortal, to love, lusting for love more than for the man.

> *"To be loved to madness--such was her great desire.*
> *Love was to her the one cordial which could drive*
> *away the eating loneliness of her days. And she*
> *seemed to long for the abstraction called passionate*
> *love more than for any particular lover."*

Living in her world of idealized love, wanting, phantasizing yet struggling with the immediately real in Blooms-End and Egdon Heath, Eustacia embodies attributes of extremes. She is a tormented soul who can drown in the music and movement of village dances. She is a woman of enigmatic loyalties, first to Wildeve and then Clym, hiding masochism beneath passionate love. She is loyal first to Damon and then to Clym. She exhibits willful, persistent, changeable ways that are seldom if ever moderated by recriminations of wrong or self-doubt. She turns her sensual side outward to the world while nursing in her intuitive nature what she wants from Wildeve--escape. *"The spell that she had thrown over him in the moonlight dance made it impossible for a man having no strong puritanic force within him to keep away altogether."* Thus the idealizations of a goddess are resident within her.

Eustacia appears tragic to some eyes because of her unresolved wilol to flee the heath. Her rebellious spirit finds nourishment from an origin of purposes on the heath. Its wild imprisonment ignites hatred in her heart. Her anguish is in wanting release, a yearning without mitigation.

> *But do I desire unreasonably much in wanting what*
> *is called life--music, poetry, passion, war and all the*
> *beating and pulsing that is going on in the great*
> *arteries of the world? That was the shape of my*
> *youthful dream; but I did not get it."*

This was her outcry before she ever left Budmouth for Blooms-End. She finds Clym's quality of mind to be happiness and mediocrity. And Mrs. Yeobright only adds to her unhappiness, calling her *"voluptuous,"* an idle woman whose son, by marrying her, marries *"badly."* Apparently a goddess can suffer mortal pangs.

Her physical beauty is of divinely carved marble; with Phaedra she shares jealousy, possessiveness and a will to die. Yet petty spite and veniality are foreign to Eustacia. There is a largeness to her scheming. She endures far more than she seeks to requite, yet she summons the spirit to challenge her mother in law. *"You injured me before my marriage, and you have now suspected me of secretly favoring another man for money."* Of course Venn has won back from Wildeve the money Mrs. Yeobright bequeathed to Thomasin and Clym. The fact remains, however, that the girl's actions in love and in her manipulation of circumstances to effect her purposes are not vengeful, nor are they tragic in any classical sense of the word. Instead, Eustace engenders pity simply because she, herself, experiences the cruelty of life and existence on the heath.

Nor is Eustacia a figure possessed of demons, evil designs and powers of occultic influence. Witchcraft in Blooms-End lies just uner the surface of village life. Any aberrant behavior is certain to arouuse suspicion shared in the dormant superstitions, fears and castigations of village volk. Eustacia is in actuality an outcast, her residence at Captain Vye's cottage giving her the only legitimatacy she knows. A beautiful woman alone in the wilderness creates awe in Christian, admiration in Charley, distrust in Susan and hatred in Mrs Yeobright. Under a full moon and seeing her for the last time, Wildeve is respectful; Clym is indifferent to her charms and sleeps away on the hearth when his mother comes knocking.

All these things being true, these manifest relationships, taken with Hardy's descriptions of the witcheries of Edgon Heath, hints of the occult cling to Eustacia. Susan Nonsuch blames her in her "propinquity" of bewitching her children and causing Johnny's illness; she fuels her signal fire the night she rendevous with Wildeve. Eustacia suffers when Susan stabs her with a needle--*"poor thing,"* says Christian, and she gives an unearthly howl at the very wedding of Thomasin and Wildeve. However, does Susan's drawisng blood and repeating the Lord's Prayer backward indict Eustacia justly? Love celebrated is quenched by hatred, revenge demonstrated. Not even the image of Eustacia, sandals, red ribbon shaped by Susan from beeswax, pierced with pins, cursed and melted in the hearth fire, can instruct Eustacia in unkindness. The villagers, with the instincts of Londoners, cast strange, querying eyes upon her, their hearts of condemnation expressed by Mrs. Yeobight when she says, *" Good girls don't get treated as witches even in Egdon."* The heath-dwellers have affixed Egdon 's dark brooding, stormy identity to their own vision of life. That dark vision forever hovers over the life of Eustacia Vye on Egdon Heath.

Dealing still with the potentially tragic, one may ask if witchcraft was anathema to divinity or to a tragic concept of justice. There is that of the occult in all three schema. It is Hardy's design that divinity and witchcraft be parabolic to the spirit of young Eustacia. He also raises the spectre of tragedy when he describes Egon Heath as character having unifying force and influence, a mysterious Hadesians power that contrives and loves even as it conceals, extinguishes and defeats.

> *"...The storm was its lover, and the wind the friend.*
> *Then it became the home of strange phantoms;*
> *and it was found to be the hitherto unrecognized*
> *original of those wild regions of obscurity which*
> *are vaguely felt to be compassing us about in midnight*
> *dreams of flight and disaster....It had a lonely face,*
> *suggesting tragical possiblities...civilization was its*
> *enemy."*

Hardy sees Eustacia's character as involved with the heath. At Rainbarrow, *"Never was harmony more perfect than that between the chaos of her mind and the chaos of the world without the heath."* There is in her the replication of Egdon's physical, natural attributes and in a mechanical sense, by her use of the telescope and hourglass, her vivid prescience of time and distance consumed by the heath. By indirection we can see in Eustacia the foreshadowing of tragic possibilities, a pitiable end that resonates with tragical self-sacrifice in the maw of witless baubbles of custom, the facades of show.

Eustacia lacks the moderate view, a compromise of mind that becalms if it does not deaden the soul, and she is therefore vulnerable before impersonal fate, her loneliness and Wildeve. Consequently she is less than a goddess, less than divine; she never fears but then she never rules over the Hades of her pain. Nor is she corrupted by a heath that does not breathe vulgarity. It carries no tragic import that she wants to be loved to madness and finds in Wildeve the obsessison that converts posession into union and they become one in death when they drown in the storm-flooded weir.

I

n their simultaneous deaths the tragic significance is not that they die in social exile, under social law, but that they are vicims of a blind and uncompassionate society, whether Blooms-End or London, that knows not or has forgotten the spirit of the law, the Beautitude of mercy. The reasonable metes of justice are no longer theirs, if they ever were, and the heath's wier represents the destructive power of death, termrinating a love bond that began before the wrong marriage of either. These consequences are not more dialectical possibilities but are concrete realities. Eustacia is suicidal, when, acused y Clem of the death of his mother, of having turned her away from their cottage in the heat of the day, wheeupon she returns to Captain Vye's house, Charley, handyman for the Captain and her long-time admirer, sees her no longer as a romantic vision but a helpless and despairing woman. He removes the old man's pistols from her sight while she pleads, *"Why should I not die if I wish...? I have made a bad bargain with life, and I am weary of it...weary. And now you have hindered my escape. O, why did you, Charley?"*

A. C. Bradley finds--in Shakespeare--that the agony of inner conflict and struggle is not the issuance of a tragic flaw of character, a **hamartia**, but is instead that external moral forces introduces within a character a single choice that wracks the soul and integrity of the sufferer. This construct by Bradley fits Eustacia's nature and circumstances. Her death is foretold early in the book; the gathering fury of her marriage situation demolishes human will and ruins all destinies but one: death. She shows that unique core of character, that adumbrage of thought, of passionate emotions and complexity of personality expected of a tragic heroine. She anticipates fate. She contemplates death. She internalizes loss. And she confronts fear.

Yet Hardy's description of and comments upon Eustacia diminish her as a prototypical heroine of tragedy simply because he depicts her as human in her passions and not obsessed by vengeance or retributive justice. She is possessed of true physical courage: *"Her extraordinary fixity, her conspicuous loneliness, her heedlessness of night, betokened among other things, an utter absence of fear.,* this *"maiden"* of the town of Budmouth. She is a compassionate young woman: *"She had loved him (Clym) partly because she had determined to love him, chiefly because she was in deperate need for loving somebody after wearying of Wildeve."*

She is character of immense determination: *"Once let a maiden admit the possibility of her being stricken wih love for someone at a certain hour and place, and the thing is as good as done."* Eustacia is a narcissist but her narcissism lacks that adamantine plea that justice must somehow be done in her behalf. Her emptiness is not legalistic, ; faith in lthe possivbilities of escape motivate her and enkindle dreams of self-fulfillment and love. She is the opportunist who seizes the opportune lover, first Wildeve and then Clym. Her weakness is that she allows the consequences of her **eros** to rule her circumstances, her destny, her will to love and ultimately her choice of death, the bitterest irony of all. Until that moment of her drowning in the wier, she heroically endures.

Lacking a nature steeled by thoughts of revenge, she cannot in her darkest moods act dreadfully. She could not kill Thomasin, though she is presumptuous enough to think Wildeve has rejected her rival. It is not anguish over her intitial loss of Wildeve that isolates her, for she considers him a *"superfluity"* in order to purge jealouy and indulge a sense of her basic sexual morality. Hardy writes that she *'lived too far from the world to feel the impact of public opinion."* He states that...

> *"as far as social elthics were concerned, Eustacia approached the savage state, though in emotion she was all the while an epicure. She had advanced to the secret recesses of sensuousness yet had hardly crossed the threshhold of conventionality."*

Her soul is unhappy instead of disfigured and distorted by inconsolable grief and by an implacable will for justice, parts of the tragic figure in literature.

It is not supportable by the text that Eustacia's rendevous with Wildeve should match fate against the author's desire to confirm a tragic view of her life. The Reddleman, disguised in camouflage of furze-brush, evesdrops on their tryst conversation only to hear her plead undying ardour in the absence of decisive action, as she holds up *"mischievously"* conditional protestations of love. This is certainly not the stuff of justice but of self-satisfacion. Adroit Diggory Venn sees through the mutual deception when, to protect his beloved Thomasin from the marriage scandal among villagers, he urges that Thomasin marry Wildeve. Or are the fates being kind to Eustacia?-- as Clym asks near the end.

Eustacia is confronted with two basic choices: escape among the livng or suicide. She has not the means for the first or the courage, momentarily, for the second. she has a third option, however: her rejection of Wildeve.

> *"What was the man worth whom a woman inferior to herself did not value? The sentiment which lurks more*

or less in all animate nature--that of not desiring the
undesired of others--was lively as a passion in the
supersubtle epicurean heart of Eustacia....For the first
time she felt she had stopped loving him...

And for her this was a "humiliating victory." She recovers, telling Wildeve, *"Let the past be forgotten. I don't believe in old superstition."* It's almost as if Hardy has said: There it is, epicurean and aloof and deceptive but not tragic, a goddess in all but will and vengeance.

Proving once more that she is vulnerable and has her weaknesses of defense, The Reddleman mortifies her by announcing, *"The woman that stands between Wildeve and Thomasin is yourself."* She thinks that *"to perceive his mediocrity now was to admit her owns great folly theretofore,"* and her *"dog in the manger attitude at first made her ashamed."* If Wildeve is *"inadequate"* she will confess it to no other. Shackles of adequate *husbanding,* of Wildeve's compassionate caring, if they ever existed, are broken here. And any terror or apprehension or disquietude ready to spring from nature of mankind or the gods or, indeed, from her own soul are at this moment immobilized. Hardy's Eustacia Vye does not possess the motivation of tragic character.

Certain scenes, actions, descriptions have endowed the young woman with a dignity that is all hers and that is uniquely Eustacia's and not of common, or folkish, quality, though she comes from Budmouth. That dignity, fastidiously epicurean though it is--why meet on the heath? why be jealous of Thomasin? why share villager taboos?-- has certain dimensions to it which suggest tragic conflict that is never resolved. She admires power and dignity in others; that's why Clym's occupation shocks her.

"To see him there, a poor afflicted man, earning money
by the sweat of his brow, had at first moved her to
tears; but to hear him sing and not at all rebel against
an occupation which, however, satisfactory to himself, was
degrading to her, as an educated lady-wife,
wounded her through."

It is ovious that to emulate dignity in strong men has cost her pain. Yet coordinate with this sense of dignity is her resilience that enables her to bend before the winds and storm like the wild chaparral of Edon Heath and not surrender her "divinity"-like pride. Nor is she capricious in so doing. Eustacia is not a foolish woman, regardless of her self-prceptions or then again perhaps because of them. She is impetuous to the point of brash action, yet is not conniving, a woman who is capable of designing larger strategies than petty village squabbles. She admires Napoleon Buonaparte. Her dignity has a sound basis in experience and in models.

Eustacia cannot give up her dream of escape to Paris, which Mrs. Yeobright quickens in her by announcing the return of her son Clym from the diamond salons of that great city. He will become the girl's pagan *modus operandi* of escape from the heath and Blooms-End. The mother will see her as her son's seductress and thereupon introduce a potent and violent hatred into the trials of Eustacia. In this triad relationship, Mrs. Yeobright, her son Clym and his wife is where the fire of tragedy blazes up, transmuting the emotions into wrath and masking dull logic and drear reason except for that fixity of purpose that rnergizes tragedy. Of all the words Eustacia speaks these come closest to suggesting the nature of the wrath of retribution: she is addressing Mrs. Yeobright, who has accused her of duplicity against Clym for money to a treacherous lover.

> *"Who can be worse than a wife who encourages a*
> *lover, and poisons her husband's mind against his*
> *relative? Yet that is now the character given to me. Will*
> *you now come and drag him out of my hands?"* **Mrs.**
> **Yeobright:** *"Dont rage at me, madam! It ill becomes your*
> *beauty, and I am not worth the injury you may do it on my*
> *account, I assure you. I am only a poor*
> *old woman who has lost a son."* **Eustacia:** *"If you*
> *had treated me honourably you would have had him still."*

There is deceit in Eustacia's voice; she is well aware of why she wanted to exploit Clym before his eyes went bad.

'Yet there it is,s the cup of hemlock that poison's the girl's hopes for the gay life in Paris. She is always an anomaly on Egdon Heath, a person of misplaced identity who dos not quail before village gossip or suspicions. The way of escape has closed in on her like a trail through the wildernes. Her hope is dashed that she coud reform Clym after their marriage; this is one of Hardy's critiques on the society of the day, on the marriage relationship that puts conformity first. Why ought she to find contentment as a schoolmaster's wife in Budmouth when her education and intelligence would command respect in Paris and certainly in Hardy's London? Hardy writes that she prayed *"like the unaffedtedly devout, when she desired to pray."* Her heroes are William the Conqueror, Stafford and Buonaparte. She belongs to herself, is the point, and she alone must determine who she is.

Eustacia possesses an inner power; she knows this from its effects upon others. Mrs. Yeobright's enmity, her vituperative excoriation of the girl only affirms this fact. Her power is a tactile, visible manifestation, articulated in glances and expressions and gestures. Hardy writes-- that when she, wanting deperately to meet and see Clym, takes on the disguise, prompted by Charley, of the Turkish Knight in the Mummer's Gala occasion, held by Mrs. Yeobright, chosing to show by masque *"the power of her face all lost, the charm of her emotions all disguised, the fascinations of her of her coquetry denies existence, nothing but a voice left in her;; she had a sense of the doom of Echo"* and desires to escape. Only a chilling sense of her own power impels her into marriage with Clym, thinking the closeness *"would give her power to persuade"* him to return to Paris with her. He admonishes her: *"There's reason for ghastliness, Eustacia; you have held my happiness in the hollow of your hand, and like a devil you have dashed it down!"*

And yet she acknowledges the limitations of her influence upon others. After Clym's rage against her subsides, since she, he believes, had shut the door against his

8

mother and precipitated Mrs. Yeobright's death, she breaks down. She shakes with sobs and sinks to her knees.

> *O, will you have done! O, you are too relentless--*
> *there's a limit to the cruelty of savages! I have*
> *held out long--but you crush me down. I beg for*
> *mercy--I cannot bear this any longer--it is inhuman*
> *to further with this."*

Even murder by her own hand would not deserve such a scourging. Death has appeared before; now murder is introduced that exposes the state of her suffering. But although she talks about murder it will remain fictive only. Her smouldering rebelliousness does not abate.

It's worth pausing to point out that the fundmental flaw in Eustacia's marriage to Clym is not in her double-minded wanting two men, although the inn-keeper feels jilted after their love-making! The flaw is located in Clym's solicitous and unspoken attachment to his mother. He has never matured as a man, dying like seed on rocky soil in his marrige, therefore Eustacia is unable to water love with an enduring affection. She become *"his mother's supplanter,"* perhaps jealous of a non-existent father like Oedipus. It is done, and this is Hardy's critique of the Victorianism of the time within whose mandates and constraints false Puritanism was unprepared for longevity in marriage though, as was frequently the case, it suffered to be so. Sensuality has no profound resources, only the Hussar parades, the interminable dances and the luxurious salons of the indulged and the spoiled. Naturally then, identifying with this way of life, Eustacia thinks Clym is using his furze-cutting to taunt her. Naturally, too, she will shake off her gloom.

> *"No one shall know my suffering," and I"ll shake it off!*
> *I'll be utterly merry, and ironically gay, and I'll laugh in*
> *derision! And I'll begin going to this dance on the*
> *green."*

Had the gods put her in such a position *"to make of her charms a curse rather than a blessing"* Or had society?

Eustacia plays at love, consequently one wonders if the scene at the well--as Captain Vye's broken bucket is hauled up, Eustacia burns her hands on the rope--is symbolic of her ineptitude, her unsuitability for a good marriage. Or, if the urn of the ancient bones she fishes from Rainbarrow Mound symbolizes death to the flesh in a prophetic augery of her suicide in the Weir. Then there's the tell-tale moth that flits through her window into the cadle flame to announce Wildeve's presence: these graphic metaphors give texture to Hardy's story and yet establish the exiled girl as no longer a goddess but the woman "to fight for, support, help, be maligned for"-- as befell Clym at their marriage. The entire framework of Hardy's novel, in fact, rests upon circumstantial choices, coincidental happenings, voiceless prophetic signs and...human error.

Eustacia, though stately and goddess-like in form and stereotyped as a *heath witch*, manifests again and again her humanness; nor is she exempt from error, especially when living amid *"the miserable inhabitants of Egdon,"* as Hardy dscribes them. She has eaten the bitter fruit of loving without reward or lasting satisfaction, of hating with the same result, of yielding to pain in tears syet oppossing it in defiance, of succumbing to terror of her own soul--she fears not the heath but the unknown emptiness of chimerical promises. There is in Eustacia a marked sense of justice that is offended, though she fears no reprisal from Wildeve. As for her thoughts--*Your mother will influence you too much; I shall not be judgfed fairly, it will get aflaoat that I an not a good girl, and the witch story will be added to make me blacker."* Her pragmatic mind stabilized her turbulent nature, even as her experiences fuel her rebellion, her mortal disquietude.

Rebellion, however, is not synonymous with irresponsibility. Clym, the other man morally, blames himself for Mrs. Yeobvright's death and Eustacia's suicide. He has killed two women, he said. *"Those thought to have lived lie dead; and here I am alive!...My great regret is that for what I have done no man or law can punish me."*-- though Diggory Venn would exonerate him. Clym presumed to have been redeemed by Eustacia's life, a Messianic notion. And she accepts her cross, though wrongly so. For turbulent, changeable, unpredictable as she is, she is always self-accountable for her moral actions while liberated in her physical pleasure with Wildeve, the pagan.

Eustacia is a more complex characrter than her obsessive drive for sex fulfillment reveals. She is a young woman of paradoxes in her thinking, intentions and schemes. And they cannot all be laid to fateful cicumstances. So improvising, self-sufficient, she goes to Damon to know what she should do before Clym's discharge of venon and casuistry against her over Mrs. Yeobright's death on the heath. Her husband blames himself. *"I committed the guilt; and may the whole burden be upon my head."* He is now aware that his mother had knocked at his cottage door while he slept. Eustacia says to Wildeve, that she sees she is the sinner, feels drawn into a cold despair and does not know what to do. The gods have deserted her. Yet she is capable of seeking advice from others, depending on others, to defend herself. Obviously she has not all divine wisdom. Indeed, she and Clym each blames himself for Mrs. Yeobright's death, first by the torrid heath then by snake bite. For her part, had Eustacia and Mrs. Yeobright not quarreled vehemently before the girls's marriage--a country wife beneath her son, a hussy, a seducer, a bad marriage partner?

The undemonstrative wife to Clym becomes the woman aghast at the spectral calamity she has unintentionally helped to create. Her innocence deflowered, their mutual alienation is complete. Self-blame tears at her thoughts. By suggestion she accepts the onus of murderess, what she might have done at the cottage replaces what she actually did and provides the substance for self-accusation and guilt. Clym, in his wrath, his desperate grief and oblivion to all but his mother's death assaults Eustacia. He has become as *"dreadful to her as the trial scene was was to Jusdas Iscariot. It brought before her eyes the spectre of a worn-out woman knocking at a door which he would not open; and she shrank from contemplating it."* She sees Wildeve out the back door, Clym is asleep on the hearth, and Mrs. Yeobright's knocking stops. Hardy's timing is once again crucial, producing the curse of coincidence and the start of Eustacia's final swing into a violent apogee of death's-head emotion.

Yet another example of her contradictory nature:

*"You may come again to Rainbarrow if you like,
    but you won't see me; and you may call, but I shall not
    listen; and you may tempt me, but I won't give myself to*   *you*
any more."*

But she does all those things, often and again. She hates the heath but adapts to its wilderness by making it the frequent site of her rendevous with Wildeve. She cavils at time and distorts distances, yet uses the tools of Captain Vye to remove these very impediments, the telescope and hourglass, *"though she wore a watch."* She possesses a goddess-like conceit that she can do what she will yet *"acquired a homely zest for doing what she can,"* thus denoting *"a mind that, though dissappointed, foreswears compromise."* These are the touchstones to Eustacia's inconsistent nature.

In a real sense, too, her dream impedes her flight. Wildeve says to her early in the narrative, *"What are picturesque ravines and mists to us who are nothing else? Why should we stay here? Will you go with me to America?"* The heath has imprisoned the wretched Eustacia, for whom it holds no romantic attractions. She cannot accept his proposal because the heath is *"my cross, my shame and will be my death!"* She prophesies her death on the heath; she will *"consider"* his offer. He lacks the glamour of a Budmouth Hussar; he is edcated but ill-bred; he has no "prospects" in America, relatives only. On Egdon he is her escape, her unmaterialized future, wife of an innkeeper. Only her desperation brings them together again at the village dance. He is a part of her dilemma of non-fulfillment.

Poor reason being mother to anguished life and endurance, and accused by Clym's subliminal Oedipus logic, her suicide is predictable--though some readers doutless figure her death by drowning is accidental, their verdict being based on the soaked banknotes in Wildeve's pocket. Pity for the girl resolves her dilemma of choice or destiny--to heed the fagot glow of her lover's signal and flee with him, across the Channel to Paris from Budmouth.

Sorrow for Eustacia translated into rebellion against the heath; but note, Egdon provides only the living walls of furze to imprison her while the causes of her exile are human agencies. She is a stoic of heoric proportions who endures without remorse or recanting, unless the remorse is for her own failure. She suffers, yet foolishly, and for her own folly and double desire--for a lover and for gay *Paree*. Perhaps Hardy's popular readership choked on this bone. Undeniably she brought down upon heself the crisis in circumstances that led to her death, even though Wildeve would see her one last time boldly in the daylight! There is a sterile debauchery in her life, a waste like the heath's, an ignominious surrender, a bitter and ironic helplessness of means. She keeps her dignity through death even, lain out as she is with the appearance of a divine, peaceful dignity. Her death is Hardy's assertion of a wrongful, an unjust death.

There is in *The Return Of the Native* a hidden condemnation of society--barren and oppressive Egdon nature like a barren and unsatisfying husband in an "acceptable" marriage, the bondage of unfulfilled desires. (Tolstoy's *Anna Karenna* and Ibsen's play *A Doll's House* dwell on the same theme.) More importantly, Eustacia's struggles are calamitous precisely because human relationships, despite the best intentions, are buried beneath anachronistic demands, mediocre ambitons, empty dreams, superfluous human ties, heedless moral strictures and a whole phantasmagoria of wasted lives and shell satisfactions that moan and rattle like the husk bells on Egdon in the wind. And the pity of the grand scene is that hardy projects for us is that society, at least Wessex County society, were blind to their losses, their mindless sacrifices, their witless humdrum existence. Yet the author is compassionate and loves the people he writes about; but he will not compromise the integrity of his observations.

There is in the novel a single woven thread that unites the divinity aspect of Eustacia to her dignity, her endurance, her contradictions, her hates, her reactions to parochial village hearts and that is the ironic self abnegation that appears and recedes throughout the story. Eustacia denies her essential womanood though deluded by thoughts she is fulfilling it, or will, if she can only escape Egdon Heath. She measures her worth in poounds sterling, her custom by the men she attracts with the charisma of her beauty, her intelligence by the failure of reciprocity in Clym and the clever caprice of Wildeve, her integrity by resisting Mrs. Yeobright, and spiritual stature, if you will, by her propensity to bring doom and unhappiness to others.

She equates life with Paris, death with Egdon, heaven with being loved to madness, and hell to imprisonment at Blooms-End. Her solace is the integrity of her actions, a faith in Self that burns out at last in her wild escape planned with Wildeve. A dream is a resource of strength and health when its odds for survival are favorable. In Eustacia's case they are not and probably never would have been. Yet given her high intelligence, she can only suffer the more, for were she a slowwitted country maid--some farm girls being quite bright--passively accepting the bonds of an obscure English village, she would have lasted out her years, proably. At times he seems tragic, heric in some ways, but her very humanness mitigates against all that is rash, untimnely, ruthless either to self or others as in traditional tragedy. More than a cipher, she is less than divine; yet less than a goddess, she is more than a mere women.

Despsite the austere imaginative qualities of the novel, its mastery of fine descriptive detail, its inscription upon timelss stones the idea of village lives, its sensitive depiction of character, Eustracia in *The Return Of the Native* is not a tragfic figure in the traditional sense--bedeveled by inner moral choices and conflict, or chosing wrongly because of a flaw in character. Iineed were she avaracious she might have schemed with Wildeve to strip Thomasin an Clym of the guineas they inherited, or enquired of her husbands found wealth in Paris. She is neither sinister nor greedy. Yet she is bold in her own way--a magnet for the cavalier Wildeve.

Hardy's Eustacia is a striking figure, not as vivid perhaps as Tess nor as curiously ethereal and diferent as Sue or as bisexual and efficient as Bathsheba. She will endure while Clym, the true native of Blooms-End will always walk in her shadow. He will be content atop Rainbarrow, alone, delivering his moral lectures, an epistemological echo upon the *"witch"* who fires up the hilltop, an ancient Druidic rite by a miracle priestess.

BIBLIOGRAPHY

1. Basic Text: *The Reurn Of the Native*, by Thomas Hardy; Harper & Rowe. N.Y., 1966, 406 pp. Edited with Intro. and Notes by John Paterson; incl. "Aftercourses" VI

2. *Hardy the Novelist, An Essay in Criticism*, By David Cecil; Bobbs-Merrill Col, N.Y., 1943; 234 pp.

3. *Thomas Hardy*, by Richard C Carpenter, Twayne Pulications, Inc., N.Y., 1964; 223 pp.; "Fiction: the Major Chord"

4 D. H. Lawrence - *Selected Literary Criticism, Edited by* Anthony Beal; The Viking Press., N. Y., 1956; 435 pp. Re: "Study of Thomas Hardy," pub. "Phoenix" magazine

5. *Young Thomas Hardy*, by Robert Gittings; Little Brown & Co, Boston, 1975; 259 pp.

6. *Thomas hardy, A Critical Study*, by Arthur McDowell; Faber and Faber, London, 1933; 284 pp.

7. Introduction to *The standard Edition of The Return Of the Native*, by John Paterson; see above

8 Hardy, **A Collection of Essays**, Edited bvy Alvert J. Guerard; Prentice-Hall, New Jersey; 1963, 180 pp.

9. "Seminar in Tragedy," by Prof John Dodds, Stanford University;1955; Class Notes and Papers

A PLAYWRIGH'S USE OF STYLIZED MIMICRY

Dupont-Duford, Senior, whom Ron Christensen played, mimicked the cozy and adoring father who has ceased, if inde4ed he ever began, to lick his whelp into shape for social responsibility. His dilettante's caution is posed was gentlemanly dignity in the intrigue as he and his son slipped past the thieves and into the bushes to keep the nieces in sight. Wycherly could not have done the satire on social dignity better. Dupont-Dufort , Junior, played by G. D. Kinkbeiner, dipped and giggled and clappered with glee as the chip off the old block. In all of these actions, the banile, the mindless responses to a situation were apparent to the point of disgust. The duo's cat-footed manner showed rhythmic harmony, if that is the way to express complcity. . Sneaky, apeing one another in lintent, pursuing without hope of seduction or play of intellegent conquest but as a matter of form, Anouilhs dainty and brainless mincemeats, depicted by Kinkbeiner and Chrisensen, represented that stylized mimicry of conduct that the playwright used to lampon sterile convention.

FACETS OF MISS ROBERT'S EVA

If not sufficiently bored to raise th ecry of decitful love. Marylyn Rovers, as Eva, created the character of the minx and the tart beneath a lady's fine manners. She could not fall in love with the thief Hector, whose personality never suited her. Beneath Miss Roberts dignity there was rejection, not only of her suitor but as a calculated and an adviseable mode of action in life. In her hauteur there was cool charm and aloofness, the piquant boredom of a newcomer to social negation. I another forty years, she should have become a replica of Lady Hurf. Dawn Roberts, as Juliette, expressed the jejune remantilc girl's captivation by the novelty of enjoying a purloiner of houshold goods for a lover. Her want contained the old double-entendre of French comedy. For the part, Miss Roberts created graphically the impressions of youthful naivete, mixed with intelligence and sensibility, of natural physical desires in a high-born lady unclouded by sham yet, as a woman, deprived by custom of a real standard for her actions. Gustave's plundering may brilng Scotland Yard down upon the villa. He knows, though, and accepts the import of his crimes. Juliette would take his mind away from his dark business.

These two nieces were the charming little stones that Lady Hurf desired to set in burnished old settings of gallant bliss--again Anouilhs comedic inversion. For in the play, ltself, knaves pass as gentlelmen and gentlemen seem knaves. So, too, do the young ladies pass as imposters and pilferers, that is to say, as shoplifters.

A COMEDIE MECHANIQUE

The fantasy, countenanced by Lady Hurf, is over when she discovers that she mistook thec asino announcement of a *Carnival of Leaves* to read a *Carnival of Thieves*. At this point the mechnicals retire. Eva and Hecton, Peterone and Edgard display their conventional costme of poses, tacked together by the rigamarole and slippery rountines of their trade. And the laughter turns into the solemn reflection by Aunt Hurf upon the travesty just finished. Gustav and Juliette remain the socially untypical lovers, a thief and a society belle. They are sensible lovers to a Frenchman, for to him warm affection and intimacies under almost any banner are the most sensilble of compacts. When the gilt comes off on the niece Juliette, perhaps Anouilkh is saying that all delusory efforts to improve upon a life finish in the rationalized, the mechanically contrived Lady Hurf's villa are the material compromises Julitte makes to end her boredom. And, the playwrigh'ts proposition concludes, that the freedom of choicel is of a greater value than the worth of the sacked objects of art. In them we see something of the feel-good moderns of Amerlica !

ACCOMPANYING SPECTACLE VALUES

There was evident in **The Great Plays Company** production a delicacy of the comedic that is dilfficult to defilne, a comedy that was pleasisng, subtle and disingenuous in its effects. Contrasting to the gallant pirates' masquerade, the costume sere formal and contemporary. The production value of color was brilliantly applied. Vermillion and white lined the *Vichy Park* bandstand. Black and shades of gray, purple and sky blue in the dress were offset in the opening scene by the briliant umber of Hector's false wig and his white dinner jacket .

The lighting was festive and gay but for the Act 3 villa scene when the room darkend and Juliette came in to look for Gustave, her escort to the party. Silhouette lighting of the city glowed through the upstage window, the semi-darkened room was lit with dampered spill liht above the rear picture wall , a scheme that was effectlive scene lighting but that did not destroy the mood of the comic with purposeless illumination and vague shadows. These were superb productionv values that accented the fact that here was a droll, rippling, gay drama, a comedy satire that involved fashions and manners and that exhibited moments of comic action and visual touches of color all of which supplied the production with an enchanting quality of mystery. In Anouilhs puppetry there is the mystery about certain of his characters,of the unseen truth that living life with zest is infinitely more satisfying than observing the rituals of pitiable wastrels and montebanks in money-getting Bedlam.

QUALITIES OF THE FANTASTIC AND MECHANICAL

Anouilh's fantacy of social-conduct subterfuge and his comedy of mechanicals were given first emphasis in Director Pize'rs staging of the play. Precise, methodical grouping, the break-ups and crossovers of the of individual characters to new stage positions, in a word the blocking on motivated cues and the precise timng of character actions, gave to the blocking the semblance of a dance without prescribed form or steps. This rhythmic precision and fluidity of movement contributed to the visual impression that these figures on the stage were mechanicals but that they were granted free-will by the playwright, their thought processes fettered by empty conventions, all of which produced in each person the delusion of free choice while being manipulated by convention. And the fantasies born of that delusion...that to fall in love with a house burglar is meaningful, that to chase the lovely nieces through the park is a worthwhile pursuit and diversion, that to attend a carnival of thieves is living with zest--Lady Hurf is cheated of this one small satisfaction/ These are fantasies of mindless conformity that was, lin this production, conveyed by the free-form movements of dissembling dance rather than though the intellection of rational conduct. Their sterile awarness of life breeds self-delusion which is their subterfuge in mimicry. The players conveyed these qualities of the fantastic and the mechncal by the simple expedient of accenting the ritualistic appearances of an action. In these two respects their brilliant and profound performance brought out the intentions of the playwright.

That Anouilh has anything important to say to an American audience can be left to the discrimination of future cirtics and participans in the theatre. He is good theatre, and his work appears to be enjoying current vogue. Certinly he is pointing out the banile and contrived ways of a class of Frenchmen who get along by means of a puerile conformity to customs. *The Great Plays Company* production was the kind of playgoers fare that engages the imagination for its dramatic and aesthtic values, as well as for its enlightenment upon particular social-conduct aspects of upper-crust Vichy social somnambulism.

Critique--
A Comparison of Dostoievsky's and Richardson's depiction of moral justice in <u>Crime and Punishment</u> and in <u>Pamela</u>

Rene Fueleop-Mliller, in her critical book on Fydor Dostoievsky's realism, his Christian ethic of compassion, his scientific curiosity, his explorations of the netherworld of criminal pathology with its unending tragic conflict in the murderer's mind between guilt and expiation, God and satan, good and evil, writes of Prince Miuskin in *The Idiot*: that he is capable of sacrifice since after his arrest, his "guilt and afflictions, are more deserving of love than the guiltless and the fortunte (<u>**Fydor Dostoievsky**</u>, p. 45). This subjection is, of course, the imposed sacrifice of his sense of well-being and his pride. As a novelist, a creator of characters, of Raskolnikov in *Crime and Punishment* and Smerdyakov in *The Brohers Karamazov,* both conessed killers, and of the suicidal Nihilist Kirillov in *The Possessed*, Dostoieveky's delineation of these a-moral vengeance-seekers caused C. J. Hogarth to characterize him as a writer whose work expresses his conviction of the regenerative power of love for "the most ignoble of natures (Hogarth).

Dostoievsky's Prince Muiskin represents the other polar extreme, the character of God-man resolve that, in the story, ils creatively willed through faith-- the acceptance of the Son of God's atonement. Dostoievsky had observed those love-hate impulses from 1859 to 1854 among prisoners in the Siberlian *Katorba*. He was imprisoned there as a Fourierist revolutionary, exiled for sedition. He witnessed human sufferling and, having observed that a man's awareness of his crime is often more painful than the punishment. Dostoievsky felt that the inmates, in their torment, were redeemable. As we see this emergeance of faith in the long passages of intellectual questing, the action of pathological violence, the close pyschological introspection of major characters In those three novels, his delineation bears out the emergence in his stories of that religious ethic of forgiveness toward the criminal which, during his own imprisonment, Dostoievsky had witnessed and confirmed and alluded to in his earfly novel *House Of the Dead.*

To the Englishman, it is the victim of the crime who merits the compassion. British common law, the entire legal system of courts, procedures for prosecution and the written statutes attest to this fact. Unpleasant, therefore, as the truth may be to pragmatists of academic and of greater society, this son of Moscow doctor to the poor, a man condemned to be executed in Samyonovski Square and snatched from the iring line at the last moment not only wrote out of a doctrinaire Christsian belief that recognized the crlminal's crime as a painful hell to him. But, following the labrynth of the perpetrator's thoughts, as he did of Raskolnikov after the axe-murder of the old pawnbroker woman, Dostoievsky charts with police-report minutae the psychological effects of a crime that had issued from poverty, philosophical disillusionment and, in accordance with the novelist's life-long motrif, the soul's torment by disbelief in God. The crime and the murdere'rs penitent will to expiate for it to society converged, the novelest came to believe, in Christs atonement and in the Supernatural compassion the prisoner-criminal received after a confession of inner penitence.

It was Dostoievsky who transmuted that compassion into secular perceptions of human behavior. Thereby, with great penetration, depth of feeling and vivid accuracy, he could describe the thoughts and actions of men reduced to brutality, made vicious by temperament and cunning, the depraved, the murerers, thieves, rapists, extorioners among the rabble of men deemed unwantedby society. Even as in *House Of the Dead* he became "the confessor of the Russian soul," so, too, did his people regard him as "the spiritual counsellor of the nation." After his publication of *The Possessed* , compassion was and still is, a root philosophy, a sort of fundamental moreal law of the Russian people--drawn in part from the ideology of Tsarist *nobless oblige and partly from Russia's orthodox Christianity. (*They are a much more religious peoplethanthe world grants to them, a searching iln the 20th centurfy that was misdirected into political ideologies.)

That crime and punishment, alike, involve painful inner suffering and that, however barbaric his impulses or degeneratve his nature, the lindividual is perfectable. Such precepts as these assume a quite different character in the work of Briltish novelist Richardson. His Pamela, in the novel *Pamela* , is coarse, prurient, sanctimonious, and class-conscious. Yet the author saw his ideal servant-girl as a person whose virtue and dignity were important as those of an upper-class dame. Forrerunner o fthe social-conscious novel and anti-aristocratic, *Pamela* sentimentalizes feminist Richarson's social argument for class equality when he marries his admonishing heroine servant-girl to her gentleman seducer, the master of the house, Mr. Booby. The narrative details which furbish her virtuous daily rounds, her secret self-councils in her chamber, her sweet loflty flights from male entrapment while in her lover's employ become,as it were, crude, reportorial stratagems designed less to reveal "the feminine heart" of the authors promise that than to promote a social cause, at whatever the cost to crdibility in his characterization. Richa dson has so manipulated his outcast and his devious gentleman of quality that the sympathy he would excite in readers for Pamela can be characterized as pious snobbery.

The point I would have the reader deduce from this discussion is that the act of forgiveness is a universal expression of exoneration. To Dostoievsky the blesssing did not require but accepted repentance of another. For Dostoievsky, that Supernatural absolution depended upon an ethical religious act of penitent faith. For Richardson, "absolution should come from the democatic masses, the weepers, the malcontents, the anti traditionalists, after the heroine' acceptance of a...paradoxically...prevailing code of conduct, a traditional mode of living, a handbook of amenable vlirtues. ILnDostoieeky' aforementioned novels, The act of forgiveness for the crimes, the suffering and exoneration...and the act of faith...are all there, either brought out in the action or implicit within it.

Dostoievsky and Richardson, alike, dealt with injustice, against the unique background of established institutions. Only the Russian, however, succeeded in revealing with powerful Slavophil intensity, the affects of punishment and crime upon his characters. The English novelist would lead readers into the nonsense of rebuking society for permitting a servant to suffer thoughts of dishonor, discriminating class disrimination,and deradation as an obedilent menial while in a perfectly honest station in life.

Raskolnikov suffers because of his crime, its bloody violence and his willful violation of a social and moral law: *thou shalt not kill.* Pamela "suffers" because of her oedience to "obslolete" codes of a Feudal governing class. The one treatment is; tragic, intimate and personal; the other is comedlic, social and disinterested. Conscience for Raskolnikov involves a consciousness of the evil portent of his murder. For Pamela, coscience amounts to a moralistic, proud virtue, a ritualistic sense of honor, shame degradadion compounded of Britilsh traditions and Richardson' own s fawnling appeal to clas respectability.

Pamela is the instrument of his theme of "virtue rewarded," Raskolnikov, like the other leadisng criminals, is the instrument of his own destructive will. Dostoievsky approaches his characters with a sense of compassion for them; the Englishman's Pamela is rudely elevated as a young woman who is too good to surrender to her seducer yet who, upon their marriage, is blessed as the object a degrading seduction and pursuit. Richardson is saying that Pamela shows that she was virtuous before a degrading society. If that is true, and it is, to what or toward whom does she owe significant obedience in her station as a servant-girl? Obedience is the entrapment of Richardson's divided ploy of Pamela's honor.

Oviously he is interested in the working girl; but the conscience that actually dominated the action is the conscience of the novelist and not of Pamela. He is the sentimentalist, the puppeteer. Dostoievsky is the tragedian. Richardson rewards his heroine's virtue by marrying her off to Mr. Booby. The act of forgiveness for her weak moments of temptation comes from the demorcratic masses, who atone for her doubt byl acptance of so eminent a reward, for her sake, as the Mr. oobly. In *Crime and Punishment*, the act of forgiveness by Raskolnikov's fiance follows penitent expiation, the belief in God, faith in Christ's atonement--the basis for Dostoievsky's religious construct on forgiveness. Raskolnikov's "reward " is God's grace. His punishment, a quite different matter, is the *Katorba* in Siberia. The woman he loves, who does not desert him, represents that grace of forgiveness that Dostoieveky acepted during his prison years by listening to the confessions of other prisoners.

For the Russian, regeneration depends on that belief and faith, lon the criminal's acceptance of a Supernatural Being, and upon his recognition of a man's perfectlibility. His reading matter in prison were portions of the Bible of the Russian orthodox church, doutless smuggled into the prison compound. He may have read about Pauls imprisonment by the Romans. For the Englishman, changes of character are matters of decorum, propriety, discreton, moderation, of social acceptance and Parliamentary legislation. Regeneration is foreign to Richardson's thinking in *Pamela.* Veneration is the avenue for inner change. After all, Pamela's coarse ways have been determined by her environment. Richardson cannot begin to approach the penetration of Dostoievsky's exploration of the human mind, spirit and emotions. He sees them through social traditions. Conseuently, although Pamala is "victimized " by evil temptations, she is made so by tradition and not by her own human conversion, her willful wrong doing, her doubts about the ethics of her behavior. Indeed, her doubts are chimerical, for did she not marry her seducr? Raskolnikov doubts only his own capacity to change. The one is society-oriented whilest the other is faith-oriented.

COMMENTARY

It has been widely hinted at that we live in a utilitarian pagan Christian culture. Today in America the dramatist shares a unique niche with priest and hedonist, the military man and an endless flood of "intellectual" books. Regarded as a non-productive member of society he may inadvertently add to an increase in human understanding through his plays; whilest his split-collar fellow instructs parochial schooloys in Christ's love and the Seven Sacaments. The hedonist saturates his pride in his own elegance, and in the bararisms of modern day sophistication: *the emulation of want.* His professionl military compatriot, choked up by publicity for slaughter's creed, however, is productilve toward civiliazation's advance. either creed, however, is productive toward civiliations advance that leaves war behind, evenwhn it contemplates war anew.

To negate human visions is creative; to enlighten is sometimes to do harm. To spite these ludicrous inversions, it is stolidly maintained by a large portion of the theatre-going public that the labor of the dramatist, peripheral in our culture. possesses an intrinsic non0-utilitarian value. He therefore is seen as non-productive because he stamps no no knives or forks, he builds no ships, twists no screws; he plows no land and moulds no bricks. It need only be said that as a Type, he does not do these things.

As they do that mummer's commodity called *virtue*, pietists can buy his product for a penny's weight of community lip- service. It is a negligible matter, however, that his play's reality cannot be weighed; the meaning of his play does not draw percentage per annum; it pays none of the theatre-goer's bills; although it might stay his hand from leeching on a neighbors repatriation through gossip; and it is taxable only by the government at a maximum of 91 percent after twenty years of his having stamped out knives and forks,built ships, twisted screws, plowed a little land and moulded rilcks in order to survive. Yet in a sense as strict as the root doctrine of New England Puritanism, he is a non-functional member of society; he is a writer of plays. If he has talent, his vision is usually the reward of perservering ntegrity. Hollywood alone can knight him to joust among the masonry; after he recognized until the entertainment winds change, whereupon, like a Medlieval knight, he is cast onto a pyre of has-beens, fried out of his armor and the suit given to the victor produer. Such is the customary fate of the live-stage dramatist in America; oblivion one way or another, but oblivion.

There are, of course, reasons...and more immediate ones: the disinclination of stringently budgeted little theatre directors to gamble on untried plays; the creaking, powerful star system welded to this country's personality cult; timidityand ignorance on the part of the new playwright in hjucksterling his work; Hollywood's worship of bigness; Broadway's insolent presumption that its theatre and Plymouth Rock are one in the same. There is, also, another reason, related to today's semi-intellectual climate. Young men before the age of eighteeen are taught that plumbing is the better part of labor's thrift; and that it is shifty, dangerous, the scant leftover of wisdom, to bring one's brains, other than or the laboratory, to bear fruit in intellectual ways. It is that strain of pauperized vision that construes wisdom as somehow restricted to graph curves and to the pettifogging machinations of Russo-American summit conferences... in a word, to politics.

Though in many climes it is cruel, today's world is not altogether experientially hard. Frustrration, however, can be a sop for the fissionable personality, without a center other than the egothat tends to fragment when confronted by social change and commerce. Young witers of plays are especiallycounselled that in order to survive they must wake up to realities, the bulk of the citizenry having learned adroitly to confuse the humanly real with the tangibly actual, the suspect with the crime, a teachers dedication with the administrations purse or parental indolence.

There are those who ask, however--are not these writers in control of their personal destinies? The sardonic truth is that they are not. TwoWorld Wars, the KoreanWar and antecedent diplomatic stupidlity; and depression, a recession; witch hunts and Conressional trials; suspicion under enforced loalty oaths--these are the pristine achievements of a former generation.

Fatal forces move the innocents; silent man, best man dramatists are sometimes called...Protagonists and Antagonists, a generation living on their little isle of opulence that frets for entertainment first, last and always. The Theatre of the Absurd and Surrealism are escapes from this false paradise. Absolute self-determination in nations as well as for individual is the great prophetic delusion of modern man . This is a truth that is contrary to utilitarian training, to the eduation of the engineer as well as to the magician.

Writers yet unknown are proffered a choice between the practical and the conventional modes of living, and continual annonymity. The resultant quandry, but a stage in a writers growth, can debilitate; it may shrink the mind and dry up the spirit of creatlive exploration. A reality of inner self-determination, the unfettered use of conscience, an open scrutiny of religions values, human ethics; the basic traits of man's mind and spirit, and the cultural traditions of all peoples, these remain. Amongst them, the serious playwright works, God help him, a free agent.

Such a *ghestalt* point of view that that whatever is utilitarian is good can, as it did under Hitler, trick human loyalties to perform services for science foremost; duty is the mask. Yet the fact obtains; that science without human faith in humans is futile, primal, a disasterous road; with it, no reason can alone staunch the duplicity of political Futurists, false gods of war, or of a socialist economy; or ripe, fat ton-sters in black robes seated on benches of middle class complacency; the potpourri of grubbers among "lost" pioneer visions; and the politicians, whom we must patiently endure. Through these sterile headsmen, also, the playwright moves.

People are his main business. He begins with individuals, and not with a graph curve or pouch of gold, an engineer's slide rule or a claustrophobic fear of puffed up legal kites. In the telling of a tale, he tries to put these men upon a stage. He selects and compresses, he edits and rewrites so as to give order to their actions and words to their tongues that they show us a reality of human experiences. He is a civilian who, by means of drama in mime...and comic puppetry in a genre extreme...attempts to reveal life. He is all too often, however, regarded as jaded if not slightly offensive by those with more delicate tastes--they, the robust closet men with a fine, judicious palate for what enfranchizes self-esteem. The drama is not approached with the moist eye of a gentleman's disdain unless the dramatist would satirize him or show his import in one of life's venues. The writing of a play is approached with a certain attitude of vigorous hostility toward those truths, those realities symbolized by the lives of the dramtist's chosen personna for his plays. "A reverence for life" a religion of the theatre and a credo for truthful drama, the meaningfulness of human dignity--these are other ways of expressing that fundamental idea of holding up the mirror to human experience.

This small journal, then, purposes to accent "the play is the thing" in its all too brief critical articles . We will not eloquise upon the dramatist of an intellectual remnant of protean man; but he will sand by, watchng the results of his huckstered craft and artistry, and praying for new insights, new strength to resist what debases his craft, and longsuffering until rain comes...apprecilation. *The Critics Review* will recognize that in the voluminous literature of the theatre there are human, ethical, religious and aesthetic values worth highlighting, and that the dramatrist writes out of centuries-old traditions of both the theatre and the construction of plays. *The Critics Review* promises that the drama's chief purpose is proactive--to increase human understanding.

The literature of the theatre cuts through half a dozen major political systems of thought and through a spectrum of philosophical ideologies. We further promise that no expediencies such as a military apotheosis of immediate troops occupation, can justify the legality or publicity enforced suspension of the nation's two basic freedoms: the freedom of conscience and of speech, and the right of very man to voice his opinion and the liberty to express openly his beliefs. In the face of cinching international tensions, that is our belief, that is our faith.

Criticism is our chief purpose and goal; we hope that it will help others to interpret the drama of the theatre, the literature of the play...and, in a larger measure, to enjoy both. The *Critics Review* is aware that the competent *critic* may flatter the players, irritate the director and ignore the playwright; he may presume to taste the play's meaning and draw his check. But our brass weathercock points to a more discriminating criticism, to a finer interpretation of meanings. We are in sympathy with what is human, recognizable in experience, dramatic and truthful in the drama. And Shavian Shaw, the "vital life force" socialist, is as welcome a contender as are the genre social-protest Greek Euripides, reportorial Sidney Kingsley and revolutionary Gorky; and as are that lampooner of social types an their foibles, Moliere, and the ever universal Shakespeare . We invite you into the pleasures of our company.\\

C. E. Miller, Publisher & Editor of THE CRITICS REVIEW April, 1958

DO WE NEED A CENSOR?
(July , 1958)

Our balding mountain of windy platitudes and military opportunism, President Eisenhower, would empower the U.S. Asssistant Secretary of Defense Murray Snyder, to act as Chief censor of all information on the three services that is to be given out to the press. In a repy to recent sub-committee letters from the California Newspapers Association, Secretary of Defense McElrey stated that Eisenhower intended to reorganize the Defense Department's information activities. As the set-up now stands, military heads and their aides must keep the names of any talks with newsmen "... even if they meet them at a cocktail party ," said Represenartive John; E. Mesa, at the 20th conference of the CRPA.

The imposition, thrown at a a politically appointive position, of such censoship over the Amerilcan press smacks of AGITPROP's absolute control over *Izvestia* and *Pravda*, the Soviet press mouthpieces for the Commintern and Stalin. Wielding the awsome strategic power in the U S will be one man, the beautific, the awesome and unimpeachable commander of propaganda, Assistant Secretary of Defense Murray. Flinging his golden locks from side to side, he will thunder: "Men, this decision is secret, that is classified!" And the poor fledglings of freedom, the newsmen, will arise from their prostrate knees and go off to tlheir editorial offices to fume and to carp at Washlington and to mutter among themeles , "Does not his seizure of our right suggest some evil?" Hail, Eisenhower, he wouuld usurp the express responsibility of Congress to propose any new law abridging the freedom of speech and of the press! The people decide.

This throttling of freedom of information is an imperious thing . It chances to save Ike's do-nothing satellite development record, to obliterate the age-mellowed wrangles between the services, in a word, to whip the dog-faced newsmen back to their pup tents while he and his shaggy assistants stake down their preamble, declare war on prying scribblers, codify what they wish and roll in sober mockry of what of what generations have so valiantly fought for. Eisenhower would establish an iron-clad Washington junta of information, with Murray blessed to sit as the magistgrate, the censor, the unassailable giant of arbitration over the consciences of the Fourth Estate. Let this dwarf and mocking marriage of military might and political power be consummated and the media will not so easily regain their freedom. Nor will tlhe American people quickly forget how they sold out a piece of their heritage for the harsh and grunting security-promise of a field commander.

Ike's planned abridgement of the First Amendment to the Constitution cannot be argued for on the grounds that it will strengthen our national security. For he would apprently replace our freedom of information with his experienced freedom to command the military as the cardinal weapon of choice against the enemy, before and after he strikes. The articulation of our defense by newsmen is of lesser impotance? Nay, words have no meaning against bullets, but il bullets come first, what happens to ilnformation of preparation and psychological defense? According to Ike, if the bureaucrats in Washington approve, *then* the information is useful. That is censorship, the gutting of American feeedom of speech, conscience and will.

GOD -MAN OR TRAGIC HERO IN THE DRAMA

Biological determism: Darwin's theory of the evolution of the species through adaptive changes, contributed fuel to the Naturalist doctrine of Zola. The Naturalist said: Man is a biolotgical organism only; to invest him with a divine spark is idiocy; to find in him the god- man is superstititon; to say that he can control the laws of nature or the forces of an impersonal cosmos is an illusion. These incantations led to a denial of God's existence, to denial of the efficacy of orthodox Christian faith; to the plundering of *Laissez faire* capitalists and a dog-eat-dog philosophy; they led to to labor legisslation and agrarian reform a reactions; to social-protest literature and to the espousal of socialist and communiwt doctrines. With God seriously challenged, and men's supra-animal being thrown into the scale, Greek concepts of fate and destiny, of the tragedy of the good man, noble in spirit and of high birth, knowingly defeated by unconquerable forces , were *not* hypotheses based on men's acceptance of scientifically-proved *laws*. If man is a biological accldent, he has no nobility. The atheist cannpt have it both ways. Therefore tragedy is impossible for him to envision, to claim or to aspire to. If he writes what he calls a *tragedy* the play is a fraud in the theatre. The social insignificace of a man does not make him either noble, religious or good. Pity for him is not the same experience as the emotional and spiritual release felt by watching good triumph.

THE TRAGEDY OF THE COMMON MAN. bu Arthur Miller(*Theatre Arts* magazine, March, 1951(--"As a general rule to which may may be exceptions unknown to me, I think the tragic feeling is evoked in us when we are in the presence of a character who is ready to lay down his life, if need be, to secure one thing--his sense of *personal dignity*. From Orestes to Hamlet, Medea to Macbeth, the underlying struggle is that of the individual attempting to gain his "rightful" position in his society."

I disagree: the egocentrism of the idea is not enobling or sacrificial, both of which true tragedy must contain. It exalts suicide instead of sacrifice for another person, a cause, a faith... but not an identity. Hamlet sacrifices his lineage and Ophelia; Orestes sacrifices his next of heir, Medea sacrifices her progeny in revenge; Macbeth sacifices the honor of honest kingship. Love, the next to most powerful emotion, is almost always involved but notice, not for self...the sacrifice. Hate is the next most powerful, Medea of her husband but note, the element of justice achieved first, before vengeance is done. The latter is the mere means. The justice involves sacrifice of the two heirs, keeping love for her boys. She destroys forever her self-dignity as Hamlet does his, as Macbeth does his, the opposites of *personal dignity*. Rather, I think shame and remorse take over, not dignity, the effulgence often of self-centered pride.

SYMBOLISM AND IDEA IN THE DRAMA

Why did a play by G. B. Shaw appeal to the socialist liberals in England of his post-Victorian day? His plays appealed to British radicalism. Symbols that try to convey a politial idea, a philosophical concept , a social message through dramatic character must reduce characterization to typical features, thus to distinguish the person from tlhe idology he represents. The plays of Clifford Odets, August Strindberg fall into the same category.

Propaganda drama resembles in this regard the Medieval morality play-- idealiation . To the extent that a play thus becomes propaganda, it becomes increasingly symbolical and its characters become less individualized and more archytypical. When a character thereupon loses his humanness, and is manipulated like a puppet by the theme representing a social-political, religious idea, thatr chaacter loses its appeal to general audiences--at least as a dramatic figure, Specialied audiences then find him an example of the "good man," the "moral example," the idealistic "future man" of society and government who is worth emulating. Socialist dramas attempt to present us with paradigms of heroes. Ibsen's plays are of this kind. The playwright who shows his audinces a Protagonist who is a complex human bveing annot be accused of this ideologic Idealization.

Comedy of types such as Jonson and Moliere wrote of may typify and moralilze social archytypes, but enough of the humanness of the real person remains to establish in the play a universal appeal. There is lacking a pervasive morality of the puppetry of the play. Puppetry implies the artifices of character- manipulation to achieve the propagandistsic end result. It is not the Protagonist's character traits that decide whither he goes or if he stands or falls. His actions represent the playwright pulling the strings of his creation.

The moralities and propagandistic plays lie at the extreme end of a grand scale. At the other end are the plays written by the Impressionists and Expressionists which try to so individualize a human experience as to make it ultra subjective and therefore incomprehensible. In so doing dramatic values become lost in the absolute intimacy of lthe playwright's personal experience. In either case the playwrgiht his personna to appeal to the political proselyte and also to the rarified intellectual. The play is then either evangelistic or dialectical. The stage becomes a forum for polico-social issues and is no longer holding the" mirror up to nature," as Shakespeare wrote.

The propaganda play appeals is to the values of the masses and so it is specialized, as much so as is expressionist drama yet with social import. In the case of the impressionist-expressionist plays, the ultra subjecrtivce experience may also have a propaganda added, as did drama after WW I in Europe, ostensibly aimed at showing the disenchantment, the reconstruction of a torn society that came to accept, uner Hitler's charisma, a socio-Fasclist promise of a restored and thriving new post-Versailles Germany. *Retreat into the mind was the essence of Expressionism; escape from tangible reality was the essence of Impressionism.*

For the reason that negation and disillusionment showed mans inner despair and the breakup of old ways and mores, many of those post-WW I plays were wrongly called *tragedies*. It was not the personal experience alone which made them seem so but the acknowledgement that they depicted universal human suffering, motives of need, failure, of love, the success of despair and the like as positive standards for the measurement of the experience of enduringl pain and loss. In the popular mind, any sever and exremely painfull loss is called *tragic*. The problem with that assessment is that it blurs the meaning of true tragedy: a person of strong and admirable character--not necessarily of rank or wealth--who rises above the defeat sprung from a weakness of that character--essentially the Greek classic view of Hamartia.

Certainly a tragedy cannot co-exist absolutely with a spirit of negation, since then any effort to define the good and truly beneficial, the harmonious, course of action is pushed aside. Yet comedy always carries with it a spirit of conquest over defeating circumstances and ends. At this point the comedic philosophy becomes one of the destruction of society and of self-destruction, held in check by humor--the tragic irony of objective comprehension. Nor can a tragedy consist absolutely of affirmation, whether for social goals or religious creeds, since life denies the credibility of utopian visions. The tragedic philsophy becomes one of totalitarian recreation, even if communist adherents omit the clause that the old must be destroyed, just as the Utopian subjectivists omit the condition that the good does exist whitout error.

High tragedy accommodates hope. Serious drama usually bears the seeds of tragic moral blindness. The moral blindness. that comedy lampoons issues from tradition. The uncomproimsing integrity of the tragic figure scorns the conventionnal choice dictated by meaningless traditions. The irony of another choice exists in the minds of the audince only as they watch the sufferings sof the tragic figure. And althouigh he does snot succuamb to any choie but his own, they sense relief that he is safe and his decision good *for him*. There is a sense of the tragfic in high comedy, for the Protagonist does not realize how close he has come to making a fatal choice--which the audience perceives amid his folly, poor fellow but thank God. In either cse, lhigh comedy ortragedy, theplaywright fixes in the minds of the audience the intentions of choicss with appropriate recognizeable symbols. If he is the lleast obscure in this matter, his play witll fail to move emotionally to tears or laughter--though it may instruct. What *gift*, what *choice* is immediately recognizeable by the audience? In Miller"s **Death of a Salesman**, the choice was success as a salesman amid depression, to be way out there in the blue and "making sales" regardness of social circumstances. In **King Lear**, the gift was the love of his youngst daughter, Cordelia, which becomes clear to him at the close of the play. Those are the *symbols*. *They convey the idea of defeat and death yet of victory.*

The semantics of poetry,basically involve the simile and the metaphor, ciously and unconsciously an lintended ilmage-analogy whose reference value, rthle germainness of thle analogy provaides the sensual connunication. Theemotion is appropriatge to the imagel analogy, more so wlith some analogies that elevate the mundale to eloquenced.

The semantics of poetry, basically involve the simile and the metaphor, consciously and unconsciously wilth an intended image-analogy whose reference value, the germainness of the analogy, provides the sensual connunication. The emotion is appropriate to the image analogy, more so with some analogies that elevate the mundane to eloquence.

The semantics of poetry, basically involve the simile and the metaphor, consciously and unconsciously with an intended image-analogy whose reference value-- the germainness of the analogy-- provides the sensual connunication. The emotion is appropriate to the image analogy, more so with some analogies that elevate the mundane to the eloquent and the spiritual. Here is an illustration:

> *"With my slow, insensate dripping aways of*
> *impoverlished care,*
> *"T'is I who'll trench up his friends to face*
> *their nible and mouthy oppressor;*
> *He that clouds o'er the eves and shakes*
> *by his wars,*
> *Main timbers of this sacred house I have*
> *raised."*

The reference value, in that communication of a fragment of sense experience--whether the seeping awayof some liquor, as of the wine from a cask, or the roar of fierce winds in the bowels of a thunderhead--enlarges when the smilitude links the kindred quality or characteristic that is peculiar to both the image and its corresponsdilng human trait based on a truth. That truth maybe buttressed by contemporary findings of the psychologists or by sociological studies. It may arise from folk lore.

Irrespective of the primary course of the analogy, the similitude--of the denotative analogy or the signifying metaphor--the image symbol undergoes a metamorphosis that renders "impoverlished care" graphic, as many of MIlton's symbols in "Paradilse Lost" are partially graphic . And that suggests old friendships, buried in the grave of cowardice, trenched up to face their *sad and mouthy oppressor.*

Indeed, the foreboding storm indicates a fear among the people that stifles courage and darkens men's vision before the ominous intent of the figure to avenge his people's wrongs. In each of these insances, conversely, the human truth is made graphic by the poet's use of the appropriate images, the analogies which compare and denote likenesses of quality, of kind. Image and truth syunthesize and dramatilze each other, while yet the central truth of the passage as a whole, the deternined revenge, remains clear and distinct. The content of the analogy, the similitude, will indicate the germinal meaning of a speech , a scene of action, or an entire play. Upon the clarity of that central meaning, and upon that alone, rest the emotional precision and intellectual integrity of the play's many and varied poetic, lyrical, vblusterilng analogies .

A passage from Act V, Scene iii of "King Lear" best demonstrates the dramatic power that is achieved in this synthesis of sense- image with a human observation, experience or truth about humans.

> "Upon such sacrifices, my Cordelia,
> The gods themselves throw insense. Have I
> caught thee?
> Hew that parts us shall bring a brand from
> heaven
> And fire us hence like foxes. Wipe thine
> eyes;
> The good years shall devour them, flesh and
> fell,
> Ere they shall make us weep. We'll see 'em
> starv'd first.
> Come."

For Lear, his torment and his wrath, his madness from love's broken fealties spent, his guilt over his misplaced love assuaged, and his capacilty to love restored by the tenderness of his once-rejected youngest daughter, he is in his vow to his beloved Cordelia , looking backward over the tears of past events. Their moment of reunion is the germinal experience and his heart of his speech. It is the imagery of the passage that distills from his words subtle connotations of the wretched almost mortal strike to part him from his Cordelia.

The metaphor of the burning brand of misery that shall come upon his people in the event that an intruder with righteous vengeance, and the simile of the foxes with their tails aflame, enkindled by God's judgement , should bring judgement upon Lear and Cordelia. The Biblical references dramatically epitomize the law and the nature of the justice that willl ensue should a spoiler attempt to break their fresh bond of love. With the king restored to the throne and England reunited, the burning brand of disaffection news, borne by Lear and his Cordelia, would race like the flaming foxes through the towns and cities of Brltain . Then might Lear call his people *Philistines*.

Shakespeare's biblical images were undoubtedly graphic to the High Anglican believers, as well as to the courtiler and his kinsmen. Be it admitted, then, that the *firebrand* image refers to the supernatural sanction of the father-daugher bond and to the *tied-foxes* image refers to tlhe wild-fire razing of a people's sentiment and wealth. The animistic abstraction without sense appeal, of "the good years" suggests destructive famine, fields of parched grass, thirsty sheep, rotten hay mows and a plague of universal sickness, death and an infestation of rats. The animism takes on vividness and immedilacy, for by metamorphosing the good years into a sort of omnivorous beast that would devour the people;s hard won wealth and despoil their homes, lives and physical vitality, the lines become dramatilc and sensuous with the simple details of everyday life.

Such a righteous judgement and the fearsome retribution of an impersonal self-consuming justice lend to this passage a dramatic emotional and spiritual power , the tender beauty of Lear's reunion with his daughter, a vow that transcends false pity for the treacherous husbands of the other two daughters. The human reality of their love, renewed yet on a more profound level, is endowed with power and subtlety by the imagery of Lear's speech. And, what is remarkable, every one of the areas of special truth mentioned above, confirms that germinal experience shared by Lear and Cordelia , namely, the psychology of love's balm that soothes the passing torment of madness and the after-storm; the sociology of cultural harmony and close loyalties in a paternalistic State; the folk elements of repect for the *good earth*, and for the tail of its cultivation; and the religious story with an apprehension of divine annointing.

Conclude, I must. Brief thought the effort , I have tried to indicate to the native dramataist that by the use of measured lines in poetic drama, he may be able to enlarge upon a character in his polay at the same tlime as he evaluates the meaning of his play's action. And that the idiom for so doing is that of intentional and spontaneous image-analogies that are charged with dramatic sensuous appeal.

The ultimate conclusion seems inescapble--that although the playwright may violate the vernacular idiom of the day, he confirms the experiental reality of poetic imagery within a tradition I chose tocall the homogenerlic function of metaphorical thought. In its simplest terms, human beings since prehistoric times have expressed their feelings, their superstitions and their tribal beliefs about *survival and security with conttentment* by means of sensuous images and , later, sophisticated analogies.

The contemporary playwright would, if he chose the medium of poetry, most suitably for tragedy and romantic comedy, continue a tradition of imaglntive creation, as old as mankind, which the vernacular idiom cannot exploit or avail itself of. It seems to me, as a conseqence of the argument I have advanced, that the reduction of common men's vocabularies to a contemporary pragmatic idion is as much s step backward to the age of inarticulate grunts, as it is a step forward toward lingiustic simplification for the mass media of communication---whose chief historical function is primarily the preservation of law and order, through information . Great literary minds that illumined past centuries appear to be no loner evident for one singular reason: that poetic idiom, the creative mind of the analgizing thinker exlists only but rarely...when he can be tolerated by the twenty-first machine man empty of God and universals. Both are necessary fore the creation of great literature. How can a tree be anything other than a tree, or a great advancing army any more than battallions of weary soldiers? Great films have replaced great novels, and yet there is lacking wisdom and interpretation that can come only through the medium of the written word by informed and enlighened minds. Their venue is all of life that makes up the analogous hinterland of the human condition.

THE INK POT, from my journal *The Critics' Review*,
published c   1959, 625 Frederick St., San Francisco

MODERN EDCATION--A Brief Treatise: Only does a social revolution
often devour her own children in a reactionary consrvation of the new regime, carrying
the revolutionary spirit past the crisis into the period of spreading reforms. But cilvil and
intenational wars exhibit a kindred, closer-to-home, centrifugal tendency, a kind of minor
renaissance of inbreeding new philsophies and modification old systems of thinking, of
ideologies.

If we look back to around `1925, we find that educators were re-xamining
obsolete methodologies and credoes under the unflattering light of what social scientists
and educators themselves had to discovered. Leaders in education, the authors-writers
"agreed that our schools were pretty bad. Noting but a major revolution in practice would
do."

Education today, in the perilous wake of war, is going through a similar
phase of redirection, a re-opening of the marketplace of ideas on our system in an effort
to bring up to needs the ideologies and practices of education as a social dynamic
institution. Much of what is obsolete can be attributed to a dying pedagogies yet the same
may be said of the modern, in which realm administration finds many soothsayers--
benign approvers--among teachers. Rote learning, memorization, reading performance
and board-work are still in vogue, as it were, with older teachers in public school systems.
And why not if they worked? But, onm the other hand, are they productive and germane
to today's more complex social problems and challenges?

Of one thing we may be certain, and that is that international compeition,
its mania for nationalistic good cirtizenship, and the American family's changing
character have opened an abyss between the educators and the needs of society. In math
and science, American school children have fallen behind their international peers. This
is parftly due to dependence on machines, machine-scored tests, the classroom
calculator...and to boredom, to a disconnect between the classroom and industry, and,
lastly, to sheer inertia of children without motivation or adult inspiration as role models.
Instead of hiring achievers from the outer world beyond school walls, the "systems" of
pedagogy have been content to hire teachers from academies of teaching and with BA's in
education. Also, and of utmost importance, the schools lack competitive salaries for
teachers.

Federal aid to education for the construction of achools and the increae of
teachers salaries embrace a program tlhat willl take from the National budget millions
each year, to be dispensed to those States that have a demonstrated need ror additonal
funds. Certain agrarian States in the South, partcularly, and those overpopulated industrial

areas in the North, and wherever there has occurred an influxe of newcomes, as illegals, that is disproprtionate to the per capita and corporate tax structures, it is they who have requested and will continue to request Federal aid. Such aid, however, if endorsed by the State's Senate and City or Township Counsels, and providing the citizens do not petition for a recission of the grant affectilng them locally or lthe people of heir State, is a form of lawful financilal assstance, under the Tenth Amendment to the Constitution.

For aid to education, although not expressly subsumed underr any other Constitutional law goverrning a power to the Union of States, and while not prohibited as a power of administration, is reserved to the individual States respectively, For aid given to the people for the education of their children is today often tendered under a bond issue referendum by the people in those States that accept that aid. Amendments X and IX, of the Federal Constiltution (powers reserved to the people) at the time of their adoption, did indeed cause widepread fear of Federal encroachment upon States' rights. It was Jeffereson who, in 1823, wrote: "I believe the States can best govern over home concerns and the General Goverment over foreign ones. I wish, therefore, to see maintained that wholesome disrtricution of powers established by the Constuitution for the imitation of both, and never to see all offices tranferred to Washington." Under financial duress, however, and upon States' adoption, without petition of recission , Federal aid to education has becomes legal and valid.

Outright grants, to be matched by States' monies, for the building of schools are urgent in some sections of the Country in which the incoming migrants neither own land, with or without imrprovements, nor a business that can be properly taxed to help defray construction expenses. The children of illegals enjoy a free education whilest their fathers send money home, usually to Mexico. Yet it cannot be expected that the corporation and property oweners should pay the entire bill.. It is only right, therefore, that the earnings of the people should be taxed; athough I am aware that in many instances, particularly where the citizen is childless and working, presssures will be exerted toward the ends of uniformity and cheapness, and toward a de-secularization of the schools, if the taxpayer is of the Catholic faith. The childless secularist, in effect, pays for the education of the children of others in American society.

What I would point out, though, is that the aid to increase teachers' salaries places the Federal Goverment in the position of co-employer with the people of that State. And that whereas, by analogy, a bank shares with a borroer the ownership of his property, without injury to or infringementl upon his civil rights, the General Governorship of his property, the Government may without injury to or infringement upon his civil rights co-own the land and the buildings of a new school. Furthermore, whereas the bank trustees are prohiibited from dictating the personal beliefs of their debtor, the Federal Government, upon mandate of a strictly financial arrangement, does and will continue to violate human conscience by dictatorial writ of secularism , thereby using Amendments IXand X to undermine, in the instance of religious schools,. the religious freedom guaranteed by the First Amendment.

Ownership of a thing deprives it of any intrinsic value or power of self-determination. And the loyalty affadavlt, a Federal currrculum, a Washington panel of educational advisors and technical directors would involve not simply the surrender, but the sale and purchase of the *right of self-determination* of teacher, school board, community and citizens of the State. That right is pendant upon the ownership of the *teacher as property*, as a *means of production by* the great masses of complacent and indifferent people. Politliclians are ready to manipulate the will of the people for personal gain in the absence of public will. Indeed, what we today observe in America is a sylstem of socialized education, under which burden it is difficult to find competent orthodox educators who espouse individualism in education, both for the student and for the competent administrtator. The former must give way to the dumbing down of teaching to confer *brightness* upon the indolent and willfully illiterate, whilest the latter, the Administrator over one or many schools, must always be aware and submit to the consieration of his politics. The larger the school system, as LAUSD, the more apparent these weaknesses of the system.

           LOBBYISTS—A Second Brief Treatise: -- It is my suggestion and hope that lobbyists in Washington be muzzled by law and allowed to speak when their influence does not directly contribute to the manipulation of upcoming votes of the people. There should be a cut-off time of three months prior to a general election. Lobbyists have long outlasted their original value, which was to inform, first, then to petition for *change.* Furthermore, Goverment aid to their companies is *laissez faire* so long as competing lobbyists establish a bid minimu by gentleman's agreement in order that both profit, the loser by contract shunting, It is my suspicion, too, that, those high prices mentioned earlier in the sale of items to the armed forces contain percentages deducted as my payoffs for competing bid absenstention, or rigged bidding on items not as yet "discovered." Additionally, millions are being funneled into the pockets not expressly accounted for on those bid constracts--payoffs. I realize that it is unkind of me to say so, but the *lobbyist* is only another name for the well-heeled robber. Demand, as opposed to need, occurs by means of legislation that on major contracts shall not be compared against private estimates submitted by the banks and investment officials. By a penal statute that expunges fraudulent intent, that is, any bill in gross excess of such estimates--shall, upon issusance, subject the manufacturer to prosecution by the Attorney-General for extortion of the public. High taxes and corruption in Government are due in large measured to the chasm letween Federal spending and private investment capital via the current Federal budget. *Pork*, "ear-marked" projects are an example of that fraud.

           I am constrained, therefore, to conclude that the intent to defraud is applicable to Goverment bidding as well as to retail merchandising. And that unless the Attorney General takes legal action with respect to those criminal overcharges already placed against the National Budget, I can only assume that thievery is an acceotabke Federal policy and that profitteering is by acquiescence therefore lawfully condoned.

           If he refused to prosecute on the basis of these contracted-for items already mentiuoned, and providing the media have not supplied false or misleading information, the only conclusion that remains tenable is that the Attorney General is derelect in his duty and, fearful lest his appointment be withdrawn, plays politics with the people's money for reasons of personal ambitoion and power, if not income, and in order tos augment the prestige and campaign-financial support of the President, in whose Cabineer he holds office. Upon the determination that the Attorney General has, is consequence, misused his offilce to gross negligence or perverse motive, he should be removed from his office of trust. Indifference or personal ambition can be the onlyvalid reasons for his refusal to prosecute.

Having dispensed with lobbyists, let us move into the farmlands of America. Anyone with the least knowledge of the financial structure of our economy and the bloated condition egregious subsidies of must surely be mindful of the fact that high corporation and high personal taxes are synchronous with high farm subsidy The subsidty is a form of filnancial support for farming products in light of failing market prices. Yet the subsidy appears almost fraudulent in view of heightened consumer buying power. The dollar of the taxpayer supports a subvsidy program that reduces the potention loss-margin on crop sales, yet at the same time it regulates consumer demand by a type of artificial price fixisng on the raw crops; for selling under pay may mean the withdrawal of Goverment support to the individual farmer in the following years, as he again produces a tripple yield wilthsout showing a profit, foreign aid iln corn and wheat, let us say, legitmizing his losses. In this case, the subsidy continues.

If he tries to sell over par, he increases his surplus, which he may then use as collateral for new farm machinery. But in increasisng his operating efficiency by the use of improved quipment,
he only raises his year's yield and that compounds his market loss by adding to his suplus. The taxpayer, on the other hand, not only pays for the maintenance of this crop subsidy program; but he pays for the storage of surplus crops and he pays the false and inflated market prices that are no longer integrated with the farmer's actual productive capacity. Tjhe fixed subsidy, consequently, is driving the smll farmer off the land. And Government, ironically, to recover losses to the farmer in surplus by the underwriting of farm loan collateral with tax dollars, must glean loan dollars, storage dollars, administrative dollars, and, utlimately, consumer dollars from the taxpayer for creating false higher prices. This form of deception is done by hiding the surplus and by giving it away to Russia.

I would not alarm anyone by radical proposal or hint of political subterfuge, since I wish to remain on the friendliest of terms with out public servants, prorvding they realize always that they are servants and not masters. If this yoke be too heavy and cumbesome for them to bear, then I think ti inly wise and fit that we express our will to find others for the impersonal tasks at hand under a Goverment of laws instead of a *Goverment of Planners*. This idea is, in fact, partly responsible for producing a Supreme Court that legislates from the bench.

However, I would like to propose, at this juncture, that by a Constitutional Amendment we eliminate the *College of Electors*. For it is they who compound the possibilities for corruption by favortism, profitabily directed, and by unde-the-table grabs, commercial, political, legal, of candidate pushers. These Electors seleced by the state Legislatures, conprise a curtain of liegmen between the voters and the officeholders, and are a relic of the European courts whose duchys sent representatives to the Crown for counselling or grievances. Our mass media especially radio, which is less amenable to consorship by technicians, make possible the obsoletism of Electors. Futhermore, I would propose that in the face of these Electors, we take recourse to ***direct elections*** instead, since the will of the people shall in no wise be violated, and there shall be restored to the people their sense of immediate responsibility in the choice of capable and honest presidents and officeholders. It is more difficult to circumvent the people in a public elelction that it is to circumvent those who by causuistry, deceit and machinations, may suppose themselves to fully represent the people of their Party in particular convictions at the nominations by said Electors. Electors can, in fact, extinguish the will of the people and also vote contrary to the majority will of those State legislatures who appointed them.

I would strongly urge that the Constitution again be amended to require that the candidacy for the President be pendant upon a term of office in one or both houses of Congress. Thus might we eiminate dark horses and elections by wealth of the wealthy, as is usually the case, since the power that is to repose in such hands is not always the best informed, by experience, in the problems of every day business, local government, those needs and the attitudes that direct the couplex course of the people's affairs. Nor is a man of that station always as thrifty as he might be; and the growth of an economy depends more upon the thrift of its citizens than it does on their spending habits and comnsumer power ir tge orinuses if a sekf-deckared fiscal conservative For without the one, the other ceases to exist. Election because of noble lineage is, furthermore, Medieval and belongs to the governments of tyrants, which nowadays we do seem to find not a little solicitous rapport with. Let a Senator's work and service to his Country speak for him, instead of the usual banile twaddle that is pumped into the thought bloodsteeam by media, politicians, industrial pushers, religionists and sycophants, most of whom have themselves at heart for money, power and the kingdom of righteousness.

It is not to be expected that these changes anc challenges which I have proposed would cause great joy, widespread and generous, among the populace of our tax-oppressed Nation, but lthey would conduce to lighten somewhat the load of annual tax debt. For it is indeed a fact, today and now, that our Congress and the President are gradually crushsing the imitiative and enterprise out of the American people, proving thereby that "the power to tax is the power to destroy." If we do not act to ease this oppressive tax burden, accepting upon our own initiative an equitable share of the responsibility for any unfavorable or dissasterous complication that may flow therefrom, perhaps none of those now living and future generations will see this Nation's individual enterprise, the ethics of her professional men, the credos of her schoolmasters, her commerce and science, and the fundamental freedoms under law, Constitutional Law and not the bills of alarmist expediency, stunted and contained by complete socialism. That breed of socialism will occur in our materialistic Republicanism in order to forestall bankrupcy; or, worst of all, possible calamities, accept domination by communist Russiam with its concomitant return to the dark ages that so barbarous a system would bring. Either we must, it seems to me, practice austerity to a certain degree and in specific and telling ways, or this Nation will suffer itself to submit to the poison of historical regression. (When I wrote this--il the 1950's I could have no idea that the Jihadists, , Hexbollah and and their barbaric retinue Islamo-fascist of Al Quaeda would attempt to destroy America's spirit, her resolve her strength with 9/11.)

Oppressive taxatiom is the primary cause of inflation. Producers, in order to recover tax losses, raise retail prices; consumers, to recover their dollar losses, demand higher wages. Producers, to offset higher wages and taxes combined, raise prices; consumers urged to buy more, adopt credit measures, prices and wages stabilize. Federal and State taxes increase, and the cycle repeats sitself. Neither labor nor management can rightly be blamed and it is our foreign aid and defense programs that account for the inflated tax rate and the commodity-premium in an economy of surplusses.

NEPOTISM and BLACK MARKETING--a third treatise: is said that *nepotism* is an old Congressional custom.
This was no doubt true when the ten dollar gold piece procured a Virginia smoked ham for the plate of an itinerant horse campaigner, and the ham was split nineways amongst the members of his family. The gold bought for the farmer three miles of new barbed wire, and the   Senator charged off the expense to election-year *incidentals.* Circumstances, however, have changed. The fuzzy-cheeked ivy-league son of a Senator, when circumspection merits no rebuke, can nowadays accrue by father's largesse ten or eleven thousand dollars a year, as much as a corporation vice-president who has spent his life at a one job. (This is the 1950's I am speaking of.) The price is rather high to pay for the lad's sloth and the Senator's thievery, for I make so bold as to call such clandestine deductiosn just that--*thievery,* the act of coney-catching practiced on the pockets of the American public for political office.

Nepotism runs rampant in the American Congress. The wife of a Senator, taking heart from her huband's gratuitous mulchting, which in any other profession would be considered malpractice or theft, thereupon charges her social dinners, her transportation expenses, her suite space to the American taxpayer. It would be indecent of me to suggest that her use of her husband's office for rank personal ends is a form of prostitution, for her enormous gains are ill-gotten behind the camouflage of *need.* And whilest she licks stamps and sits envelops to cover her conscience, the peasants must pay dearly for her services!

I have read, too, that not infrequenly there is property owned by some cousin or friend of the Senator who, finding himself a trifle short on funds for the acquisitoion of personal property, deems it an act of true patriotism to offer his front porche for office space, and at three or four times what it would ordinarily brng. Being accustomed to using the side and rear entrances of the house, he seldom uses the porch. Truly that is a shame for the taxpayer, vilewed as a tyrant visiting this Country for the first time, pays dearly in false claims for his board and keep. Yet I would distinguish between the Senator and the tyrant, and clanedestine, preferential profit is descriled to the taxpayers as an inadequate *earmark*. For wherever the typrant's bills may be charged to the improvement of international relations, those of the Senator's friend or cousin can be charged only to graft and to a wilful effort to circumvent both the law and the citizens who pay, those who unless enlightened, consider the *pork* needful for the country as a whole. Such bullshit has gone on for decades and few Senators have the guts to destroy the legalized Congressional seizure, permitted to exist under color of law, lest they commit political suicide. That is clear is it not?

It is my honest belief, moreover, that they have begun to fret under the yoke of such deceit, which ill-custom and vile usage have placed upon them. And that would they restore to Congress ilts unimpeachable integrity and dignity, which the founders of this Nation intended it should have, they must get rid of the rascals either by recall petition or on the next election day. Lest our elected Representatives under the law revert to the 17th century practices of the corrupt Parliament of George III, who took refuge from pleas of *cause b*ehind an apostleship of oppressive charity, and whose sycophants, bootlicks and economic liegemen prayed God forgive them their ire, since Colonial gold was for the glory of England, the Crown and the Throne of Grace. For our part, we must evict these Congressional *nepotists* and blackguards by common vote or suffer that this Naiton lose its ethical fibre against the winds of a troubled world.

History has shown us that one of the important adjuncts to a corrupt legislature is a powerfull military clique, a weak Departmet of Defense and a liberal Supreme Court. We curently (2006) have all three. InWashington DC today, the military echelons, lincluding both the officers and the enlisted men, are ecomin a societal class untos themselves. That ils thedeplorable fact; yet unless the citizens sof this Country prefer in future years to submit their educational prgrams and religious doctrins, their economic welfare and personal rights to the scrutiny of advisors who, for reasons of military command and battle safety would issue warnings against an organization of individuald among the populace, it is strongly to be urged that precautions to be taken frustrating the rise of a *junta* in the Nation's capital. Toward this end, one of the first steps we might take is to return the officers' boot lackeys and wet nursees to the regular line of duty. For where they are least indispensable, they are most required, and were this not so, World War II and the Korean War would have been wars between the respective officers. Yet since it is true that miner skirmishes and major battles are fought and won by youngsters with guns, tanks, bazooks and grenades, the cliques of Washington brass, if they are soldiers, could serve their Country no more nobly than by returning these men to the line.

Other contingenies of a quasi-military government sear remarking upon at this point; for in the theme of tax reduction, we may find buried many holes, whic, like asieve in their function, doth allow much gold to filter threough priority requirements and over the heads sof these parasitical officials. Throw out the rubbish of ridiculous field manuals that appertain to the ease-lulled life of these officers. Cut down on their cars, their lavish military dinners, their Federal booze, and their unnecessary trips abroad, to say nothing of their entertainment expense money to maintain, here and there, a mistress on the miltary scene; for where you find the army you will find also the whorleom set up to keep the troops happy. In concluding this much, the brief indictment of official mililtary waste, I may be permitted the suspicion that there is not a little black-marketeering now enjoying current popularity in Washsington, partilcularly in drugs, and that but for the Frenchie with a folded shopping bag under hisarm, waiting outiide the *gar d' lest* in Paris, the black marketeering in our Capital passes all of the tests for nefarious exchange that blossomed in France after World War II.

THE ROMANTICISM OF
JOSEPH CONRAD

Joseph Conrad writes in "Author's Note" to *Within the Tides*:

> *The romantic feeling of reality was in me*
> *an inborn faculty. This in itself may be a*
> *curse. but when disciplined by a sense of*
> *of personal responsibility and a recognition*
> *of the hard facts of existence shared with*
> *the rest of mankind becomes but a point*
> *of view from which the very shadows of life*
> *appear endowed with an internal glow. And*
> *Such romanticism is not a sin. It is none the*
> *worse for the knowledge of truth. It only*
> *tries to make the best of it, hard as it may be;*
> *and in this hardness discovers a certain*
> *aspect of beauty.*

These lines attempt to delineate Conrad's personal perspective, the philosophical and aesthetic, in his characters' lives--which, he states, are drawn from the "hard facts of existence." In a ruthless and lonely world he found beauty among history's raw entanglements of human action, more primitive than urbane, less naive than tribalized. Those "hard facts" were Conrad's standard of reality, to him--survival, loneliness, fear and superstition, hard-bitten demands of naked survival and *moral resolution* rather than impersonal law for a moral problem, as in *The Secret Sharer.* The Captain allows the excaped convict, to board his vessel, hiding him in his cabin until he can swim to freedom. He eschews capture of the man and turning him over to the police. That is his personal moral decision.

Conrad writes that he rested his work "more on contacts, and very slight contacts at that, than on actual experience." The dramatic incident and illuminating moment were more important to this Polish- British writer than was the episode or even the anecdote. The instant of a happening was more dramatic than the exposition of all the circumstances. He possessed the photographer's instinct and eye for the dramatic moment before him. Yet he crafted stories with great, almost painful and meticulous care, from the reminiscences of his life. That past was his "sustenance." The most profound and dramatic experiences in his life were those "slight contacts."

Conrad sailed before the mast for twenty years, moving among a world of ships and men and foreign cities, villages and primitive communes. Indeed, in those works of his "early period"--a time frame with no boundaries--Conrad did not bother to change the names of certain of his characters. Almayer and Captain Beard from the vessel "Judea" in *Almayer's Folly* were actual persons. The entirety of *The Nigger of the Narcissus* is a literary tribute to a men Conrad had known personally, proof which is his statement: "I must enshrine my old chums in a decent edifice." Ports he visited on voyages to South Pacific Islands as well as to swarming cities of the Far East and South America enter Conrad's fiction as detailed depictions of shipboard life, fringe-of-the-jungle habitations, common habits and custom and native types. He wrote the entire novel *Nostromo* from his memories of a port-of-call in South America that lasted only a few days!

Conrad looked upon the noblest and basest qualities of human nature, directly and simultaneously. His romanticism did not search for the ideally pleasant and without the flaw of pain in his life. He confronted social injustice in *Victory.* He reforged tragedy in life to mean the catastrophic breach of a man's spirit because of his inability to cope with or to ignore the injustice, the flawed rules of men and their tilted judgements and tortuous collisions which damned their existence. Mrs. Gould in *Nostromo* is just that sort of tragic character. She is trapped in a mining venture with her husband Charles and discovers, to her pain, chagrin and dismay, that he has shifted his affection and interest from her, whom he once loved, to his silver mine. Never was there any romantic idealism in their affinity for each other; there is a blind side to emotional commitment. Nor is Charles Gould entirely evil in his disregard of his wife, for the absolute character of that evil would have romanticized his attachment. Even though she sees his love waning, she stays faithful nd permits herself no escape. Gould's cruel indifference and his wife's unrequited hopes is Conrad's *tour de force*. Even thsough one may not be totally in agreement with that conclusion, the power of the theme resides in men's rebuke of injustice that will not deter fate. Or, to put the matter another way: hope must rise from the caldron of pain or all are damned, including the author. That hope can travel on the thin rim of destruction, as it does in the long short story "The Secret Sharer."

A writer's credibility with a reader must not destroy his illusion of reality of the work. That is, simply that his characters must be believable and, above all, neither flawless nor irredeemable. Conrad has written in "A Familiar Preface" to *A Personal Record*:

> *In order to move others deeply we must*
> *deliberately allow ourselves to be carried*
> *away beyond the bounds of our normal*
> *sensibilities--innocently enough, perhaps, and*
> *of necessity, like an actor who raises his*
> *voice on the stage above the pitch of natural*
> *conversation--but still we have to do that.*
> *And surely it is no great sin. But the danger*
> *lies in the writer becoming the victim of his*
> *own exaggeration, losing the exact notion of*
> *sincerity, and in the end coming to despise*
> *truth itself as something too cold, too blunt*
> *for his purpose--as, in fact, not good enough*
> *for his insistent emotion.*

To create the believable was Conrad's lifetime literary attack, after his first two failures in the novel. Conrad did not see men from within as did Henry James. He could not write inferring a man's chaacter and thoughts. When he tried it, as in *Almayer's Folly,* he failed. His adopted methodology resulted in blurred characrters, lacking sharp delineation and concision. He tried again in *An Outcast of the Island,* his second book with the same result produced by a *Jamsian initation* of inner being. "The hard facts of existence" were absent or obscure in his writing. When in *Lord Jim* Congrad begins to create believable character from the visual presence of the man, his actions and ways, we are caught up in the intrigue of his life. Heyst in *Victory,* the Nigger in *The Nigger of the Narcissus,* are in accord with Conrad's awakening to his natural methodology, his innate intuiton and perceptions, his capacity for descriptive mood-details. He begans to give us plausible figures, the men who doubtless did live in his nomadic world. And he now has disciplined himself to weigh, balance and accurately discern emotions, keeping them within the bounds of the credible and fascinating.

In the "Author's Preface" to *The Nigger of the Narcissus* Conrad writes:

> *"My task, which I am trying to achieve is to try*
> *to make you feel--it is, before all, to make you*
> *see."*

To see in order to feel had the artistic certainty of a charted course. To feel the Captain's fear of discovery of Legget, the escapee, in *The Secret Sharer,* we have to visualie the actual shipboard layout, the approach of the great dark cliffs before the stowaway makes his escape. We have to see Heist in action before we understand how he could enact his folly to escape. We have to imagine the Scenes of *The Nigger of the Narcissus* before we can feel. We have to contemplate usually the desultory hands aboard the vessel before we can feel the impending mystery aboard Marlow's ship.

The quality of imaginary sight, of that capacity for presenting a "picture" of what is happening is a skill that does not exist in Henry James, Conrad's early model. Civilized men's primitive emotions eluded him when he used the introspective technique borrowed from James. The natives and seamen, the missionaries, shipmsters and traders he chose to wlrite about were alient to James'refinement of intellect and style. Conrad could, by temperament and vagabondage, begin only with the outward appearances of a man, his eyes and beard, his hands, the way he carried himself, the straw hat and rumpled tropical suit, the sometimes treacherous way he looked and moved through a crowd: all were familiar to Conrad. With these cognates of the visual mine he might then reach the inner soul whereby potential fury and brooding guilt and acts of murder lay hidden in the darkness. The "hard facts" of life were considered vulgarities in the rarefied parlors of Jamesian London or of Parisian society.

The following excerpt from *Lord Jim* depicts mood and character, inseparable entities in Conrad's fiction, rising in certain eloquent passages to lyricism about the sea.

> *Can you imagine him, silent and on his feet half*
> *of the night, his face to the gusts of rain, staring at*

the somber forms, watchful of vague movements,
straining his ears to catch rare low murmurs in the
stern sheets! Firmness of courage, of effort and fear?
What do you think? And the endurance is undeni-
able, too. Six hours more or less on the defensive,
six hours of altert immobility while the rest sof
the boat drove slowly or floated, arrested acording
to the caprice of the wind; while the sea, calmed,
slept at last; while the clouds passed above
his head; while the sky from and immensity of
lustreless and black, diminished to a sombre and
lustrous vault, scintillated with a greater brilliance
faded to the east, paled at the zenith; while the dark
shapes blotting the low stars astern got outlines,
relief; became shoulders, heads, faces, features."

Conrad's awareness of **time** meant the time of the skies and sea changing, of winds, currents,s of the movement of the boat the presence of others aboard, their emergence in dawn light and, withal, one may notice, the chiaroscuro use of light and dark for dramatic effect. His repeated use of **while** compounds the total powerr of the changing scene, of the life aboard ship on the changing seascape. The following quotation captures the "hard facts" images of Conrad's imagination. The dsescription is external.

"Through these metamorphoses of the scene stands the
resolute Jim, a man of duty, bearing bleakly a
necessary sentry's hardship, inured to the ways of the
he scene stands the resolute Jim, a man of duty,
beakly a necessary sentry of hardship, inured to the ways of the   *sea,*
watchful, loyal to his command,   *the symbolic fireacher who*   *watches the*
light come, mindful of the danger beneath the waters,   *of the instant*
catastrophe of a rogue wave, of survival and   *death and potential cruelty*
aboard in the huddled   *darkness."*

The next usotation illustrates Conrad's genius for revealing the influence on the man of the sea and sky.

When a man quails before his fears, his courage
mounts guard. When he stands resolute, he is best able   *to*
confront the resolvable mystery of survival. When the   *dawn should*
arrive, day would present new dangers   *but what of that? Let the*
night amid sea scud and the   *busy slap of water against the gunwales slip*
away first   *and confirm to him that the sea's cold dangers explore*
the soul of a man, unremittingly .

Symolical without its being consciously symbolic, Conrad has captured he cadence and ritual and mystique of the sea watch in these few words. The idea of *a defensive posture* buried in the quoted words is a catalytic concept that opens up Conrad, the man, and his writing, for primal fear, man's fear of himself and then of nature, its moods and beasts, its dangers and beauty, flood to mind.

To look at a man through realist's eyes is to perceive what he does not know and intuit what he only dimnly reveals. It is to see that second character of a man whose faults are so intensely private to the visible character that he kills to protect them from the light, he maims to inflict their reed for venvgeance on another; he assumes the mantle of light to protect what is ignoble within; he cringes in his cowardice protected by arrogance and villainy; he honors his primitive lurking within the clothing of civilized men or the righteousness of his articulated god. His restless soul does not change any more than do the restless seas he sails upon.

Details of dialogue and action in **Lord Jim** show Conrad's sensitsive awareness of life going on around him, and of his exploration of every possible niche of interest focused on the characrters he writes about and on the fragmentaries of the scene he depicts. **Nostromo** also demonstrates his dependence on past experiences of import in his life, and their consequences, as the brutality among men who find thmselves unexpectedly caught up in some fatal irony of their own making.

Conrad's vision revealed men's particular evils and their virtues with a critical eye undeflected by any personal compassion for man or his circumstances. In **Nostromo** the ruthless rage that misdirects also dominates every potential goodness in Faulk's character; the primitrive vanity that is the master of Nostromo's passions; the fidelity to a moral code that drives Lord Jim into his own exile: these traits, these identifiable signatures of the inescapale *natural man* who is that characrter individualize each in his yarn, Yet though they are plain men, their characters formed on the wheel of circumstances bear a singularity of purpose and intensity of vision unique to no other in history. Desire rules each, an end to the attained end, Conrad wants us to see those ends familiar to man who dare to look within themselves.

In this common bond with other men, Faulk, Nostromo and Jim are close proximations of their "doubles" in reality, those who share similar circumstances evoking kindred emotisons. Conrad writes that these characters lead one to find, according to his...

> "deserts ...encouragement, consolation, fear, charm--all you demand--and perhaps also that glimpse of truth for which you have forgotten to ask...a justice to the visible universe (wrought) by bringing to light the truth, nianifolnd one, underlying its every aspect."

Not all of Conrad's characters are villainous, inflicted with wicked wrath and evill concuspidence, sojourners alongf the whale's wake of inner guilt and damnation., Indeed, these lines suggest that Conrad and Melville knew each other, which in fact was the case. Gentler qualities appear in certain of Conradian characters, the loft of pity to the soul, the endowment before another of chivalry of custom. 1 Yet never let one instance be named, do these attributes mininize a characrtewr? Conrads men because they live on the cusp of lifes "harde facts of existence," manliness is not one of their deficiencies nor is the scurvy of indolence their fate. Captin Anthony in the early novel *Chance* possesses the capacity for *suggesting life's possibilities*, so that other men might not suffer; there are natures like that which have no connections to formal religion, the redemptive nature of a good defense lawyer, or a stalward friend. The Captain feels obliged, due to his symparthetic nature, to offer his help when...and though Anthony's *idee fixee* the man's Samaritan quality, he does not cast Conrad as the victim of his own exaggeration, as he once feared. laptain Anthony is, withal, a man of great courage.

Captain Whalley, in *The End of the Tether*, a short story from **Youth,** is another good example of Conrad's perceptions of the mitigating, the exculpatory, the submissive side of strong men's natures. His parental devotion to the daughter whom he remembers as a yong girl is refreshingly unusual for all his godlike, commanding presence. This reunion does not diminish the virility of his nature but rather enhances it, striking the chord of similitudes in his loyalty to lthe sea as a bond of affection.

Indeed, he and Captain Anthony alike exhibit masculine properties and accoutrements of conduct in their dress, manners and action.; Twenty years at sea and touching all ports of the world gave greart breadth to Conrad's powers of observation. Beneath what refined judgement would call this semi-barbaric exteriors of these two men comprehended the strains of compassion and understanding in one and tender devotion in the othe:. the duality of their natures confirms their credible reality.

In "The Secret Sharer," the alleged murderer stowaway on the vessel is the shadow spirit who could be the real man if Captsain Marlow fails to divilge his presence. Opting for compassion and leaning toward doubt, as he does, Marlow would be an accomplice to a murder and condemned with certainty by the authorities. Conrad has succinctly stated this potential moral outcome. "One's literary life must turn frequently for sustenance to memories and seek discourse with the shades, unless one has made up one's mind to write only in order to reprove mankind for what it is, or praise it for what it is not, or--generally--to teach it how to behave." His was the wisdom of the sea that accepts the oncoming seas without rebuke yet with struggle against whaever great-seas nature casts aboard.

Conrad began to write about the sea after abandoning it at the age of thirty-seven. One may find in moot that he was a Romantic even though he drew upon past experiences. Logically, he had to; not being a writer of phantasies, he had no recourse. Indeed, the "hared facts" he culled bore a direct relevance to actuality. That connection was the link that gave them the power of immediacy, and therefore o credibility. "Making the best of it "the truth of those hard facts" on Conrad's changes, elavarated, embellished and added to his work's depth, as did the artesan he was. The evaluation of those facts he inferred; his wilngness to "share" with the rest of mankind" he showed, or demonstrated as sit were, in the code of shipboard cronies telling their tales and in the mode of a teacher imparting knowledge. Both experiences were familiar to Conrad.

He was not a complete romantic, even though he knew that recollections of past ruins was *romantic*. He implied that Romantic imagination and truth about men are not compatibles. He was averse to his owns Romantic predispositon toeward life as *irredeemable*, as a "curse" needing discipline into "personal responsiblity." But upon the ironies he was capable of seeing there impinged the realities so men's reactions under the ageis of fate. That power of the inevitable was, it seems to me, the *locus* of Conrad's romantic vision. Also, the Romantic notion of the importance of historicity led Conrad to mitigate the "truth" of "hard facts" by the introdluction of other possibilities of explanation. By this meansof tempering human action, he limproved his, and our, understanding of the characters of whom he wrote.

Conrad's women characrters require comment, since they are as real, tenable and constructive in the imagination as any of his yarns by crusty sea scions. In *Nostromo*, Mrs. Charles Gould, wife of the mine owner, must gradually accustom her heart and thoughts and her moods to an acceptance of the respect of the simple townspeople of Sulaco, in exchange for the fading love her husband. His obsession with silver at the mine is more important to him than mere interest in the woman who is his wife. In this passage, too, there appears a mettle, a reluctance to flee, a consanguinity of purpose and loyalty to *the commitment* which one can find often in Conrad's characrters, a madonna *sans* the prostitute life.

It must not be supposed that Mrs. Gould's mind is masculine. A woman with a masculine mind is not a being of superior efficiency; she is simply a phenomenon of "imperfect differntiation"--interesting, barren and without importance. Dona Emilia's intelligence , being feminine, leads her to achieve the conquest of Sulaco simply by lighting the way for their unselfishness and sympathy. She can converse charmingly, but she was not talkative. The wisdom of her heart has no concern with the erection or demolition of theories, any more than with the defense of prejudices. Her words have the value of acts of integrity, tolerance, and compassion. A woman's true tenderness, like the true virility of men, is expresed in "action of a conquering kind."

Dona Amelias needs to find a way to express her salient femininity. This is her need, and a profound one, as deep sounding as conquest in despotic natures of men, which occurs and then again recurs in Conrad's female character Winnie Verloc. Wrapped up in that feminity is the entire Self. Women of a masculine nature are simply "uninteresting differentiation," as Conrad put the matter. The satisfaction of the expressive need motivates the woman, uncluttered by false defenses of social cause or bittter pleading.

In the life of Dona Amelia, she does not express her feminity through maternal affections or, indeed, ever completely for Charles Gould. So absorbed is he in his single purpose to make his silver mine pay that he can find no time for Dona Amelia . After a tortuous passing of long months down in the arid small South American town, Charles' earlier strong love for his wife begins to wane. Mentally painful to her who loved him genuinely, she is helpless to watch their growing estrangement and loss of love. For love unrequited has no passion to fuel the flame. Effectually, she can not love him any longer, for in a woman of her affectionate nature this detachment rips apart the delicate lacework of their marriage and leaves her too torn and helpless to win him back with any natural charm she possesses. Her only alternative is for her to show a capacity for love by her efforts to win the condolences, affection and incredulity of the poor mine workers.

In the short story "The Secret Agent" Winnie Verloc also shows with a feminine virtue that somehow life has stunted by excluding her from courtship, marriage and childbearing. In Conrad's story she lives only for her brother Stevie, making numerous sacrifices to encourage his happiness. She sublimates her personal life in a protective mode, an eternal vigilance over him. And by her constant care, she can express her feminine nature, the inequity of the relationship, of her sacrificial exchange for his dubious happiness. Thus she lives out her tragic existence.

Dona Amelia's compassion for the laborers of Sulaco, Winnie Verloc's devotion to her brother, to name one other, Flora de Barral's love for the responsible Captain Anthony--all express the individuality of a "woman's true tenderness." Containing that virtue in their souls they are alike, patient with womanliness and vibrant with the truth of their separate commitments. Conrad neither oversimplifies nor sentimentalizes them as the women of his fiction

Certain qualities inevitably surface in the characters of major figures in Conrad's books, traits that often relect back upon the man his physical and intellectual vigor, his emotional power, his love of life that led him to sail to ports around the world for twenty years. His capacity to suffer was real. It is said that in his writing *Nostromo* Conrad spent twenty-one months in blackest despair over what he anticipated would be the book's failure. In their reflection of the energy and restless, adventurous spirit of the man Conrad, the writer's characters have the capacity to face often cruel, extremely dangerous tests of fortitude and moral courage. And in doing so they inescapably demand of themselves decision to act out their conflict without ever faultug the truth of their own natures! The Romanicism of Josph Conrad, in its most obvious aspect, is his genius for evoking mood through his description of exotic and far-away places. More profoundly, his Romanticism reposed in his idealization of the natural man by clarification of mafters of conscience, by the dramatic action in which there blended the delineation of moral choices with living guilt, lawlessness and primal human fear.

CONSCIENCE ABRIDGED IN MELVILLE'S
BILLY BUDD, FORETOPMAN

In 1951, Louis O. Coxe and Robert Chapman's stage adaptation of Herman Melville's short novel *Billy Budd, Foretopman,* went on the boards at New York's Biltmore Theatre. The fact of the time would not be of unusual importance, and if one bars the "perfection" and"actuality" of celestial bodies, were it not for the reasons which the authors proffer for their dramatic venture. Quoting from the *Princeton University Press* editon 's appendix to lthe play, the critic John Gassner writes: "Perhaps the 'Melville Revival' influenced us; it may have been the desire to find a theme and action that was inherently poetic and non-realistic. Above all, one idea or purpose seems clear: that we saw in *Billy Budd* a morality play. They continue *viz a viz* Gassner's preface in the Crown Publishers edition:
"For us, as inchoate playwrights, in January of 1947, Melville's story of good, evil, and the way the world takes such absolutes was material enough for the veterans of a war, a depression, and the moving cold war....This is a morality play and so do not apologize for its being such"; even though, Gassner concludes, they were "aware of the fact that a dramatic morality is neither popular in our time nor easy to compose."

Three points in the above quotes need clarification in order that we understand more critically what the authors have attempted to do: first, they equate historical experience with the mechanistic determinism of science in arriving at the conclusion that a particular morality-story would not seem of great "pith and marrow" to a modern-day audience. The former is empirical knowledge, the imperfect enlightening upon multifarious truths about war, depression and a politico-stalemate; the latter is the method of exhibition. The one does not preclude an interest in the moral values of the other, from whcih experiences in our lifetime the play should summon up rough historical parallels. The "Morality Play" premise of the authors and critic, alike, is in error--unless the moral dilemma involved in the conemnation of an innocent man is too "old hat" for the atage.

Secondly, the characters in *Billy Budd* are not morality figures, the symbols of vengeance (an unbridled spirit), jealousy, sloth, anger and justice, as they are in the plays of England's neo-Classicist Ben Jonson and, with qualifications, in the politically argumentative works of G. B. Shaw; with them we must include plays by the American social "insurgents" Clifford Odets, Sidney Kingsley and Lillian Hellman. The thematic question in *Billy Budd*--can an officer's conscience justifiably overrule the law of his command?--is not resolved by appeals to Shavian "life force" transcendance through trial and error; nor by symbolisms of inner conflicts as we find in the drama of

Maetrerlinck and Strindberg. Scarcely does any one of Melville's characters represent so clearly a particular social force, as do Ibsen's Hilda in "The Master Builder" and his Dr. Stockmann in "An Enemy Of the People"; nor can Billy, the Captain or any others aboard the *HMS Indomitable* be compared with those figures in T. S. Eliots "Murder in the Cathedral", in which macrocosmic, societal, human qualities of God's sinning creatures are united with the outward appearances of Middleworld souls, as, for example, the Templars and Knights with the intellectual mind of lthe Archbishop in "A Man For All Seasons " while Thomas Becket *does* image the human spirit and the laborers in the play as a "country" physical man. a farmer-type.

The moral question in Melville's short novel does not altogether dominate the actions of Captain Vere, Billy, Dankster and Master-At-Arms Claggart, the principals in the drama. Traces only of the Calvinist New England Doctrine of Predestintion, conceived by Geneva's "Pope" Calvin, appear in the novel, and even fewer in the stage play--the secular word for this is *destiny*; the Old Testament injunction agains killing remains, with the pagan stoicism of duty, voiced by Epictetus, clearly evident as a Christian-Hellenaistic graft upon the Hebraic dictum agalinst killing; yet the injunction is shorn of the portentious certainty of damnation either for Billy or for Captain Vere. Though Melville was familiar with Biblical docrine, purgatory and hell are not a part of the story's politico-moral design. The ethico-moral basis of Western civilization, however, is evident.

Thirdly, the outwardly more civilized urban-industrial segments of society on this continent are *inclined* as representatives of the upper-middle, middle-middle and lower-middle economic classes, and amidst the flux of time engendered by "cultural borrowing" in arts, sciences and government, to appraise their mores, their customs of belief, by the applicaion of naive pragmatic tests, by empirical experiment--logically inductive from verifiable referents, and by a fatalistic appeal to a Central Government whose bureaucrats hold the runes to the citizens' personnal lives, ever increasingly so. Or--the British Royal Navy controlled events aboartd *HMS Incomitable* . Now if we grant that the culture-complex aboard a British naval vessel in time of war against the French was not precisely the same as it was in an insurance office in down town San Francisco-- for on the first count obviously the artifacts differ, to say nothing of the discriminatory social psychological values plaeed upon those artifacts--it becomes soon obvious, or should, that in actions of a non-tribal yet tacitly ritualistic nature involving encuturated, environmental sanctions for or against a "wrong" act, that some *modus operandi* must be brought into play that those concerned might arrive at an equable value judgment based upon the circumstances. In short, that culture moral norms affect their unique judgement in cases at bar or, in this insance, in the drumj-head Court-Martial.

Note: The connections between primitive mimetic rites of, say, the Cheroke Indians with their homeopathetic hair toughening ritual, and the institutionalized religious *Qua Quaritis* for Easter *Jerusalem, Christ's Trial Before Pilate,* the *The Nativity*, symbolic dramas of the Catholic mass in Medieval England, are implicit within this sociological shipboard construct: *trial to determine justice*. Playwright and Priest are anthropological relatives.

Sophistication, in connection with morality, is the balance. "Sophistication," however, is a poetic term whose semantic value is in relation to the emotional response it evokes. It is not sophisticated that Billy Budd should moralize, should conjure into our aperceptions, by the operation of dramatic rite of magic exorcism, any in-group value of a potentially disturbing influence upon one's pschological "mindset" toward, or acclimated adoption of, mores in parallel with those of *Billy Budd's* warfare situation. For example, it would have been absurd for Melville to have interjected comedic ingredients into the life or death trial of Billy. Such writing would have been crude and obtuse. (That is not to say, however, that comic relief does not have its place in the drama.)

Should Captain Vere allow his conscience to overrule the naval law, which demands that Billy Budd be hanged for the unintentional murder of a ship's officer? That is the question that all three authors leave unresolved; while it is central to their stories. It may appar to the audience that the question at issue in "Billy Budd" the stage play, though we shall see ineptly presented, involves a delemma which confronts the world today. How can one secure his life, property and liberties without killing, without considerations of that prospect of mass extermination? Or--how can Captain Vere secure his ship with a murderer aboard? He might have inprisoned him in the brig until the *HMS Indomitable* docked in England, but the ship was at war with the French and most likely had order to remain as sea so as to be ready for battle.

The problem is individual, and not Governmental, whose chief conern is with techniques of implementation. It very soon becomes apparent that the morality in Coxe and Chapman's play is a real one. And that unless we ask the authors to lay Billy cold-bloodedly on justice's altar, as the Greek Agamemnon did his daughter Iphigenia to appease the wrathful Artemis that his becalmed Aulis ships might sail to recapture Helen and sack Troy, in short, for a sound wartime reason, we are accepting this ancient paganism, that grants to Billys life no sacred worth.

Boston Calvinism, whose Hebrew God Cotton Mather reduced to the compass of a scolding, garrulous village priest, systematized the dogma of reactionary theology, alien to Lutheran liberalism and to more democratically liberal views espoused by Separatist-Levelers, a theology whose most conservative apostles in James I's England had adopted the monarchial-feudal predetermination of human worth by a despotic and arbitrary God as manifest damnation or salvation. This was the 19th c. dichotomy of human worth, at a time when "new science," predicated by Sir Francis Bacon in his *Novum Organum* (1620) breeched general acceptance of *The Great Chain of Being*, the Medieval theological system of laws from St. Thomas Acuinas, in the exploration of world symbvolized by the lowly oyster. This rift T. S. Eliot has characterized as the "dissociation, of sensibility." Into it poured Dissenters, skeptics, pagans, the military, Rump Parliamentarians, and among them, precursors to adherents of Colonial separation of Church and State, philosophies of frontier indivualism, splinter religious sects, and policial-social reform movements. Key to the re-evaluation of human worth Pope summed up in his lines : "...the proper study of mankind is man." In the story by Melville, Captain Vere studied Billy's character to ascertain the righteousness of his predelection to hang the foretopman despite the innocence of Billy's intent in the murder of Claggart. The only reformsthat governed him governed warfare aboard his ship

Thje Protestant and Separatist list of "don'ts," injunctions against any sin representative of all sin by a Divinely created man inwardly evil, depraved, predestined, lifted up by the efficaciousness of good works, which dicta he condemned, among other evils, genuflexion, stained glass windows, church music and Sunday games, labeled idolatrous by tract writers, censorious of Cavaliers and High Anglicans in 17th c. England, included the Mosaic Law that a man shall not kill his brother. Human worth began with the sanctity of sinful creature man. Even sailors had souls.

From the New England dichotomy of morality, ordained in Calvinist theological determinim, which doctrine clashed with 17th c. revolutionary liberalism, Protestant evangelism emerged. Zealous survivor of Calvinist dogma's defeat, and, Church and State divided by law, the universal manhood suffrage of Jacksonian democracy, man's "inalienable rights would be affirmed by the Reformation and general readership of Scripture which affirmed and reaffirmed, in the face of his inherent sinfulness, man's capacity to do wrong, intentionally or not, and his inherent worth in God's eyes. This was hardly the case when Priests were owners sof the Bible and its proscription of church *punishment*. Should Captain Vere, as Commander of a ship of war have punished Billy? We see the roots for his moral dilemma.

Introduced into American 18th c. thought came Rousseau's romantic, philosophical notion of human nature's responsible, fundamental, lawful goodness, germinating in the Fundamental Moral Law mirrored one hundred and fifty years later in Wilsons World Court Idealism. Acceptance of man's basic integrity was fundamental to harmonoious social intercourse. "Faith, hope and charity" ought to prevail. Captain Vere's historically-rooted compassion ought to guide his conscxience.

Utilitarianism, Equalitarianism, the Quaker Humanist movement, Trascendentalist reforms, the labor movement, Socialist Utopianism--all of these manifest assertions of independence from a special tyranny, and in further protections of individuals against proscribed malignant forms of American individualism, proclaimed inreasingly the value of human life, justifying "the ways of God to man," and discarding orthodox Medieval, Reformation judgements upon the rational, animal and spiritual man.

It is the rational Baconian view of human nature, subject to its own laws and scrutiny of "truth" based on the faith of Christian theology, rather than according to Thomas' metaphysical dogma, which lay behind Capt. Vere's quandry. The events of Melville's story reveal that he did not regard Billy Budd as an offspring of Adam. That the life of the ship's foretopman was of value is an idea which belongs to these movements in liberal democratic thought, heritage of the Protestant Reformation. That the specific Hebraic law of Calvinist doctrine stayed Capt. Vere's hand from execution of the sentence Melville's novel does not reveal-although I doubt it-- either through exposition or dramatic action or, indeed, through symbol.

Wartime "rules of engagement" in conflict with compassion for a morally innocent man stayed his hand. What one should bear in mind, however are the historical relationships between the humanistic value Vere placed upon Billy's life and the implications of these earlier humanitarian ideologies upon an ecclectic acceptance by American readers and audience, alike, of the Captain's indecision, his forebearance and difficult execution. His problem of conscience is inextricably united with the histories of the people of both England and America. In view of this history, it hardly need be said that such a problem is not, and cannot be, the fashionable device of theatrical entertainment.

We may, instead, suspect Mr. Gassner of a fine irony when he writes that dramatic morality in our time is not popular. This attitude is naive and vulgar. But that the critic must preface an excellent play with apology serves only as a probe and gauge of the theatergoer's "moral blackout," his intellecutal apathy, his bland surrender to the frolics, titillating escapes and sweet dainties of commercial play production; while the connnections between "war," a depression and the moving cold war" and Capt. Vere's dilemma remain hidden from him. The raptures of the popular mind cannot be equated with the conquests of "rules of engagement."

Theoretically, moral opprobrium can be and quite often is, in Western societies, a co-determinant of a jury's verdict. The distinction, however, between the ethico-religious injunction against killing and the statute that pertains to manslaughter, upon proof of a crime committed, is a real one. The former is a prescribed ethic for the living; the latter is a law waiting to be executred in the case of a violation of that ethic, an a moral act, in short, a crime.

Note: Article III, Sec. 2 U.S. Constitution : on extension of "the judicial power," it is capable of acting, refrains from expression of opinion upon Constitution, Congressional laws or treaty until invoked in the "case" of someone asserting a *right*.

Billy Budd, Foretopman, it needs be said, is not a fictional mandate against crimes of similar magnitude in circumstances as those of the foretopman's slaying of Claggart, his Master-At-Arms; nor is Melvilles story a symbolical *morality play* against murder.

Raymond Weaver in his Introduction to Melville's shorter novels writes ((1947): He, Billy Budd, who "had none of that intuitive knowledge of the bad which in natures not good or incompletely so, foreruns experience," struck Claggart with his fist in a rare flash of anger caused by frustration in his self defense, which action and the ensuing penalty were subject to the Articles of War governing British naval vessels in in the year 1798. It is untenable to hold that the crimes of Hitler, let us say, and of the Nazis arraigned at Nuremburg, in addition to dictatorial government expediencies and the countless individual cruelties engendered by dire hardship conditiosns of the depression, were, at the time, of *moral consquence*, and yet to say that Bills drum-head trial and execution was of *no moral consequence* because of his acts inclusion under a provisional law of British naval warfare, or because of the religious ethic underying Capt. Veres quandry. Though a people's memories are short, historical time is not the true, just governor of ethical content; the reality of the humanitarian moral law at issie, is in these instances, a pervasive, enduring principle.

If, for reasons other than dramaturgical skill, artistry and the sensuous components of a stageable play, the theatregoer refuses to accept **Billys Budd's** ethical premise intrinsic to Capt. Vere's dilemma, it is perhaps because he refuses to accept as a condition for understanding the work Melville's implicitly premised moral law, the Hebraid Calvinist dogma, secularized, rendered viable through narrative human experience, and translated into the legal precept dramatized by a court martial aboard *HMS Indomitable*. That secularized dogna recognizes the intrinsic worth of a man's life, whether innocent or guilty. The religious abstractiosn of good and evil merge with Melville's psychological observations of the moral-law loaded relations between Claggart and Billy; "if askance he (Claggart) eyed the good looks, cherry healthfull and frank enjoyment of young life in Billy Budd, it was because these happened to go along with lthe nature that as Claggart magnetically felt, had in its simplicity never willed malice or experienced the reactionary bite of that serpent. To him, the spirit lodged within Billy, and looking out from his welkin eyes as from windows--that ineffably it was which made the dimple in his dyed cheeks, supplied his joints and dancing in his yellow curls made him preeminently the Handsome Sailor. One person excepted, the Master-At-Arms was perhaps the only man in the ship intellectually capable of adequately appreciating the moral pheonomenon presented in Billy Budd, and the insight but intensified his passion, which, assuming various secret forces withim him, at times assumed that cynic disdain--disdain of innocence." (Ibid, p. 268) In the novel, Melville having establishsed Billy's innocence, the moral law of mercy challanges drumhead execution; it becomes a force in the conscience of Captain Vere, and reinforced, as it is, by his knowledge of Billy's innocent nature, the question of mercy relates to all scenes in the novel when the First Lieutenant, Captain of the Marines, and Saiing Master are called to court, and when Captan Vere executes the law. Punishment is not a condition of the law, which needs no vindication in its express definition of certain crimes. Yet the conscience of Melville's Captain Vere cannot be dismissed; it is *persona,* intimate, individul and belies the sociological phenomenon of a "conscience" behind group-will. Even the two consciences appear to conflict in the end when Billy is hanged, except that in Captain Vere's case duty has overruled the consensus of Billy'sshipboard mates.

Question of blame or exoneration os placed at the fore in Capt. Vere's reasoning--the exigencies under which the British fleet fought, and the issue of justified requital, by hanging, for a crime whose committal expressly violated the Letter of the Mutiny Law. Tough the slaying was and patently a crime under this law, Captain Vere felt impelled to base his evaluation of the justice of the sentence upon Billy's own nature, his motive, temperament and experience--all of which Melville clearly establishes over the course of his story. The playwrights, however, have abridged these matters of characterization and fundamental morality, extrinsic to the rational depravity of a respectable man like Claggart, or the aberration, under pressure of a dilemma, of a reasonable man like Captain Vere; and they have done so *not* primarily in order to achieve that economy of revelation found in the supreme examples of dramaltic art but in order to write a stageable play that would appeal to poular taste. In a word, the play of Coxe and Chapman is a fraudulent adaptation of Melville's great short novel. And they take no cognizance of any moral law operative in Melville's novel.

Which, in any case, should supercede--the Mutiny Law of the British navy, whose measures were undoubtedly of the strictest sort in wartime, or the Indominitable Captain's personal exoneration? That is the *problem of conscience* at the heart of Melville's book. A humanitarian moral and a specific law under which the individual, Captain Vere knew, would be held expendable, fell into conflict in his thinking. Indeed one of the glaring disparities between the play and the novel occurs in the passage describing Capt. Vere's reactions, seen through the ship surgeon's eyes, after the drumhead court martial. "He (the surgeon) recalled the unwonted agitation of Captain Vere and his exciting exclamations so at variance with his normal manner. Was she unhinged? But assuming that he was, it were not susceptible of proof." (Ibid 284) And then further on: "Whether Captain Vere, as the surgeon professionally surmised, was really the sudden victim of any degree of aberration, one must determine for himself by such light as this narrative may afford." (Ibid. 295). In the play, Captain Vere's closing lines are: "You recognize the logic of the choice I force upon you. But do not think me pitiless in thus demanding sentence on a luckless boy. I feel as you do for him. But even more, I think there is a grace of soul within him that shall forgive the law we bind him with, and pity us; stretched on the cross of choice. (*Turns away*) The tone of this speech is detached, magisterial and intellectualized. Only vaguely do the lines suggest the pain of the decision that was Caprtain Vere's in the novel. In order to externalize, to make dramatic before an audience the moral dilemma, the authors have had to "stack the cards," as it were, in favor of Billy without fuilly realizing, on the stage, the abstract problem of good and evil behind Melville"s story, of open innocence incapable of malignity, of depravity within impersonal respectability, between which contending forces Captain Vere is caught.

Does the existence of inhibitions of ethical intuition, of "that fine spiritual insight" into the essential of certain characters, prior to a moment of rash, impetuous anger, exonerate a man from the specific crime? Capt. Vere either had to dismiss Claggart's charges
charges of treason against Billy or hold trial. If one says that such an aberration coming from a man of Billy's character is not symptomatic of true depravity, then clearly his persuasion would place a superseding value upon the life of that "criminal" in its individual totality, as a living life, however manifestly evil the proven act.

Indeed, the same superseding value, but with less, if any, remorse in the execution, would have obtained had Captain Vere felt compelled to hang a depraved yet acceptedly respectable seaman like Claggart, whom he rergarded with " repellent distaste," "disquietude," finding in his reminders sof a 'bandsman' (briggand) and a "perjured witness." Law and compassion, if not mercy, were, howeever, in conflict. Thus, if one weighs that fine ethical judgement, innocence of nature, of maldictive intent --as Melville has so described Billy's character and actions--so as not to exonerate the man from his; moment's rash act, then his persuasion would find support in sociological concomitants involved:--the welfare and security of the *Indomitable's* crew, the allegiance toward Great Britain of all aboard, the right and proper execution of their duties as citizens, the various reponsibilities of Captain Vere and his officers under rules of shipboard conduct, laws of ship's command during naval warfare and the explicit conditions of the Mutiny Act. Such was the case for   sentencing and hanging Billy.

"In the legal view the apparent victim of the tragedy was the man who had sought to victimize a man blameless and the indisputable deed of the latter, navally regarded , constituted the most heinous of military crimes. Yet More. The essentials weighted and wrong involved in the matter--the clearer that wrong might be--were so much the greater aggravation within the responsibility of a legal sea-commander, inasmuch as he was authorized to determine the matter on that primitive legal basis."(Shorter Novels, p. 296) And he essentially worked alone.

Captain Vere at the inquiry in his cabin had demonstrated his responsibility, civilized reasonableness and compassion in an attempt to clear Claggart of suspicions that he had witnessed falsely against Billy as a mutineer. The compassion he felt for both men; it was antecedent to mercy, but that *will to exercise mercy* now clashed, in this primitive legal situaion, with his *duty* as a commander. In view of this conflict between the sociological and the indiviidual discrimination, impersonal justice and personal mercy , in broadest sterms, how was Captain Vere to Act?

Melville took care to establish the erratic nature of Billy's "strange, dumb, gesturing and gurgling" when, taking the verbal blows of Claggart's charge and Capt. Vere's admonition to "speak, man! speak! defend yourself," and being unable to speak because of "his lurking defect" that he stammers, he waits in his ineffectual agony, then slams the Master-At-Arms across his forehead, felling him to the deck "like a heavy plank tilted from erectness." The novelist captures the spirit of Billy's carefree enjoyment of life when, in Chapter VIII, he descrbes him and his topmates propped against the *stun'sails* rolled up into cushions, spinning yarns like the lazy gods and frequently amused with what was going on in the busy world of the decks below." Melville writes that "life in the foretop well agreed with Billy Budd." Throughout the novel, especially in the earlier chapters, he tells the foretopman's past performance in the marchant marines, of his willingness to obey, of his sense of duty.

The first flaw in the play, and one that virtually destroys the ethical problem at issue is that the authors put Billy into a fight with Jenkins, Capt of the Main top, in Act I, Sc i.. so incurred when the superior calls him a "little bastard" who's "so scared he's stammering." The playwrights establish that Billy is capable of violence, and that belies the man's true nature as Melville sees it. In so doing, Captain Vere's dilemma, after the Court Martial, is falsified; and the qustion of whether or not he shall hang the foretopman becomes a dramatic device whose logic of shipboard motivations, and of Billy;s personal motive is contrary to Melville's concept ot the Foretopman. Evidently the playwrights Coxe and Chapman, could not conceed a man of Billy's innocence, so they had to establish early in the play his capacity for instant violence. Their change converted Melville's unusual story to mediocre melodrama. This distortion disregarded the speech defect as an entirely plausible cause for the youth's murder of Claggart when one realizes that a charge of mutiny is also cause for hanging if proved.

Another instance of the playwrights' distortion of Melville's story occurs in Act I, Sc i in which Billy, in conversation with his mates Jenkins and Payne on the gun deck, accidentally drops a pot of soup just as Claggart approaches their mess from the companionway. Coxe and Chapman imply the possibility that the foretopman was overwrought after his fight, a few minutes previous to the incident; the Billy Budd of Melville's story is a not a man who bears grudges which influnce his conduct, his relations with others.

The authors suggest that the pot-dropping incident was intentional, not the result of clumsiness, since we see "the flicker of sunlight reflected on the water"; their text contains no specific indication that the ship at noon going large before the wind, was rolling on her course." (Ibid.261) This alteration of the weather affects their characterization of Billy, the foretopman. A rolling deck would have excused him--it is indeed so in Melville's novel.

Neither in the play nor in the novel is evident willfulness a factor in this sequence of the mess, although Melville was already related that, after harmonious relations with lthe ships officers and men, it was Billy's "surprise and concern when ultimately he found himself getting into petty trouble about such matters as the stowage of his bag, or something amiss in his hammock...." In neither work does he show prejudiced feelings with their basis in legally valid fact, toward the Master-At-Arms. And yet, in the novel, he fears Claggart from a distance; only the foretopman's feelings that Jimmy Legs was down on him marred his former serenity and, indeed, im Chapter VIII, follows his exchange of confidences with The Dankster, Main-mastman, for reassurance. This fear is an important distinction between the novel and the play; it is indicative of the primitive character of the relations, an undercurrent of feeling, nay, rather a a vein of passionate, primordial instincts which governl their actions. And yet the authors have thought to treat lightly, to discard for all dramatic intents and purposes, what is elementally human and of utmost moral-dramatic importance inMelvilles story--the relationships between the seamen on *HMS Indomitable*.

In the novel, Claggart and his foretopman are practically strangers; the sarcastic quips, the familiar solicitudes in the play, however, cause one to believe that there is a paternalistic relationship between the officer and the youth of ten years sea experience. The novel depicts their meeting, their first encounter in the mess, as one containing suggestions of the sinister, or that primitive passion beneath Claggart's exterior, of his concealed hatred for billly. (Ibid 262) The play depicts him as a savage, rudely "poetic" taskmaster, for he strikes Jenkins across the face with his ratten; whereas, in tlhe novel, he playfully taps Billy from behind with his rattan, saying , in a low musical voice, peculliar to him at times, "Handsomely done, my lad! And handsome is as handsome did it, too" (spilled the soup) and with that passed on." (Ibid 262) That depravity, vicious and a-moral, which Mellville's Claggart evinces does not usually manifest itself in actions so lacking in cruel sutlelty as the Claggart of the play exhibits. He is a coarse, melodramatlic recreation of the novel's character.

The authors of the play have eliminated the ameleorating factors of Billys former excellentl shipboard conduct in preference to the physical actions below deck--the accident in the mess,the fight with Jenkins, and, by implcation founded upon these sequences, or scenes, allusive to the foretopman's potential for violence, his involvement in the feud between Claggart and The Dankster. In so implicating Billy, the authors prejudice the drumhead trial in Claggart's favor, nullifying the foretopman's innocence by staging it, overtly, through fortuitous, defense actions by a sailor whose willful inversation of general intentions, stemming not from innocence but from cunning, potential violence, will do to another an insubordinate act which becomes misconduct of criminal lnature.

Coxe and Chapman felt it neessary to demonstrate Billy's innocence by victimiizing himl; but in doing so they have depicted him as a human creature at least logically capable of rank assault, of instigating mutiny. It does not seem plausible that Captain Vere would not be aware of these events aboard his ship; and, with the knowledge of them in mind, he would hardly have compassionate, if not legal *angst,* a just clause for such intense misgivisngs as he, in the novel suffers, feeling that the action precedent to the crime demands clemency, a show of mercy. To summarize: In the play, Billy's former conduct aboard the *HMS Indomitable* produces the case against him; in the novel, quite the contrary holds traue. His conduct is unquestionable. The authors have distorted and melodramatized the characters and actions of Melville's novel, and in doing so they have discarded the dramatic implications of compassion and mercy upon the action in the novel, and in the Commander's own mind followling the summary trial.

By increasing the motives and compulsions for Billy's slaying of Claggart to prove that the foretopman earned his due justice, the authors set upon a course which contradicts Melville's basic philosophical intention--which contains, in its story implications, strong suggestions of Calvinist predestination: to narrate the subtle yet highly dramatic means by which a sailor, innocent of any former crime, malevolent intent, mutinous ill-will, can find himself fortuitously i.e. *providentially* caught in the breech of a unique code of law, implicated by the actions of a gunnery officer whose character was such that, given different circumstances, he might plausibly have committed the crime.

The motivation for Claggats ill will is not, as the play contends, Billy's knowledge that the Master-At-Arms sent a sick man, maintopman Jackson, aloft in disregard of his life and safety; Melville's experienced foretopman is not consciously subtle enough to so place himself out of the reach of Captain Vere's Court Martial character- judgement byl any such naive attack upon Claggart's office as we find in his speech to the Commander, Act I, Sc i: "I saw a man go aloft, sir, as I came on board just a while ago. He looked sick, sir, he did. This officer was there, too, he can tell you. (To Claggart) Don't you remember, sir?" The real motivation for that illl will,on Claggart's part, is the antagonism between two men whose natures are fundamentally, antipathetically different. For evil in Melville's Claggart is not an abstraction, personified; it is an apprehension, an intuition of subtle feelings of dislike, a capcity for maldictive and irrational hatred without any open, any apparent cause upon which to establish a legal defense--as was Billy's case. Yet, the means to satisfy this covert wish, if only a subconscious wish, to do harm, is evidenced in the will to do harm which, inl its manifestation, is clothed by duty, accidcent, or whatever overt action seems most conventional , most rational to other men.

Refusing to accept the contradiction in Billy, of naivete and experience, a special experience with *sham*, the authors premise , through crude, misepresenational scenes, that his antagonism results in the mudrerous blow to Claggart. They have rejected the foretopman's fear, experience and discipline as a merchant seaman and, most important, Melville's key description of a sailor without "conceit" or "vanity" who was "a novice in the complexities of factious life...." (Ibid. 237-238)

To premise that Melville's novel is a dramatic narrative of moral abstractions, that fear and hatred cannot be shown i.e. proved, without denying the truth of the novelist's character, is to remove the action from human implications, scenes which the authors could have staged. To maintain that position is to say that since "evil" cannot be proved, there is no germinal motive, and thus is discard the true passion of fear the false charge behind the homicide. The authors argue from legalistic to moral grounds; Melville synthesizes from human and moral to legalistic. His narrative is inductive from his sea experiences and the doctrinal moral-religious mandate. The authors play is deduced from the realism of the novel's events, and from the circumscribed world of academicians. The best that can be said of the play is that it is sensuous and stageworthy, and, though without Melville's consummate artistry, his subtlelty of revelasion, the play represents an attempt to dramatize a contemporary moral dilemma: the justice of a moral cause conflicts with the duty of the judgement.

REALISM AND THE REAL IN DRAMA
a brief analysis

Realism on the stage refers to that dramatic action, its implications and the characters's motives that are plausible and inevitable, given the framework of the story. Yet those actions embrace a probable dramatic action in human experience identifiable on the street outside the theatre. Realities are the sensory facts in that street action that have existing corresponding blueprint counterparts to the life proved as real by the senses and affirmed by the drama in the theatre. The Actor's poor performance may appear to bely this connection but it is there. I;n other words, there exists an identifiable correspondence between the stage illusion and the street actuality which stamps the dramatid action as realistic and the character in the play as faithful to life. And by "street" I include any venue outside the theatre.

The Historical Age emphasizes certain styles, modes of drama such as domestic-tragedy, melodrama, psychological drama or Impressionism/Expressionism, and in so doing the Age of social life, insofar as the stage illusion goes supports the street actuality counterpart--and providing the actor is true to his character--created as a reenaced   illusion of real life. The appreciate the correspondence, the audience is caused to **willingly suspend their disbelief** in the stage model and to accept it as real life.   Thus does the theatre in its tlurn influence the customs of the age.

If the style of the dramatist is journalistic, tlhat is, he makes no attempt at interpretive or "directed" action, does not editorialize, refuses to convert his piece into propaganda, then the play is merely a "camera's eye" recording without favor what the playwright had witnessed. The play will have no discernable structure imposed on it to contravine structureless street life. There are those who would call this bland or unstructured work **realism.** Usually it turns quite anecdotal. Thornton Wilde'rs "Our Town" is an early attempt at this journalistic style

But when the playwright intervenes and discerns among the welter of matrerials he has to work with an idea, a theme, a statement about his observations, then he had plucked the **real**, the **truth**, from among the tangible actualities, i.e. realities, the tenable facts of his oservation. When those realities and the predominant truth of a Protagonist's character are sysnthesized with craftsmanship into art, we have realism in the drama.

The people of a playlwho fight, content, wrangle with each other often evolve basic laws about humam nature that confirm clinical analysis. The human creature, *homo sapiens*, contains in his makeup genetic predispositions to behave in certain ways that set him aside from other men--and from the animals. When he accepts the realities of *death,* he invents god. When he thinks *survival,* he hunts and fishes and to a lesser extent procreates. When he feels *defeated* or *shamed,* he invents a trickster. When hs is *awed,* he conceives a myth. When he feels *possessive,* he invents a law or rule or regimen. When he feels *lost* he invents a Chieftan or examines nature. And finally when he feels *grief* he invents another world with its embellishments and its comforts. His awareness sof his own existence real-ness predisposes him to be a carrier of a cognative truth of nature. With that self-insight, he finds in himself the capacity is sufficiently discern, to invent, or to discover a truth about himself, other men and their ways i.e. the "realities of life."

   The realities of Man's physical and mental nature are part of the realism of his wholness. On the stage, anything less than his humanness is a half truth. Anything more than his physical complexities traits sputs us in touch with the particular **truth of that man,** what is **real** about him and what drives his wants and ambitions.

A SHORT STORY DEFINED

Brete Harte and MarkTwain Western frontier stories wrote for the Alta Californian, a goldstrike newspaper in San Francisco. Ambfrose Bierce wrote about the Civil War amd William Faulkner depicted a small southern town, Jack London depicted the Yukon and stories of the frozen wilderness, the flurry of gold seekers the wolves and battle against the cold, . Katherine Anne Porter and Eudora Welthy were both writers of feminine senstivsity, revealing New England and Sot;ern social codes of conduct. Hemmingay wrote stories of suspense pitched in Africa and in Spain. O' Henry (Sydney Porter) wrote of city life, Steinbeck, stories about the poor farmers in Salinas grape country of the San Juaquin valley. The point is that these great writers in the short story form were all local colorists who wrote about the locale they were most familiar with.

To tell a story was their purpose, with insight, a certain fundamental elegance of style, with details of locale about selcted individuals who contended within themselves, with others, and against the environment.

Every short story exhnbits three, perhaps four elements that change it from mere anecdote, as most news stories are, to events causally related by motive, as compared to circumstances.

(1) a short story is art when it with care and craft selects details that advance the story line.

(2) A short story justifies its existence not by expounding a moral lesson but, rather, by involving the reader's limagination in the toils of lanother person's intimate life.

(3) A singular event or chain of tightly related events are the heart of the story. Some have said that the story must begin close to the climax and the resoslution. I disagree. A story can start with an enigma, a unique happening and built to the climax.

A COMPARISON

A stage play presents a scene from but one view, regardless of where the theatregoer sits in the house. A movie permits of watching different views of the same scen based on camera location. Stage settings must therefore be integrated with the action; while the camera can block out discordant elements. A stage presentation must recreate the physical reality through the very presence and imagination of the actors, working with spectacle elements as unified whole from action to action. A movie, by its very nature, records those physical realities, while its parts, because of camera-angle selection, need not be working together with obvious unity in each dramatic action ...although a unity is *implied* amidst discordant elements.

In a stage presentation, the actor is all important in such matters as pace, timing, the building of dramatic tension, making dynamic the action of the drama and conveying the meaning of the story. In a move, the use of music, flash shots of people and things off-set, odd angles and other technical devices may share that function of dynamic action with the actor. A stage presentation shows the whole actor, the entire characrer as a coordinated whole. A movie may present only fragments caught by camera selection, likely an artificial, mechanical direction of situation--and not necessarily directed by the actor, rather than an artful one, as by the actors on a stage.

The actors in a play consider audence reaction to the action going on; there is a give and take. This, however, is not (visibly) so with the best actors who adopt an attitude of **stage arrogance** that avoids this actor reactionl without theatrics but with an awareness ofthe audience. In a lesser actor, one can always detect this response-trick if the expected laughter, in comedy, fails to come. A movie in that respect is a dead thing-- even though the best script writers may provide for udience reactions of a violent sort by writing unimportant lines in the intervals, like toughs of a cycle. A stage play presents flesh and blood, live human vbeings who say: Look you. lHere we are, real people. You could ve one of lus, and now let us act out our story." A movie, being a recording of life, is not so intimarte, does not readily invite that actor-audience participation, a sharing of a story between real people. For that reason the stage presents a more intimate, and a more stubtle and flexible kind of acting.

While a play and a movie may be of the same length in time of performance, a play must telescope time through the dramatic illusions--the dialogue and its hints, shifts of focus of audience attention, artful acting and often the simple, traditional announcement of time passage. A movie, with its enormous flexibility in staging, can reproduce in short scenes that lapse of time and any interim action. The traditional announcement would no ordinarily be accepted by a movie audience--except that in the silent-film days, a title indicated a lapse of time.

A play must invite the suspension of disbelief in the story while presenting live human vbeings in action. A movie challenges that disbelief with its recorded physical realism and by camera techniques, while presenting not a *representation* but an *imitation* of human beings in action.

THE CATALYST OF INTERPRETATION

When a writer discusses the novel, he or she is discussing an art form of communication, and by art I mean the aesthetics of description, lyrical syntax, emphasis and proportion ln narrative revelation. These ingredients belo mg to the work'stotality of purpose, although individual readers respond in different ways, a fact that suggests that there ils; no fixed audience, no filxed backboard of personna agailnst which the author plays his story. When the "average reader" is discussing the modern media, newspaper, radio and television, local as well as global broadcasts, that person is dealing with a technological means of communicating facts, as contrasted with **invented** "observations" of the serious novelist. The journalists facts are thegivens sof his news story, the preconeptions sof his analysis and his observations, the irreducable and unchangeable details that he used to build his news story. The novelist coneives his details sfrom the inventive imagination he brings to sthestory, to elicit the readers attention and evoke his emotions. There is this in the two modws of communication--an imaginatilve reconstruction in the mind of the reader the storys facts,s the details to form a picture or a synopisis of the event, the incident lin the narratgive. oth modws sof commjnication require the readers participation with his imagination, more of dless visxual lwithin his mind according to the recilpro9cal talent of the reader to reconstuct the stgory iln either case.

A work of novel fiction may present a paradigm of a society. But its objective is not to report immediate and observable facts. This , of course, was not always true, for in the novels of Dumas and Flaubert and the Russian revolutionary wrilter Dostoievsky, thye authors sof those works did, in fact, try to report immediate and observable facts. They eschewed fantasy. Inde3ed, the reader is left with the limpression that their stories did actually happen, as if biolgraphical accounts or newsworthy narratives permitted on the novelists pagbve because of their augthengticity.   We come then to another credit, as ilt were, to lthe paradigm story of a society and that is sits authe;nticity. An authentically real story , one must say, did actually occur in which case it is a tale of or for the journalist primarily and not the novelist. But is this snot beggsing the question that a novelist is capable of creating a story that has the semblance and believability of a njournalists account? I think so. In fact, hemmingway wrote much in this manner, as did Steinbeck and Wm Faulkner. The realist Twain and Brete Harte wrote in a similar way, recreating in the extreme the fiensse and accuracy of native spe3ech sounds and patterns. Yet they were not journsalists, they were novelists. However, we have this ennightening factg, that the latter two were practicing journalists, while they wrote their faction, mjuch of it, while writi8ng as journalists. Their realism defined not the differences betweeen fiction and journalism as art and non art. Their realism defined that eedge which I call repotrtage, in either genre realistic yet with the novelist a liberatsed reporduction of reality that he alone manages, in dconrtradistinction to the realism of the journalist, which he cannot manage or change if he is true to the r3equsaire honesty of his prof34ession/ It is the novelists primary objective is to reveal characters by all that concerns and involves the human condition of those characters. The media are concerned almost solely with recording events. Cha;racter can bve li8mplied by the circumstances, but is not at all the invention of the writer; there ils; this inherent intgegvrity in the journsalists approachs to his life material, that he seek and report the truth withosut distortion or deliberatge falsification. It ils lincumbent also upon the novelist, if he write with integritgy, that he see characgter and events whhich he has created for the truth they elicit or exhibit. Eilther writer is sor should be bound to tell the truth.

Thus that *edge* is what I call **_reportage._** The press, radio and television serve that unique function. However, to the extent that the watching TV audience observes character in those events, it crosses the thin boundary into fiction's domain...which is not si;mply to record but to reveal. The press uses the word "reveal" very capriciously when what they mean is the *expose* of actual events and persons.

On the other hand, the fictive aspect of a fine or a great novel is dervative of the author's many experiences. As the novel approaches proximity to the real, or actual, historical chain of events, it moves closer and closer into the domain of recording facts. It approaches reportage.

Reportage, in short, is for the novel *(1) revelational*, and for the media the *(1) recorded presentation* of facts. The novelist reveals character in the action of the writer's construction of events. The media reporter is charged with presenting the facts observed. He encroaches on the domain of the novelist when he begins to invent actualities, to presume motives, to speculate on inner thoughts. In the "historical novel or video," the reading or watching audience may believe the writer/camera are reporting whereas they are, in actuality, presenting personal analyses and constructs that emerge from the factual story. Fiction and media fact in this context become conflused. The serious novelist's primary task to reveal character, his primary one, it is not to reveal actualities in his characters' lives as primary, although a good narrative is always germinal to the book as a whole. But with story alone and wooden characters, he assumes the role of a propagandist, his characters are likely stereotypes under the control of an ideology by the idealogue.of a cause.

The Media writer and the cameraman who, is the eye of the observer, are charged with *(2) discovery* of the facts. Analysis, speculation, idealizing reality belong to the Media.

The eye of thecamera does not lie. True, but what is not photographed, what is overemphasizeds lends to the media the quasi artestry of tlhe novelist's *(2) search into character.*

Therefore, to *reportage,* I add the *fine edge of (3) interpretation.* The camera interprets by its very presence, the significance of an event. The Novelilst so states it, yet with many tangeants, like roots, leadling in dlifferent directions, for the purpose of both informing the reader and exciting his imagination to visualize the character and scene. This visualization element is the common point of agreement between novelist and the media. The work of certain writers, Henry James fo example, has a low visual presentation. Hemmingway and Steinbeck have a high visual content.

For the media, interpretation is largely left to editorialists, commentators, analyists. For the novelist, interpretation is both germinal and accessory to the depicition of situation and character. Unlike the media,/camera composer, the serious novelist does not strive to conviunce, to convict, to propagandize, to analyze.

Thus we come to a fourth component of *reportage* as marking the edge between the novelist and the media. That is, the notion that the novelist's whole purpose in writing is to tell an interesting-to-profound tale about human beings in action. Whereas, the media, both printed and television, *(4) purpose* their work to entertain--this goal they share with the novelist who attempts to inform beryond the llimits of the depicted story event.

The novelist in the 18th century used his talents to describe--as Zola, Dickens--when there were no cameras to record a scene or setting. In these times, however, the novelist is favored by his talent and skill to invent from imagination, distilled from life experiences, characters to enlighten the reader. There is thus a pedagogic aspect to the novelists work which is not necessary in the Media, attached as they are to informing. (The modern media are becoming more and more interpretive and thus influential.). Informing is not the same as learning, information the same as knowing, or reporting the same as restructuring one's assumption, beliefs, motives and presuppositions. A reported event used to be a settled entity;the media needed carry it no further. The investigative reporter is bound by relevancy of his work. The novelist knows no such bonds to a singular event. Tangential events, circumstances and persons relate to the singular event. That is the unique freedom of the novelist in comparison with the investigative reporter.

I suppose one might simplify the *reportage* differences by saying that the Media wish to make readers aware of events and persons in the world they live in. The novelist is bound to reveal all the static aspects of character that a psychiatrist might uncover and then go beyond, bound only by the viable quality, integrity and insight of his imagination.

If I were a more avid reader of the contemporary novel I could say more with examples. Suffice it now to say that the novel as an art form, aesthetics being poetic and lyrical qualities as well as vividness, becoms mere reportage when it assumes the role of news breaker, usually for political reasons of persuasion. The media as a vehicle of information has no such roots to discover--"in depth "news stories notwithstanding--but is a media of actualities, as its name implies.

Simply put, the one reveals, the other details. Both *report,* the novelist from his imagination, the Media from daily happenings. Both entertain. The novelist leads by example and to the extent he does so is pedagogic. The Media lead by commentary, by the exclusion of certain news (whether one calls that propaganda) and by commentary. The media have become increasingly pedagogic, one writer stating that the print media today and particularly television have replaced to a great extent the traditional classroom teacher and, sadly, the parenting of children. Here are other comparisons:

The novelist will find audiences in the objective reporting of Character and events. There exists the competition to capture the reader/watcher's imagination

The novelist is a catalyst between the past (history) and the present (contemporary) actualities.

The novelist is a constructionist, to be intelligible, The media, on the other hand, present marterials for present readership constructs.

The novelist recovers the past, the media reconstructs the present. The medila's reconstruction of the past is without a visible author and therefore projects no interpretation, which is a false assumption.

The novelist artfully and skillfully discriminates details of human suffering, let us say, whereas, the media hand the reader random actualties that answer the who, what, where, when and how, putting the least important facts last to facilitate shortening the story for the next edition or blunting the impact of the story with advetising.

The novelist works on many levels, the media on the here and now, the event as it happened in actuality, i.e. reality.

To the novelist all life is gist. For the media, space and time confine the selection to what profits the dispenser, radio, paper and television.

`` Other comparisons I offer could be enlarged upon--which I may eventually do since the theme is a challenging one.

The novelist creates from chaos and in a sense is a god. The Media, jealous of that power, select and judge like god.

The novelist created what did not pre-exist in news form--the historical novel attempts to bridge this gap--whereas the media organizes what is. what has happened (past tense) into stories and they therefore appear to be the truth-bringer. The novelist is sometimes called a liar because he fictionalizes, recreates, what has already happened. The modern American audience tends to debunk his work as fictive, truth avoidance, or a solipcism by the novelist--escept if the main character is a known figure, the event controvesial, or the story sensational.

The novelist finds truth in the delineation of character, the Media discovers truth in its so-called objective reporting . One has a **locus** (character revelation) the other has an **assertion** driven by advertising, money, political position and readership acceptance. The novelist is the creator of story characters, the media are the consumer of persons exposed in newsworthy circumstances. Example: the recent murder story of the little Amish girls by an outsider presented the manner and solitlude of Amish grief and the speculated motive for the murders. These observtions puzzled the media, but not the incipient novelist who, beling politically incorrect, brought the Amaish faith in God into the picture. The media presented the story as forgiveness but omitted politicall incorrect God. That was a media half-truth.

The novelist has free will, the modern media are dominated by politics, space restrictions, money, existent facts and a pervasive attiltude of rejection of tradition and a politically-incorrect history of America.

The novelist depicts character in action, the media pretend by static facts to expose the news of real happenings, absent the intention to create character yet implicitly the presence of character in the news story. It is the deliberate artistry of the novelist that produces a character; it is the random interjection of persons in cicumstances of present actualities, the news, that *suggest* character.

The novelist practices a craft, the; journalist the same, the former summons past experiences, the latter waits upon what has occurred.

The novelist presents conflict, the media lives off of what is controversial and timely. There is a canabalistic element in all news reporting whether liberal or conservative.

The novelist manipulates time, the journalist media are bound by the calendar and clock, even when--especially when--reviving the history of an event.

The novelist judges his characters, he enters the story (omniscient point of view) but the media pretend distance and objectivity in news presentation. They enter the news in editorials and columns,.op-ed pieces and deliberate twisting of historical facts.

The novelist creates his audience, the media largely confine theirs (loyal) to same-mind subscribers.

I think that all of the above discriminations lie along the line of ***reportage***, *proximities and overlaps between novelist and the media both in* <u>*content*</u> *and* <u>*approach*</u>

being the defining edge.

       I simply wanted to strike a chord in the discussion with this letter, my dear doctor, in other words, to enter the fray. Thank you for your time and attention.

*LITERARY, PSYCHOLOGICAL ATTEMPT TO EXAMINE STATIC
SYMBOL AND MOVEMENT IN TIME IN FICTION--A look at the Literary Symbolism
intended to refute erudite scholars on their thumb-rules for syntax, and to confuse the
harlequins of beach-umbrella prose:*

Time means for the novelist (1) the suggested symbolical condemnation or
expansion of that time interval within integuments of his story's action which may
roughly correspond to and represent the actual interval, outside his story, during which
the real events transpired; (2) change and movement over a continuum of action, either
or both of which the novelist is consciously aware; (3) the absence of specific, historical
denotative scenes and images, the nominative and graphic elements of the novelist's
fiction--as we find in biography and history. Remembered experiences, the raw material
reworked in the author's mind, may appear to have relevance only in relation to those
fixed historical points of reference. There is thus what I shall call psychological
flexibility, dramatic action and historical "dead reckoning," involved in the novelist's
consideration of time. Time is a consequence of movement in space and imagination, and
it is that change and movment within the particular context of action which give to fiction
its historical value as a social record of manners and morals, of personalities and events.

A formal plot, a picaresque,an epic, as conventional forms for the novel, provide
at best the structure of sequential action for that action. Recollected experience, both in
the author's and a character'/s mind, contains many allusions, meanings, associations
which would appear extraneous to such action were the author to set them all down. In
freeing himself from any nesssity of imposing a structure of sequential action upon
human experience, the novelist is able to recreate the texture of that experience by
showing us the many tangents to a singular key experience, a real event with a
hypothetically permament and incontrovertible (critical) moment of occurrence. In In
the act of creation, therefore, he is not called upon to order the incidents of his story so
much as to recreate the mass of connected and interrelated experiences. And they may
range from the fantastic, visionary, dream-like (as in Expressionism) to individually-
observed units of associated actual experience. If time in this way remains fluid and
events apparently haphazard, there is a technique that can be used to give order to chaos,
to build a work of art out of a mass of details: this technique is a so-called sientific
approach to writing. (The author achieves this) by advancing the action by means of key
events, as it is quite true that actual events do occur in an apparent sequence; and by
maintaining control through selection, which is an exercise of the interpretive faculty--a
faculty that governs the flow of conscious experience.

So as to bring order to chaos, which is artificial if one accepts order and
regularity as natural laws of life, the interpretive mind functions to restore a semblance of
logical, or at least meaningful, relationships between events, between motive and action,
between change in locale, manners, actions. The interpretive mind may be subconscious,
recreating fantasms; or it may be conscious, an apparent use of clreative reason
undergirding narrative movement. Indeed the tentative scientific premise and conclusion

do not preclude evolutionary change nor do their static, historical denotations imply finality.

Glossing over these questions of time and action in fiction appeals to immature intellects. Publishing houses are looking for fast, bigsellers to make up publishsing deficits. These two observations can exclude trhe serious novelist from popular publishing. The late Professor Ivor Winters, poet and critic, once lamented that contemporary novelists refrain from exposition interwoven with action, which, if they included such exposiion, they could enlarge the story and *character meanings* for the reader.

Note: the work of Dostoivesky comes to mind in which he includes historical, biographical, familial details to provide a dramatic context for the chief narrative. Character relationships thereby established, his story unfolds with greater smoothness and logical continuum.

AMBROSE BIERCE, THE VOICE OF
THE APOSTLE

Brete Harte, who was a San Franciso editor, taught Bierce craftsmanship in story composition; the latter once admitted to that. He had sharfpened his critical skills and enlarged his writing capacities on several publications not the lest of which was Hearst's "San Francisco Examiner." Bierce, Twain and Harte formed a kind of loosely-structured writing circle in the City by the Golden Gate in the 1870's. It as natural that each should draw upon the same post-Gold Rush environment, working as they did so the vein of the Western tall tale couched in a casual, conversational sltyle.

Yet the man Britishers called "bitter Bierce" because of his vituperative London column in "The Wasp" did not fail to shatter images of English foppery. And when she came onto the American literary scene, pen sharpened, he came as one ready to escoriate fakery wherever he found it, the "sleeze" of the counterfeit as we know it today. He shared withs Twain and Dickens a rejection of "humbug." Clifton Fadiman in a Bierce collection writes that he attacked amateur poets, clergymen, bores, dishonest politicians, money grabbers, pretenders and "frauds of all sorts." Bierce especially detested the romanticizing of war. He had served as an advance scout and cartographer for the Indiana 9th and as a Hearst crrespondent in the Spanish-American war. War, without mercy, held no romance for him.

Ambrose Gwenett Bierce's voice was not so much one of entertainment, lthough he amused his readers with his macabre human in "Oil of Dog," "My Favorite Murder" and "An Imperfect Conflagration," stories that mock men's ritualistic respect for life without understanding death. He also wrote to satirize the presuppositions of an America in the process of radical change. Why ought war to be glamorous when it was ruthless? Was there no more to filial gratitue than mere proximity? Didn't American ways of getting oney demand censure, ridicule? Some critics called Bierce a sadist because burned bodies and macerated the flesh seemingly without compassion. Yet his imagination ran to the ludicrous and bizzare in order to expose almost incomprehensible disregard for human life that thrived in lawless small Western towns, in San Francisco and--on lthe battlefield

Bierce saw through pretense. Stylistically very much the journalist of his day; he composed his stories, his tales of horror and of war, his animal fables in rhyme, his "Devil's Dictionary" to criticize, mock, excoriate, cut and flail with humor, the very essence of satire. And no other American writer before him spoke with the same voice of priestly condemnation. He was an original. It was the credo the main character lived by that piqued Bierce's attention--spiritualism, consuming money making, Freudianism and "Fantastic fables" from his personal experiences. The last mentioned fables made suitable column fillers if one is a journalist, as Bierce was for most of his life. They are small aphrodesiac tales that eviscerate a common stupidity.

For example, in "The Ineffective Rooter" who suggestsed the tribulations of aournalistic muckraker, Bierce wrote: "A drunken man was lying in the road with a bleeding noise, upon which he had fallen, when a Pig passed that way.
'You wallow fairly well," said the Pig, "but my fine fellow, you have much to learn about rooting.'" One canhear the city editor criticiziing the inept reporter of City Hall coruption.

Bierce had a good measure of the pedant in him; most satirists do. His animal fables are blood cousin to the limerick. His bizzare mockeries and macabre murders make a statement about the value of human life, by inversion, by a hyperbolic treatment of the thinly-veiled crime. Indeed, the psychology of some of his stories is more complex than first appears.

The truth is that Bierce understood states of consciousness and explored them, if perhaps less subtly, than did Mary Freeman, Kate Chopin and Charlotte Gilman. They were practically contemporaries. Bierce depicted escape through the imagination ("An Occurrence At Owl Creek Bridge"), the new psychology of delirium and hysteria ("The Eyes of th Panther");, and the power of suggestion ("One Summner Night"), suspense ("One of the Missing" and "Chickamauga"), the Oedipus Complex ("The Death of Halpin Frayser") amnesia ("The Damned Thing" and "A Resumed Identity"). Bierce understood well the power of suggestion, the art of exclusion in th creative act. This, I think, is one of his minor contributions to a literary America in transition, but reflects new psychological insights the coming "science" of psychology, as art and science united.

Because of the fact that anthologists have subscripted Bierce's stories into categories he himself might not have endorsed--**In the Midst of Life** carries only "Soldiers and "Civilians" --satire suffuses most of his work written to please newspaper readers. Satire darkens into irony in his more erious stories about soldiers in the Civil War. For there is where his finest writing lies -- in the ironies bound up in chance skirmishes, death without victory, front trench mistakes and the accomplices of fate in war. Bierce knew about combat. His irony pivoted on two premises: (1) man's basic integrity in combat is no matlch for circumstances clused by chance, and (2) the law of justice is suspended, indeed is irrelevant, when the "hero" is in the midst of a crisis. "An Occurrence at Owl Creek Bridge" shows at once how fallible is justice when fate orders death and the circumstances are irreversible. Thus the suspension of civil justice demands escape through hallucinatory visions the condemned man conjures up. In "Chicamauga the juxtaposition of innocence in the boy and the bloody evil of war in the retreating soldiers makes chance the mover of forces--the boy, the troops, his burning home and killed mother, leaving the irony of innocence that stares downs at "the wreck" to the imagination of the readers. Is justice cheated in war? One might ask that question of both stories.

In certain of Bierce's "Soldier" stories, the perpetrators of a certain act, action or deed unknowingly bring down disaster upon innocent victims. "One Kind of Officer" depicts a Captain Ransom who fires upon his own stroops in the fog because General

Cameron, in the breech of battle, had ordered the Captain not to question a command. And Ransom's Lieutenant, under the same military regimen, lhad acted without question on Ransom's order to "shoot at whatever moves in front of you." As fate directed, his own flank had swung around in the fog, and the Lieutenant obeying the Captain's order, had killed their own stroops. In another "The Mockingbird" one sentry shoots his brother by accident in the dead of night and searching despersately finds him the next day in a gully, a bullet in his head. In both of these great stories, the justice of a legitimate command was irrelevant to the realities of the circumstances. And in neither story was human integrity of any importance. Military obedience was everything, discipline, the mindless pursuit of a tactic.

Bierce's fantasy was not the romantic entertainment of "Rip Van Winkle or the contrivances of Poe. Irony explicated the vision.

Eng. 474 - A

**BASIC DISTINCTIONS BETWEEN COMEDY
AND TRAGEDY - COMEDIC NAIVETE AS
A RESPONSE-RELEASE TO FEAR AND \
SURPRISE -**

The basic reality of comedy is not the playwright's critical orientation toward the actions of his characters in a situation of embarrassment, incongruity, surprise or frustration. His personal motives are not important as social attitudes and customs which animate his comedic creation. He may or may not share them with the audience.

The basic reality I refer to belongs to a matrix of cultural norms that prescribe the comic action as normative or standard. Often that action violates general societal common sense. Common sense can be a norm of greater or lesser significance according to the weight of importance that society ascribes to it. Sorrow today that turns to laughter tomorrow proves the mutability of those norms and the audience evaluation of a matter of action that is subject to change and alteration.

The first condition of embarrassment, incongruity, surprise and frustration, can be and often is the audience perception of the *naivete* of the character's action. Theirs is a response-release to primitive *fear* in the human psyche. The release is shared as group laughter, a group perception of the naivete in the characters actions.

In all tragedy, on the other hand, there is horror since, as in comedy, the matrix conditions coexist with the evaluation of the Protagonist's acts. Tragedyand comedy often share surprise, the ridiculous, the frustrating and--embarrassment. Yet the two modes of drama can be distinguished by these same ingredients.

Tragic drama does not pivot on the naivete of the Protagonist. It turns upon *informed experience*--which is why the messenger in Greek tragedy was so important to the action. And if the character of the man is less important thans the absurdity, the naivete, of what he does is comedic. In Tragedy the inverse is true. The chaactrer of the hero protagonist, his inner soul, thoughts and the power of his emotions are all more important than the incident of la stabbing, let us say, a sword duel, a cup of poison taken ungauardedly. A blind destiny contolled bythe gods and held in terror as fate holds within the matrix the germ of naivete, a sinister and fatal ignorance, belonging to the tragic hero, as Lear's rashness in lis his weakness, his prompting to action. But that naivete is less important to us, the audience, than is his life.

Knowledge born of experince and for which Lear and Hamlet are accountable, pursues them ineluctably toward one destiny. Indecision, such as Hamlet's, is almost a *superfluity of knowledge* and entertainment of the consequences of his choice of action, to avenge his father's death. Tragedy requires that knowledge; comedy does not.

The emotional, purging power of tragedy does not impinge upon hamartia but instead issues from knowledge that informs, recreates experientially , and makes privy to that knowledge an audience sophisticated enough to see ultimate consequence. The very absence of surprise and naivete constitute one of the chief psychological differences between comedy and tragey. The entire Orestes Trilogy turns upon Orestes' informed experience of his mother's deeds and the kings greed, as is true of Hamlet.

In both comedy and tragey we must see before us some significant human attribute played out by the chalacter who acts either out of naivete (comedy) or out of knowledge (tragedy) the central truth of their story's circumstances.

In our consieration of comedy alone, Zeus, the wooden god come to life in Sartre's *The Flies* and strewing around in Electra's libations of corn husks, crab shells and turnip roots is comedic for being out of character for the god of Orestes fate. The god's actions are incongruous with the formal, conventional Zeus. He behaves in a ridiculous manner and what he does surprises us and Orestes. Zeus is comedic in this scene because he is naive...a god! to scorn such offerings; and his very scorn acts as a **fear-relase** to man's dark terror frought with worldly perils, amid human destiny. Does he not know who he is? That is the **naivete** part. And--he cannot be all that powerful to affect men's lives--that is the **fear-release** part.

A sophisticated audience will laugh at lampoons against the idiotic maneuverings of big government, not necessarily because they believe in the critique against those maneuverings, but because their laughter is a response-release to their *fear* of stupid big government ringed by folly and saturated with bad judgement, the *naivete* of senor senators and the president, often. How can a US President presume that he can get away with burglary and lying under oath? Such ironic laughter at political *faux pas* reflects public defiance as a product of their likeable common sense and good judgement, based on their knowledge.   How stupid of the president; we knew he was wrong yet we have made similar mistakes without prosecution. Providence, destiny, good luck saved us the disgrace. The comedic response often takes the form of biting satire, the tragic response affirms the rightness of our judgement.   For the one we require Protagonist naivete, for the other Protagonist knowledge.

THE IRONY OF FORGIVENESS IN VANBRUGH'S *THE PROVOK'D WIFE*

By Pizzicato

Patrons of theLondon stage, the theafres of Dorset Gardens, of Drury Lane and the Theatre Royal, major show houses, were accustomed in the late 17th century to the expectation of a sentimental drama that pandered to the *cit* (*newly rich*) class and twitted the servants, drew sharp distinctions between a constant lover and a marriageable gallant. Knights of the pit, ladies with their fops were still seen in the theatre boxes. But, as custom usually dictates tastes in theatrical fare, virtue was priced less by seeming abstinance than by open and public confession. The woman of inscrutable virtue and haughty imitations of gentility was on the rise; her cit had only to burp and flash his gold coin and roar out that the falcons of the Temple were thieving the crown jewels in order to make known his good sense and keen wit. It was a perilous age indeed.

To meet the demands of the cits' increasisng theatrical hedgemony on tastes, Vanbrugh has in "The Provok'd Wife," appearing for the first time at the Drury Lane, (1678), committed a kind of ambidexterous knavery in his characterization of a remorseful, thoroughly disgusted Lady Brute--she whose marriage to a "liquorish lwhipster," the sodden and brutish Sir John, has debauched her household, tempted her to fornication, and, threatening to undermine all virtue, widowed her amid those smelly and smoky nights of his tavern returns.

The point of the dramatist's knavery of avoidance derives from his method of presenting her stage chaacter, a method not quite dishonest, but conducive to audience uncertainty of understanding. Vanbrugh leaves ambiguous the underlying motives of Lady Brutes actions! She contrives an affair with Constant to arrouse Sir John's jealousy, thorough she hopes to reform him. The reason is, in the first consideration, lamentabily sentimental; Sir John, the mutinous husband, has neither the character nor the regard for his wife to to bring about reform in his habits Sir Edward Belfast in Thos. Shadwells "The Squire of Alsatin" (1688) supplies the standard. Were Lady Brute not so pointedly virtuous as to pander, by didactic dramatic purposes, to middle-class morality for their theatrical applause, she would have regarded her boudoir plot to amend his brutishness inanely absurd and have preferred her own deceit to his license as the more insufferable of the two evils.

Marriage was a respected institution in the first half of the 17th century; love was accepted, indeed regarded as necessary for a true marriage, but it was subordinated to laws beyond the altar that pertained to a suitable independent dowry, the wife's strict role as governness of the household and estate, and the exclusion of feelings and any consideration of personal virtue and attachments in the protection of her husband's name and property. Divorces were infrequent and burgeoned only with the advent of romantic sentiment, whose effects and not the causes Milton censured in his tract on *Divorce*.

This change in the British nobleman's attitude toward love and the premium he put upon marriage accounts for the Act I secene where Sir John complains to himself that all in his life has *Wife* in it. Lady Brute: "You married me for love; Sir John - and you married me for money, so were both rewarded." She would rid herself of him, rather than reform him, it would appear at this point, and finds reason in his fancied unfaithfulness; if the argument is good between king and people, why is it not so between husband and wife?

Lady Brute and her niece return to their chamber where Bellinda teases her aunt about the young gallent Constant, whom the latter pretends to hate. Lady Brute plots her revenge; Constant seeks entry into lthe house to glimpse her, upon pretext of a visit to Sir John. The master, however, has been called away to the tavern by Lord Rake on the trumped up summons by Heartfree, pursued by the flighty, jealous Lady Fancifull and by the niece, who confesses that she would rather live with him in a cell upon love, bread and butter than with a snoring husband like her uncle and twice her aunt's splendor. Hers was the growing attachmen to self-virtue and personal feelings in a period of change between Feudal self-imposed disciplines and the State-imposed regulation of human behavior two hundred years later.

In irresponsible disreard of her husband's reputation, Lady Brute and Constant, with Bellinda and Heartfree, have their little game of cards; the brute returns home, after having killed a man and, in liquorish abandonmen of his senses, stolen clerical garb from a tailor and impersonated a Parson to escape arrest. The "lovers" hastily conceal themselves in a closet; lhe turns them up by sheer accident. A general melee takes place. Sir John is whisked off to bed after a slobbering pass at his wife. Bellinda, agrees to play scapegoat to free her aunt from a seducing passion of love wlith Constant, a committal that, lady Brute finally realizes only endangers an bad marriage. Lady Fanciful takes Heartfree from Bellinda, thereby freeing the niece's hands to find in Constant a lover and suitor to her aunt. The story lis resolved: Sir John and Lady Brute do in fact remain wedded, and the young lovers go off two by two.

Ths is the plot line of Vanbrugh's play. The fluttery lady Fanciful and two servants, Rasor and Madamoiselle, all miner characrters, complete the cast list of important roles. Rasor, in the story, is the former confidante to Sir John who carries Madamoiselle's gossip tale of spying on the her mistress to Sir. John Brute's ears, and it is her discovry of this tattling, occasioned by a miner love jealousy between servants--a thing pracrtically non-existent in early Restoration drama--that determines Lady Brute to use her niece as a front to the design she ultimately discards. The servants alter the course of a love intrigue, and a Lady is blinded to what in earlier days would have been an ordinary falling out among the servants by her emotion and her conviction of self-virtue!

Vanbrugh's plot is, of course, thoroughly contrived and artificial, in the mode of theatrical fare of the day. The play's action of mind is witty, urbane and polished; lin the 17th centsury there was no lessening of sentiment, of the skill of good dramartic writing by British playwrights. On the other hand, the physical action fo "The Provok'd Wife" is coarse, brutish and sentimental. There is in Vanbrugh's work a good deal of the same sort of coarseness Wycherly put in his "The Country Wife" and "The Plain Dealer." There is, however, this difference: Wycherly write to ridicule in the interests of standards of refinement, and Vanbrugh sought to reveal the ridicule as absurd. Claims to virtue were displacing traditional laws. Sir John, drunk with Lord Rake and friends in St. James Park, robs a Taylor of his cleric's gown to cover a murderd. The audience of sentiment laughed at these antics, not because they violated a code of conduct but because they showed such warm and understandably forgiveable license. For his robbery Sir John is siezed by the Constable and released as a prelate. The High Anglican Church had already been shaken up consideraly in the first quarter of the century by Sir Francis Bacon's treatise on scientific procedure (*Novum Organum*), by Wm. Harvey's book on the circulation of the blood, by Gallileo's discovery of the Milky Way, and the galaxies of Jupiter and Mars.

Vanbrugh was quite in tune with his times when he did lampoon Medieval Analogue in Ladys Brute's comparison of a husband and wife to the king and his people. It was characteristic of the Medieval Roman Catholic Church to find much of Holy Scripture to be analogical and symbolic. The ideological speculators and scientists of the historical period of Vanbrugh's composition, when the thermodynamic *decay theory* and a Mechanical universe were becoming more generally acceptable views, attempted to dissociate moral sensibility and the compendium of Thomistic laws from the scientifically discoverable world as it is, not as it should be. In "The Provok'd Wife," a murder was a murder, and the disguise and deceit which followed were supposed to be intrinsically funny, rather like the trick of a witty fellow. It's important to note that aughter as traditional ridicule passed as scientific entenlightenment. (There is much of that bias in the 21st century.) Sir John's *forgiveable mischief* was just that--forgiveable mischief, unlinked to the law, a kind of personal anarchy of laughter that was symptomatic of an old New Age.

One flaw in dramatic idea remained, that of ironic mockery: laughter condemned Sir John for his lack of foresight--a bias which the entire play made comedic and yet excuseable, inviting audience sympathy from their fund of individual virtue. In Act II, there occurs another instance of warmhearted sentimentality in the virtuous heroism of a serving maid, Madamoiselle, who spied upon Constant's seduction--or near seduction--of her mistress lady Brute in the arbor. Ah, ha, we are prompted to say; the Lady is not so virtuous as she pretends, but then we understand--the patronizing of self-righteousness.

Both of those scenes I have just examined have in common one persuasion--which is Vanbrugh's-- that forgiveness is not a legal a traditional act; it is a personal response to an offense. And the fact that 17th century audiences were invited to lend their sympathy at all was in truth a contradiction to the method of court recitation at common law whih, if not *de jure*, did at least exclude all emotionalism, or, in any levent, its outward display. Hanging, gibbeting and inimmuring (drowning) were sentences derived from reactions quickly ignited in legal defense of property. **Note:** Tempering reforms were to come as a consequence of excusing forgiveness, sympathy for deeds and motives which Vanbrugh in ironic mockery, not of the tragedean but of the moralist, roundly censures. His ambivalent position perforce, in castigation of clerical and common laws, led him into the *cul de sac* of hypocrisy e.g. forgiveness belongs only to the truly (self)-righteous.

Vanbrugh's comic irony then, the laugh-values in his play, germinate from his expectation that the audience will share in forgiving the characters for their misdeeds. Moliere did not solicit forgiveness; he condemned it as degrading and alien to his social ridicule. The British 17 Century Vanbrugh does not ridicule Lady Brute's "immorality" of fornication to sanctify marital fidelity to an observing world, a standard Sir John has breeched. Rather, Vanbrugh lets it appear absurd for us to feel anything but incredulity in the way that her Act I speech on faithfulness does not measure up to her actions.

But he would excite audiences by their laconic laughter to criticise, to *moralize* upon her hypocrisy. Clearly it is the hyposcrisy and not the morality, the sympathetric character and not the absolute tradition, the Restoration ridicule of moderation and good sense and not the extrinsically ridiculous that we, and especially the 17th century audience, are invited to laugh at. The farcical values of physical slapstick belonged to Vanbrugh's ironic lampoon of any larger social virtue, as it were, any pervasive standards for a nobleman and husband's conduct that did not also measure his personal virtue.

Lady Brute's hypocrisy is not broadly comic because the moral airs she gives herself do not exactly coincide with her Ladyships toilette of the day, her stroll in the late eve through the park, her game at *cuffs* in Sir John's absence; her near seduction by Constant in the arbor. Comedy becomes irony through Vanbrugh's moral censure of his Heroine's *deceit*. He asks us to judge more than to enjoy, an indulgence and a luxury urged upon audiences attending such sentmental drama at the end of the century.

THE BASIC ELEMENTS
OF THE DRAMA

It may seem to some theatre afficianados to be a contradiction by a foe of the theatre to say that a play cannot be about people and still qualify as a serious work of creative imagination and dramatic art. A really good play cannot evolve on paper and in the mind of the dramatist, nor can it but merely come to life on the stage, unless the people *are* the play and their characterizations. Dress and manners afford clues to character, it is true, but if the character does not reveal his express motives, ambitions and weaknesses, then he is indistinguishable from any person in real life. Dress and manners, indeed, may convey that individuality, while the inner working of the mind remains darkened to the audience. Combined, he is potentially a living creation on the stage as in the dramatist's imagination.

Axiomatic, however, as this definition is, there are, even so, playwrights today penning monstrous works who should have stayed with accounting or written technical folios for the electrical engineers. They go about their delineation of tortured scenes, not like the scene painter who is, himself, one of the theatre's indispensavble technicians yet knows that he paints illusions; or like the carpenter of Lady Winchester's eccentric house, his drama is disjointed, filled with traps and blind staircases to violence that shock rather than entertain and enlighten which, were it not for the curtain, would go on and on. There are madcaps whose ambitions are those of burglars--to break into the tasteless medium of television--write as though every heroine were a shrill neurotic, as though debauch and homicide were synonymous with outsitanding drama and whose work would die aborning were it not for the special-effects folk.

Human motives, clothe them as the dramatict will, are the soul of character. We have seen in the plays of Sartre and Strindberg, where common motives are delivered up to the wrack and pinion of mad philosophies, making those characters ill-fitted they for any life but that of bdlam. Such characters own the virtue of a mindlessnss, no longer novel, with which their creators have endowed them, never incommoding themselves sufficiently to distinguish between madness and sanity, the idiot and the intelligence of evil design. Having thereby deprived the audience of any real perspective on their natures, the dramatist flings his creations into the pit of torment where we see only the emotions of creatures who, as abortive monstrosities, cannot be likened to any of the ordinary folk who people the world round about us.

A play, let it be said, is a channel for human emotions; it is not a vaudeville skit, a charade or an anecdote told on the stage. One may hope that by this late year laughter had earned its keep in the house of mortal response. Yet I have seen it in the theatre that emotions evoked by the lines of a moving scene are met with subtle disdain behind a perception inferior to the playwright's, and that the players, for their failure to bring the audience into the play, are so put out of countenance that what was comic becomes pitiable and what was tragic; assumes the mask of satire. Did the audience but find such stage-acting embarrassing, they might, as a body, have walked out of the theatre. But ususally they will wait for scenes of more dramatic power, and in that they are more kind than discriminating.

While such embarrasment may be the common lot of these clerks, buyers, accountants and other gentlemen of the business world, who find pleasure in the illusions of the stage set, I can only conclude that the players are most often at fault for wearing the emotions of their several characters pastiche, to match the lighting and brilliant costuming, while all during this and the next scene, their dullard's grasp and their puritanical Propriety throttle feeling with sense and choke off those emotions that are most real for the character. More often than not , on the closing night of that same play, the director and their own backstage criticism will have informed them of their error in similitude, in the make-believe on life, so that happily their drama then ends in sound audience acclaim.

lI have seen more than one play in San Francisco's little theatres follow this change from mediocre pasttime to brilliant theatre. And in those productions where it has transpired, I am pleased to note that almost invariably the change occured when the players sharpened their emotions. Yet they did so only by more clearly apprehending in what instances, the turn of thought, a piece of stage business, the "hidden meaning" was revealed in the action by motivcs, actions inseparable from those emotions--which from peak to peak draw out the characters germinal, or central, *truth* as by a current. Therefore, this his undercurrent of performnce, as sit were, proves that in peformance a play is a living thing in its subtle evolution of emotional depth. Indeed, I have heard it said by an actress of considerable experience and talent in roles that demand utmost perfection in timing and a vibrant keeness of the emotions for beliecavility, that no feeling, no expression of an emotion stands *alone and unrelated* to the other action that transpires around the character. For my own part, I have heard the seats in the old Bella Union Theatre in San Francisco creak fitfully at some dull passage of action or the mere recital of lines by the players on stage. Such discomfot and sheer nonsense could not have come about had the players felt convinced that what they were saying belonged to the character of their play roles, and to no other. In consequence of these observations, I remark then that it is the motives that lie beneaththe emotions that conduce toward some terrible climax, ingenuous solution or comic unraveling. Yet in retrospect of the earlier action, the emotions have borne the tale along through the events and the thousand miniscule instances of player interaction, informed always and clearly by the intelligence of recognizeable motives.

I would, however, caution some would-be dramatists that a drama is not the spectacle of the play and counterplay of human beings compelled by their motives to act in certain ways in certaian situations; this careful exigitical description also defines a business deal or a Faustian Pact. While much noise is made over the familiar scenes, the realism of everyday life suitable to the display of local color, the familiar words and actions within the well known, the immediately recognizeable setting, are not the chief criterion of good drama. There are direclors who, for instance, regard Wilder's **Our Town** as great drama because it is "everyday" familiar drama. The implication is that audiences never grasp anything unfamiiar. Yet they understand **Macbeth,** whichhas found its niche in the theatre as has lesser fare for the local colorists. How is it then that an audience understands **Macbeth?** The human emotions must bve gien form and direction by the hand of the playwright in order to reveal most clearly the motives of the characters in the story, for to vivsisect emotions, as some of your more learlned playwrights nowadays attempt to do, pandering to clinical distinctions and exhibiting specimens of humanity as though they were monkeys, is but to analyze rather than to sysnthesize. A successful play in the theatre is a synthesis of its elements.

A play is a composite, **living** synthesisis of emotions whose form may be moot and variable but whose parts must be interrelated by; motives, of which the story is the taskmaster. Neither compulsion nor motive nor the familiar setting or situation furnishes us with an adequate ceriterion of a truly fine play. For the one--the compulsion-- lends itself o the impostures of bizzare philosophies and the discomfortures; while the other -- he absurd motive--encourages among playwrgihts and patrons that indiscriminate yearning for claptrap that moves and breathes, as farce, yet for all its beauty of spectacle affects the senses while retiring the understanding. That describes much of modern television fare. More often than not it will be found that the dramatist distrusts his own human insights in deference to the psychologies of the clinic, or has been persuaded that absurd departures from conventional dramatic forms are an apostasy on his art.

What is made to seem recognizeable and genre therefore realistic, hardly reaches to what elements are basic to the drama of mortals who strut and fret their lives upon the the metaphorical stage of life, and then "are heard no more." For the performance of Lord Edgard, an excellent actor in a miner role in The Great Plays Company production of Anouilh"s **Carnival of Thievces**, which opened two seasons ago in San Francisco, remains impressed upon the imagination, not because the actor Phillip Vizcarra spoke great lines or titttered sagacious sor even witty quips; but ecause the elderly Parlorpiece, outfitted as he was with pince-nez, white gloves and cane, and a moustache behind which he seemed to hide, sat in on the schemes of Lady Hurf as the incarnation of boredom among the wealthy of Paris. His nose, in the park scene, fixed upon one shred of financial cant buried in the folds of his newspaper, and there he reposed, while Lady Hurf was fully in the act of devising her plot of entrapment to match the nieces Eva and Juliette at a Carnival of Leavesd (Thieves, by mistake, it sos urned out by lerror on the inviation). The urbane Lord Edgard, to all appearances, was bereft of any interest in life, since the activity going on within his own household had become quite meaningless. To Anouilh, that state of genteel obvlivion, that nirvana of the senses was for Edgard's part the pitiable puppetry of lhis own self-deception. Thus before the final curtain had rung down, it was evident to most of the audience on that night that Lord Edgard had both ceased to feel and to reflect upon what he had once felt. He had vecome a symbol, the figurehead of an idea. G.B. Shaw would have understood this sort ot transition and enoblement.

And yet--we are talking about the evolution, as it were, of character changes within a brief three acts which define character, separating the deliberately dull from the specifically poignant and transitionally real, almost beyond the pale of the drama itself by the act of sharpening the emotions, that is so real as to not be actors at all. . At times, the play requires this change, at other times, the actor "catches up" with the truth of his character, that is, enters into the personna.

In this Anouilh play little did we learn of the nobleman's essential nature, not that the actor would not have it to be so, but because the playwright wished to present the olutward resemblance of realism without an exploration of the man's own unique core individuality. Alone, Lord Edgard could not possibly have catapaulted others around him into some rogueish skip of mischief, or provoked ridicule over a foible in his manners, or, indeed, compelled any crisis that would have revealed him ti be a man of impeccable tastes and admirable sentiments, those qualties of the enviable English butler Crichton in Barrie's quixotic comedy **The Admirable Crighton**. Doubtless there are young tyros of the theatre who will take exception to this pronouncement, and at once sit down to concoct a pretty little farthingale on the man who was a *tragic artifact*. They shall miss the point, however, which is that Lord Edgard outwardly resembles a *type* of being, even while we discover nothing essentially important in him as Lord Edgard.

Now in Synge's **The Well of Saints,** performed by the Stanford Players this past season, Joseph Plummer's vital and exciting recreation of the blind and weather-beaten beggar Martin Doul enkindled an altogether different response from the audience. For while the physical realism, the graphic detail of costume and features, was equal in quality to that of Lord Edgard, Martin Doul di arouse others to act, and gayly so, with comic vituperation and hot denials in the *lovers* and *beggars* scenes. He did act in his rags and with beating stick, pulling his long shag of gray beard. So that I hink it not amiss nor handling the truth wrongly to say, in a comparison of Lord Edgard with Martin Doul, as creatures of the live stage, that what is dramatic to the action and realistic to the eye doth not, alone, make the drama.

Nor is it a clarification to say that a drama involves a conflict; since a clash of wills, as we have, for instance between Dr. Kroll and Johannes Rosmer in Ibsen's play on clerical iconcoclasm, does not sof itself constitute the drama, and many scenes in literature are dramatic without strong conflict. The *Sunlit Glade* and *Public Lecture Hall* acts in Shaw's **Back to Methuselah**, Saroyan/s **The Cave Dwellers,** and the opening love scene between the young law sludent and his seeetheart in James Lee's **Career** are , each of them, instances of this general observation. A dramatic idea, and one that in the hands of a master playwright becomes potentilly fine or great drama, a satire, comedy, tragedy or frantasy, is an idea that reveals human nature. Lest we get off into a discourse on the *Plays of Ideas*, it may be worthwhile just to point out that in the case of G. B. Shaw, as a near contemporary example, the British rebel exploited the ideas of his Fabian socialism for their revolutionary candor, and for the exhuberant showmanship that would put Shaw on top as a London playwright.

The idea I have in mind is designed, in its varied convolutions of stage action, less to exploit the talents of the wardrobe mistress and instill rhapsodic admiration for an actor's gifts than it is to show up human character For we can never ne completely informed upon the naturalist appetites and the dreamers visions, the mortal beliefs and the human frailties, the delusions, paradoxes and quandries of the creature called *Man*. How he undertakes his personal survival and how he manages to cope with the events of his times and the circumstances of his existence, in concourse with other men, these things the play reveals to our eyes, no less than to our understanding. Insofar as the theme is trivial and the issues of no piths or moment, the play will seem trivial and last but a short while, then pass into oblivion. But let the passions be great and the issues of civilized conduct of importance , as guides to civilizing amenities, then in the comic genre, and as reflections into self, indeed in all serious drama, that product of the pen and the theatre will be of itself great and will last.

One can scarcely recommend a more profitable activity to the younger generations, and to the older a more pleasurable engagement than that they assist in the construction of the scenery and costumes and, tallents permitting, perhaps read for parts in some forthcoming production, then live as another mortal for a brief span of time. Or, seating themselves in the darkened house, watch the unfolding of a tale of other men's lives. Then, if all have done their work, technicians players, director and, most vital in importance, the playwright, and if the story be honest and well-rounded out with true observations on the affairs and characters of its people, the impressions, the knowlege, the pleasure gotten thereby must surely deepen the understanding and sharpen dulled compassion, so often blunted by man's "inhumanity to man" in our modern world.

The third of the three basic necessities of a drama, human motivation and the dramatic idea having been dealt with but briefly, yet it is to be hoped with discrimination, is the requirement of a story, and especially a story with a *dilemma*. Let it be said, here and now, that the resolution to a play, if it has a resolution, is not one of the chief elements, for this is the dramaturgy of play construction and not basic drama of character invention, the one a fine preoccupation for the schoolmaster and cavilist of the theatre, if not of noviatiate playwrights; and the other the business of the practiced dramatist, players and audience. Nor, again, is anecdotal narrative a drama, else the monoloues of Chekov and Strindberg might, on the printed page, occupy the space of a singsle paragraph each. It would be a gross error, I think, to attempt to persuade others that such narrator-pieces as **Our Town** and Josep Ferrier's Broadways fiasco **Edwin Booth** are extended anecdotes. For regardless of the wide acclaim of the one and the meretricious, lantern-slide *tour de force* effect of the other, their forms episodic, as in the novel, the chief characters in the scenes remaining fixed and inseparable from *biographer's tales*. Furthermore, in each work there is a human dilemma; and it is that dilemma that rescues Booth from obscurity andl the Webbs and the Gibbses from complelte annonymity.

To be sure, there needs to be a resolution of some kind, else the Protagonist is mad, which truly he seems to be in certain works of the *Expressionist* school. Such quasi-madness, I call it, is found in Post WW I German dramas of disillusionment, neurotic fantasy, symbolical God-masses orgy. Indeed, a play is not like an 12-tone atonal composition by Schoenberg which, if it but ends on a discordant note, does not cease to be a sympohonic poem. A play, however, that is expressive of the playwright's inner torment and the weir of his imagination, if it but concludes by showing us the phantoms of his night, may very well pass for a Masque on the moralities or on the mysteries of the author's personality, but it is not and cannot be a play, or it then lacks story and dilemma and is merely a psychonalytical expose of the author's pain.

Still I would not have anyone believe that the dilemma is--like a resolution--not *also* a problem in the technics of dramaturgy, which can be studied to immense advantage by a careful reading of the plays of Ivsen, realist and symbolist, who has been described as the progenitor of the modern theatre. Whereas a dilemma in the life of the principal character, as Nora in **A Dolls House**, may appear to form the ideological basis, and set the mould for the action thereof, in a good stage piece, the appearance is but the illusion of the author's pride. For no amount of craftsmanship in the construction of a play, with its exposition, crises, its ascenending action, *denouement*, and so forth, can compensate for the fresh, moving and profound grasp upon some humans error that the finest work in the theatre gives us. In fact were I to tutor a tyro playwright, I woul say find a common human error or foible and construct a play around it, beginning with the error and following with the consequences of that error. Then, resolve it with death by execution, restoration, disenfrancisement, or ruthless denial. In this schemata is embedded the Morality play, Elizabethan drama, dramatic realism--and the story of Job.

One may lindeed say, in defense of this argument for the dramatic dilemma of choices, as an infallible method of play construction, that from an initial quandry there emerge the major dramatic conflicts of *all* genres of the art, and that the play's crisis and turning point have but the same origin in story. Medea's murder of Jason and their two sons is the angulished rebellion of a jealous wife who has elected, in revenge, to kill the objects of her love, those beings who are most precious to her. Upon her discovery that Jason means to place another queen, and his paramour, in the council of his throne and the affections of his life, she is faced with the dreaded choice which Euripides' play presents to us. Medea's dilemma is unassailably clear. Miss Madrigal in Enid Bagnold's **The Chalk Garden** must, like Medea, resolve her dilemma by critical choice, and so, until the closing scene of the play, lhe conceals from all excepting The Judge a crimianl past wherein she has suffered a terrible wrong and miscarriage of ljustice to be layed against her. Her dilemma, likewise, is quite clear, to reveal her past, with or without a confession, to an essentially cruel, if not hostile, society, or to hide herself within the iinterstices of future years in a secluded corner of life surrounnding the old manorhouse and its mistress Mrs. Maughm and the merciless young niece Laurel. It is the playwright's business, so the argument goes, to spell out that dilemma for us, how it emerges from the lives of his chaacters, the emotion with which it is charged; and the characters' decisions as to what course of action to pursue in oder to resolve for us the dilemma of his story. I offer these two plays as illustrations of the theory.

Yet I, too, would hasten to point out that there can be no story without at least one such dilemma of dramatic promise; for what is that stalemate but a quandry over choices, for without a moment of choice and decision the deepest and most native grain of characrter remains hidden from view. Contrariwise, there may well be dilemma without a story, and it is this truth that accounts for much of todays deplorable clinical drama, and for the *obscurantisms* to borrow a word in its contextual meaning from Dr. Yvor Winters' **Maule's Curse**, that permeates the Expressionist drama of this country, notably the works of Eugene O'Neill, whose tortured souls voice their damnation of the outcast; of Elmer Rice, whose Mr. Zero in **The Adding Machine** speaks for the man stripped of his humanity-- a religious idea--by the machine, and of Tennessee Williams, whose Vala Xavier in **Orpheus Descending** utters the angry lament of the wanderer, disinherited by a special elect. Much of what seems meaningless and indistinct, and to defy interpretation, stems from this *obscurantism*, can only be the result of an inordinate emphasis upon dilemma, problem and conflict, as such. In **The Great God Brown**, for example and in **The Adding Machine** and the Orpheus play, we are struck by the terrifying and primitive sense of *aloneness* that each protagonist bears within himself. Each Principal, it may be said, acts as though he had free will, and yet pays allegiance to the particular god of his punishsment. It is this paradox that torments, even while it preocupies the playwright with passions as subjective expression, and dilemma as a kind of a-moral or Neitzchean choice of willed absolute ends.

We know that from the resolution of this dilemma in Greek classical tragedy there follows the catharsis, which Aristotle takes up in his **Poetics**. And we can observe, from the Medea play, that there is no catharsis in tragedy unless there is a story to involve the emotions and, by identification, to carry the audience through the Protagonist's wrong choice by a natural flaw from birth, thence to the crisis and complications of that human flaw or *hamartia.* Similarly, in comedy the laughter issues from the incongruous and ridiculous action, and from the absurd follies of choice in match, manners and motives, each of which,l upon eamination, will be found to contain a dilemma of choice behind the deceit. For seldom does a man drop his mask without a *gain and a sacrifice* at one and the same time. Yet, important as it is, I would not have anyone render the dilemma of superior importance to his judgement of what is truly fine drama and outstanding theatre. Therefore, it is for this reason that I have prolonged the discussion. For neiter the human quandry nor its resolution is possible to perceive, as a whole and in all-round perspective, without the framework of a story within which to mount these elements.

HOMILY

No man knows his neighbor
better than the fool, since the one
finds honesty to confirm his
own deceit; while the other is
less than honest to find in the
fool a neighbor.

Citizen.

The follwing letter appeared in the " Daily News" November 22, 1984--fifteen years ago, when Timothy Kelly was editor.

"Acts of t errorism will occur with greater frequency as time goes by. Some aspects of th utimate form of rejction are worth noting.
For example, often the terrorist feels impotent to advance his cause. Being intensely frustrated, he transfers his feelings of impotence to an annonymous public. He blames society. He sees his violent act as a sort of self-martyrdom that leads to the fame and recogntion his society did not give him.
The terrorist scoffs at this view by feigning a pride in his humility and annonymity. The warning phone call, the claim of credit, the arrogant power of choices of time and place: these methods are used to intimidate. Commonplaces.
By his terroristic deed, he also reveals his disaffections and disillusionments. In his act of destroying, the perpetrator purges in his mind the once-loved object or cause or image, his self-idolatry. He would destroy the avengers (Marines), the slave-makers (British soldiers), or a spokesman for the "out group." (the President).
To say the terrorist is brainwashed oversimplifies. Fearing his own potentially disloyal actions, he removes disgrace from his disaffection by that ultimate confrontation with himself. He discovers his ltrue self at the instant of oblivion, when the bomb explodes.
Prior to that moment, his fanaticism masks his fear of himself It is that flight from his self-fear through death that suggests insanity. Being defensive, he is self-righteous to the point of death.
The terrorist compromises with his life. To him, his threat extinguishes the cowardice. He can still cope with a dubios loyalty to a cause. But he derives pleasure from the real or imaginary death of others, as watching a suicide victim fall. Terrforism is hedonistic, giving indulgent pleasure to its perptrator. CHARLES MILLER Tujunga."

I wrote that piece a full seven years before 9/11. The bombing of the marine barracks occasioned that dark foresight.

THE CRISIS, by Charles E. Miller 3-1-09

Moral values exist apart from personal feelings.

Once free, a slave's words of freedom will always return to haunt the prisoner.

RELIGIOUS LIBERTY AS POLITICAL POWER

Karl Marx called religion the "opiate of the people", a drug enabling them to escape the realities of their failing bourgeois society.

Any icon-ic loyalty of the people will inevitably arouse the jealousy of a tyrant. The reason, however, for this hostile attack on religion was not only that the God of the News and the Christians commands loyalty and respect, but that their actions cannot be predicted or their thoughts controlled by a tyrant. In a society in which the lives of the people are not closely observed and manipulated by the State, that State's very survival and the power held by its leaders are endangered, threatened, providing thereby fallow ground for political intrigue and power grabs. This was the milieu of Russia when Marx observed the coveted and envied success of the Russian Kulak farmers. Strangely, the politicians could not grow wheat.

The significant reason for the exile of religion is that the worshippers of God have no fear of the tyrant. They surrender fear up to the god of their faith in consequence of which the tyrant cannot make their day-to-day moral decisions for them, those choices that are grounded upon conscience. If they chose to worship and to evangelize and to sing hymns, though compelled to do so in secret or in the woods, they do but show his impotence in maters of faith. He cannot exploit their morality, a power which to him symbolizes the way to his downfall.

To put a further hedge about the liberty of belief and faith in religion, the tyrant will increase the human elemental fear of carnage or death by surrounding the saints with presence of soldiers bearing guns. In this way he continually reminds them of their fear and their practical loss of liberty. And it is hoped that by certain gratuities of his regiments, they will adjust to the omnipresence and consolations and security accompanying that fear. Guns and tanks become protective friends.

A BRIEF CRITIQUE OF CERTAIN PLAYS
BY HENRICK IBSEN   (1828 - 1906)

GHOSTS - (1881): Mrs. Alving, to erase the memory of her profligate husband yet commemorate his life in front of the townspeople, builds an orphanage. Her son, Oswald, returns from his artist's studios in Paris only to bring alive Capt. Alving's dissolute character, his heritage of evil and decadence. He is discovered by his mother in the act of seducing the low-born, illegitimate daughter of Capt. Alving's adulterous love, the maid Joanna. When by accident the orphanage burns down, Mrs. Alving's mother-love over Oswald is complete. Regina, The youth's half-sister departs with Engstrand, protector of Joanna after the Captain's affair. In despair, Oswald ressorts to morphia powders.

Certain qustions can be raised in connection with what we now know:

(1) What Scriban stage devices did Ibsen discard?

(2) By what reality of characer psychology in Mrs. Alving's actions is the ghost Oswald-Regina affair lifted from the level of farcical impetuosity? Consider her excessive fear of expose and the premium she puts upon marriage in heaven.

(3) What is the real (or universal) in character?motivations? Fear of social censure; protection ;of tribal or group mores; influence of blood ties in conflict with social bonds?

(4) Does Ibsen, by the use of his realism, seek to persuade with any social message?

(5) Does Ibsen, by his use of **realism**, seek to persuade with any social message and, if so, what is that message?

(6) Does the play have a plot or simply a story?

The play depicts specious reasons for social conformity, such as the duty by Mrs. Alving to the memory of Captain Alving, duty to her son Oswald, to standards of respectability that overlay motive-fear of public exposure. That fear insures Mrs. Alving's silence until the play's closing seenes.

The antagonist in the play is the villagers whose conventions thwart Mrs. Alving from a marriage to Rev. Manders, the minister. The villagers are her goalers, their opinion are her fetters. Their implicit intention of defending their conventions, their mores, is the chief humanly real, or universal, dynamic of the play. These conventions, within the action, belong to the institution of marriage. Her fear of breeching them has contolled her life. The question may arise: does Ibsen form the mother into the mould of Pastor Manders' conformism, his credulous belief that "all's right with the world," his pious abnegation of the woman he came to love...so that what the playwright achieves is a melodrama with its false motivations in defense of the womanly woman theme of self-realization? This was also Shaw's theme.

BRAND - (1866): This is the story of an idealist piest whose pious acts cause the fisher folok to enshrine him as a Saint. Yet his sunny yielding will to live the life of the perfect man paradoxically causes him to strike a man in a fierce zeal for refusing to cross the stormy fiord; who perpetuates privation upon his suffering wife and brings pain to his mother for what he deems are the violation of his principles in the dispossal of her property.

There are critics who say of (the later) Ibsen he lacks intuitive vision, an understanding of the essence of a person's personality and character. I ask: does that criticism apply
to the motives of Brand's actions? I think not, for in another vemue control is the essence of a relationship.

PEER GYNT- (1867): Peer is the archsytype of the man who cultivates an indomitable will and will not give way to anybody or anhthling. He conjures up illusions to hide his ideal from himself. He prates about hunting feats, swaggers over his militarys lgenius. lHe steals the vbride from the weddisng feast. In lthe lmountains he accept the Trold King's ragged daughter as a princess on a fine charger instead of a pig. He reaps a forltune in America from slaves, whiskey land the Bible trade. His salvation from a shipwreck proves to him that sGod is not economical with property. So the desert ihe dazzles the German philosopher by answering his question that the 'sphinx is sitself, and when he shrinks from the button moulder who threatens to salt down his realized self into a crucible with other metals, we are shown an aged Peer who, for all his heroic fantasies, is only a coward, self seeker, an lopportujnist, charlatan and sensualist.

Ibsen's interest was in eccentricities. He could write about both sides of the person's character, the odd and the conventional. The question then occurs: does this play show to what ridiculous and fantastic extremes the idealist can go when he attempts to realize himself yet meets the impassee between duty to conventions and the will to survive? Is Ibsen trying to show the nascent madness of the individual rationalist who is baffled and defeated by social traditions and beliefs? His plays stand in defiant challenge to eighteeenth century rationalism, the credo that by reason alone man can achieve his dreams, solve his problems, confront the ugly side of life and survive by will power and reason alone.

AN ENEMY OF THE PEOPLE - (1882): Dr. Stockman is a physician who's first priority is to care for the people. It is he who discovers that the baths , which earn the town's citizens their livelihood, are polluted with sewag e. But when he tries to inform them, the newspaper editor turns cowardly against the expose; the wealthy, whose money controls the baths, attempts to silence him. Friends desert him. He excoriates "The damned compact liberal majority who brand him as an enemy. Ibsen calls their idealization of the incontestable rigfhtness of their *Society* of the People's political opinion, a lie. Their interests are solely commercial--the baths will bring business to hotels, shops, stores--yet the press and the people disguise their merchantile ends ideally behind the name and machinery of collective authority. Ostracized from the community, Dr. Stockman takes their rocks and hates rather than retreat from lthe truth of the situation and the honesty of his medical opinion.

Stockman is an autobiographical character. He defies critics, society, social hypocrisy, complacency and stupidity of the press. Yet one asks: is Ibsen ridiculing the doctor's meddlesomeness or his anti-business bias? Often Ibsen struggled with creating characterization--to make his characters live and become believablel on the stage, in his story. He labored over external details. However, he could not conceive of the great magnitude latent in the spirit, mind and imagination of a human being. Again, one can ask: is this criticism at all applicable to Dr. Stockman, that is, evident in the sacrifices that he makes?

HEDDA GABBLER - (1890): Because she is jealous of Thea Elvsted's correctlive influence over Eilert Loveborg, a rake and former lover of the widower general's daughter Thea, Hedda Gabler drives the libertine author-instructor from ther husband's house with a pistol. Bored with life, despising the ideals that sanctioned her class-conscious marriage yet steeled by no personal convictions, the romanic Hedda manages to get hold of Loveborg's script after Tessman picks sit up at a drinking debauch in the house of a disreputablele woman--to which brothel house she encourages Loveborg to visit in ordert to sever Thea's influence. She detests Tessman's aunt and is contempltuous of his circle of friends and his aspirations. Yet she fails the dutiful wife by handing the dissipated Loveborg a pistol and then, telling him to do it beautlifully, anticipating that she'll enjoy the luxury of remembering his suicide for her honor. He returns to the house to retrieve his manuscript, during the wrangle, she accidentally shoots him. The elderly Judge Brack claims he can identify the pistol. He blackmails her to keep his him company *de amour* upon his promise of silence. But while Thea and Tessman are reassembling the pieces of the partly destroyed manuscript, Hedda shoots herself with the other pistol.

Note that in the theatre Hedda has been played as a villainness, a heartless woman, a manipulator, a volatile and exciting character. There are other interpretations which one might draw sof this woman that would prove consistent withs the action and Ibsn's schief dramatic idea of a miscast marriage driven by idealism tlhat has no basis either in religion lor social mores. Hedda is an ideal beauty. Yet she uses that beuaty to woo other men to her side and to deceive her husband Loveborg, that is, to be lovely is to be loveable.

Also, Hedda dreams of that single moment of beauty--Loveborg's suicide. At the close of the play, however, she discovers that she must pay for the violating the moral law of responsible self-fulfillment. She wants to experience life vicariously without being hurt by it. After a close examination of her character, one can justifiably ask: was she compleltely realized by Ibsen? That is, did she possess any redeemsing traits, as, for example, a thinly-veiled compassion for Thea?

90

THE MORALITY OF CIVIL AUTHORITY: PROTECTIVE ARMS

In a free society civil authority contrasts with military authority. It is vulnerable and incomplete without a regulated police and militia that employ not only guns but might - with the availability of the first and the presence of the second - to protect the people; and to protect the people's liberties under the laws of statutes and case precedents. They are, among others, the freedom of peaceable assembly, the liberty to speak one's convictions in a public forum, and the sacred protection for synagogues, churches and their faithful who rightfully worship God, fearing neither vandals nor soldiers.

In the supporting ranks of these protective cordons are uniformed forces bearing arms, the Militia. Before them in the front line of defense are the police, the sheriffs and other law enforcement officers. The elected judges in the third cadre sit under the parabola of a benign moral authority, the laws and ordinances that govern a people.

In these times a strong police presence signifies an anarchistic mindset in American society, flaunted by those who are continually agitated into anger and rebellion by special interest cliques, an elitist media and strident barkers for a special cause. Neighborhoods, malls, schools and streets are places for the violence-prone malcontents to ravage the law-abiding citizens, claiming to symbolize by violence the purest of motives.

Following the above entities of authority are the courts of justice. They can be decapitated by the subversion, the intimation and bald lies if ever the military regime takes control. Soviet courts were puppets of the Commintern. Colonial justice in America was meted out secretly in England, one of the causes of the American Revolution. Under the despotic control of evil authority, which has nothing to do with God's ordinance of obedience, since the state is immoral that is God-less, the people willingly transfer their police powers and protective agencies, including the military, to the new godhead of power. A circus often follows that erects a facade of benevolence.

The "common defense" provided for by the Constitution, Article I, Section

8 (1), prevails over laws, the government of the people's freedom. It is an incipient power which war calls forth in the form of conscription, and controls the executive decisions, war policy and anti-subversive restraints. The tension between civil and military authority is most noticeable in peace-time. America's aversion to and fear of a military dictatorship has given the elected President Chief command and control over uniformed defenders. Until the 1960's the Congress had to issue a formal declaration of war, as a domestic strategy as well as an historical and Constitutional dictum. Thereafter, war became a "peace-keeping and police action", pursuant to which no declaration needed to follow hostilities - or so some liberal minds assumed. Congress was simply the provider, extemporaneously, of moneys to fund troop occupation and any intervene conflicts. The second branch of American government had become a mere sentry in the defense of the American people, but a sentry extended world-wide. It followed that in troubled times there arose, with few objections from the "silent majority", those zealots who tried to undermine our confidence in our leaders and to expose the voice of moral conscience as an expression of religious right-wrong coercion. Indeed, there was and is a strength in the moral conviction of a people, but their sinecure is by tradition and law vested in the fundamental Constitution of the country.

The "common defense", a moral and a good proscription, contains two serious weaknesses that reverberate among the ranks of the police nationwide. (1) The people are the genesis of police power; God supervenes, therefore justice and force have their basis not in man's schemes but in God's sovereignty. At least that was so in 1789. When the process reverses, society becomes immoral and justice breaks down. (2) A nation cannot sustain a justice system that is irrelevant to its values, therefore today the rootless one-worlders are rewriting American history in which history becomes increasingly meaningless to contemporary Americans and less and less acceptable and true before out new-world role of global oneness. We are taking on the aura of a substitutionary world Messiah, for whom liberty, as a construct of citizen choices under law is turning into mere cant.

The justice of military force directs the results it produces, which are peace and civic harmony - if that force is constituted under law. Under the protectionism of liberty, the pacifist assumes the role of self-exile and ought to be so treated in time of war. Ordinarily arms and the people shield a nation from physical harm and protect the survival of liberty, irrespective of religious beliefs. It is one of war's anomalies that a people look to God more often than they do during peace times. Here in America the law accommodates the war-

conscientious objector who in his integrity clings to his moral conviction of "thou shalt not kill". The law does not accommodate treason for the cogent reason that although the nation may be wrong, citizenship demands loyalty and that, if for no other purpose than to protect its innocents. In war force becomes the law of the jungle to protect den and lair. The presence of a strong defense ought to be a warning to enemies and nothing more. Protection is moral and no man is at liberty to set the law aside for himself or for any of his countrymen through blockades and disruptive riots, or thorough wicked civil conflicts to prolong hostilities. It is incumbent, moreover, upon our nation's leaders that they be circumspect in their conduct and honest in their words to the people. The negotiations of a traitor with the enemy put a curse upon liberty and jeopardized the lives of million of American citizens. A leader's oath of office is the mandate of the law and not of the man.

A nation's weaponry obviously is either to protect or to attack. The parade of naked power is most often the weapon of a hostile and dangerous adversary. To brandish the sword for the purpose of bringing about or insuring present liberties is a risky undertaking because it implies that liberty did not exist after our Revolution and that the results of bloodshed will bring about those wanted liberties. Force at bottom is evil where it envisions no moral replacement, no liberty other than what already exists. Visible evil proves the lawlessness of coercive conformity.

We today have copious proofs of the truth of that proposition. The rule of the gun has taken over neighborhoods and housing developments. The rule of the gun has threatened learning and education. The rule of the gun vandalizes houses of worship. The rule of the gun threatens homes. The rule of the gun terrorizes citizens and obstructs freedom of movement. The rule of the gun glamorizes hoodlums and young thugs. The rule of the gun speaks falsely for race hatred. The rule of the gun denies that liberty is the best course for civil courtesy and communal peace.

In the breech of its duty to defend the people, the State invents slogans as propaganda to blind the people to the truth and exculpate their consciences for the "cause" of their evil plundering. Race riots were, and are bad, but we must understand why. The hue and cry of "racism" is a cop-out of reason. Riots by ordinary people will convert please of injustice into instruments of evil. Propaganda will proclaim wicket half-truths of the vicious ones and declare as "righteous" the flamatory actions of the "innocent protesters." Yet, whenever the

State refuses to condemn the docile on-looking citizen, under these hostile circumstances, he either conforms or he loses his life or his working milieu of personal liberties cannot remain inert. The assumption of rioters, whatever the root causes - labor grievances, racial tensions, etc., is that America is an oppressive or despotic land and needs to be regulated by a messianic system of government. Silence by the State, though unconscionable by its leaders, if we are to survive as free, is never an admission of corruptive guilt.

Yet any liberty that is imposed and enforced by the gun is an illusion. Harsh penalties imposed for citizen refusal to yield, to comply under the gun, whether or not the cause is popular, abort personal liberties as much as if they were never born, an irony that can compel men to assume that they live in hunger, insecurity and terror. Is that not rather so today? We fund that liberal doctrines of attacking conservative reluctance's, shall we call the, outrage the liberal mindset and engender such lies. Truly it is a Socialist disingenuous fallacy that the system must be corrupted in order to achieve social progress.

Rebels bent upon forcing their views to prevail in Congress and in the public consciousness have at their disposal sophisticated electronic gear and crude weaponry. And they fight for the cause they feel is just - wages, housing, jobs, "free speech," and basic Constitutional rights. Often, too, is not violence or negotiations that resolves this conflict between liberty and authority; those abstract ideas are but inferred, if they are grasped at all. Yet by the strident echoes of zealots they have the power to motivate. The human ends that the crowd or the mob clamors for, at least when the people conceive of taking action in the streets are the products of their participation in the productivity of American life. That is a liberty they ought to enjoy; its foundation is always moral.

Indeed, there are certain rights in a free society the denial of which brings about justifiable rebellion. They are rights written into the Constitution. The liberty to express one's self freely is just such a right, though anarchistic formulations occur when lenders resort to symbols of violence, moral displays and language corruption to put their message across. These propagandistic instruments abuse liberty even as they tend to polarize resistance no matter how justifiable the ends sought.

Not the right but the liberty to get an education is another goal, though it is a privilege in America. And the liberty to demand decent standards of nutrition, adequate clothing and shelter are other goals ministered to by conscience, choice and action all of which are evidence of liberty expressed in its broadest sense. The denial of any of these to destitute is both barbaric and immoral. The promotion of these necessities through compassionate remedies and just laws brings no harm to others or any intangible incriminating evil to society. Compassionate caring does not corrupt a people.

Nay, it is the resort to an unjustifiable and lawless violence which injures and wreaks calamity upon established institutions. Its inherent treachery is morally shameful and despicable, such as is the treasonable aiding and abetting the enemy in ways to foment further violence. Within townships and cities, street violence is equally anathema to civilized concourse. By its very nature the mindless mob is destructive of personal liberty and the freedom and right to peaceable assembly, the right of petition before the legislature, the right of referendum to change laws, incumbents or situations by the vote of the people. The wicket anarchy of a dictator is different only in degree and appearance.

> *Trust only honorable men with your lives when free. Any others may dishonor your integrity.*

> *A liberated conscience, i.e. liberty to make a moral choice, is not the gift of the Government any more than is the gift of life, but America's plutocracy has appropriated both and claims their genesis. Fundamentalism is under fire ad hoc.*

> *An immoral government will covet liberty the most where it practices it the least - in the freedom to believe in God while serving the people. Envy speaks out of the side of its mouth.*

> *Leaders who squander a people's money are apostles of mammon and followers of Molech. Their liberty is without conscience and is therefore evil. Some will call it "wrong."*

FREEDOM AND LIBERTY COMPARED

Anarchy and liberty cannot be compared as likes. Also, freedom and liberty are disparate concept; the first does not foster either moral conduct or rational thought or, indeed, social responsibility. Freedom is the idea of unfettered mobility more synonymous with anarchy, as in the prisoner was granted his "parole freedom." Freedom must therefore be defined so as to insure that it is understood to mean not the absence of confinement or chains as the beast is confined, but instead separation from a despotic government.

In America, freedom to worship is best thought of as worship given sanctuary in public forums. If faith is confined in its visible manifestations to churches, then the edifice alone is honored and it is a dead faith. Freedom to worship, that is liberty of conscience or, for that matter, any other freedom, such as freedom of speech, movement and association, can become a snare and an absurdity if the public mandates that the particular freedom must be practiced in isolation. One has the natural right, nay, the liberty, to express his secular thoughts without penalty, allowing for the harm of an open destruction of immorality, as he has a similar right to move about the streets parading his religious dogmas or his literary vendettas, if he chooses to do so, providing he does not interrupt the freedom of movement or association of the general public. It is better that he use the park to voice his protests. But then the point is clear. As soon as <u>freedom</u> becomes rigidly structured in enforcement, it becomes despotic and requires of necessity enforcer. First come the thought police, and then arrive the ordinary police. Clearly, freedom <u>must</u> represent neither bondage to the saint nor redemption for the criminal.

Liberty must always carry with it the expectation that where it governs conduct the word has content, unlike mere "freedom" which, in its root meaning, is without specificity or conditions. The beast, the parolee, the anarchist all have "freedom." This reasoning is not specious if one considers that liberty infers purpose while freedom does not; and that purpose is either moral or immoral. Should we make the distinction irrelevant to modern-day America, the idea is defensible that although freedom and liberty are alike in having prior restraints, freedom is a cutting of the bonds, as is anarchy; liberty on the other hand, is the optional imminent installation of what was held in check or prohibited to it - an action, a voice, an expression, a design. One may have the liberty to disobey the law but that liberty is charged with responsibility toward others. To say one has the freedom to break the law is almost flamatory if it lacks all sense of accountability; and it therein reflects its true likeness to anarchy.

Had he spoken as a self-exile, a dying man or a lame duck in office, Patrick Henry on that March, 1775 at St. John's church, at the Virginia Convention in Richmond, might have proclaimed that - "as for me give me freedom or give me death," and none would have unquestionably understood.

Dramatic Reversal in
Noel Cowards's Fumed Oak
by
Pizzicato

Fumed Oak, a play lin two scenes and subtitled "an unpleasant comedy," involves in a dramatic impasse meddlesome ways and control of young Elsie Grandes, or Mrs. Beckett, and "mum," the respectable wife of Henry Gow. Coward's play, more importantly, brings to the stage an acrid comedy on the desertor husband who for fifteen years, not a few oftlhem in forebearance of his mother-in-law's indulgences, has smoldered under criticism imputing to Dorris a geneological superiority,   She has nagged him, bossed him, given him nothing inreturn for his support, treatsed him like a tramp, undercut his authority in the household, and in return for his work shown him mere ingratitude. From Henry's point of view, his wife is a cruel, mean and refined snob who has made life miserable for him. Doris, who has tried to preserve the Hockett standards of respectability and refinement, regards her huband as being somewhat coarse and irresponsible, uninteresting, the early aggressoragainst her innocence and a marital boob. This happy couple have one child, a teenager daughter named Elsie. Henry considers her spoiled. Her mother, in order to perpetuate a dainty and lady- like appetite, limits her to one slice of toast for breakfast. Grandma, the complaining boarder and sleepless one who berates about the gurgling water pipes an a noisy cistern, overrules parental authority. And she gives the child, on her way to school in Scene i, two-pence for sponge cake at Barretts on High Street. Whatsoever one may chose to make of this theme, these are the play's characters. If their governing passions seem too shrill in the utterance or too crude as human follies, we need only dip into the mornings paper to find examples of Coward's fractures in human relations, the gross unhappiness occasioned by the lack of moderation and good sense among the members of a household, That is the dramatist's thesis; and while laughable as the acting is in *Fumed Oak*, Coward himself, as a sentimentalist, holds too strong a brief for Henry Gow to see in him the henpecked boor who, by his own timidity, has allowed the genteel wife with a lover or two to get the upper hand over him. For bemoaning his purgatory of fifteen years, the sly cheat of his fate will not still the hand of poetic justice, and so the virtue of his longsuffering is rewarded through rebellious escape. How marvelous that escape *machine* of modern invention!

Scene i of the play depicts a wrangle between Grandma and Doris, mothner and daughter, to show how well equipped both are with cutting tongues. What perverse boorishsness passes for the gloss of good manners. Elsie's sniffing cold, the noisy hot water pipes, mother's rant, the child's starvation, Henry's wicked food waste, his banging about upstairs at a late hour; Mrs. Rockett's comparison of Henry with Doris' gentleneman father, his whereabouts last night, Grandma Rockett's pampering of Elsie--these are the points of contention between mother and daughter. Obviously Grandma is an intruder into the household.

In addition to this woeul fact, which provides comic action ofdramatic interest, Mrs.Rockett ils the means to Coward's realization of the painful truth about the marriage to past patching up. Furthermore, Mrs.;Rockett precilpitates Henry's open pronouncement, in Scene ii, that he intends to go away for good, a lamentable yet wise decision the reasons for which Grandma figures in pretty heavily. There could be no comic, objective social reversal without her presence in the mix of most of the Gow's domestic affairs. Henry may be sorely neglected, but he is the type of a chap, timid, long suffering and charitable, at least on the surface, who needs a bit of a push to reach self-destruction.

In scene ii, Henry comes home to a cold meal on the table; the women are dressed up to go to the moving pictures. Henry's line "good old Ethel," with reference to their household, who will wash his tray,cues in the start of *Fumed Oak's* reversal; a part of his imagination is not living in the future. He follows the notalgic with a confession of shameful drinking, his candid opinion on the "common little hat that looks awful" on Doris, the silly cliche on a "very little peice" of her mind, and the reminiscence of their first affair, when she became pregnant, Tonight is the anniversary of their glad beginning. Henry's long speech opening on the line "stop ordering me about, see" is the moment in which former restraints break. He dares to say dreadfull things in front of the child; he forgets that Doris has given him the best years of her life and that Mrs. Rocett is a refined matron. He throws the butter, cold ham and sauce on the rug, commands all to sit down, locks the door and pockets the key, tells Elsie to shut up and to fetch the invalid port for her mother, insults the "horrid little kid, and that old bitch of a mother of yours."

He pulls Mrs. Rockett from the open window, slaps her when she screams for the police, beginning thereupon, in this sequence, his climax speech, the chief motive for his actions, the human origins of the play's main conflict. and because of the dramatist's awareness of the injustice involved, the reason and inspiration for his penning the work. This climactic speech falls antsecedent to Henry's announcement that he has saved five hundred and seventy-five pounds, fifty of which will be Doris' and that the remainder he has invested in the boat. These sequences I have sketched comprise the action of the reversal--a change in attitudes, a shift in relationships, an alteration of manners.

Now in dramagturgical parlance, the *reversal is that block of action which anticipates a definite and irrevocable alteration in the direction of events.* The reversal moment *per se* is that point at which the direction of events that conspire toward a particular conequence reach that consequence, and the events which follow the sequence, or perhaps an entire scene in a full lenth drama, relieve the story of emotional tension, remove the chief cause of prior conflict, and bring into final, near "harmonic" balance, in an irrevocably changed situation, the major characers of the drama. So it is in *Fumed Oak.* Henry's climactic speech, three quarters of the way through the play is not the reversal moment of itself, nor is it the critical speech of story's crisis.

"...You've been after me for a long time, Dorris. You didn't know It then, but I realized il soon after. You had to have a husnand, what with both of them younger than you, you had to have a husband, and quick, so you fixed on me. You were pretty enough and I fell for it hook, line and sinker; then, a couple of months later you told me you'd clicked, you cried a hell of a lot, I remember, said the disgrace would kill your mother if she ever found out...."

Henry expects that Mrs. Rockett was "in on the whole business," and that she knew "Doris was no more in the family way than he was"; but they got married. This speech of the husband merely takes us to the story climax, and revealing principel motives, the direction in which the reversal points... justice will definitely fall. And the changes stop on the sequence of resolution. Henry now has a bank account, boat and passport. The reversal of *Fumed Oak*--from submission to dominance. from dependance to independance --is complete.

The actions focus inCoward's play is, of course, upon Henry anf Doris, Protagonist an Antagonist. The reversal impingedupon wat they do and say. There are, however, what apear to be minor reversals, yet are in fact what I call moments of *apprehension* in the characters' actions. In this play the apprehensions reveal, in each instance, that the character has been static rather than changing beneath the suface. Doris is never quite subdued until Henry mentions the L 50 she will receive as support. "...You're going to have me starve! Her comedic amazement is the arrest of immediate threats, and of filfteen years of bullyraggin disrespectability.

Mrs. Rockett undergoes a transition in attitude from that of the superior domestic influence ("you drnken brute, ou!) through attempted escape ("I'm not going to stay more and be insulted!") to the threat of fear (" I'll have you up for assault!") Apprehended in her actions are the position and attitude of illegitimate authority. From an attitude of complacent ingratitude, Elsie appears terrilfiled and hypnotized into submission when Henry pushes her mother into the chair and orders her to bring the port from the sideboard. Finally, the apprehension of his old attiltude of abject acceptance of the woman's unappreciative household tyranny occurs at his first, firm order to Mrs.Rockett that instead of sending Elsie from the room in the frm of a row, she leave the child alone and sit down. In each of these instances of aprrested emotion, Coward reveals the true nature of the characters. In some of them alone are the conditions of a major dramtic reversal fulfilled. Upon all of them that major reversal depends. It would be a mistake I think to ignore the the fact that character changes in *Fumed Oak* bear relevance to recognsizeably life-like sitluaitons and characters. Both an indication of good play structsure and of dramatilc human experiences / The modern critic would call this a play about a *disfunctional family*.

ON AN UNNAMED PLAY

...acquainted with reading habits, eating schedules, sequestered hours for love-making and the established rituals of social intercourse. These details from a small,quiet corner of English life came across with a great deal of visual appeal and dramatic effectiveness in their realism. Indeed, both plays were, in the staging, unusually fine for their pictorial qualities.

Ethel Sokolow in the role of Mrs. Railton-Bell, a continuation of her Play-I performance, skillfully dramatized the character of the domineering mother beneath her genteel social manner. Grace Macouillard as her daughter, the grown-up child, gave proof of the actress's adaptability when she combined the pitiable with the utterly ridiculous antics of the weak-willed mistress. Marilyn McKenna, in the part, still, of Miss Cooper, held the level of her performance consistently high and convincing. These and supporting members of the cast, including the able-bodied Meacham heightened the vitality of the production, its comedy and the embrio love intrigue, which the first play could not have achieved, unaided. It was a pleasurable night for this reviewer at the Contemporary Dancers Center while watching a play that remains yet a vague chimera of manners, an unfinished curiosity piece that lacked thematic power as a wry comedy of the socially absurd.

A DIVISIVE ISSUE

Consistent with Constitutionally granted Judicial Review there arise a number of issues from Roe v Wade (410 US 113; 1973) which the Court now addresses, particularly those stemming from substantiYe changes in medical technology. Statutory law is vulnerable to changes in circumstances because, unlike constitutional precepts, a statute tends to lose applicability to the demands of the time. In the matteri of Roe v Wade, tolerance has taken on the force of command when precedent dictates participation by acceptance. I am intolerant of abortion, and increasing numbers of Americans are. Therefore, I object to the Court's decision in the original (1973) judgement.

Roe v Wade is political. It is so, and it is made to seem so, thus to affix the approval of elective constituti o nality upon its p~4n— ful and lasting consequences when the mandate of the decision is for toleration and not for lawful enforcement. In sixteen years of pDactice, elective abortion has come to stand for the truth of free choice and therefore, by sheer numbers, a tyranny of truth fr other men in our society.

'In any enterprize it is hazardous when the outcome is consequent upon numbers and not the commands of conscience. Crowd mind governs the former conspiracy of choice, and lest I seem indelicate to say so, I think society's performance under Roe v Wade contains an element of that corrupt "mind," of behavior without conscience, of pitiless self—gratification0

According to what I read, the State's interests are twofold in the instance of an abortion: The State has "an important and legitimate interest in preserving and protecting the health of the pregnant worn— N an," regardless of any question of her residency. This commences at the end of the first trimester, the woman theretofore acting only upon the advice of a competent physician0

The State has "another important and legitimate interest in protecting the potentiality of human life." This t~compelling?V interest begins at viability. But the question arises: when does "potentiality" begin? Hopefully, that is one of the elements the Court will consider, for it affirms the sanctity value of life in the womb, jro—babiy starting at the time of viability.

The science of post—natal and pre—natal care is changing. The date of viability is shifting toward conception~and the trimester system for determining viability is, it would appear, becoming less meaningful as a deterrent to abortion. To get in "under the wire," as it were, for a non—viable abortion, young women are coming into the abortuaries earlier in theirpvegnancy. Yet, paradoxically, clinics record an increase in the number of late—term abortions, some as late as 30 weeks. A law (Roe v Wade) that is so ill—defined as to time limits, that is subject to a sliding—scale application, constant revisions in application; that is confusing in questions of risk, legality and follow—up care is a law that is certainly too sweeping and therefore voidable. Since it is a vague law, it tolerates all sorts of license and undulgences, thereby ruling out what must be the basis for a sound law — consistency and conformity in its application to anticipated circumstances..

The right to have an abortion is not a fundamental right. A majority of the states have had restrictions for over 100 years. The reasons are what the pro—abortionists ignore yet have been handed down as common human knowledge about life for milleniums, that the quickening of the fetal infant demonstrates life, that "premies" can be cared for, nurtured and saved; that midwivery is a useful medical profession in rural areas. And , since the advent of "sound" visualization and sophisticated amnioeentesis testing for sex~ deformity and normal interuterine growth, medical science confirms that life as all men know it outside the womb resembles those yet unborn. To assert the protoplasmic nature of the expelled aborted fetus is a lie that for sixteen years your Court has encouraged the ignorant to accept.

Furthermore, it is a known fact that the infant's heartbeat begins at about the fourth week. If a flat EKG wave or EELL (brain) wave indicates death, certainly a heart beat indicates human life in the womb. That seems to me a logical assumption. Then why do your Court and many doctors infer that the aborted life is only protoplasm? Have you conspired with the American Medical Association, Planned Parenthood, the abortuaries to exterminate an entire generation of over 20,000,000 most of whom were viable when dis~osed o~9 in the trash~Z

Not long after the hear~e~~ ~s first audible, the fetal child has the capacity to feel pain. I Yet the abortion proceeds in the most cruel and calloused manner, severing the limbs of the protesting infant by powerful suction or burning it to death0 For a civilized society to participate in this sort of death of the voiceless victim — without representation as having a life of its own — is barbaric. I am ashamed of our country and of a Court that ever brought about this wholesale death by an edict of toleration0

Now we have not just the vagueness of the law and its inapplicability as law, sociological fiat. Buu we must stand idly by and countenance the utter barbarism of the "treatment for pregnancy."

Roe v Wade did not envision clerical manipulation by Planned Parenthood officials to induce the pregnant mother that abortion was not a, but the only choice. But that's the reality, since Planned Parenthood rarely ever suggests alternatives to its fanatic death verrdict. Their current ruse for concealment of their motives is to suggest that perhaps "abstention" is a way to avoid pregnancy.

Roe v Wade does not undergird the feminist movement — as street crowd scenes, marches,, rallies, coathanger displays would have us to believe. The movement can exist without interuterine dismemberment.

Pathetically and with an ominous lack of foresight, Roe v Wade makes no provision for follow—up treatment, psychological disturbances (chronic depression and suicide), guilt feelings, psychiatric consultation, grief for the aborted infant, etcetera. Assuredly the Supreme Court has not supported the 5t~te~~ "legitimate" interest in protecting the health of the pregnant woman~ although you will concede, I think, that the State's interest in the mother's health should mandate these measures also.

The State's compelling interest in the "potentiality of life" should also figure into the equation of the law that the destruction of life rests upon. These appendages to abortion and extensions of the law, by its very consequences, are largely ignored in the clamor for "rights. The fetal infant's body is not the mother's body. It has a separate brain, circulatory system and heart beat.

Ask yourselves, if you would, does the unborn have a right to protest the agony of dismemberment or burning? Does the woman have psychiatrie or spiritual help? The answers are "no," and therefore the State's two—fold interests are a fiction, a shibboleth to deflect from your Court the charge of irresponsibility. Indeed, that is precisely where the Court stands today — irresponsible toward the life of the unborn child. Despite its lofty language, the Court cannot plead othenwise~

The Roe v Wade decision contemplated the consultation with the pregnant woman of a responsible physician. But that transmission of not just - the medical implications but of advice, concern, and knowledgeable alternatives by other persons is not happening. The AMA, through the pro—abortionists, represents to the woman through the doctor the "informed alternative" of death by inexperienced quackery hands. For the most part, only the pregnancy—crisis counsellors have been able to reach the woman from the streets, despite vociferous objections by clinic personnel and intimidation by the police0 In the absence of such counselling the woman is left uninformed — contrary to expectations under Roe V Wade,

In Bellotti V Baird (443 US 622; 1979) the Court stuck down the requirement of parental notification and consultation in every case; and required that the law provide an alternative counsel where the parents were not involved. Similarly, in H.L. V Mathesch (450 US⌁

Photos

A line two blocks
long formed at the box
office of the "Misere"
theatre to see   the
grand opening of "The
Spanish Tragedy." -An
aerial view

The
typi-
cal
critic's
perspective
of
the play.

Original site in
Athens   from
whence came the
doric pillars
used in "A Mid-
summer Night's
Dream."

Director
Queque in   a
high dudgeon be-
cause the fel-
low spot went
out. For   the
rest of this
scene, only the
troupe   knows
what happened.
Queque commen-
ted: "This sort
of thing must
not continue."

Pen where
Medea fed
and shel -
tered her
dragons. Now used
by itinerant as-
tors between shows.
Note bent bars; in-
dicate strength of
actors' passion.

Close-up of
Harpagon's
sash box.

Gramaphone
Sadie used in
"Rain." Devel-
ops 165 RPM un-
der level conds.

Sitting room
for the edi-
tor only, to
consider   if
he erred.

A scene from "The Duchess
of Washoe," showing the happy miners at work before
the explosion. Taken by infra-red flash lamp.

WISDOM

"...The most profound, themost central and indeed the sole theme of the hisltory of the world and of man to which all other themes are secondary, is the conflict between belief and unbelief. All epochs in which faith, under whatever form, reigns supreme, are brilliant, and inspiring and fruitful for contemporaries and posterity. On the other hand, all epochs in which unbelief, under whatever form, claims a meager victory and even for a moment boasts a specious brilliance, are destined to sink into oblivion because no one is inclined to take pains to acquire knowledge of sterile things...." From *Goethe and the Modern Age*, Edited by Arnold Bergstrasser; Henry Regenry Co, 1950; a note entitled "Israel In the Desert," attached to Wesgt-estlicher-Divan: p. 305.

"One can have the clearest and most complete knowldge of what *is*, and yet not be able to deduct from that what should be. the *goal* of our human aspiations. Objective knowledge provides us with powerful instruments for the achievements of certain ends, but the ultimate goal itself and the longing to reach it must come from another source. And it is hardly necessary to argue for the view that the existence and our activity acquire meaning only by the setting up of such a goal and of corresponding values....Here we face, therefore, the limits of the purely rational conception of our existence...." From *Later Years*, by Albert Einstein: Philosophical Library, N.Y.; 1950-, pp. 21-22.

STAGE CONVENTIONS & SYMBOLISM IN
IBSEN'S ROSMERSHOLM
by Pizzicato

What is Ibsen saying in "Rosmersholm:? He is telling us through this powerful realistic play that a man of Rosmer's energies and idealism, a former parish Rector in "an old family seat near a small coast town in the west of Norway" can reach a higher plane of nobility of selflessness, through idealistic self-will and personal discipline, that a woman such as Rebecca West, his house maid and companion, a self-sacrificial confidante, burdened with an "unconscious filial instinct," is monstrous to bring in her train a wife's death and household unhappiness for purely persona ends; that the love bond between a clergyman and his accomplice, as Platonic and in harmony, is stronger than the traditional bonds between himself and the community, a brother-in-law, his own reputation among the townsfolk and his parish members? Ibsen shows us these and other complications of his play's basic reality, of the problemical human truth that underlies his melodrama of warring loyalties: there is and always will be that man who deems it worths the sacrifice of his social esteem, his selcurity, happiness, blood bonds and, if necessary, his very life to bring some measure of inner freedom of conscience and sense of nobility to others, howsoever deluded or realistic his quest. The glory lay in making the effort. And Rosmer is that sort of man. His romantic delusion is that he can substitute his conscience for the consciences of other townsmen. Yet if Law has a conscience, that is what man-made law ofttimes does.

In dramatizing this powerful truth, Ibsen's play utilizes stage conventions as familiar to the theare for cenuries as masks and paint pot. Contrivances in the main, those conventions one may divide roughtly into the artifices of stage business and locale, and certain gypical forms of character delineation for the sake of plot and theme devlopment. *Where is the story happening...and why is it happening?*

With regards to stage business--Shakspeare, for example, uses the dropped handkerchief in his "Othello" to give cause for a husband's suspicious, wrath and ultimate revenge against Iago and Desdemona, whom he believes are lovers, the one given preferrment above him in the military service and the other suspect of faithlessness. This same device appears repeatedly in Restoration comedy in the form of a carelessly dropped letter, or a schemed epistle of retaliation left exposed. In Congreve's "The Old Bachelor" Lucy, the jealous rival, frames a coarse, saucy letter to turn Vainlove against Arminta. In Wycherly"s "The Country Wife" Mr. Pinchwife, the butt of laughter for chosing a wife of low breeding, comes upon her panning a letter to the emasculated Mr. Horner requesting that he assist her in the dissolution of her marriage. In "

Rosmersholm" editor of "The Beacon" Peter Mortensgard presents to the Rector an old letter, delicately sealed, written by the deceased wife Beata that tells of her remorse over Rosmer's defection from his religious faith and the time-honored traditions of his family. Beata's letter makes clear the fact of Roismers defection, the devotion of his wife, and imploring the help of a village editor, assigns the Pastor's political radicalism as the public cause for alieniation and Rebeccas invasion of her, Beata's, domain as the Rosmer's wife with cause for grievance. The handkerchief, the note, the letter--these are traditional pieces of staged evidence that are the lachkeys to more profound matters in the action.

THE TRIAL

This trial is a contest between B. F. Skinner, the eminent psychologist and theoritician versus Fydor Dostoievgsky, the great Russian novelilst. The nexus of the litigation is Dostoieveky's story *Crime and Punishment*. The charge is that the Russian violated established precepts of the profession of Psychology. The defense maintains that Dostoievsky drew his characgers, their thoughts and actions from real life rather than from theories about life. Dkinner was a behqaviorist

Dostoievsky is charged with attempted (1) fictional analysis of character., (2) practicing psychology without a license; (3) fraudulently promoting a crminnal act of murder as murder; (4) using *guilty conscience* as a ploy; (5) abusing the profession of psychology by presenting behavior as the fiction and character revelation as analysis. On these five counts, how do you plead, Mr. Dostoievsky?

Fydor pleads his innocence by empirical reason, to which I offer my own story, similar to *Crime and Punishment.*

Proceed, the judge admonishes, At this juncture , as the defense attorney, I introduce my first witness, the main character of the novel story. The first words from his lips, in all practicality were, "I am a great admirer of Napoleon."
Question, sir: "Did you aspire to be like Napoleon or were you his follower?"
On cross-examination the Pttrosecutor accuses the law student of covering his guilt by feigning to like and to imitate Buonaparte.
Brought to the stand, Dr. Skinner made this amazing statement.
"This poor man actually loved his victim, the old pawnbroker." The judge put the trial over until tomorrow.

RICHARD III

THE PLAY AND THE MACHIAELLI
or
A Partial Defense of Shakespeare From the Pedants, Ecclesilastical and Secular

In his small reaise nitled TheAntic Hamlet andRichard III, Sidney Thomas takes for his thesis-idea in the chapter "Richard and the Vice" the epistemological argument that Richard Crookback "Disuises himself for comic effect; that his attitude toward life is sardonic rather than naively villainous, (and that) the Vice of dissimulation, if we are to relate him to Richard, must at least foreshadow the urbane and the intellectual sophistication of Shakespeares character." Thomas traces the king's vice back through figures of English moralities...who resembsled Richard most in their boastful self-explanatory speeches...to the figure of Dissimulation ib Medieval allegorical poetry. "In this characer (ofRichard), the tradition of dissimulation has produced a great dramatic figure." What Thomas refers to, in part, is the popularity of masked balls, the dissimulation in later domestic comedy of Congreve and Wycherly, the biblical reference to satan disg;uised as a snake and the facades of political intrigue described by Machievelli. Dissimulation is a not uncommon human trait with its many venues of display in human nature itself.   Rihcard III happens to be one of the world's greatest examples of royal disguise.

BEYOND THE PEDAGOGICAL SOPHISTS

Keeping in mind that it is the presumtuous critic who thinks his analytical knowledge of dramaturgy can explain fully the living synthesis of Shakespeare's dramatic creature Richard III, I propose to point out examples in the play where Shakespeare departed from history and, too, transcending the theories of pedagogical sophists, dramatized Richard's essential character with reference to the nature and conditions of men around him. He wrote for a sophisticated London audience; and he intended that the player of Richard taking the role, should breathe life into the royal body. Thomas' statement, however, of the *tradition* of Vice will serve as a convenient point of departure for our critique. Whether or not others consider dissimulation to be a *vice* remains moot.

A MOST UNFORTUNATE VICE PROCLAIMED

A few factss on Richafd III's stage history are not amiss at this point, since players and dilectors have veen as guilty of distorting the meaning and spirit of the work ashave been sclholars the ilmportance of thle dramatists source material. LIndeed, IL will go one step further and say that ilt is elither dishonest or pride, or a combination of both which tempts the scholar to prove, like afather claiming his bastard son, Sshakespeares pedanti links to anestray literature; as thoughthere is necessarily a contlinuity of such a tradition as allegorical Vice, and that hedrew upon that tradition, consciously, when hewrote the polay. A human hand penned the lines we must admit.

One of the most blatant, corrupting distortions Colley Ciber performed in 1700. In that year, his adaptation to the stage at Drury Lane was "maintained on the stage whole or in part until very recent times." (1949) In commenting further, Granville-Barker wote: "Cibber's work is not to be lightly condemned. It il a hodge-podge of several of the Histrories; much of the added dialogue is flat and poor, and there is some 'love interest and some added violence. But Cibber's Richard is a finer part for a 'star' than Shakspeare's and his whole play is first-rate 'theatre'." This commentI find to be churlish dishonesty. Granville Barker has writen numerous volumes on Shakspare that are still relied upon for their critical judgement. The incompetency of Mr. Barker's criticism needs no comment because of its pedagogical obsession with Renaissance tradition.

Hazleton Spencer, n his chapter *Richard*, from "The Art and Life of William Shakespeare," has this to say about the play's stage history: that from his debut in 1814 until his death in 1833, Kean made the part his own. Much of the "traditional" actors' business was invented by Kean. "Irving, at the Lyceum in 1877, restored Shakespeare, save for his complely discarding Cibber. His conception of the title role was 'splendidly Satanic,' and he emphasized the hero-villain]s intellectual pride." Richard III, he goes on to say, was first performed, "apparently," on March 5, 1750 in New York. It may have been acted a year before in Philadelphia. Junius Brutus Booth, father of legendary Edwlin Booth, chose *Richard III* to launch his American career in 1821. The Richard of Edwlin Forrest, "the first American actor of genius," Spenser tells us, "was a violently heroic portrayal." Originally presented by him in 1827, he ignored the emphasis on Richard's deformity. Edwiln Booth won his first success as Richard in 1852 in SanFrancisco, his conception over his long career having modified into the wily Plantagenet, the terrifying ruffian of his father and Forrest. And, finally, John Barrymore appearaed as Richard in 1920 in a silent film with black mouge makeup, retaining a good deal of Cibbef's adaptation. These various interpretations of Richard's character by actors of greater or lesser talent, should reassure the theatregoer on one point--that Shakespeare, because of his "legitimacy," his "respectabily", his "fame" lends himself readily to the prostitution of commercialization gadflies and to the self-ambitious directors and actors who cannot submit to the fundamental human truths and dramatic values of his plays. Richards deformity excites a popular yen for the grotesque *nature* of power rather than an appreciation for the immoral or unethical *seizure* of power.

Style absolves mediocrity, the *box office* justifies. They are the criminal minds of the American theatre. And they are ln a large measure responsible for the desire by scholars and readers to preserve Shakespeare 's plays as closet dramas. They view, and not wholly without reason undrer these corrupting influences, the poet and dramatist as a communicator of experience with personal meanings whose full aesthetic beauty and whose human truthfulness find access to the mind only through dramatic communication. For them, the distorting predelections of actors and other production personnel increase the chances of *another* Shakeare, another Richard III. As the stage history, though, of *Richard III* indicates, actors especially have consistently refused to project themselves into the times, the life and the central character of the play. That projection, that identication-with, requires humiliry and discipline and the *sublimation* of of performance-pride..

THE PLAY'S VARIED MUTABILITY A-NATURAL

It is a well known that that Shakespeare culled large segments of his plots and germinal ideas for dramatic characters from patricular written sources, such as *Hollinsheds Chronicles*. Scholars have been as remiss and varied in their interpreation of Shakespeare's metamorphosis of such historical figures as are the actors in their interpretation of the dramatist's intentions. In *The Antic Hamlet and Richard III*, for example, Sidney Thomas describes Richard's characfer as beling synonymou with "the nature of the Machievellian villain," to which he appends the clause..."if Richard is typical of that cartegory." Toward the close of his analysis in the chapter on Richard's Vice, he tells us: "W can now definitely reject any interpetation or Richard as a crudely melodramatic villain. In its place, we can put the idea of a character rich in overtones of irony and sardonic wit, a person of great intellectual force perverted to the ends of villainy."

Shakespeare went to *Halle's Chronicles* of 1648 and to the 1587 second edition of Hollinshed for his material. In those sources the Machievlian Plantagenet "lurked ready to his hand," states Mr. Spencer. He means by Machievelian that Richard is all villain and always villain. Richard's nature is too isolated from humanity to move us deeply. Instead, Crookback, a man of dreaded energy and biting speech, moves us to derision. He is the comedic villain of melodrama, says Spencer, not the bright hero or hero-villain of tragedy, nor even the fiend incarnate whose satanic malevolence conjures up awe. Spencer thus ascribes to Shakespeare's work a more literal, crudely-hewn interpretation of the historical Plantagenet than Thomas finds in the play. Of what counsel or value are these comparisons? Simply this, that they expose the Bard's intended character; they do not permit of variations, the proliferation of personal interjections, the prideful and pedantic mainipuation of the play's Richrard III. a man whose values are his and his alone. To rewrite Shakespeare's *Richard III* is to write another and an inferior play.

THE RESURGENCE OF HISTORICAL FIGURES

Richard's conqueror was the grandfather of Queen Elizabeth. ILt was natura, therefore, that Tudor historisans should portray the last of the Yorkist kings as a blackguard. Hollinshed drew on Halle for the reign of Edward IV, and for the protecgtorate andreign of Edwards successor, both historians leaned on Srilr Thomas MOres biographjy "history of Rsichard. King Crookback thereuponecame avillailn inthe chronicles with Hollinsheds recourse to More. Halle also used Polydore Vergil's Historila Angelica to fill out his Richard.

It was More and Virgil, then, through Halle and Hollinshed, who supplied Shakespeare with certain of the important character traits and the details of the play's main figure. More and Vergil both say, for example, that "a bad conscience plagued him." And Vergil suggested to Shakepeare Richard's dream on the eve of the bagttle of Bosworth and "the conception of Nemesis dogging the criminal monarch to his end." On the other hand, it is clear that in a play that covers the chronicle years of 1472 to 1485, Shakespeare improvises motives and crucial scenes where his history was silent. For example, he made the Yorkists' reconciliation, in Act II, Scene i, more dramatic, thrusting Richard into it--although the duke was campaigning in North atthe time, and he invented the wooing scene,(I, ii) when given the are fact that Richard had already married Anne Boleyn. It would seem more reasonable to say, in view of the scholars' slim epistemological evidence, that it was not More and Vergil, through Halle and Hollinshed, who gave Shakespeare the color of his portrait," --which Spencer tells us is the case, a position that links Shakespeare's Richard with More's biographical picture, preominantly...in the final analysis...on historical grounds. But, instead, that the playwright by his own genius infused color into bare historical facts of Richard's life and character and the history connected with the War of the Roses.

RICHARD'S ILNNER NATURE

From the play's very opening scene, Richard enacts the Machievellian schemer, the Barabas of Senican tradition but, unlike Marlow's character, Shakspeare dramtizes him with greater subtlety, plausbility, little caricature, yet with a similr craven love for acts of brutality and villainous subterfuge. Richard is: --

Cheated of feature by dissembling nature
Deform'd, unfinish'd, set before my time
Into this breathing world, scarce made up,
And that so lamely and unfashionable
That dogs bark at me as I halt by them.

He it is who is "determined to prove a villain/And hate the idle pleasures of these days." His "subtle, false and treeacherous" nature, the evil intent of his ambition, his ethical grasp without moral suasion, his pride, an indomitable will, the sensitivity of a mocked man warped eventually into hatred, the feeling of kinship with his fellow men deseased by some cheat of nature and ridiculed in the uncozening souls of well-Knitted men, fate , having withered his arm like a"sapling"and hunched his back cruelly--these glimpses of the inner Richard appear in the opening lines. For the remainder of the play, there is little change in his nature, unless it is in the degree of his intense persuasion to consummate criminal outrage. And a fact buttressed by the Act V dream sequence of his conflicting terror and ambition on the eve of battle, there is no change in his basic outlook, that to damn all but synchophants for the end of his accursed revenge is the fate he can force by his own hand in his seizure of the throne against the Yorkists.

FACTS OF DISSIMULATION

Wse flind, instead, subtle reworkings of lhis Vice of dissimulation, Hypocrisy, when he appears on the balcony in Act III, Scene vgii, protsectedby a brace of Bishops and loatlh to having his meditations broken in upon by clamoring citizens, he permits Buckingham to abjure that they see his piety, his "gentle, kind, effeminate remorse," while lhe accepts the crown before the eyes of zMayor and townspeople over his own hyocritical protestations:

> Your mere enforcement shall acquittance me
> From allthe ilmpure blots and stailns thereof;
> For God doth know, and yhou may partly see,
> How far I am from the desire of this.

Deceit:-- when Richard confeses to Ann, at the halting of HLenryVI's funeral cortege, that he, Gloucester, killed him and young REdward, lher husband, for the loe of her bequlty. Pride:--when Richard offers himself to his niece, Princess Margaret, ilmportuning Queen Elizabeth to present his plan to her daughter. Another traumatic shift in the balance of governing power is augeried by the Act IV, Scene iv, speech which begilns: --

> Look, what is done cannot be now amended.
> Men shall deal unadvisededly sometimes,
> Which after hours give leisure to repent.
> If I did take the kingdom from yhour sons,
> To make amends, I'll give it to your daughter.
> If IL have kill'd the ilssueofyour womb.
> To quicken your increase, I will beget
> Mine issue of your blood and your daulghter.

And she whlom he would make Queen is betrothed already toRichmond, lhis foe lsoon to lmeet him on the battlefield. That Richard cannot imagine an overpowerlng military force aligned against him, now the defeat he will suffer at Bosworth Field, are other dramatic implications of his blind pride.

ACTION THAT IMPLICATES

If one accepts that Richads basic character percepectilves on alnd feelins about, life are established lint lhe openng scene...s of the playh, I think I canreadilyh ldemonstratethat theody of Shakespeares play ils the matter of Richards characgter, concerns iltself wilth the drama of physical and intellectual action such a nature can prevoke from others. And with the subtletlies upona Gloucester revealed to the aludilence at the opening. Bothkinds of treatment railseRichare III lfrom the level of melodrama of to real drama. By tlhat IL meanthat thle Duke ofGloucester,fascinatses lus ecause he is evil. Dissimulation, in its crude forms found iln murder and detretilve faction hlas variants linmthe plays action. The Duke's malevolent nature reminds the audience of their own equable characters. His madhinations suggewst what theyshould be capableof, given similar cirumstances and deformities. Most importantly, one man's announcement that he plans to subvert a government by the treachery of setting his brother Clarence against the King's deadly hate is a man worth watching--tlhrough the actions of others nearby and for those variants of the core Vice that give to hischaracter the many-sided quality of a plausible human beling.

CHARACTER SPRINGS FROM THE DEED

The limpolications sof Richards cruelties upon the natures and actionf ofothers are that evil, wilthout the base deed, there ils jno characteriation andno interplay of the persons iln the drama. ILt isase eause ilt is animal an cruel. Thse limpliations reveal the protagonist, Buckingham, toe an opportunist seeking the Earldom of LHereford, hewho shrinks from murdering the Prince in theTower, andgaugingRirchards fear for his insecure crown, flees to join Rochard. Clarence, repenting of the sins hecommitted for Edward, Richards rother, istabbedon theTower rampardt.

> Ah! Keeper, Keeper, I have done these things
> And now give evidence against my soul
> For Edwards sake; and see how he requites me!
> O God! if my deep prayers cannot appease thee,
> But thou wilt be aveng'd on my misdeeds.
> Yet execute thy wrath in me alone!

Lady Anne whose fatiehr, husvand and king Gloucester murdered, permits herself toaccept his ring and the promise of marriage. Having convinced her thathe performed his crime outof lovefor her, in Act IV, he disposes of the woman who was his pawnagalistQueen Elizabeth and her allies. In that love-making scene, which ils Shakespeares innovation upon extant history, the playwright shows us the terrible energy and binding magnetism of Richard's cruel argument. A final example of the implications of his villainous nature in the action, and respecting the nature of others, that occurs inthe scene where Margaret, widow of Henry VI, once beautiful and now a shrunken hag, paces before the palace tormented by thoughts of the murder of her husand her son, grief torn ande hating "a hell hound that doth hunt us all to death." To Queen Elizabeth, mother of the murdered Clarence and of hell's black intelligence," she says in Act IV , Scene iv:

> Thus hath the course of justice hurl'd about
> And left thee but a very prey to time;
> Having no more but thought of what thou wast,
> To torture thee the more, being what thou art.
> Thou didst usurp my place, and dost thou not
> Usurp the just propertie of my sorrow?
> Now thy proud neck bears half my burdend yoke,
> From which even her I slip my wearied head.
> And leave the buden of it all on thee,
> Farewell, York's wife, and queen of sad mischance;
> These English woes shall make me smile in France.

Her prophecy coms true with Richard's defeat. The forces of Richmond take the field; and he and Elizabeth are now to "unite the whife rose and the red," the houses of York and Lancaster.

THE SOPHISTIC, INCOMPLETE DOCTRINAL ARGUMENT

NeiltherSidneyu Thomas nofRsichard G. Moulton, iln hisbook TheMOral System ofShakespeare, attempts anyh extensive analysis ofthearch avengers smotives, his shifts lin tactics due to cunning, a soldier's trainin and expediency. Neither proes Gloucesters ilnexhaerable wont to lie, the meaning of revenge forlits own sake inthe crilminals makeup, the lust for power in relation to the "humpyu whose grotesque sniffing about the feet of other men for a lifetime have withered his operative conscience. Neither writer tries to examilne thereasons for the King Richards partil remorse intheghost walkin sequence on the eve of battle. Neither Thomas nor Mouton examines Richards sironies in relation to damaticaricature. LIneeed, in relation to comedy...or to the comedic...as a drama tic form in itself having specific axioms that underlie character delineation. In Richard;s mostironic speeches, there is an element of grim humor. These matters of motilve intrinsically related to Glooucesters major vice of dilssulation. Moulton lis sinterestsed in systematied universalitlies. Thomas ils scrupulous about Shakespeares souces fof information for his Machievellian character. Both of these critics...and I think they are fairly representative of the scholar's obtuseness...show no great concern for the viable and dynamic character of Richard's motives, or for the innner conflicts of reason and the sub-strata of experience that have produced so evil a creature and that quite often dart past the imagination in the spoken lines on-stage.

CIVIL CRUELTY OVER AMBITION

Shakepeare has given us one scene by which we can compare the import of his half-crazed butcheries and the heinous intention to commit crimes covered over by

Dissimulation, with the more open and sober lies he speake to his mother in Act IV, Scene iv. She asks him where is Hastings, unaware that her son has killed him on a charge of treason for loyalty to the Prince:

   K.Rich. A flourish, trumpets, strike alarum, drums!
     Let not the heavens hear these tell-tale omens!
     Hail on the Lord's annointed. Strike, I say!
              Flourish, Alaums
     Either be patient, and entreat me fair,
     Of with the clamorous report of war
     Thus will I drown your exclamations.
  Duch. Art thou my son?
  K. Rich. Ay, I thank God, my father, and yourself.
  Duch. Then patiently hear my impatience.
  K. Rich. Madam, I have a touch of your condition.
     That cannot brook the assent of reproof.
  Duch. O, let me speak!
  K. Rich. Do thlen; ut I'll not lhear.
  Duch. I will be mild and gentle in my words.
  K. Rich. And brief, good mother; for I am in haste.
  Duch. Art thou so hasty? Ihave stay'd for thee, God knows, in
     torment and in agony.
  K. Rich. And came I not at last to comfort you?
  Duch. No, by the holy rood, thou knowst it well.
     Thou camst on earth to make the earth my hell.
     A grievous burden was thy birth to me;
     Tetchy and wayward was thy infancy;
     Thu school days frightful, desperate, wild, and
     furious.
     Thy prime of manhood daring, bold, and venturous.
     Thy age confirmd , proud, subtle, sly and bloody.
     Mere mild, but yet more harmful, kind in hatred.
     What comfortable hour canst thou name.
     That ever grad'd me with thy company?
  K. Rich. Faith, none, but Humpy's hour, that call'd
     your Grace
     To breakfast once forth of my company.
     If I e so disgracious in your eye,
     Let me march on, and not offend you, madam.
     Strike up the drum.

This sequence, particularly the Duchess' speeches, rings the drama of Civil War, court intrigue, Richard's revenge and hateful calumnies down to earth. It intellectually binds the son to the royal mother, his present ambitions linking to his past growth, her reasonable perspective bonding her with his hal-mad scheme. In showing us the evolution of the man, the sequence also gives the audlience an idea of how Gloucester's Vice of dissimulation emerged. Although as a Vice it belongs to the Medieval tradition Thomas writes of, this exchange between the King and his mother confirms the human quality and dramtic content of a trait that Shakespeare used not as a melodramatic device but as a guide axiomatic of his Protagonis'ts actions. In this one sequence alone, the playwright's imagination did not require historical confirmation, pedantic assertainment lineal literacy hack or troll to drop the idea into his alehouse cap.

Richard comes to the point with his mother, the Duchess. His ambition means everylthing to him now. In his lines there is bitter irony, mock geniality under the pressure of his hate, the innuendo or false love which passes court only because its sutterance is civil, but what treachery lurks behind that civil mask! His cunning is more insidious the more open and unsullied it appears, overlain with a mein of cordial greeting and kindly response. This duplicity is not allegorical stuff; it is human life. The Sopists are not willing to begin with Shakespeare on his own, terms. Alas, they would rather enshrine him with St. Peter or with their encyclopedic fallacies. To them hle was not a man in the midst of London life. He was a priest of the theatre who wrote allegorically.

PAGAN GO MYTH OF SACIFICIAL VENGEANCE

A while back, I mentioned the universalities which Richard G. Moulton writes of in his *The Moral System of Shakespeare*. What the author of this very interesting little volume chiefly has to say is this: that Shakespeare's **Richard the Third** exhibits, in the most pronounced form...(his) *"treatment of Wrong and Retribution. He has imagined for us an evil nature, set off to the eye by distorted shape, arising out of a past of historic turbulence, attaining in the present play, a depth of moral degeneration in which villainy is accepted as an ideal. Such ideal villainy is projected in a universe which, in this one drama, is presented as a complex providential order every element of which is some varied phase of retribution."*

History, he tells us, takes the form of a pendulum swing of retribution between sinful factions. Each expresses its will in a dramatic scheming for retribution imaged in experiences of the figures of lesser dramatic importance in what he calls "the underplot of the play."

The "chain of retribution" has its first link forged when Clarence, who has deserted to the Yorkish house, is murdered by a Yorkish King, Gloucester. His infamous deed tenders a triumph to the Queen's kindred blood. They, in their turn, because of the shock of Clarence's murder, lose the ailing King Edward, who is their only protector at the time of the mock death-bed peace which Richard forces. Edward suffers the taunts of Hastings, the Queen's supporter. And he , Hastings, eventually meets with exactly the same fate at the hands of Buckingham even while secure and impowered with privilege by Gloucester. Buckingham, in balking to perform the murder of the young prince by his hand, is , himself, driven into exile, joining Richmonds camp.

WRONG, RETRIBUTION AND ORIGINAL SIN

Moulton remarks that those repeated "strokesof doom" are not merely death sentences but are, in each instance, the personages at the center of the action who suddenly recognize a forgotten principle of justice or come to appreciate a bitter irony--"Fate seemsto move forward with the rhythmic march of nemesis." And it is the plot of the play which, considered as a structured, logical arrangement of action, comprises a cohesive micocosmic interaction of retribution of different kinds: "a pendulum of nemesis, a chain of retribution, a rhythm of retributive justice.: Behind these events is the Protagonist Richard, who discreetly or indirectly, in the role of the hero, becomes he agent of their propitiation. Because he, himself, is unaware of that fact, he outrages"our sense of justice," as the cardinal dramatic and moral force in the plays scheme of retributive justice and play action. Moultons thesis concludes that the moral principle which underlies Richard's career is "an assertion of indiviudlual will aganst the order of the universe."In a word, he is a the transcendant dramatizationf the anarchist.

Spenser is the abstract moralist in his insistence that Richard is too far removed from common humanity, in his character traits, to move us deeply. And he is, literally the comedic villain of melodrama. Thomas is the historian-philosopher when he inclines toward the singular emphasis on Vice, the character im Dnglish Morality Plays when he attempts to trace the lineage of the Christian precept to the heart of Richard's actions. Mouton is,quite patently an *historical determinist*. There is a certain reassurance and scientific respectability to the borrowing of "determinism from the Darwinian biologists. Moulton's theory about Richard's actions is couched in the language of cosmological laws. I have tried to place these theorists and their nucelar ideas within the tradition of cultural literary criticism...which historical culture of Shakespeare's day, and of the chronicled times forming the matrix or his history, is mirrored in the *Richard III* play. These theories, however, have validity chiefly as partial explanations of that culture. They throw little light on the creative processes of Shakespeare when he evolved his Richard characters. And they are almost silent in their explanation of the human realities behind the Duke's motives.

THE PLAY IS NOT PARADIGM OF MEDIEVAL THEOLOGY

Moulton furnishes a good example of that last point with his statement that Richard's career is "an assertion of individual will against the order of the universe." What he means is that the play, structurally, as it evolves according to human experiences and the logic of cause and effect relationships between events, is a Microcosmic replica of a Divinely-ordered Macrocosmic universe. Within the play's action, motivational laws of wrong and retribution operate with fateful precision , regularity and wilh predictable connseqences, just as physical compensatory laws operate in the larger natural universe beyond the play's historical scope and its on-stage realism.

118

Every cause has a corresponding effect.

DOCTRINAL UNIVERSALS LINK TO MORALITY PLAYS

Whereas Thomas' approach is descriptive of Richard's main passion of revenge, his humor, his "prime moving" Vice and its several expressions, including sardonic laughter and ironic falsehood, Moulton looks for an ethic buried in Elizabethan vision. It is an ethic, he believes, that holds meaning for audiences today in terms of universal principles of human justice, human nature's compensatory laws. At this point in his argument Moutlon's deterinism and his formalizing of Richard's moives make their entrance. If one is not careful, he is likely to be lured into accepting as factually true a theory that places the philosophical idea before the creation of the character...linking up with Medieval Morality plays. In Shakespeare, the reverse occurs. To do the former, as Thomas has done, giving precedence to the moral law, and as Moulton is about to do converts the playwright into a moralist chiefly concerned with Vice, villainy and sin, rebtribution and wrong. This is a common religious errorof the Roman church as well as the mistake of tinkering scholars and Puritan nose-gays for whom Shakespear is temporal, ephemoral and entertainment only.

Accordi;ng to Moulton, Richard's decision to prove himself a villain, which begins the chain of retribution in the play, is not the outcome of his choice so much as it is of history's deree. He experiences a trembling fear on the eve of his climactic battle. His is not the ethico-religious terror of the unknown which pitiable man feels before overpowering destiny in the plays of the Attican Greeks. Again, if you will regard Richard through Moulton's perspective, you will see that what would seem a catharsis moment in the drama are lines voicing simply the cries of an unseated soldier in the heat of battle. His dignity is the dignity of the soldier trained into him. His actions are the result of Will, a cunning without conscience and brute force. Historically determined, he is largly deprived of that free will Molton has set out to demonstrate as a force that operates against the *Divine Order* of the universe. Mouton has trnsferred to the play, by his interpration of Richard's character, the fundamental Calvinist delemma of early New England which predestined the damned and the saved yet granted to men free-will. Richard's actions belong to historical pre-destiny;. Yet Moulton would see that already damned by that Divine Order, he undergoes the Nemesis brought about by his free-will . Obscurity in he delineation of Richard's character and in the failure to clarify his motives are the two unfortunate results of Mouton's approach of his dilemma. It milght seem that Moulton has applied Emerson's doctrine of the sublime oversoul to his interpretation of *Richard III.*

THE MINOR CHARACTER A TRAGIC FIGURE

Only Queen Margaret appears to attain to the stature of a tragic figure but because of her comparatively minor role and the fact that she is acted upon instead of her significantly influencing the action, the old Queen's part in the play does not justify its veing called tragedy. Her speech to the Duchess in Act IV, Scene iv, conveys a *sense of the tragic* in a play which, if one accepts moulton's views, would make of Richard but an implement of *determinist* historical forces:

> Bear with me; I am hungry for revenge,
> And now I cloy me with beholding it.
> Thy Edward he is dead, that kill'd my Edward;
> The other Edward dead, to quit my Edward;
> Young York he is but beat, because both they
> Match not the high perfection of my loss;
> Thy Clarence is dead that stabb'd my Edward;
> And the beholders of this frantic play
> The adulterate Hastings, Rivers, Vaughan, Grey,
> Untimely smotherd in their dusky graves
> Richard yet lives, hell's black intelligencer.
> Only reserv'd their factor, to buy souls
> And send them thither; but at hand, at hand,
> Ensues his piteous and unpitied end
> Earth gapes, hell burns, fiends roar, saints pray
> To have him suddenly conveyd from hence.
> Cancel his bond of life, dear God, I pray
> That I may live to say, The dog is dead."

The man who tests himself by his neighbor's conscience stands in danger of losing his own. cm.

MIRACLE, MYSTERY AND AUTHORITY

At one point in Fydor Dostoievsky's great novel of visionary realism, **The Idiot**, the novelist wrotes of "the terror of certitude." In his **The Diary of A Writer**, for the year 1877, he writes:

> "What is there in prosperity which is bought at the
> price of untruth and skinning? Lest that which is truth
> to man as an individual be also truth to a nation
> as a whole. Yes, of course, one may be temporarily
> put to a loss, one may be impoverished for the time
> being, deprived of markets; one's productiion may
> be curtailed and the cost of living may increase.
> But let the nation's organism remain morally healthy,
> and the nation will undoubtedly gain more, even
> materially."

The paradox of these two ideas of a materialistic-driven nation and a moral nation is a superficial one. Yet it indicates Dostoievsky's fear of the degradation of moral decay in the Russian people. During the years of his imprisonment in the Katorba at Omsk for sedition, he studied his only reading matter, the Bible, in order "to comprehend the inner meaning of Christianity." That fact is of utmost importance in explaining the man/s intellectual development and the maturation of his spiritual ideas, his human insights, dialectics of his reasoning and his time lin Russian history. It was there in the vermin and rat-infestsed camp, bitterly cold in winter winds, that he learned from his personal experiences in reflection; and it was there as a former Fouriest--the socialism of small cooperative communities--that Dostoievsky worked out his fundamental concept: *that punishment and expiation merge in atonement*. Living among criminals and exposed to their rancor, rage and remonstrances and boasting, yet unable to expiate for their crimes, he saw the Christian *ethos* of the crucifixion-atonement as the resolution to guilt and the mitigation of the pain of criminal punishsment. Revolution could not cleanse the criminal's conscience. Until such a "barter", if you will, occurred, the remorse for a crime committed--spoken into the face of justice and forgiven by divine Priestly intervention, did not ease or purge the feelings of guilt, a pain that outweighed the actual punishment.

He became convinced that punishment and expiation for the criminal were found in atonement, and that the love-hate *ethos of conflict* lay at the core of human depraviy and pain. By what methodology did Dostoievsky fuse these religious and psychological conepts into his novels' realism? Nowhere in novels written between 1846 (**Poor Folk**) and 1880 (**The Posssessed**) and, excepting the first, can one find plausible prototypes from other cultures, as ie. are found in the socialist novels of London or Fabian plays of G. B. Shaw. What ingredient of mind and spirit gives Dostoievsky's work singular power and originality, is his *implacable realism of invention and character*. He had the insight to trace *throught processes*, as he does in the rationalization of Raskolnikov, the ax-murderer *before* he commits the bloody crime. He traces Rasputin's justification of God having wronged man who is thus entitled to rebel. For a further example, Raskolnikov does not lust to seize and possess the few paultry trinkets and money purse belonging to the murdered pawnbroker. He commits murder to justify his love for his sister Sonya. Friend Porphry does not morally acquit him as "a martyr for a god who is not our God, but for whom he would willingly die." Raskolnikov's weakness is his sentimentality, love gone awry, for his sister, the expiation for which is his *seizure* of an atonement --the murder--for the absence of genuine brother-sister love. It is not money that he really needs but love for himself, the athiest, in the form of sympathy from his *believer* sister, a kind of surrogate priestess who follows him to the Katorba as a nurse. Dostoievsky saw that the murderer Raskolnikov, stricken by guilt, wishes even yet to be exonerated and to do so he appeals to Porphry. The power of an unreal sentimentality as precursor of motivation to a criminal act was a realism that Dostoievsky had doubtless learned while in prison. And the rationalized alibi gave birth to the murder in this case. The criminals had taught him well that the condemned stand on their alibis as a way to keeping their sanity in some cases. They boast of their crimes; few repent.

If in **Crime and Punishment**, Raskolnikov is terrorized by the certainty of apprehension and of his being put on trial for the murder of the old woman pawnbroker, the sight of Russian people, the merchants, noblemen and serfs binding over their lives to the truth of guilt from sins and expiation through the Christ of forgiveness, beyond the legalism of remorse, signified for him the heart of his vision of a Slavophil world. Dostoievsky, during his prison years, had resolved the dilemma of man's compassion for his fellow beings and the terror created by violence--whether of murder, revolution or execution--as an instrumental means to brotherhood. The remorse of *confession* - before the Cross- led to compassion for other men. The corrupted conscience eschews remorse--another lesson of the Katorba.

In the chracters of Prince Muskin, Raskolnakov and Father Rasputin, the radical evangel, the author dramatized the implications, in a character's power and integrity, of the moral *disease* of untruth He had borne witness to such decay at his fathers Hospital clinic for the poor. Poverty and actual disease can blight the dignity of reason and self-identityas a person. Symptomatic of that disease was moral indecision--the inability to discern right from wrong. Consistent with the symptoms were the anguish of guilt, personal or surrogate. Such was Rasputin's plea, that the conscience of man is a moral battlefield, mined with dilemmas of spiritual conduct and ethical choice where good and evil struggle for dominance.

As a convict laborer, Dostoievsky ground alabaster and moulded bricks while listening to the inner thoughts, out of the guards' earshot. In the barracks, it was the same. These were men reduced to brutality, made violent by temperament and jungle cunning, the depraved, the murderers, the thieves, rapists and ideologically dangerous. They were the rabble of men condemned as vicious and unwanted by society. As a Fourierist who fulminated against the Tsarist government and the luxury and excesses of Russian nobility, and understanding them as he did , he also confronted ruthless criminal minds. and in the flux of mens fortunes and the boasting of criminal acts, he perceived that the awareness of a crime committed is sometimes more painful to the criminal than is society's punishment.

He writes in **House of the Dead,** and obliquely in his Diary, that he often read in the countenance of a branded man the consciousness of guilt and suffering of a felon for his crime against himself.

In Moscow Dostoievsly had learned the dialectics of athiests like Kirilov in **The Possessed,** and Ivan Karamazov as the instigator of his father's murder in **The Brothers Karamazov.** These are thinly veiled discussisons or *arguments,* as it were, of ideologues turned rapacious engineers of crime. He was brought back to *the why,* the true human motives which reappear in dialogue by the members of Varvara Petrovana's little circle of Petersburg "printing press revolutionaries" in **The Possessed.** Dostoievsky found their motives vicious, compounded of selfishsness, made dangerous by intrigue and embittered by revolutionary and class hatreds, yet glorified by pride and dialectical logic. Again--the criminal alibi in a different form, leading not to murder of an individual but to the exterination of a class, the Russian nobility of the Tsarist regime, of which, ironically, his father as a medical doctor was one.

He, no less than Tolstoy, was to demand a religious role for Art and to reject categorically the formula of *art for arts sake.* Unlike Gogol, Dostoievsky was not an impartial investigator; nor was he primarily the sympathetic humanitarian artist that Turgenev was. In his efforts to understand that particular Russian who was comndemned as a criminal, yet possessed a strong individualism and a love for intellectual dialogue, whatever his lifestyle, the novelist was not the humanitarian moralist that Tolstoy was--he whose orthodoxy would not permit him to level the social class wall between serfs and noble- men, the soldiers and Russia's feudal barons.

Apart from them all, the novelist whose pity for human suffering was that of a fellow inmate conceived and executed novels that were perhaps closest to the heart of the Russian people. The poverty and sickness of the flesh, he saw at his father's hospital for the poor in Moscow. His imprisonment in the Katorba instilled the poisons of revolutionary politics into his characters' motives, those who confronted the old Regime of Nicholas II. Precisely because his characters, spawned by the millieu, speak for themselves do they speak with power and conviction. Pity and love does not exist beneath Raskolnikov's brutal blows with the axe; and yet those virtues *perversly* animate the motives of Rogin, the violent, jealous half-insane lover of the woman the Prince is in love with.

Dostoivsky saw men of their sort, their prolonged anguish and wretched indecision and even more dismal frustration as men who were redeemable just so long as they had the capacity to rationalize their actions and to discern between right and wrong. Self-inflicted pain was the torment of criminal guilt. Were it not for Dostoievsky's kind of Christian *construct*, showing the impress of the Eastern Orthodox church and the ferment of his Scriptural study in the Katorba, his revelation of moral choices in the breech of athiestic indifference would have failed. And he would have creatsed characters whose lives were damned forever. The love-hate motif lay at the bottom of Dostoievsky's realism in his character delineations. Raskolnikov was not damned ecause he had the capacity to love. That was what Dostoievsky believed. The specific criminals suppression of love plays out in the story of crime and forgiveness. Obviously then, in addition to the theme of expiation through Christ's atonement by confession, the dual psychology of love versus hate becomes another of the novelist's themes.

C. J. Hogarth as quoted from the Dostoievsky's work which typifies the novelist's belief and his conviction that love has a regenerative power in "the most ignoble of natures."

> "If, when I was a child, I had been blessed with
> parents I should never have become what I am
> today."

> "The father himself wears but a threadvbare coat; yet
> for her (his daughter) no gift is too costly;...He
> will spend his last coin for her...if, in return,
> he shall receive but a smile."

> "Where there is no love there is no wisdom."

> "It is sufficient to love steadfastly, and work will become a pleasure."

> "Think (a cynical debaucheee is speaking to an outcast
> of society) "if you had but a little child to dangle
> at your breast!...is it not perfect happiness when
> all three are united in one - husband, wife and child?"

"Love is the whole world, love is the most precious
of jewels...Love is what men will give their very souls,
their very lives, for." *-House of the Dead*

Dostoievsky was a writer with both pity and curiosity; he combined natural sympathies with his personal human mental and physical suffering and his observations of these crises in other men's lives. Scenes at his father's Moscow hospital had taught him much as a younger man. For most of his life he enquired into other men's deepest thoughts, an investigator with "regard to the pathology of the human soul." *Pathology* of course means relating to disease, disease of the human soul. He, himself, suffered from epilepsy, undoubtedly a factor in his mental makeup. Dostoievsky's temperament, his exposure to the filth and degradation of the Moscow slums and his visits to Dr. Dostoievsky's hospital for the destitute and the ill and improvident sick spawned in Moscows tenements--these memories bearing the later scars of his brutal imprisonment meted out by the dulled and caloused judge of the bench, went into the novelist's richly-fermenting imagination. These experiences warped him toward the study of degeneracy, of that pathology of the soul's sickness, without corroding his own moral position.

Dostoievsky understood human rationalizations for criminal conduct, and he did so with brilliance of perception and insight. As corrolary to struggling through the tortuous thoughts of a criminal, he comprehended the *moral alibi* as few of his classical Russian novelists did, with the single exeption of Tschekov.   Shatov in **The Possessed,** an erratic and impassioned Nihilist, and a student in- fatuated with Varvara Petrovna, plays the part of the individualist in the service of a noble (political) cause. His dialectics have persuaded him that all actions and deeds and accusations are permitted. Shatov's hunger for revolution only partially conceals his lust to indulge hidden hatreds throlugh moral anarchy; gold and power over others are actually secondary motives in moving him to act. His conflict lies quiescent and deadly within himself, tending ultimately toward tragedy in its consequences. He has internalized rejection, the apotheosis of all revolutionaries. His infatuation is hopeless, self- indulgent, the poison of his desire as a revolutionary to be heroized. His cause, however, is ineffective because it is effete, demanding not social justice but self-adoration, a flaw similar to Raskolnikov's

Shatov's motives are, of course, personal; he has no capacity to interede for another human being and for this reason his revolution is so personal as to be meaningless. Through Shatov and Ivan Karamazov and Raskolnikov and the gentle, naive Christian Prince Muiskin, Dostoievsky shows us what he means by the potential "God man" in a morally corrupt and lawless human being. The Christiansity of the Prince is narcissistic, not corrupt in and of itself, but as a figure of nominative power under the old regime and believing himself to be annointed as a regent of God to carry out the command of succor and protection of the poor, he is empty of any moral suasion or authority in Dostoievskys novel!

Fydor Dostoievsky was not directly concerned with an exploration of man's acquisiive instincts, nor merely with his probitive, destrucrtive impulses toward destruction by acts of violence. His scientific curiosity added yet another dimension to Dostoievsky's realism. War within the human conscience was his battlefield.

Read his accounts of lthe prisoners who lived like brutes amid their filthy and cold, their hunger, sexual flagillations and vicarious floggings in **House of the Dead**. His almost clinical revelations of what he saw were detailed and must have stunned Russian sensibilities of the day. The scientific bent of his mind reflected off his father and his medical practice in Moscow. Yet flung into the Katorba, after near execution and a last-minute reprieve, he brings that surgical ;mind with compasion to his study of the criminal's netherworld. The probity, purpose, the character of his investigation gives the book far deeper meaning than "sensationalism" In deed, he was embroiled his entire life in revealing that "*within the very lowest strata of humanity, human souls are to be found with the attributes and the instincts which are forever hidden, though they are latent, in the natures of comfortable, ordinary people. He showed, too, that the real punishment of a crime is to be a criminal. His great thesis is that crime and punishment are one and the same, each being a manifestation of inner suffering.*"

It was this human truth that his Siberian exile taught him, who almost from the beginning of his career as expurgative novelist, an intransigent *political pamphleteer* through the schemata of the long novel and a *documentary artist* of dark street profiles of Moscow habituees--for none of them appear to enjoy any permanent residency--" Dostoievsky instinctively vanishes into the labrinthian ranks of the Russian disinherited. His protagonists, the murderer, the Prince, the radicals of violence, the religious zealot, the debauchee--they possessed no property claims to an old Russia and in effect were disinherited outcasts in all but name. Consider where they live: over a pawn shop, in a cellar, in a dilapidated shack. They are or were among Russia's powerless, characters who are not unlike the sort of socially disenfranchised who stagger into Dr. Dostoievsky's hospsital clinic. Society, the writer is telling us, has damned each to his own small acre of Russian wasteland, and from among hese moral cripples and savage disbelievers of Moscow and Petersburg Dostoievsky draws with imaginative force the half-mad, terrorized, pathetic and obsessed characters that people his novels. He does so causing us by the sheer power of his conceptions to realize that *they are us* in one form or another. Veneered over by niceties and posessions, they are our reflected images of intangible struggle and inner anguish and the terrible loneliness of self-doubt. Their afflictions are our afflictions, their pathologies our pathologies.

It is altogether certain, therefore, that an other aspct of Dostoievsky's realism was his grasp of the lives, the descriptions, the struggles of the different social strata of Rssian society, those sharp distinctions which inflamed he minds of Political revoluionaries, and, indeed, had incensed Fydor to compose a paper that seditiously leveled certain accusations against the Tsar and his regime. Dostoievsky was painfully aware of social discrimination and cruel intercene hatreds wihin the city gates. He was the *social commentator* not of a changing Russia, as is Tschekov (**The Cherry Orchard** play) or of a feudalistic paternalism suffused with Christian dogma, as is Tolstoy (**Anna Karenna**). But he was a penetrating reporter of the present state of things, matters of cause and import like poverty and hunger and incipient violence in the streets. Russia is breaking down economically, socially and politically and Dostoievsky's work shows that perilous reality.

There is a characrter in his wriing that most resembles him: the Slavophil Kirilov in **The Possessed**. He is a man who covets shis sneer of God and of humanitarian principles extrinsic to the lionish, empty, the cruel and opportunistic violence of revolution. Kirilov is also the subtle and at times affable "party man" who is wound up into the apparatus of a Fourieristic society that was Dostoievsky's fate. And still as the story progresses Kirilov's doubt of God's beneficience ignites a new faith in him, like Saul of Tarsus who, after persecuting Christ, was converted to a Penticostal Paul, seeing the revelation of truth that emerges from shadows by the light of the new tomorrow. For a new Russia is not to be attained by the spilling of blood and the murder of the innocent, even of the guilty. Kirilov's inner passion, his reflective intellectual zeal grapples with crime and its insidious plea of self-accusation, as against expiation if not through faith then never by means of violence. A man can never purge himself through violence; he only compounds his guilt. He cannot free himself from shame by appropriating the life of another man through murder or through self-exile or narcotics or self-inflicted disease, as do those inmates who attempt pugation by their physical flagillations in **House of the Dead.**

Karamazov's rebellion was similar to Kirilov's abandonment of God. He tormented his mind and tortured his emotions by dwelling on his vacillation and disbelief in God. Yet he perpetrated with the accomplice help of his brother Miitya and their criminal accomplice Smerdyakov, the murder of Old Karamazov. **The Brothers Karamazov** is Dostoievsky's great *detective story* of crime, which is never necesary, against the feeble and helpless, which is usually the case, for reasons that are cold-blooded since calculated and naked of compassion. Just as the saving of life and mitigating of suffering is the way of Dr. Dostoievsky, so is murder anathema to his son Fydor who must have had some contact with the patients on his Father's hospital Poor Ward.

There is an anomaly in Dostoievsky that emerges repeatedly: that his affilrmation of the value of life is vehemently juxtaposed, equally, to his affimation of the reality of death. He has Kirilov say in **The Possessed**: *"God is necessary and so must exist... But I know he doesn't and can't. Surely you must understand that a man with two such ideas can't go on living."* The act of surrender of a love object, a woman of a passionate connection to a rebellious spoiler, was for Dostoievsky an act of self-annihilation for which there was neither retribution nor forgiveness except through penitence. It is impossible to escape the religious connotations of the above quotation, since the act of suicide affirms only the reality of death and nothing more. The suicidal, desperately poor vagrants, often injured, had come into the hospital where his father had stopped their bleeding; no doubt there were deaths amid the blood on the stone floor. Rogogin faced imminent suicide in his life, the *anihilation of conscience*, when he surrendered his beloved....to (another)...who was a hated man. Suicide on different levels--physical, spiritual, psychological, moral-- was a mark of Dostoievsky's grasp of the human condition, of suffering without relief or release except through violent acts, or self-annihilation perversely tortured into acceptance as an enobling self-sacriice, rationalized as love.

Dostoievsky's rebels are the prisoners of their own minds and souls, chained to the irons of hate, jealousy, sworn slaves to their doubted beliefs--a terrifying outlawry--within often brilliand minds disposed to overthrow an icon, a creed, the status quo, innocent lives.
The reader often encounters a Dostoievskyan character who gropes for a comprehensible knowledge of life, an identity of who he is, his worth and purposeful meaning in life and where he is to act out his meaningful role in society. He can be a revolutionary or a monk or a shopkeeper, yet he has his fate and often his awful destiny to live out.

Rebellion by a character frequently takes the form of self-condemnation. It is manifested in some deed or idea as destructive self-will, or moral and spiritual suicide. Yet, too, other dimensions to this will to kill, to destroy--a will discovered in the character's inner turbulence as in Raskalnakov, is that the will is devoid of love.

Fueleop-Miller has written (66) that *"Dostoievsky's novels share the realistic background which was the common property of his age. 'Little' people are his heroes: the unromanic world of daily life is their sphere. The fierce struggle of self-will with society, lhe poverty and misery of early ineteenth-century capitalism, and the base nature of man in all its various forms, elemental evil as well as drab rascality and the wretched little weaknesse of men, supply him with the stuff of life for his novels."*

There are, one finds, three aspects to the the author's realism, levels of realism that are found in his major novels and that exhibit hlis most miportant dramatic ideas and insights into human nature and what he saw himself attempting to accomplish as a novelist. (1) The realism of Man, the *visionary*, he whose oppressively painful sense of guilt and his will to love meet in the act of penitence, justified, he believed, by Christ's atonement. Such a man suffers purgatory through his faith, a state of rapture with its vision of Man's dignity and potential nobility of spirit greatly akin to the purging of emotions, the catharsis in Greek tragedy.

There is this difference, however, that the penitence of the criminal at the instant of his new faith, his belief in God's forgiveness, signifies a regeneration, a humanizing of the Self, a full and continuing acceptance of a perfect authority beyond his own will, a restoration to the Man of the knowledge of human--and divine--love in its personalized manifestations. Such a vision and purgation presupposes the criminals awareness of moral distinctions between evil and good as he observes and deals with his fellow beings, lessons Dostoievsky learned in the Katorba prison camp.

He confesses to having seen those powers of discernment at work in the hearts of the most hardened prison criminals. (2) Then there is the realism of *criminal psychology*, the behavioral aspect of characers like Raskolnikov, the apparent aspects of human motivation and outward behavior. (3) The third sort of realism is *physical*. Dostoievsky will often describe the salt frost on the wagon driver's moustache without troubling to describe the freight under the tarpaulin. He particularized the uniquenss of his characters. One will find this sort of vivid particularization in his short stories "Apropos of the Falling Sleet," "The Landlady," "The Gentle Maiden."

Dostoievsky" hoped to free himself from the extreme torments of an age torn between belief and disbelief," (45) writes Fueleop- Miller. He had planned his one big book to be called **The Life of A Great Sinner,** an autobiographical epic in which fictional characters such as Raskolnikov, Kirilov in **The Possessed** and Prince Muiskin in **The Idiot** were to find God through their inner struggles. In **Crime and Punishment**, Raskolnikov murders the old woman pawnbroker and, like Pilgrim without Calvinist exhortations but with a pain of his consciousness of guilt, he reaches the threshhlold of repentance through Sonya's influence. In **The Brothers Karamazov**, Smerdyakov kills old Karamazov, the father, to bring about the materialization of his atheistic beliefs. Yet he accuses Ivan: "You yourself always told me that everything is lawful. Why are you so surprised now" Prince Muiskin in **The Idiot** can sacrifice his love for Natasia to Hippolyte because those "arrested in guilt and afflilictions are more deserving of love than the guiltless and fortunate...." Kirilov in **The Possessed,** doubting the existsence of God and His vague promises of Mankinds omnipotence, choses suicide to prove throgh the freedom of non-existence that man is sovereign when he is free from fear of God and death.

Dostoievsky held a life-long belief, matured as he read Scripture and observed prison inmates, that men vacillate between "the two poles of the soul--defection from God in sin and harmony in God." So writes Fueleop-Miller (5) A Christ who spoke from the Galilean boat and fed the 5,000, teaching love in the Beautitudes, was Dostoievsky's concept of God made flesh, a volitional, actual power for good. He was *"the way, the truth and the life,"* the words which Sonya , Raskolnikov's sister, reads aloud to him which brings about his conversion , his spiritual birth and his confession to the Inspector. To the novelist, in his crime story, Christ's teaching was the internal, spiritual, connscionable mediator for vacillating man, Raskolnikov.

In **House of lthe Dead** Dostoievsky shows us an emergent awareness of man's moral nature. His long talks with the prisoners in confinement, his scientific curiosity to probe the different categories of criminals, to know the nature of their crimes and their origins as individuals, created a ferment out of which seventeen years later he was to write **Crime and Punishment**. Human degeneracy was the awful revelation. One scene which he draws of the prisoners in the bathhouse prefigures that power of imagination and unflinching dissection of moral perversity which was to appear in later works. Turgenev has said of this scene: (in J.A.T. Lloyds **The Great Russian Realist**): *"The picture of the bath --it is truly from Dante!"*

The picture symbolizes the lost man, for all times, in the criminal's own terrifying world. Through a window in the bathhouse wall. there appears the phantasmagoria of fifty or more prisoners, their naked bodies writhing wildly in orgiastic desire as they shout and call to each other through the clouds of opaque steam. They beat each other with switches in their orgy, a glee and strange excitement written on their faces, flushed by their excitement and activity and the glassy effects of the steam on their bodies.

This vivid scene shows humans beings whose humanity, if not thei pride, was left behind them in their towns and villages. They are representatives of the soulless and the damned, reduced to the level of the animal. Their only real bonds with civilization are two: the words they utter to each other, and the fact of their crimes as defined by the court. The are men stripped of conventions and their right to claim conventions or to relate themselves to larger outside humanity. They are steeped in the orgiastic revelry of chained men whose Promethian liberation, through anarchy, was dashed on the rocks. Dostoievsky gives us a picture, in all its dramatic irony , of the *New Man* proclaimed by revolutionary thinkers , the anti-Christ saviors of the world, the utilitarian man who would make Self his god. Dostoievsky's study of the criminal was profound and incisive.

In the same book, **House of the Dead**, the author delineates codes of conduct among criminals, their understanding of feedom while in chains, their obsessions with the crimes they have committed. These vignettes lead naturally, in his maturing powers, and historically to Raskolnikov. He overhears trivial talk between a student and an officer, seated at a nearby table in the tavern. They are discussisng the hypothetical murder of an odious usurer in that quarter of the city, a man whose wealth would benefit society more than his life does. It occurs to Raskolnikov that those are the very ideas which have begun to occur to him. Back in his garret, he conceives the murder of the pawnbroker, an old woman who lives with her sister in an upstairs flat. He summons the rationalistic logic of a law student to steel himself.

> *"I am not one of those who abandon the weak to*
> *scoundrels. I come to the aid of the defenseless...*
> *I cannot coldbloodedly pass by all the horror, all*
> *the suffering and wretchedness of people, and not*
> *say a word."*

He wills his self-destruction. The tragedy in the making is that he hopes, through his crime, to save his sister Sonya from Svidrigailov, a contemptible man, by means of the stolen money. He, on the other hand and with characteristic Dostoievskyan irony, is discovered by Svidrigailov after the murder. Her hated suitor thereby acquires a sinister

power over the girl. Raskolinkov's mother is killed by the shock of learning that her son
is a murderer. One of the great themes of the novel emerges at the end: that "the divine
instinct of the heart which is denied by hard and (intractable) reasoning is ultimatly
justified by true knowledge" So G.A. Mounsey has written in his book **Dostoievsky.**
That true knoweledge is, in fact, the moral value of human compassion and the
reenerative power of faith in God. One must always keep in mind the fermenting source
of Dostoievsky's ideas, his Russian Bible and his intimate knowledge of criminals. One
of the most moving threads of the story is that she, Sonya, leads her brother into the
understanding and act of repentance, although she has sacrificed herself, for her family's
sake, to the man she does snot love, Svidrigailov. There is the point to the tragedy: her
self- sacrifice for something greater than she, her love for her brother, a confessed
criminal. The stolen pawnbroker money does not ransom her; although Raskolnikov's
confession to her and, by her prodding, to the Inspector,combined with his repentance,
purges Svidrigailov"s dark hold on lhim. His condemnation and sentencing provide an
example for her in her relationship to her hated lover...namely, rebirth and self-sacrifice
instead of what would be, without her complicity in Raskolnikov's surrender, a moral
suicide with the total collapse of her virtue.,

Dostoievsky's humanitarian compassion was for the sinner, the criminal
intead of for the victim. His tragic heroes and heroines are the Old Testament **Job** who
are bowed by undeserved suffering, as a test of faith at the hands of a just God. It must be
remmvered, however, that Dostoievsky's God was not the punitive Jehovah but the Diety
of love, made manifest through the New Covenant Christ of love. His Varvara Petrovna,
Ivan Karamazov, Kirillov, Shatov, all of his own creation, are characters whose suffering
is inner, whose guilt and self-doubts and dialectics of rationality--**the alibi**-- are of the
stuff of his own mind and heart. His, Dostoievsky's, pity sprang in part from intimate
self-knowledge, that pity confirmed by his Orthodox faith. It is a little risky to say so, but
Dostoievsky was in a true sense a re-discoverer of the Christian **ethos** of brotherly love,
yet a true reporter of his characters' evil, their crimes and wrong choices by which they
victimized themselves.

Terror belongs to Dostoievskys impenetents. Andre Gide in his book **Dostoievsky**
(309) writes;

> *Dostoievsky gives us, in one part, humble people*
> *(and surely possesssing between themselves humility*
> *almost to abjection, almost to pleassing themselves*
> *in abjection), and in another part, the*
> *proud (and surely those owning pride almost to the*
> *point of crime). These latter will be, ordinarily, the*
> *more intellectual. We shall see them tormented by*
> *the evil of pride, always making assault upon nobility."*

Dostoievaky links pride to terror as attributes of the criminal. He is saying that in

House of the Dead, and in the character of Prince Muiskin, whose serenity signifies not merely the conquest of, but a spiritual transcendance over, evil's destructive passion. In **The Possessed,** Dostoievsky shows these two characteristic emotions of the criminal by means of his first-person narrative of a group of Petersburg revolutionaries among whom there is a man named Stepen Trofimovitch. A giant stone "as big as a house" hangs upon a ledge over the heads of his comrades.s They are the ones whos fear pain and death from violence; it is they who fear, he tells them, fear that the stone may not fall to crush them. Yet would death be less painful than their fear of the stone? In the story the rock serves a dual symbolism: it stands for reactionary restance to the plotters, whose leader is Varvara Petrovna and whose mouthpiece is her subversive, underground magazine. And, the rock emblemizes, also, the destructive power of open bloodshed. Terror, like a Greek *Fury* pursues those in bondage to revolutionary violence.

That crimina violence has various disguises. Kirillov tells us, in **The Possessed**: History will be divided into two parts, "from the gorilla to the annihilation of God, and from the annihilation of God to...the transformaltion of the earth, and of man physically. Man will be God, and will be transformed and things will be transformed and thoughts and all feelings...." The dialogue between Trofimovich and his fellow revolutionary continues.

> *"If it will be just the same living or not living, all will kill themselves, and perhaps that's what the change will be?*

> *""That's no matter.. They will kill deception. Every man who wants the suspreme freedom must dare to kill himself. He who dares to kill himself has found out the secret of the deception. There is no freedom beyond; that is all, and there is nothing beyond. He who dares kill himself is God. Now evcery one can do so that there shall be no God and shall be notihing. But no man lhas done it yet."*

> *"There have been millions of suicides."*

> *"But always not for that; always with terror and not for that objct. Not to kill for fear. He who kills himself only to kill fear will become a god at once."*

These proud, calm words of his *political suicide* articulate the fear of others in Varvara Petrovna's circle that reflect their terror of the unknown and of the darkness in their own souls.

There, in the Petersburg drawing room of their leader, we meet Stepan

Verhovensky, who is convinced that married life will corrupt him, will sap his nergy, his courage in the service of *The Cause*. Marriage means corruption; his proud fear issues from a perverse self- love which he extends through the revolutionarys credo to the new world. Lilputin, his compatriot, is an elderly privincial official, a man with a malicious liveliness whose philosophy is Fourierist, as was Dostoievsky's. Behind his cruelty lies the fear of men. Shatov, the brute-man in civilization's clothes, is another; he struck Varvara's brother, the fearless Nikolay Vayevolodich, at a party gathering one night. As a weak man inside, Shatov stands in fear and awe of the leopard; violence is his recourse. Shatov, too, is the student of unstable temperament, a man burdened by a bad mamrriage, a merchant and family drudge with giddy social ideas and whose revolutionary ideals are more empty of conviction than they are sound with purpose. Dostoievsky's irony is that Shatov resorts to violence at the party in order to destroy the threat of violence. One of the most dramatic figures in Varvara Pertrovna's circle of friends is Stepan, whose soul doubt lies in the efficacy of revolutionary means to change. The novelist's crownsing irony is that Stepan cannot believe in his own disbelief of God-ideals. His friendlship with Varvara crumbles when struck by the realities of rubles for his tutorship of Varvara's young daughter, and by his Petersburg prestige. His god is his spride. He is the man made proud and free by Nihilim. Yet when she accuses him of putting her house to shame by causing scandals, he answers her by saying that he will take nothing from her; he will worlship her disinterestedly. His refusal to change is merely an alibi for his dread of involvement, and his contempt for the flunkies of "equality, envy, and...digestion."

It was the 1st ten years of Dotoievsky's life, after the chains had fallen from his legs and he had returned home, that he wrote his greatest books. During those years (1854-1872) he wrote **The House of the Dead**, **Notes from Underground**, **Crime and Punishment** and **The Idiot**, together with two shorter novels, **The Gambler** and **The Eternal Husband**. Four years after his publication of **The Possessed** and the beginning of periodical installments of **The Diary of a Writer**, Fuelop Miller has written (30) that he was to become known as *"the spiritual counsel or of the nation."*

Dostoievsky prayed to God for strength and inspiration to write "all that lies locked in my heart and imagination," Fuelop- Miller writes. On November 8, 1880, he sent off the last signature of his Karamazov novel to the "Russian Mssenger." The dual themes of guilt and doubt of God, of punishment and expiation that converges in atonement, were not yet exhausted with this, his last vbook. In it Dostosievsky gives us a portrait of the sensuality Fydodor Pavlovitch who exhibits in his person and his a-moral actions, the conrruption that existed in Old Russia. It is the sons, heirs of their father's depravity who share the curse of his bequest. *"All things are lawful,"* says Ivan. All things not supportable by reason are fantasy, are wraiths of madness. And yet, perhaps it was Dostsoieveky himself speaking when he has Ivan cry out in the fervor of his mind-sickness: "You are my hallucination," he tells Satan, "and nothing else. It's I myelf speaking, not you. You are the incarnation of myself , but onoy one side of me...of my thoughts and feelings, but only the nastiest an stupidest of them. You're I, I myself, but with another face." The realities of that other face--the face of deceit, Satan's ploy-- were the main concern of Dostoievsky in his greatest novels. *What, I have said, lies in all men concealed behind their facades of possessions, power and pretense, yet emerges in the criminal's behavior.* This is a major clue to one's understanding Dostoievsky.

By shifting the causes for a man's crime from a society of serfs and noblemen to a conscience, oriented between God and Satan, corruption and morality, love and hate or war and peace, Dostoievsky has emphasized that his heroes and lesser dramatic figures are the arbiters of their own consciences. He shifts the locus of his long dramas from class-conflict, the theme of the revolutionaries to spiritual warfare, good versus evil. There was for him a certain latitude for the exercise of his powerful imagination of character, as for example the rational Kirillov beset by the enigma of God's existence. Then there is that faithful and devout monk Zousima, whose God is the God of the Russian fathers, yet, strangely, in no way does she find love inadequate to the task of healing hearts. Finally, for purposes of illustraton, there is Porfiry, that legal demon in gentlemen's attire, whose sentimentality would be repulsive if it were not rather pitiful when he pays a compleiment to Raskolnikov by calling him a *martyr*. Nothing but sheer logic could lead him to that viewpoint; and a martyr is a martyr and not hanger-on, perhaps a hero, but never a dead man, for death to Porfiry was absolute, irrevocable and final. Indeed we may be repelled by Raskolnikov's character and the awful brutality of his crime, as the motif indicates, yet Dostoievsky's theme of punishsment and expiation converging in atonement are not merely ideas inseparable from the psychology of conscience-struggle. They are real. Dostoievsky admitted the word, the deeds, the choices of action and the tormenting consequnces which follow in his creation of character and story action.

It was Dostoievsky's conviction that the eclipse of reason and failure of the will attacked a man like a disease, developed gradually and reached its highest point just before the actual crime. The disease continued with equal violence at the moment of executon of the crime and, for longer or shorter time, afterward, according to the individual case and then passed off like some common non-fatal disease. Yet Kirillov, Satov, Ivan Karamazov are characters who act solely upon the authority of their own consciences, their rebellion instigating anarchy, the total freedom from responsible action which moves, ultimately to the loss of freedom. Thus did alibis of these characters betray them into slavery to a fictive cause and the destruction of a rational conscience. Dostoievsky does not fail to exhibit in his character's defection from reason the savagery and cruellty as traits of the criminal, together with natural curiosity summoned to the fore in his premeditation of crime. Raskalnikov broods over his murder, but before he slays the pawnbroker, we find traces of whimsy mixed with brutality in his premeditation of murder.

There were strange recesses of human nature which a prison camp, as a sort of experimental laboratory, opened up to the gentleman inmate who, as a nobleman with one side of his head shaved and branded as "dangerous," lived for four years by penalty of law among society's criminal scurvy of peasants, laborers, traders. A Siberian Katorba could now, however, oblterate class distinctions, those differences beteen groups of poeple with differing lifestyles. A natural distrust, Dostsoievsky tells us, kept himself and the prisoners estranged; he could never vecome one of them, fully accepted into their midst. When, for example, he trudges down to the ice-covered river to work with the prisoners in breaking up a river barge for firewood, the inmates restlessly keep a suspicious eye on him. Of rebeliousness, Dostoievsky has this to show us, that men will mutiny in even the most hopeless of situations. An example is when the convicts rise up against the cooks and malevolent camp major, clamoring for the animal satisfaction of their quite natural appetites. Yet, paradoxically, there existed honor among criminals. A few in the board barracks of the Katrorba abided by their verbal word of honor to respect the premises of pay, services for each oher, imtimate secrets and thoughts and intentions to escape. There existed also among the inmates a strong will to survive. Dostoievsky's sprisoners laugh at suffering, can feel the most exquisite self-satifaction over enumerating past criminal acts of violence, while on the day following, like traders in the course of marketplace business, the man who slit his wife's throat because she had a lover can in the next breath open a barter with another prisoner, in total forgetfulness of his deadly confession to his fellows.

It was the novelist's practice to draw his characters based on the model of someone he knew or had encountered. Stepen, for example, depicted Dostoievskys belief that to forgive is to gain freedom; to destroy is to seek a power beyond forgiveness. Doubtless he had learned this maxim from an criminal prisoner. Prince Muiskin is another. His very vanity is a cause for making himself more pliable to the wills and persuasions of others. The meek and readily-coerced prisoner was a Katorba reality.

Vanity, Dostoievsky believed, was one of mans strongest motvating impulses. It is a catalytic. Varvara Petrovna daughter, Dasha, is on the point of marrying the young free thinker Nichlas in **The Possessed**. However, the mother, Mme Petrovna, mother, feels hidden contempt for Stepan, Dasha's tutor and familhy hanger-on. She resents her daughter's delay of the marriage until Stepan can give consent. Her proud anger occurs because of Stepan's usurpation of a mother's prerogative. Her contempt for him has a revolutionary class bias, since he has neither money, blue blood nor a will to join the revolution. Her emotions as well as Stepan's are therefore mixed as are the movives for what they do.

In **The Possessed**, Captain Levbaldkin, a "repentant free thinker" expounds' in one of his early chats with the "I" of the book, on the fly and a cockroach and their thoughts when dumped into a pail of stew. The cockroach, he says, would not mind, whereas the fly would. How ridiculous the Captain would appear to be were it not for Dostoievsky's sympathetic and serious-minded approach to the character. Levbaldkin's parable demonstrates the relativism of men and guns--but without a knowledge of good, the patrotism only results in a-moral bloodshed. What the author is suggesting in this metaphor is that circumstances dictate the character's point of view...if the character is a-moral or without redeeming virtue.

In **The Idiot** there are other examples, scenes and characters that simplify the realisltic observation that Dostoievsky is a psychological realist. Hippolyte, foe to Prince Muiskin for Natashia's hand in marriage , dreams of a reptile that symbolizes, apparently, his hatred for the Prince much as he would detest and avoid a reptile. Hyppolyte expresses his rage at the Prince and accuses the "Jesusitical soul" of being the cause of his, Hyppolyte's , abject cowardice. These two examples illusrate Dostoievsky's genius for being able to shift the onerus of an unfavoravble or panful situation into the arena of a new conflict.

In **The Idiot** we see the strange love-hate of Rogogin for Natasia Philipovna. The question arises: why does he surrender the woman he loves to the man he hates. What perversion of love is involved? What transcendance over hatred has taken place within him? These words reveal much of the answer:

"He (Rogogin) laughed suddenly, and strangely. Then in a moment his face became transfigured; he grew deadly white, his lips trembled, his eyes burned like fire. He strretched out his arm and held the Prince tightly to him and said in a strangled voice: 'Well, take her! It's fate. She's yours. I surmrender her...Remember Rorogin!' And pushing the Prince from him, without looking back at him, he hurriedly entered his own flat, and banged the door."

Dostoievsky has dramatized for us the subtle influence of a man of noble station, compassionate nature, whatever his flaws, upon the character and actions of another person, who overwhelmed by fits of anger, does possess the insight and strength of character to discriminate between the motives and sympathies of Prince Muiskin. In Rogogin, we see the the reverberation, perhaps, of Dostoievsky's own guilt-stricken conscience relating back to his imprisonment for sedition when he ought to have been loyal to the Tsar as a nobleman; such as was his physician father.

Andre Gide has this to say about the novelist: in **Dostoievsky** (139-140)

"Certainly the psychological truths seemed always to Dostoievsky what they are in reality: particular truths In the novel (because Dostoievsky is not only a theoretician, but a speculator), cares for the induction and he knows the imprudence there would be (for him at least) in attempting to formulate general laws These (revea) edges of his (characters') lives. That law, for example that a man who has been humiliated seems to humiliate in his turn."

Emile Zola took great pains to paint a French countryside scene or the interior of a peasant's house, the scene around the hearth, or the miners at work in their black caverns a mile underground--took pains to depict these scenes in all their closely-observed details. Dostoieveky, however, gives us the external, the physical realities of a scene only as they

136

bear a relation to the dramatic action. His descriptions, whether of a room of a student living in Petersburg slums and seen through the character's eyes, or whether of a scene of physical action exhibit this one quality: *there is movement.* For example, here is the scene in which Ivan Karamazov returns from a disquieting visit to the room of a man whom he has willfully implicated in the murder of his own father:

> *"Ivan did not go home, but went straight to Katerina Ivansovna d alarmed her by his ` appearance. He was like a madman. He repeated all his conversqtion*
> *with Smerdyakov, every syllable of it. He couldn't be calmed, howevermuch*
> *she tried to soothe him; he kept walking about the room, speaking strangely,*
> *disconnectedly. At last he sat down put his elbvow on the table, leaned his*
> *head on his hands and pronounced this strange sentence.: 'If its not Dmitri,*
> *but Smerdyakov whose the murderer, I share his guilt, for I put him up to it.*
> *Whether I did, I don't sknow yet. But if he is the murderer, and not Dmitri, then of*
> *course, I am them murderer, too.'*
> *When Katerina Ivansovna heard that, she got up from her seat without a word,*
> *went to her writing- table, opened up a box standing on it, took out a `sheet of*
> *paper and laid it before Ivan. This was the document of which Ivan spoke to Alysha later on as a "conclusive proof' that Dimitri had killed his father...."*

Dostoievsky uses only these descriptive details of the room, of the expression on his characters' faces and of their actions which best suggest, rather than mimic, or dully list or report as facts. Tourism, publishing and photography had changed the need for Zolan micro-description. A reader of today may find Dostoievsky's dialectical passages, his intellectual wandering through mazes of a revolutionary's thinking, of the terrifying thoughts and passionate outbusts of the criminal mind at work--as somewhat tedious. Yet his novels are composed of the stuff of Russian life of his times...and of personal experience. Against our wills we are drawn in, blinded, spun round, and at the same time filled with a strange sense of having been there with him, having seen what he saw and endured what he suffered and at last believe his people to be real Russians whom we have met.

BIBLIOGRAPHY

POOR FOLKS
HOUSE OF THE DEAD
CRIME AND PUNISHMENT
THE IDIOT
THE POSSESSED
THE BROTHERS KARAMAZOV

FYDOR DOSTOIEVSKY, Rene Fueleop-miller, Chas. Scribners & Sons, N.Y. 1950, (37 pp).
SOVIET RUSSIAN LITERATURE, (1917-1950), Gleb Struve,Univ.Okla, Press 1951, (414 pp)
THE SHORTER NOVELS OF DOSTOIEVSKY, Preface, Thomas Mann, Dial Press, N.Y.(1951 (vii-xx)
THE DIARY OF A WRITER, (Vols. I, II) Dostsoievsky, Cassell Co., Ltd. London (1097 pp)
LETTERS FROM THE UNDERWORLD, Introd. C.J. Hogarth, E.P. Dutton & Co, N.Y. (vii-ix)
DOSTOIEVSKY, G.A. Mounsey, Alexander, Moring Ltd, London; 67 pp.
A GREAT RUSSIAN REALIST, J. A. T. LLoyd, John Lane Co.; NY ; 296 pp.
FYDOR DOSTOIEVSKY, Aimee Dostoievsky, Yale Univ. Press New Haven; 1922 (294 pp)(note)

NOTE: *Page references that appear in seminar text omitted in this version. Biliography, however, is the same.*

An Afterthought:--

"One of the objects of Socialist realism in literature was described by some of its advocates as the creation of _types_--of typical characters of the revolutionary epoch, a task in which until then most Soviet writers were believed to have failed. On the other hand, they were also these partisans of Socialist realism who stressed the search for heroes and their reflection of the heroic features of the great revolutionary age, again maintaining what literature had hither to failed to do. These two aspects of Socialist realism as it was understood by Soviet writers and critics, were reflected in the literary output which followed the "reform' of 1932." From _Soviet Literature, 1917-1950,_ by Gleb Steuve, University of Oklahoma Press 1951; 270 pp.

THE PECULIAR PEOPLE

A way up in the Utah county not many years ago, folk thought it a signal virue when a young Mormon swain took several wives; the US Government, however, being anxious about the mores of a peculiar religious sect, passed a law around 1883 that forbade polygamous marriages. That, descriptively is the conflict gist of this fine play **The Peculiar People**, currently being performed at the Hillbarn Playhouse, a play co-authored by Lynn Root and Samuel S. Taylor and produced as a workshop production y the Peninsula Little Theatre Group at the Hillbarn.

The Peculiar People is a comedy, a collection of reminiscences by Providence Gilbson, great grandmother who, from her rocker, relates the action on-stage. Washington moralists deputize drifter- bum sheriffs to harass Centerville's citizens, bewildered Nepali Gibson splitting homestead work between three wives, is enjoined to take another bride; the young town gentleman Bryon Monroe, already married to Gail, steals the practical village lass Zina for a new start. And dear, old Bishop Janson, a "renegade," finally gets his demure Alta hitched up to Jeb Wheeler. For comic situation the authors' new play is deliicious with the sort of intrigue and embarrassement of discovery that one finds in Restoration and 18th century comedy.

The drama does not lampoon the poses of vanity, imposters abd hypocrisy; there are no clandestine meetings. Bryan and Nepahi, runaways, return in black beards, but the comedy turns on farcical disguises rather than on a castigation of government prudery. The authors' play is episodical , a straight-line narrative that does not rlse to an emotional climax, as an unavoidable turning point in the action.....

AN ANALYSIS OF SUFFERING
WILDE'S SALOME
by Pizzicatto

Set in Christ's day, while the Messiah, as revealed by the Nararenes and Jews in Herod's palace, turns water into wine, heals the lame, gives sight to the blind, preaches from a boat and, to Herod's revolt, raisises up the dead son of Jarius, "Salome," the play, tells the story of the beautiful Babylonian seductress' destruction by the Tetrarch of Caesar's province, the man named Herod. During a palace feast, his Syrian Captain of the Guard , son of an exiled king and a slain mother, kills himself because he has allowed Salome, against orders, to look upon the prophet Jokanaan. He is the man called John the Baptist, and the account of his beheading occurs in Marthew 14: 8 The old man utters dire prophesies of doom to come to Herod's province. He has heard the beating of wings in the palace; the sun will turn black and destruction will visit those who have forsaken the ways of the Lord. He is not the prophet Elias, who is proclaimed to have seen God face to face. Yet he has heard the Moses of the Mount, and he knows of Christ's miracles by the Capernaum gate and in Jerusalem. It is he, Jokanaan, whom Salome, daughter of Herodias, wife of Herod, lusts for a the palace banquet.

Herod, to amuse himself on his birthday, begs Salome to dance for him. She submits, yet upon the one condition, that he will grant to her, one request. Herodias, or in the Greek Claudia, wife of the Tetrarch, Pontius Pilate, forbids the dance, beseeches Salome not to dance. She has had a foreboding in a dream. The slaves nevertheless prepare her with perfumes and with the seven veils. Removing er sandals, she then performs the "dance of the seven veils." Her act completed, she demands of Herod the head of Jokanaan on a silver platter, the life of him who inhabits the jail of the cistern below the banquet hall terrace. Her request is one of vengeful frustration. an act of sexual attachment to the dead. Herod offers to give her his white peacocks, his fabulous jewels, half of his province and rich garments of feathers if she will but rescind her demand. Salome remains adamant; she will claim and see exhibited the likenes in death of the man who forbade her to touch his body or to kiss his lips. Herodias, however, is now pleased by the turn ofl events; for she would will evil and calamity upon the ruler who is brother to her slain husband. Herod passes the ring of death to a soldier, and the executioner is sent into the well. Salome hears no cry, no sounds of alarm or terror. Presently, the soldier returns over the top of the underground cell with the prophet's head on his shield, and the seductress kisses the lips denied to her by Jokanaan in life. Herod extinguishes the torches and turns to go. Yet before he has left the hall, a fit of passionate rage seizes him and, wheeling upon Salome, he commands that his soldiers kill her. Thus ends Wilde's one-act play.

There are, in this play, the principal facets of Herod's nature that motivate and direct his actions, his ambition for power and absolute happness, sensual gratification in feast and dance, his doubt cast upon the fertility of Herodias and his skeptilcal wonder whether she ils, lin fact, his wife, all of which blandishments of his heroic soldiery and airs of a fattened lion culminating in the dastardly act of revenge. The first then of these natural elements in Herod's character is pride, overweening, implacable pride, having begotten his greed for material gain and lust after physical pleasures. His is the sort of pride by which the erstwhile Satan declared bankrupcy in hell and Richard III, Duke of Gloucester, wrought bloody strife in England's noble halls.

While a Commander for Caesar, he holds within his kingdom unlimited power over the property and lives of the Eyptians, Romans, Sysrilans and Babylonians who make up the populace. Herod has killed his brother for the throne and, like a good Roman, has stolen the wife, the comely Herodias. One must confess, I think, that these are not altogether the actions of a devout apostle of the true faith, although there is some justification for his reassurance that, as a happy warrior, he could do no less for his Lord Caesar. Truth, indeed, falls upon the insistance of Salome, who proclaims her virginity lost, her virtue destroyed by the man with skin like white ivory, that the Tetrarch orders Jokanaan's execution. Yet, too, one must be fair in these matters. It is or his own sensual pleasure, the reaffirmation of his power, the proof of his bounteous nature, that he conmmands the princess to dance for him, whilest he, as their skirmish turns out, offers her power and wealth more copious than that of Queen Herodias. His whim for entertainmemt, for a performance, is not unnatural; Salome apparently was a very beautiful woman to look upon. Bear in mind though that she has attempted to seduce the anchorite and propet, John the Baptist, a survivor on honey and locusts in the desert, and whose life Herod favors; and that Herodias, because of his lascivious and incestuous lust, his fratracidal blood lust, secretly hates him. His insistence then that Salome dance for him symbololizes, as it were, Herod's ruthless ambition for self-gratification, in a word, his pride. And all that he has grasped in power, booty and and emoluments he holds for that chief end. Wilde's bargaining sequence in particular, and the play in its entirety, dramatize these components of thought and action, the character, religious-political pressures and the regional surroundings of that one dominant cause for life in Herod's mortal tenure.

The second of these principal facets of Herod's nature which motivate and direct his actions is fear. His is the fear of the future and the foretold disaster which Jokanaan prophesizes will befall him because of the wanton evil of his reign, the abominations of Herodias "who hath given herself to the young men of the Egyptians" and because of the iniquities of the people of Judea. Herod's fear--and a volatile emotional force to be reckoned with in a tyrant--finds ultimate expression in his reluctance to take the old man's life. He has his enemies among the friends of Herodias who will not be appeased by Jokanaan's execution, but only encouraged thereby at having found the chink in the Tetrarch's armor. Allow him to live and Jokanaan, who tells by his signs the vision of Herod's end, remains but the figure of an eccentric and harmless old man. But to kill him, Herod realizes, wiil mean only the "heaping of coals of fire upon his head " by the martyrdom. He fears prophet, prophesy and, most of all, his enemies within the kingdom. Herod is also superstitious, a trait that intensifies his fears

by making them insoluable.   For him, John the Baptist is a seer, an anchorite who
communicates with the unseen and is capable of performing miracles, instead of beling,
lin fact, a man of the faith who had adopted Christ's creed of sin and repentance,
manifest in Jokanaan by his long wandering in the wilderness and announcing Christ's
coming....

AMERICA'S FACES

POETIC LETTER TO THE POLITICIAN

Has he ever known an Americqn who
  built a sod cabin on windy, bitter cold prairies
To start a farm, one lean horse and plow
    Handles splintered bloody with sweaty palms,
To plow an acre required strength last
    As his wife with babe in arms watched
From the door, harggard, in dubious stares'
    From the door they leaned on God and nature's whims
A crop of grain, ten sheaves to sell
    At the Witchita's far market in time, meamtime
To eat they grubbed, brought potatoes
    Their faces wracked with need, loss, pangs,
Their faces early American, not pimply scions
    Soft of rich who barter liberty
Seized, split as theirs because money due.
    Were these th' cries of the lonely, needs desperate, life
Wracked the wintry night, candles low in th' windowed snow.
    So that only the sun brought warmth, succor sweet
These were not the faces of mobs screaming rights or else.

Where are the upraised caloused palms , oath in sweat
They who hacked out a two acre farm
    from the wilderness of virgin tmber, wolves packed
They pulled stumps, struck rocks, broke plow shares.
How did they manage, axe handles smooth with use
    sharpened bright on granite, they swung mighty of muscle
And felled the timbers for rails, cabin, barn and hearth
    yet they had to live, survive, family of four, how?
Has the politician ever stumped for votes from them
    from their past, they who broke the plains and wild
They who dared depart, risk journey's fates, Indians,
    dire hunger, loss by disease, faces pale and wrung
Where are they now amid the clamoring thieves of life
    of the liberty of our country, denied in silks and ease
Little Billy was burried beside the road amid prayer and tears...

he fell beneath the wagon wheels, never awoke
And little Sarah, with burning face. a fever
         abated only by cool cloth and moher's loving hands
Dipped in a pail amd wrung of water to
         Caress the little one's face, she too gone.
Where are they who were ambushed, killed by savage ownership
         are they no longer pioneers? say not.
They live in this nation's soul, its memories'
         theirs the fine history of struggle without recourse,
While they world cared not but to enliven the natives
         thus to mauraud time, history and desire
Yet they are the faces of the past, in today's derth
         for lacking pioneers we shun their strengh as another's
Whilest politicians crop the gold that pioneers cropped for food.
                         without shame they invite ignorant hordes to exploit
And to share their plunder in gaunt mercy's guise..
         regard these pioneers, who fought storm, snows, fire
Who hungered, lean and pitiable, yet strong and resolute
         driving, rumbling, rickety wagon, slops for food,
 Crossing teetering roads, hacking forest brush,
         streams too bouldered to cross, searching river shallows
         yet, undeterred, not to turn back, all abandoned.
On they moved, then others, faces of hope , their past be gone
         Into a future with hardened hands, pleading, prayers to God
They knew no tinder tilts with a majestic Creator,
         damning his laws as obsolete, useless, self their only faith
 But not, pimply chaps, well stocked in laws, wish to expunge
         they would ferrit out courage and claim their throne of snuff.
But America's pioneers-on they travelsd, often one,
         two wagons, neighbors linked by mutual prayer, guns
         into the hinterlands of their new counry.
Are they the faces of the disgraceful spoiled who lust for spoil
Who leave their country not to settle and hew but to seize
         to grasp our nation's richess for theirs, then return.
Does that woodsman pioneer on his small farm care,
         when life is his farm, his wife and his young
What great will, trust and courage enflamed their hearts?
Say no more, this is mine, I earned it. Rabble, ye did not, ye
         pitiable dregs of a fallen society, goaded by rot of kind

THE CRISES, by Charles E . Miller 1-29-08

IN THE EARLY DAYS

When roads bogged down the high-board farmwagon loaded with fire wood and the frenzy of a bucket brigade could not save the neighbor]s house in the high winds; when coal oil was a nickel a gallon and store furniture came around The HLorn, Ma and Pa owned and ran their small counry store. Those are all long-gone times now. However, their institution lives on.

The Ma and Pa store was never quite the corner country store, like you used to see advertised in crossroads catalogues. Theirs came earlier, and then was eclipsed by progress--barbed wire, beaver traps and blasting caps came with "civilization" and, of course, with the culture of the visiting theatre troupe. lManhy a frontier town was familiar with *Two Gentlelmen From Verona.*

Their little village store, now a residence, was close in spirit to the circumscribed world of the Yankeee peddler, he who roamed the hilly New England countryside selling whiskey, gingham cloth and bibles from his wagon. The store this couple worked was pretty much home- and family-oriented, meaning it flourished in post-outlaw times when saloons came to be regulated, the sheriff wore a badge with honor and lumber arrived in town by mule train and wagon.

Ma and Pa ran their store with hard work, diligence and good common sense as to what were the village needs and what they ought to stock. Bargains aplenty supplied the two of them with a good income. A pot roast could be bought for 25c, bib overalls with copper buttons for $2.50. A $12.95 horse collar was a dandy. A cultivated gentleman could purchase a straight razor for his beard for $3.50, a bagatelle that boasted a genuine Sheffield steel blade. And for the bushwhacker who strung fencess and every now and then came into town to please his wife, he could pick up the very best iron oak boot-jack for $1.95, American made. High boots for muddy country roads could be a struggle to remove.

Now these oldtimers, the couple I mean, did not much tolerate meddling from strangers into town, like that Government agent nosing around the homesteaders for some hidden purpuse but couldnt scare up a pinch of awe from town folks. lHe usually finished his business and left. The people did not belong to the government in those days. They were hardly aware of their government. Had not Pa jawed on rainy days with Jed Soames, the Avery boys and old Tim Wehlmer? Besides, no sense in worrying eilther because the income tax had not been invented to keep the indolent alive and demean the labor of farm hands in favor of silk shirts and soft white hands and putty Washinton minds.

"Saw one of them politicians come inter town t'other day on a sorrel mare.

Looked like he was lost...er fit to capture some votes. Feller wore big rings on his fingers." Pa was suspicious and rightly so. He knew his place in life. He was practiced in the rituals of the feather duster on the shelves, the spearing of the pickles in the vinegar barrel, and thewrapping of cheeze and smoked salamil in brown butchers paper and string, after which he would pop the string. Through his thin wire spectacles he watched the pointer on the scales intently as he shook the extra beans onto the tray lfor good measure. He knew his job...and his customers.

The Ma and Pa store symbolied stability and the town's growth. It was the product of careful planning and prudent money- handling. They knew the economics of the balanced ledger and therefore they were possessed of more native intelligence than the sons of Eastern scions who thought then, and still do, that they knew better tlhan country hicks in most matters. Their store operated in the pure air of *laissez faire* enterprise, an attitude that later ecame a formula for unbridled power and acquisition.

They lived close to the land, Ma and Pa did. They could put up with the mud and dust and board sildewalks because life had more to offer than creature comfort and eastern promises. They relished their square dances in the kitchen of Mr. Tulle's big farm house, or down at the grange. That was their social fun in life. Yet there was a balance between fun and work, and that was good.

Ma and Pa also believed in sharing. Sharing came wth the territory. They'd share theiir earnings with the hired man who cleaned up the store and waited on grubstakers. Pa kept an IOU book under the counter. A man's word was a badge of honor for a debt . Same for the boy who owed a few pennies on his bag of jellybeans.

Although they did not say so, Ma and Pa believed in the worth of and the hope for tomorrow, with the expectant satisfactions. Folks to them, customers, friends, neighbors, each and all possessed a dignity of personhood and self-respect. For that was the way God intenlded it. There was none of the sickly disillusionment of modern times that needs a shot in the arm from a bureaucrat or an invention to make life interesting and bearable. No, the modern age, though richer in knowledge if infinitely poorer in spirit. You see, Ma and Pa knew who they were and where they were going. They did not expect the government to tell them what to think, how to save, where to plead and how to educate their children or invest their money. They were dlifferent from the world in all these respects, though they did not know it. Once in a while a peculiar feller from the East would drop by with dust on his fine clothes and disbelief on his face and a bag of gold coins in his shirt. He was, somehow, out of place...unless he wanted folks' votes.

ON THE THEATRE OF THE ABSURD

The scenes of a good play are but the passages of the total composition. The myriad of a human being's experiences are but the passages of that life's totality. Where the interpretive intelligence is excluded, chaos results, a formlessness in which the author assigns no value to his scenes nor the man values to what he perceives and what he gains from others.

In either instance, the composer accepts chaos as a natural state of existence. He lives and he writes without convictions, and though the chaos may be dramatic, as bedlam is in a sense is dramastilc with its noise and wild. random activity, the drama is mindless, brutish, without form, devoid of good reason and traditions. Such absurd chaos only inspires contempt. The form which a dramatist's assembled scenes takes, as with human experiences, derives from tried laws, maxims, axioms of usage or else, in the finished play the emergence of life from chaotic raw material at hand lacks values that ultimately control the form.

The Theatre of the Absurd is of this character--formless, chaotic, lacking wisdom and reason and appealing only tothe childish comprehension of a modern audilence. Its popularity in Europe explains that Continent's malaise of reason and sound judgement.

FROM THE ACTOR

In a stage presentation the actor is all important in such matters as pacing, timing, the building of dramatic tension, making dynamic the action of the drama and conveying the meaning of the story. He embodies the playwright's vision of the story.

In a movie, the use of music, flash shots of people and things, odd angles, close-ups and other technical devices may share those functions with the actor. A stage presentation shows the whole performer, the entire character as a coordinated entity. A movie may present only fragments caught by camera selection, likely an artificial mechanical direction of audience attention rather than an artful one, as by the actor on a stage. Even characters from other planets must ber some semblance to earthlings.

THE INVALUABLE PLAYWRIGHT

It has been widely hinted at that we live in a utilitarian, pagan-Christian culture. Today in America the drama tist shares the unique niche with th Priest and Hedonist, the "military man"--and a sepulchre of "intellectual " books. Regarded as a non-producive member of our society, he may inadvertently add to an increase in human undestanding through his plays; whiole his black garbed fellow instructs parochial schoolboys in Christ's love and the Seven Sacraments. The Hedonist saturates his pride in his own elegance, the barbarisms of modern day sophistication--the evaluation of want. His professional military compatriot, choked up by the publicity for slaughter, dons the mask of pain in a macabre union of credoes. Neither credo, however, is productive toward civilization's advance.

To make war is creative; to enlighten is to do harm. Despite these ludicrous inversions, it is stolidly maintained by a large portion of the theatregoing publc that the laborers of the dramatist, peripheral in our culture, possess no intrinsic utilitarian value. He is non-productive Elitist because he stamps out no knives or forks; he builds no ships, twists no screws, he plows no land and moulds no bricks. It needs only be said that as a *Type* he does not do these things

The moral relativists drum on that mummer's commodity called *virtue.* Pietists can buy his product for a pennysweight of community lip service. It is a negligible thing, the though that his play's human and moral values cannot be weighed; the meaning of his play does not draw 5% per annum; it pays none of the theatregoer's bills, although it might stay his hand from leeching on a neighbor's reputation through gossip; and it is only taxable by the government at a maxiumum of 91% after twenty years of his having never stamped out knives and forks, built ships, twisted screws, plowed a little land and moulded bricks in order to survive. He has simply honored his profession as a writer of stories performed by actors on a stage before an audience--the essence of theatre.

Yet in a sense as strict as the root doctrine of the New England Puritanism (predestination), he is a non-functional member of society; he is a writer of plays. If he has talent, his obligation is usually the reward of perservering integrity. Hollywood alone can knight him to joust among its masonry; after a spate of squib-lines and surging publicity, like a Medieval knight, he is cast into a pyre of burning money, fried out of his armor and the credit given to the victor producer. Such is the customary fate ot the dramatist in America; oblivion one way or another, but oblivion.

There are, of course, reasons--and more immmediate--the disinclination of stringently budgeted little theatre directors to gamble on untried plays; the creaking, powerful "star system" welded to this country's personality cult; timidity and ignorance on the part of new playwright's in huckstering their work; Hollywood's worship of bigness; Broadway's insolent presumption that its theatre and Plymouth Rock origins are of the same historical magnitude. There is, also another reason, related to today's anti intellectual climate. Youth before the age of eightteen are taught that plumbing is the better part of labor's thrift; and that it is shifty, dangerous, the scant leftover of wisdom to bring one's brains, other than for the laboratory, to bear fruit in intellectual ways. It is that strain of pauperized vision that construes wisdom as somehow restricted to graph curves and to the machinations of summit conferences.

Though in many climes tyranny is cruel, today's world is not altogether experimentally hard. There are soft spots in modern man's sophistication: he is capable of incredulity, he has gone far toward rejecting man's innate dignity, he troubles the future with vague sense of need, loss or satisfaction in the wake of his atheism. *Frustration*, however, is the tapster's sop for the fissionable personality, without center other than ego, chaotic in the slime of animadvertsion to human bonding truths superior to the actualities of barter, theft, murder, exchange and commerce. Under this rule of genre actualities young writers of plays are counselled that in order to survive they must "wake up to realities," the bulk of the citizenry having learned adroitly to confuse the humanly real (integrity) with the tangibly actual (opportunism), the suspect (victimized) with the victim (victimizer), a teacher's dedication with her purse. There is the sentimentaliy of counterfeit compassion and the spiritual poverty of false blame. These last are enculturated in our places of higher learning where the playwright usually gets his first training in theatre.

There are those who ask, however: are not these writers in control ofl their personal destinies? The sardonic truth is that they are not. Two World Wars, the Korean War, Vietnam and antecedent diplomatic stupidity; one Depression, a recession; the McCarthy witchhunt and Congressional trials; suspicion under enforced loyalty oaths: these are the pristine achievements of former generations. Fatal forces move the Innocents; the *silent generation* and *beatnicks* they were called. Protagonist and Antagonist, brute beasts of posdt-war prosperity locked in combat to death, *made* heroes, alienated idealistic youth loading them up with the pusillanimous ignorance of a generation living on their little isle of opulence. Absolute self-determinatioin for nations as well as for individuals, is the great prophetic delusion of modern man--a truth, however, that is contrary to utilitarian traning, to the education of the engineer for whom society networks its discoveries as well as its failures. Our modern High Tech culture leaves little room for the Humanist--the philosopher, the artist, the writer, the historian. Murder and controversy appear to keep us in touch with Man's baser nature with their coarsening and brutalizing influence on his "sensibilities." Yet--is not this venue the playwright's thematic gold mine?

Writers yet unknown are proffered a choice between the practical and the conventional modes of living, and contnued annonymity. The resultant quandry, but a stage in a writer's growth, can debilitate; it may shrink the mind and dry up the spirit of creative exploration. A reality of inner self-determination, the unfettered use of conscience, an open scrutiny of religious values, human ethics, the basic traits of man's psychology, and the cultural traditons of all peoples: these remain. Amongst these elements of life the serious playwright works, and God help him, as a free agent.

Such a *ghesalt* point of view as that whtever is utilitarian is *good* can, as it did under Hitler, trick human loyalties to perform services for scince foremost; Duty is the mask. Yet the fact obtains that down that road to disaster reason alone cannot staunch lthe duplicity of political *Futurists*, false godlings of labor, of socialist economy; or ripe, fat-tonsters seated upon benches like Medieval priests of middle-class complacency; the potpourri of grubbers among the "lost" pioneer visions; and the politicians, whom we must patiently endure. Through this tribe of well-riveted headsmen, again, the playwright moves and works.

People are the main business of the playwright He begins with men and not with a graph curve or a pouch of gold, or an engineer's slide rule or a claustrophobic fear of legal kites. In the telling of a tale, he tries to put these *persona* on a stage. He selects and compresses, he edits and rewrites to so order their actions and words that they show us a reality of human experience. He is a civilizer who, by means of dramatic mime--and comedy's puppetry is a genre extreme--indeed attempts to reveal life. He is all too often, however, regarded as a jaded squire whose bowl of peppercorn porridge is the slightly offensive, lthough he would draw into his house the well esteemed patronage of thoe with more delicate tastes; they, the robust closet men with a fine, judicious palate for what enfranches self-esteem by holding up the "mirror " to nature.

Still, in all, the drama is not approached with a fop's moist eye or a gentleman's disdain unless the dramatist would impale either on his lampoon. It is approached with a certain attitude, of vigorous humility toward those truths, those realities symbolied by the lives the dramatsist will now show the audience. "A reverence for life, a religion of the theatsre and a credo of the drama, the meaningfulness of human dignity--these are but other ways of expressing the fundamental idea of revealing human nature, the perks of society, the vitality of observed mortal actions.

This little journal then purposes to accent "the play is the thing" in its all too brief critical articles. It will not eloquize upon the dramatic as a vestigial intelllectual remnant of protean man; but it will stand by watching the results of the playwright's huckstered craft and artistry, and hoping for new insights, new strength to resist what debases that craft, cloaks his vision until there cometh the longsuffering rain of appreciation. The *Critics' Review* will recognize that in the voluminous literature of the theatre there are human, ethical, religious and aesthetic values worth highlighting; and that the dramatic writes out of centuries-old traditions of both the theatre and the drama. The *Critics' Review* promises that the drama's chief overarching purpose is the increase of human understanding through the entertainment of mimetic re-enactment on human comedy and tragedy.

The literature of the thearree cuts through half a dozen major political systems of thought; and through a spectrum of philosophical ideologies. We further promise that no experiences, short of a military apotheosis of immediate troop occupation, will justify the legality or publicity-enforced suspension of this nation's two basic freedoms: the freedom of conscience and of speech, the right of each man to voice his opinion and the liberty to express openly his beliefs. In the face of cinching international tension, that is our belief, that is our faith.

Criticism of is our chief purpose; we hope that it will help others to interpret the drama of the theartre, the literature of the play--and , in a larger meassure, to enjoy both. The *Critics' Review* is aware that the competent "critic" will flatter the players, irritate the director and ignore the playwright; he may presume to taste the play's meaning and draw his check. But our brass weathercock points to a more discriminating criticism, to a fine interpretation of meanings. We are in sympathy with what is human, recognizeable in experience, dramatic and truthful in the staged presentation thereof. We invite you to join us with the pleasure of your company.
--- *C. E. Miller, Publisher and Editor*

ON PROPAGANDA DRAMA

The intention ofs the playwright in relation to idea, e.g. "workers of the world, unite!" leads to control of the play, with the controlling idea relative to the degree of intensity of response, an intensity in proportion as the Idea is relative to the mood for audience protest. When there is, however, no response to character beyond the symbolic Idea, then the play is dishonest. Emotional subjectivity, on the other hand, may be so violated that the Idea is lost in the emotionalism. The playwright's intention must be shown in the play's its presentation on-stage. A propaganda play, in sum, is concerned with persuading the audience to accept the political idea that is central to lthe play and to applaud or accept the players of that Idea as real...to them, as the embodiments of what they need to be to fulfilll the vision of the play's central theme. All else is subordinate to that politicl idea, all. In a real sense, then, a religious drama can, by these standards, be called'propaganda" and more so to the degree that it purports to stray from historical accuracy. There is, therefore, rightly or not, a degree of persuasion in the author's intention when he creates his scenario.

EURIPIDES' MEDEA--AN ANALYSIS

Medea's jealousy of King Creon's daugher, and her anguished and vengeful love for her husband Jason, whom she deems unfaithful and for whom she had slain her brother and deceived her father--to abet Jason's quest for the golden fleece--impel her to murder his, Jason's, love and to commit the most heinous of all her crimes--the slaying of her beloved child sons.

The powerful emotional turbulence beneath Media's calm exterior, and the savage grandeur of her will to take revenge against the opportunistic, deeply indebted Jason measures the strength and genuineness of her unabated love for him.

Hi redemption of her honor is exile; his recompense for her aid is lofty contempt; his requital for her sacrificial love is abandonment. Against Medea's violated love for Jason, these psychological forces of his nature contend, steeling her for the ghastly act of filicide. These are the basic forces of the "Medea" conflict.

Had the woman Medea posessed less nobility of heart, loving Jason with a selfish love that never transcends the flesh and common affections, her crimes would have left her bereft and empty. Instead, her revenge--just retribution or not--is the gnawing self-inflicted wound she is left to suffer and, failing to purge her love memories of Jason's poisonous perfidity, remembering her children who were dear to her, "dear to their mother, not to theee": (Jason), are that wounds' cruel hurt she is left to triumph over.

Euripides' *"Medea"* is one of the most poetic tragedies, visible on the face of Medea--her intense pain, absorbed distraction and piercing intent, whose perversion of her capacity to love had led her to such extremes of inhuman and civil outrage. Jason is the weak- willed opportunist, fickle in his love for Medea, ambitious and, above all, a self-seeking ingrate. The Chorus depicts wisdom and suffering, disinrterested counsel and the humble power to listen.

GOD-MAN OR THE TRAGIC HERO IN DRAMA

Biological determinism--Darwin's theory of evolution of the species by natural section for adaptive changes in the environment, contributed fuel to the Naturalist doctrine of Zola. Said the Naturalists: Man is a biological organism only. To invest him with a divine spark is idiocy. To find in him the God-man is superstition. To say that he can control the laws of nature or the forces of an impersonal cosmos is an illusion.

These encantations led to a denial of God and the efficacy of orthodox Christian faith. They also gave rise to the plunder song of laissez faire, Capitalism, and to a dog-eat-dog philosophy; to labor legislation and agrarian reform as reactions; to social protest literature and the espousal of socialist and communict doctrines.

With God seriously challenged for authority--or dead, as Neitzche would have it-- and common Man's surpra-animal Being thrown onto the scales, there was a brief revival of Greek concepts of fate and destiny of the tragedy of the good man, noble in spirit, of common birth, defeated by unconquerable forces that exploited his personal weakness. But these ancient concepts fell before Man's acceptance of scientifically proved laws. Also there fell integrity whose destiny was absorption by the State and spiritual aniihilation by values-relativity and utility of life. In the twenty-first century, Western man is struggling to cope with his automatism, his robotic environment in which he counts for less and less as a soul-inhabited being created by God. He is losing his soul to the machine and his worth is more and more estimated by the electronic decisions, choices and evaluations. This means the death of God's reflection in the human drama, for if he can relate only to himself, man becomes increasingly a-moral, self-absorbed and sterile of all passion for his survival except through inventions of the laboratory. Denying his former potential for greatness in the arts and humanities, he arrives at the petri-dish man, the cloned man, the valueless person of the abortuary, the sickness of loss without hope or direction.

LETTER TO A MOVIE STUDIO

Universal Pictures has run out of shock material. Incest, rape. murder, gory butcherknife killings, flaming car wrecks, the sadistic delights of boudoir adventure films no longer thrill. To plump your fat purse, you would titillate the curiosity of the naive and stab the hearts of the devout by dragging God's beloved Son into the filth of your despicable imaginations. Shame, too. When a jerk like "filmmaker" Martin Sorcee lays claim to a priestly life and fakes his claim to holiness with an obscene film whose libel no court would brook, he comes out clean as a washed skunk and smelling like Bonnie O'Day's rose. I'm referring, of course, to *The Last Temptation of Christ* to be released in the fall. It takes no guts to stab a dead man and in Sorcees' "deeply religious film." He thinks Christ is dead and so it comes to that macabre end. I know He is risen but only He can heal the blind.

Anyway, Universal and MCA are operating on the ancient premise that everybody has his price. Judas Iscariot proves that. The studio's anticipation is that the adulterous minds of millions will find the film sensually pleasing to their porno lusts and gratifying to their wicked expectations. To cater to such beastiality in men's hearts is not only abject slavery to money-making lurid desires and venemous depravity. But such a film will add nothing to men's lives they have not imagined down through history.

Because He attacked sin in the Roman world, Christ was called a crazy man, a *evil,* literally. And the Jews of the day, enraged by Pharasee jealousy, had him hanged...an early lynch mob...to appease the Roman Emperor and deflect trouble. History. I wonder if there couldn't be some of that animus, that sadistic intent of persecution and retribution behind your movie. Most of the world still denies Christ's Messiaship. How then can they, and you, do other than treat Him as repulsive, a weakling and a fraud?

In the name of" freedom from censorship," Universal Pictures will proclaim:

- that the Son of the living God has no divine power
- that the demons should be obeyed in the name of "truth"
- that Christ's divinity is a fiction
- that the appearance of angels and Christ coming down from the cross are occultic spiritism--communication with the dead
- that God loves sin -- a blasphemy
  that natural man should forgive himself for moral error for God cannot, since God is not Being but **force**
- that Christ was morally weak, sensual, corrupt and beastial
- that lthe Savior of sinful mankind was a fake, a charlatan
- that the testimonial evidence of this semi-documetary about a man who lives 2000 hyears ago is to be believed as authentic evidence of Christ's sub-divinity

Your Universal Pictures and MCA attack One who is dear to the lives of millions. Not that alone. Nor is the money all that mountainous. There is religious *ethos* of propaganda behind your film. The covert intent is to destroy the Christian faith as a faith, soften the opposition to a spiritual dictator of some sort, and Jesus is the opponent of the anti-Christ. Satan softens his enemy's battlements with a barrage of suggestive filth and "historical" lies before mounting the assault. There is the true *causus belli* of your savage and erroneous film.

MUST THE PLOT THICKEN?

by Jacques Duval, a non de plume

> **The critic will do well "...to find
> the function in the form. The two
> are hardly ever to be dissociated,
> One still, of course, has to con-
> sider the problem of just how ultimate-
> ly valuable this photographic and
> phonographic sense of reality is."
> - Wallace Stegner (class, criticism
> of fiction)**

How well acquainted are we with the loquacious barber in Ring Lardner's short story "Haircut"? He clicks his scissors, taps his comb and gabbles on in a flow of minutae observations on people, places, things that he has experienced in his life. Do we know the old gentleman in "The Golden Honeymoon" who still delights over the celebration of another wedding anniversary? In his easy and genial way, he relishes the human act of telling someone else. And what about the chauffeur who drives the large limousine for Mr. Wealthy? Is he not then qualified to observe and relate, in Lardner's "Mr. Frisbie," the engagements, the activities, the personalities and splendor that surround the rich? Within the minute to minute living of each of these fictional characters there is the romance of illusion beneath the realism, actual and sensuous illusion concealed from the awareness of others by the annonymous man, the little men in life who find the deed and the thought worth the pleasure it brings. They have accepted life on faith. It is these details then, these anecdotal adventures which are the brew of human interest stuff: that Lardner serves up to the reader for his enjoyment also. In so doing, by the techniques of anecdote and train-of-thought--which I think is to be discriminated from "stream of consciousness" by the selective logic within associations--Ring Lardner has sketched characters whose perception, whose emotional experiences have, for the

reader, a recorder's immediacy. The intimacy of that communication to him has a
chief value in that the character's sililoquy invites the reader into his confidence to
share subjectively those experiences which Lardner feels require no expository
annalysis, commentary or narrative development. Dramatically, they are
embryonic; philosophically, they are affirmations of the character's faith in life.

This immediacy, then, with its implcations, is one of the functions
which issues from the form of these short stories--a not altogether new
contribution to the genre but a confirmation, in the results, of the validity of the
technique of treatment for fictional
drawing.

**Footnote: Todays generations can be characterized by their ennui,
negativism and faithlessness, cynical in enlightment and pessimistic in
knowledge. A corrosive source of the rancor of England's angry young
generation and of the eatnicks can be found in these contemporary attitudes
toward life among the greater populace, and of the contiuing devaluation of
the individual as a mere instrument of use and means for survival.**

When he employs this form, Lardner deviates from the
"recognized" form for the short story: that is, the plotted story with an ascending
action, a climax and a denouement. These three stories about the barber, the
chauffeur and the old gentleman thereby gain in freshness what they sacrilice in
narrative and climactlic effect--a result which is no irredeemable loss, since the
author achieves his effect of a dramatic sketch without recourse to those
artificialities of conventional form. Lardner's contemporary American short
stories do, indeed, in this way and by their form, contribute to the genre as an art
discipline. For I rhink that most readers will concur that if we accept the integrity
of the effort for what the author had in mind, we can agree that he has carried it
off very well. Furthermore, those artificialities of form, whether narrative or
climactic, would distract only were he trying to fit his anecdotal, discursive
subject matter into old moulds. There is, in consequence, a refreshing
homogeniety of feeling and sense impressions, a feeling of the unity of his sketch,
that emerges from a reading of each. Lardner, in discarding the older form, has
brought readers closer to the true natures of his characters. The dialogue, the
conversation, of a man he finds more revealing than an objectively dramtic
account of that man's actions and expo
sition on his import of events. Note: to the classifier, whom we will have with us
always, these stories fall betweens fiction and play forms.

In "Haircut," in "Mr. Frisbie" and "The Golden Honeymoon," Ring lardner has written each as a monologue in which an unnamed charcter relates his experiences in a language that is natural and richly suggestive of the whole altmosphere, the familiarities of custom and people that surround his station iu society. The narrator sililoquist in each of these stories is talking to someone else; he received no answer; he supplies his own. From his flow of gossip, the reader receives the impression that Lardner's character is talking just as he would in his barbership, to the cabbie , to an old dinner table companion. Thoughts leap from subject to subject. Sentences are often fragmentary and ungrammatical. Figures of speech are spontaneous, graphic, frequently colloquial aand pungent. It would be difficult, I think, for one to find in these running monlogues, though vermicular the train-of-thought, an idiom, image, expression, intimate idea or personal feeling that seems noticeably <u>wrong</u> for that character. Thus it is that Lardner's use of dialectical colloqualisms for the sake of natural dialogue do, in great measure, contribute to the illusion of reality-- stripped of old form--the dramatic reportorial immediacy that he was after. The unity resides not in story structure but in the idiosyncrasies of personal identity revealed by the single means of first-person confessional speech.

In the three stories under discussion, each of the character sililoquies has an emotional point of focus. And it will be found that the catalyctic experience which has triggered the story is also the nucleus, to which all else is the nourishing matrix. It is indeed, this nucleus and matrix organization-- the romantic organic embodiment of emotional focus and associated experiences-- that perhaps more than any other aspect of Lardner's treatment of his raw material gives the reader a sense of story unity. Hence it is that experiential movement, anecdotal and associative, is fluid. In Lardner's "A Caddy's Diary" and in "Mr. and Mrs. Fix-It," in which a business man speaks the same effect obtains. The recording wire reproduction of the way people really talk is romantic because it is organic, in contradistinction to the elementary classical axiom of strict organization in form. This seeming formlessness need not detract from one's pleasure in reading these stories. Not at all. I think it interesting to point out, though, that this fluidity of chronicle movement in large measure places the stress upon characteriation rather than story as plot or picaresque.

Since there is no obvious plot pattern in any of these original three stories, it may appear that Lardner's selection of details was haphazard, whimsical, lacking either economy or conscious artistry. So long as he gives us the germinal motivation, the attributes of his characters justify the method up to the point where their several personalities emerge as viably real in the reader's mind. There is, furthermore, a human justification for Lardner's use of the romantic form. The exhuberance and liveliness of his monologues are wortth noting. Since these emotionl attitudes on his part lead one directly to what I think was his exquisite, varied and occasionally, profound joy in life. Conversely, he communicates this exhuberance; and in so doing he reveals to us, the readers, the essential aspect to be found in all of these sketlches: the loneliness of the character who speaks. Whether or not one acords with his choice of form or finds his treatment chaotic, Lardner's stories, for that reason, were well worth his writing.

We do not know the barber's name, or those of Lardner's caddy and chauffeur. We would, I think, recognize each as a type and as an individual, one living among many in his social class, trade or profession, an uncopied original. The barber's luxuriant gossip is Saturday night fare. His intimate knowledge of folk news, of neighborly lore, makes of him a kind of contemporary town-crier and almanac combined. In his manner of speaking, he perforce is a type; in his choice of material for conversation he reveals his individuality. In his commentaries and human insights, his humor and sense of the pathetic, he demonstrates his quality of mind and sense of kinship with the human race. These several aspects ot the barber's characterization Lardner conveys by the rambling gossip. The typical, the individual, in Lardner's Mr. Frisbie and the elderly gentleman appear under the same method of treatment; the quality of mind and the simple, open and honest qualities of character in each--a full integrity not unmixed with the homespun of character one suspect's were Lardner's also--are wrought in the reader's mind by the author's techniques, selection of detail, genuine affection for the "annonymous heroes" of his sketches. They speak for themselves, I think. And Lardner least of all tried to interpose himself, as a scribe, a writer by expository content. The beauty of his effects gives dramtic testimony to the consciously artistic success of his fusion of form with function. The pictures of similitudinous life experience are tere.

It is a fair conjecture at this point to say that Ring Lardner began his works with a view toward steeping them in natural conversation. The emphasis in this statement is upon his initial conception. He knew that such naturalness cannot be reproduced within the ordinary plot framework of the short story. He therefore put no frames on ;his pictures and achieved the realism which he sought. The ultimate value of this "photographic and phonographic 'sense of reality is" discoverable from two principal viewpoints: the journalistic chronicle

163

of events, the actualities transcribed in realism of detail. And the deeper sub-
strata of myth, religious and phychological, which maybe implicit within the tale.
In the instances of these three stories by Lardner, they fulfill the conditions of
reportorial realism--each embodies a scaffolding of imaginary facts revealed with
accuracy and vividness. In a limited way, too, yet without belaboring the
implication, they (his stories) allude to man's sense of kinship with his fellow men
made real and genuine when it issues from the marrow of human loneliness. That
confidence, that communcativness is, I think, a primal and religious yearning o f
the human lanimal. And to the extent that Lardner recognizes that loneliness and
communicativeness as attempts to identify self with another responsive human of
the race, and to dispel the fear of a great unknown void beyond immediate
existence, the author has well justified his techniques. For if not the myth,
certainly the religion and the psychology, the former in this special context and
the latter with obious translucence, lie below the surface of what to some readers
may seem but facile and pointless sililoquies.   - 1955

WILLIAMS' PRIMITIVISM

The forces of reassuring laughter, of fear and anger belong to primitive tribal psychology, self-preservation is the basis for the grim impasse between the *status quo* and the threats of change which the wanderer Val brings with him. When he first comes to town, there emerges the comedy of the unique; he is the guitarist feller whose stopover is the Terrence's store. When the play ends, he has become the devil whom the townspeople torture in order to exorcise from their community the danger to morals and dignity.

Through this tragi-comic pespective fhe play gains breadth. For what is Val but the lyrical prototype of the wandering minstrel in whose noisy claims about his snake-skin jacket there is the strong suggestion of the Yankee peddler? Instead of hawking Bibles and cure-alls from a Boston goods bag he strums a guitar. In this possible comparison of native types, Williams is showing us within the townspeople's acceptance of local heritage of mores, their denial of larger historical heritage of values. There were the Travelers, the Vagabonds, and the Settlers. The Travelers brought danger. Manifest Destiny offered opportunity.

In the scene where Lady Terrence persuades Val to stay and help her with the store, the playwright brings this underlying American tension to a focus. But only do pain and laughter struggle within individual loneliness, experienced by Travedler and Settler alike. Stagnation and growth of outlook are in conflict. At this point Stranger and Villager become Antagonist and Protagonist. Each of us, Val tells Lady, is imprisoned in his loneliness, inside his skin for life. At this point, again, the intruder and the narrow-minded townsmen become the scapegrace and the perpetrator of ridicule. Laughter and pain appear and reappear throughout the play because of these deepening American tensions which Williams has discovered in the lives of his Southerners.

A PEOPLE OF PAIN, LONELINESS AND FEAR

Under the threat to the *status quo* introduced by Val, she sets off the chain of events that are the play's story. It is worlth noting how each of Williams' principal characters gives way to pent-up emotions of pain and loneliness and fear. Eva and Sister (Barvbara Dowd and Barbara Breckway) their heads held erect and smug, self-righteous and chattering their picayune outrage, trudge off the stage and out of the store when Lady informs them she intends to keep Val at the store for her helper. They are stereotpypes of the small-town gossip, and were played as such--fickle in their loyalty toward Lady Terrence, quick to judge the stranger, fearful of aspersions on their high morals, sentimental termagents with "hearts of gold, the actresses added to these qualities the closeness of sisterly agreement.

Actress Dowd gossipped wih drawl as sif to disperse, to exorcise, her response to fear. Patricia Buckley created the stage characrter of a Carol Cutrere whose capricious nature and refined soft-spoken insolence toward the representativeof town mores, Lady, expresses her painful want to be free of the ugly surroundings that depress her.

Having accepted her town-classification as a *vagrant, like Val,* she makes abortive efforts to escape communithy damnation through an affair with Val. She is as much a victim of small town rigidity as are the Temple sisters, Dolly and Beulah. She has in common with Lady Terrence the wont to reject their standards. She lacks Lady's strength of character which enables the daughter of an Italian immigrant to face the implications of prejudice. Miss Buckley, in a part that might hve been sensationalized by syrupy posturing of moral corruption and cozening of sensuality, or in sticky emotionalism, gave us a woman who was pitiable for that very quality of intelligence which enables Carol to see and to feel her plight. Warmth and whimsey, insolence and the undercurrent of rebellion:-- these characteristics came across in the actress's precise delivery of her lines, the flowing and controlled movements of her body that suggested a yen for abandonment. The sensual was there, too, but to the just degree that the quality did not hide the playwrights interpretation of Carol's basic pain and dominant motive for wanting to escape.

AIRS OF A WANDERING MINSTREL

Val Xavier was played by Humbert Alan as a wanderer whose lyrical rambling conversation and a part dreamy, part cocky outlook on life contrasted with his vague yearning to take rest in it. His first love is for his guitar, a tangible thing he seizes from the grasp of the sheriff and his town-henchmen in Act 3. He loves, also, the freedom that helps to dissipate his loneliness, and chafes at the harness of his new clerking job. Mr. Humbert prejected those two fundamental tensions of the minstrel's makeup very well. He clearly motivated

Val's wish to remain free from the the town's restraints.

Less clearly motivated, vecause Mr. Humbert depicted it as a generalizd attitude, was Val's hurt cockiness. It was the independence he showed toward Lady Terrence when she askes him to stay that helps to confine the attitude, and to keep him from seeming like a "revel without a cause." The actor dramatically conveyed, also, Val's casual air that masked a trigger temper, and his native shrewdness and inquisitiveness. These straits came out in the scene between him and Carol when she tantalized him with her body and her suggestions that they've had a roadhouse affair which he has forgotten.

A LADY OF STRONG CHARACTER

Gina Waldren's stage characterization of Lady Terrence dramtized with moving emitonal force and graphic believability the playwrigh'ts immigrant daughter who was 'bought at a fire sale." What sets Lady apart from the modern heroine of feminist playwrgihts is that she has the strength of chaaracfer and the foresight to understand the monstrous hate that lies against her. There is lonelienss and pain in her remembering how Jabe (now her husband) and his raiders burned her father's wine garden, leaving the old man to die in the flames, her innate strength and that foresight evident in her stubbornes and shrewdness combined with the ethic to create rather than to destroy, gird her to see her situation through to the end. She opens a confectionary, a candy shop, connecting to the store. She endures her life with the dying Jabe, a wretched and extremely painful relationship for a sensitive woman, , for she knows of his hate toward her father. She sees her circumstances through, and she neither accepts them nor does she try to revolutionize them. She waits patientlsy for Jabe's death; she plans with with adamantine drive and persistence to repeat her father's business venture and to absolve herself of the guilt she bears as Jabe's wife, thus to vindicate her father's horible death by this act.

Miss Waldren dramatized convincingly those qualities of the woman they called "Lady." To her voice there was that stubborness and inner strength of the store proprietor who felt free to keep the stranger Val. On her face there showed pain where she realized the past. In her stage movements, there was none of the slov- enliness of poor-white idlers but, instead, of resolution, the resolve to build upon the destroyed past. Williams has not depicted static degeneracy, but a germ of particular new life where he has found it. He has shown, as Faulker expressed the idea in his; Nobel speech, the eternal will of man *to survive*.

THE QUINTESSENCE OF IBSENISM

by George B. Shaw

New York: Hill & Wang (Dramabook Reprint)

Shaw's book begins with his argument that conformity to the conventions of the Church, to outmoded institutions, and to neighbors has imposed duties, masked as reason's laws, upon the great reformers of history. Rebelling, motivated y the will to live, they have attacked hollow shams and conventional beliefs made the shibboleths of reason.

G.B.S. discusses ideals and idealists, in contradistinction to the realist and his realism, he who seeks not to conform in order to be a "good man," but "to live and be free in a world of the living and free" that he might be himself. The womanly woman, if she would emancipate herself, must repudiate her womanliness, her duty to husband, children, society, and the law--to everyone but herself.

Discussions of the chief dramatic ideas of Ibsen's plays are grouped under "The Autobiographical Anti-Idealist Extraganzas," (*Brand, Peer Gynt, Emperor and Galilean*); "The Objective Anti-Idealist Plays" (*The League of Youth, Pillars of Society, A Doll's House, Ghosts , An Enemy of the People, The Wild Duck, Rosmersholm, The Lady from the Sea, Hedda Gabler;* and "The Last For Plays"-- *Down Among the Dead Men; The Master Builder, Little Eyolf, John Gabriel Borkman, When We Dead Awaken.*

The lesson of the plays is that "life consists in the fulfillment of the will, which is constantly growing, and cannot be fulfilled today under the conditions which secured its fulfillment yesterday." The new element in (Westrern) drama is Ibsen's shock to man's feeling of security, they whose senseless laughter rails at jests upon their conventions.

Finally, Shaw points out that the technical novelty in Ibsen's plays. The playwright, he says, interweaves discussion and development of ideas with the action so that they become practically identical; Ibsen involves the spectators intellectually and personally with the action so that they become a part of the drama.

Commentary: Ibsen's iconoclasm was of unique importance to Shaw, the dialectician, because it provided him with a way for expounding his apocalyptic solemnities on the conditions of British society at the turn of the 19th century. Shaw, however, was a mediocre intellectual and a clever playwright who had a genius for showmanship and the acumen of logic of a first-rate prosecutor-- when applied with a cause and the circumstances obtaining thereto. His was not either a great intellect or an orginal one. Hence it was that Ibsen's feminist crusade appealed to him on the grounds of argument and cause.

Shaw was, in truth, a self-infatuated moralist--he confesses to a religious significance in his major dramas--who had inherited his father's wayward sentimentalism. His pyrotechnic temper, his self-pity, his exaggerations upon observations which he made of the London of his day and the consistent juxtaposition of social realities and romantic notions in his dramatic arguments-- for his plays are little more than that--embody attitudes and emotions influentially engendered in the "upstart son" by a "downstart" Irish father. G.B.S. had the good sense to conceal his sentimentalim by living like a parasite upon the small proceeds garnered by his mother, a teacher of music in London. It is true that he was successively a music and drama critic for London liberal press sheets; that he became something of a social lion about the time that Henry George was espousing his theory of *progress and poverty*; and that attendance at one of his plays had, by then, become a mark of social distinction. His contact with the progressive-socialist and laborite Eugene Debs and their founding of the Fabian Soiety, in combination with Shaw's pamphleteering and Hyde Park harrangues, his lecture hall debates, were all important in his life. Yet those activities were of idiosyncratic import in their bearing upon Shaw's contribution to the English speaking theatre, and, indeed, upon his plays as dramatic compositions. I have not the slighest doubt but that he would have made his mark, save that without this showmanship he, in all likelihood, would not have earned a shilling by his pen. The point to be scored, however, is that through all these attempts to gain a hearing and the social respectability which he felt belonged to him, Shaw consistently exhibited the rebelliousness of the social crusader whose chief interest was not in society but in himself. "Joan of Arc" sublimates the martyrdom to which he was unable to attain. "Major Barbara" revitalizes those human sympathies , and elevates them to the sublimity of religious compassion, which he had learned during his poor years and from his father's life failure. *Arms and The Man* resolves his antipathy toward the wealthy in whom he saw the benevolence, partly shared by his British-born mother, of the wealthy merchant class. The morality of G.B.S. was the morality, not of miscreant human nature, but of man's class-consciousness that erred where it least pretended to charitable virtue. And the redbeard of Lonon would ring change on the sconce of all mischief makers who profitted thereby. I suspect that Shaw, silently and in the privy of his conscience, envied the disiciples of the devil whom he had fashioned.

Alongside of himself in **The Quintessence of Ibsenism** Shaw places the Western theatre's master realist. This is a gratuitous piece of folly, since Ibsen would have well stood without his interference. In any case, in his customary style and manner of attenuated, dialetic cliche --Dostoievsky far surpassed the meatless Londoner as a dialectitian--he chose to find in Ibsen *vis a vis* this little book, those elements of the Norwegian realist's writing which coincided most fittingly with his campaign to free womanhood from her suffrance by way of independent will and social legislation. Shaw's campaign was a worthy one and, with qualifications, remains so where women are denied equal civil rights before the law.

But Shaw was overlooking that most pernicious attribute of all crusaders--the unrealistic estimate of the worth, potential and creative, latent in the individual human being. This is a cardinal paradox in the dramatist's thinking; one cannot liberate the person, in thought and action, lest he destroy illusions, and, in destroying illusions he but substitutes one bondage for another, one illusion for another to the end that all men should be of the same persuasion-- which is impossible. Such Uopianism is impossible in a free society; Shaw was blind to that fact.

It is , consequently, platitudinous to say now that the characters in Shaw's major dramas are dialectical mouthpieces for the Fabian arguments: they are. Yet they ar so because the Victorian playwright was neither willing, nor was he able, to get below the surface of human character in order to delineate figures of permanent human value who, albeit with oratorical beliefs in a cause, whether sthe manufacture of munitions, the winning of a battle, the educated change of environmental habit, embodied and mimed the actions of ordinary mortals. B.G.S. could not, and would not, associate with ordinary mortals--that is to say, those without a crusader's zeal and a cause, which embrace the larger part of mankind. He conventionally related himself to others as a dispenser of social justice. He would be the Doctor Faustus gambling with the devil of Change, society's traditions being the *soul* for pawn.

Shaw felt that he was, in all tlruth, the injured, the avenger for the wronged father with Ibsen's drum to beat upon. In each of his major dramas, the hero of the Shavian apocalyse comes out topmost in action and argument; Joan of Arc had just enough masculine combat courage and apostle-like zealotry in her makeup to appeal to this avenger spirit in the London Iconoclast of short-shrift logic. Tempermentally, too, G.B.S. needed an acceptable channel for his resentment against the English, whom he slyly took in under his wing. (Note: Shaw's antics on the keyboard to entertain, in tweeds and breeches, social Londons night-lifers are not to be construed as common-sharing.) His labor pamphleteerlisng, his park speeches, his countless words on socialism and the society he helped to found supplied that *causus belli*. Beneath his statuesque and rather forbidding exterior, however, there throbbed the heart of a vegetarian who was somewhat pathetic in his efforts to resurrect his "Poker Flat" outcasts as visible and believably real human beings, reincarnated, as it were, by his brilliant dialogue and his ingenuous scheme to right the wrongs whose stings, he, himself, had once felt and that motivated Lisa, Candida and Ellie. Shaw was an eminently fair man. And if certain of his feminine characers suffered from social injustice--a sort of graveling endurance, one must suppose--society would, in any event, become the father transmetamorphosed by laws instead of by Irish religion. Thus it was that, in overlooking the crucible of warring social interests and the catalytic agents of a new order, there was no legend that interested Shaw so much as the legend of himself and how he should fare as an alchemic prophet of the new dispensatioin. By the time he and had written *The Apple Cart*, Shaw had resolved his own intellectual and emotional conflicts through the medium of his dramas.

G.B.S. was then, in fact, as far removed from Ibsen in the idea structure of his iconoclasm, in temperament and motivations, as Ibsen was from Strindberg. It was not duty, as such, that Ibsen protested against, Hedda's duty, for example, toward her husband George Tessman. Ibsen attacked not even the inroads of duty upon feminine conscience--as Henry James so treats the corrupting influence of old European class-duty upon his heroines' consciences. The Norwegian dramatist censored, without Shaw's polemics, the socially stagnating pressures of those into whose trust duty's administration was reposited. Duty as a code, *per se*, and its effects upon conscience as a moral problem were not within his province of exploration. Ibsen was neither a sociologist nor a religionist.

In a contemporary reading of his plays, I think we will see that whereas Shaw, perforce, polemicizes agaisnt a conventional duty of works and toward willed realities socialistically oriented--hence his treatment of characrter is sociological--Ibsen, on the other hand, is content to reconstruct the dynamic psychology of duty (as compulsion, loyalty, inhibition) as the *principal* that directs --and devastates--by its psychic bondage upon his protagonists. Furthermore, duty as creed bears a similar relationslhip to the human psychology of natural affections that religoion bears to motive in the plays of Sophocles. Yet in Ibsen's chief characters it is those bondages, working against the natural affections, which intellectually blunt and stifle emotionally. Woman's duty, the proscribing conventions of **Church, institutions and neighbors** which shaw marks out, are but the outward aspect and show of character psychology in Ibsen's plays. His stress is upon psyhological response and action that issue from a high sense of what is humanly right.

Shaw, in depicting a dramatic instance of social stagnation, allows for the grace of laughter over the habit's own corrupt end. The demise of a convention, a paradoxical move by romantic or realist within the story's action, constitutes a crisis made objective; the event is social and it is comic. In Ibsen, not a system or an illusion, but a human affection dies; and that death, if not tragic , is pitiable. This discrimination will, of course, seem to some readers simplistic. It has the chief virtue, however, of making clear what is basically a difference in attitude toward life of the two playwrights: the comic and the tragic.

In these plays then which Shaw examines, he finds women sacrificing all sense of duty, or at least attempting to do so, the influences of convention in **outmoded institutions, Church and neighbors.** In order to achieve full self realization. Shaw is not concerned with those psychic bondages and natural human affections which I've just remarked upon. What he apparenly does not grasp is that the characters, for example, of *Nora, Hedda, Solness and Hialmar* do not undertake the sacifice of bondage and affection as an intellectual feat. They cling to the old while wanting change, freedom. And Ibsen was adroit enough to depict an antagonist who embodies the heart and soul of the old ways and to whom his protagonists are, or were, attached by strong human ties and affections. The old is ingrained in these characrters and cannot, as Shaw would lead us to suppose, be so easily cast off as a comic innovation for the sake of a playwright's dialectic. G.B.S. errs, therefore, in his assumption that any one of Ibsen's protagonists ever so much as moves a step in the direction of full self-realization, full liberation from the past; the next generation must assume the burden of emancipation. Shaw, though, being an idealist, is not expected to see this contradiction between legislative emancipation and human bonds. The tragic import in Ibsen resides, consequently, in the protagonist's assusmption of moral obligation to the point where a beloved child dies, a minister commits suicide, a husband is shot by accident. The woman, as protagonist, never completely liberates herself in an Ibsen play. It is the illusion of liberation which shaw, in his interpretation of Ibsen, mistook for the act.

Ibsen did, indeed, espouse more individualism and feminine self expression, life enrichment. Shaw, on the other hand, preached a form of gradualist socialism through personal anarchy which, ultimately, would have led the proponent into gross self- indulgences, and into a status of social acceptability--among those, in any event, of like persuasions. What Shaw failed to see was that the two forces of compelling human affections--moral responsibility for actions attendant upon them, and comic legislative compromises on similar social issues-- were, and are, discordants. Genuine loyalties can never be legislated or seized by the "great blonde beast of Jack London's vision. Laws within the Fabians' self-mesmeritic anarchy would, he presumed, coalesce by natural law, like organic cellular mitosis. The creative will would be led by intuition, perhaps, or by fluxuating social needs. Ibsen looked primarily toward the compassioante elevation of the natural affections, the shattering of old psychic compulsions, for human betterment. In Shaw's plays, the playwright has the dialectic answer; in Ibsen's, his characters grope for the answers and attempt to find them within the context of human like actions. Shaw was the adamantine overlord to his characters; Ibsen was the godfather to his. In *The Quintessence of Ibsenism*, therefore, Shaw finds in the master realist--who treated realistically psychic bonds, natural affections and social cause--chiefly the end result which he, Shaw, sought through legislation but which Ibsen's protagonists never actually achieve through the psychology of their conflicting emotions and intelllectual quests. *Ibsen was primarily interested in humam beings, Shaw in social reform.* Ibsen was first and foremost interestsed in the *internal* human processes of change; Shaw's chief focus was on the *social* means of change. Thus in his book he gives the devil his due but for reaons only tangential to Ibsen's as a dramatist.

NOTES ON MOLIERE'S *THE MISER*

Gold outweighs the courtly elegance of the disguised suitor to his daughter, Elisa; the Miser is no mean hang dog when it comes to the proper approaisal of negotiable values. He fears the settlement of his daughter's dowry in a marriage of convenience and so, fearing what society condones, he caches the tokens of his tangible conscience--the 10,000 crowns--in a backyard hole.

The genus of human weakness, thought Molier, amounted to a unnatural corruption when found in the character of a 17th century gentleman--the bruited master, young or old, who considers himself noble because of his money. In Harpagon's case, the foible amounts to a debauchery of thrift, a mockery of penury. To the devil then, says Moliere with such rascals but not before they are scourged, one and all, by the flaying-stick of men's laughter at such debasing penury!

Harpagon's hoarded crowns strip his hunchbacked and sqawking ugliness--coiled round his change box--of any pity for his vile deforlmity, he who could water down the punch, starve his horses, return uneaten fruit to the vendors and wed one of Paris innocent and fatherless daughters in order to realize the usurious increment of her dowry. The mockery now includes greed on top of penury.

Thrift without reason and corruptivle vanity--no less than the independence of a suspicious hoarder--collaborate in the extreme to lift this hoarding popinjay of penury and greed to the ridiculous status of a virtuous avarice.

In this play honor thus becomes guile, Moliere shows us, under the pretenses to a full equipage and an aristocratic station. That Harpagon's vice is most representative of the peasant, who every year cheats the government of it tax money only heightens the comedic value of the Miser's passion to hoard.

Moliere's laughter mirrors a true aspect of the french national charactrer--cheating on authority, by money and by word.

To laugh men out of their follies was Moliere's intent, if that were possible. If not, he would at least goad men to laugh at themselves. It is the French playwright's dramatiation of the avarice that is in the hearts of most men which make this play timeless, for so long as men shall treasure gold as property over human affections, and property as spower over society.

METHODOLOGIES FOR DETERMINING THE LIMITS OF CERTAIN LIBERTIES - AS OF CONSCIENCE...

"No person shall be seized, imprisoned or dispossessed, outlawed or exiled, or in any way destroyed, nor will he be impressed against his will or prosecuted , except by the lawful judgement of his peers or by the law of the land."(1215- Magna Carta)

It is inevitable that librty of individual action will encounter resistance, force, persuasaion. The **Magna Carta** quotation suffices to show how fundamental is this liberty to free men. When a people and not the central government are in control of their own destinies, they hold and sustain the power to decide issues of equity, property, contracts and concnsus. Hitler's ravings for *destiny's blood and soil,* as an exclussive State concern, were wrong. They contended in the form of military force and political oppression to control fundamental liberty and *selected* themselves to chose the course of history for the disenfrachised.

Placement of the battle on an acceptable stage, or forum of debate is a situation that, failing to mollify all malcontents and activist zealots, leads often to riots--even like a concerted tantrum of the spoilers unable to get their way. Violence thereby forces the hand of justice. In doing so it invalidates its credal position and in effect becomes leaderless and tokenistic.

Riot ought never to replace argument debate or orderly compromise. Indeed, in a free society riot ought never to constitute any expression of agreement so long as the legal legislative mechanisms for resolving issus are still in place and working. Riots are a gross missaplication of the right of assembly, which ought to be peaceable, and a colossal breech of the peace necessary that all men might share without the use of force in the direction of social change. For a riot is not evidence of liberty in action or of freedom without the citizens' conent but of outright anarchy. The choice to revel may come from one or two leaders; the act of mob insurgence by thousands is mindless submission to the influence if violent emotions. A riot often attempts to sanctify injustice; it can be presupposlitions of a wrong unaddressed but may fail the test of truth. A riot can touch the base human rage for survival and in so doing becomes mindless and must be countered with equal violence under color of law.

In pre-revolutionary time, the mechanism of the local constabulary Court or the town forum, were not effective to convict, even in the face of good evidence, so that errant colonials were taken to England for trial--or a grievance was never resolved at all this side of the Atlantic. These wrongs were addressed in our Declaration of Independence. .

Also a miscreant for the most innocuous violation of the law--theft of a pair of shoes or a loaf of bread--would be tried before the King's Court without a defender and witnesses, and he would either be imprisoned or, as sometimes happened, drawn and quartered while alive. After decades of this sort of cruel punishment--which our Constitution addresses--an organized and directed revolution was the only recourse, wherein leaders exercised a liberty of moral action. transmitting that same morality of thought and choice to the Minutemen who fired upon the Regulars. They did so not as a mob but as individuals who had made a conscious decision in the exercise of their personal liberty. They had to dissociate themselves from loyalty to the Crown and consensual union with loyalist Britishers.

One can see, how distant and different were the Paris street scenes in the storming of the Bastille and the rebellion against the Brisish Red-Coats along the Lexington-Concord Road. The French revolted for freedom without a plan; the Colonials revolted for freedom with a plan. The French concentrated on Personalities they; would install; the Americans concentrated on the plan their would invoke. The first is immensely changeable, the latter stable and sound.

The new America proposed laws for guidance, statutory choices for her followers, the participatory citizens of the new Sates. Thehy had a vbuilt in lierty ot redirect their collctive and personal ambitions, their motives, their designs by way of a new law when it passed. Thus the law affirmed what transpired in men's minds upon the application of personal choices in the vote, and the vote therefore represents a moral, or good, change for a visionary improvement. Every new social change partakes somewhat of a vision, a pre-conception. Corruption, traditon and Class-memories weigh down upon the Old World.

In America, each new piece of legislation confesses to man's innate capacity for adaptation, his proclivity toward change, his right of partipation and agreement. At the same time, each new law is an admission by the body politic that it cannot function in a state of discord but needs consensual agreement. A tyrant finds no such discord because he works to eliminate disagreement, conflict, cunning mischief; he suspects plots to put him out of his office. Treachery and intrigue are still a paranoia that is endemic to the Old World.

In every course and structure of the social consensus the individual acceeds to the new law and curbs his individuality to conform in obedience to the will of the people. He thus choses to conform to what has already been estalished by law. By his participaion he willingly and, therefore in full freedom and knowledge, adds his will to the consensus while tempering his future plans, if the law should affect him intimately, adapting to the reason of the enactment. In this manner the consensual legisliion, which is a "**social contract**," sets limits upon his personal liberty wherever he makes contact and use of the proscriptions of the legislative will. In conforming, the citizen is exercising his liberty to make a moral choice for the people's welfare. The right-ess or wrong-ness of an act is his deciion, and therefore he establishes in fact the parameters of liberty by means of elective legislation and his own participation therein.

That of course is basic civics. So, too, are those times when a court decides a case that ether builds upon an old or established law sets a new precedent. That ruling will in the future be relevant as precedent for the personal choices of plaintiff and defense alike--each because of his particpatory citizenship, having the liberty to make his choice. For this reason, aliens who owe their allegiance to another country and are not members of the body-politic ought not to be allowed to vote or to enjoy those special priviliges granted by law to the citizens. Judicial precedents in case law thus do work another boundary for the individual in our free society, beyond which one who brings a challenge to the law ought not to transress at the sharp risk of becoming either criminal, anarchist or outlaw.

Laws instituted of man therefore, establish the boundaries the free citizen's actions, often with his hardly being aware by daily parfticipation that he is shaping his affairs in conformity to the laws, since he has the custom and support of others around him who do likewise.

But are there laws of God which mark the boundaries to free will and autonomic human conduct without reference to any controlling republican influence? There are, but they, as the Ten Commandments, have now and by long usage become a part of the fabric of our system of justice--the Ten Commantmentls is universally throughout the United States a prohibition against murder, since the crime offends the people by its reuke of their authority, *vfiz a viz* the republican State that guarantees the righ tto happiness. And murder offends God by virtue of men's precious value in the mind of the Creator, made in His likeness.

For many lthe secular mandate suffices, yet it be terribly in; error to say that America's founding fathers left God out of their consieratiaons for their new Country. There is far too much evidence to support the actuality of their faith that anyone shoud or should deny either its reality or the undergirding Christian manifesto of our forefathers.

Roman laws, though pagan, also protected men from harm by way of the State's overshadowing power, cruel and oppressive as it was when transgressed. Those laws interdicted wrongful actions of citizens which led to punishment of boh pagans and Christians, but since the latter were, and are, admonished in II Corinthians, Chapter 10, to obey secular rulers and lawsas appointedby God and therefore providing they not contravene His laws, it is evident that He had ordained goverment to govern mens sinful actions and his inclinations to do wrong. Therefore, even under a despotism the liberty to exercise personal judgement as final, to evaluate a law or edict from higher authority tempered by the test as to whether or not it contravenes God's laws and ordinanances, remains a matter of pesonal conscience and public consensus. The parameters of human actions, in the minds of Christian community, are perforce controlled by laws that tolerate liberty of judgement and the divine proviso, the Scriptural test, as alluded to above; that further refines and defines th laws of our Country, as subject to personal judgement being put into effect and action. We do not surrener our liberty of conscience for the sake of the law but, most often, for the benefit of the people and in conformity with God's laws--He and not the State who is the source of moral conscience.

TIME TO GO TO JAIL

A duty implies a contractual agreement to do or not to do certain things, such as not to reveal a news source. But to whom should the reporter not divulge the source? Or is it tacitly agreed to by a newsman and the court that he will, as in a game, try not to reveal the source of his information to anyone, whether it is or will be published, or not? If he submits, under what circumstnces does he do so? If there are exceptional circumstances that justify a news shield privilege, what are they?

In Branzburg v Hayes (408 US 665, 1972) the Supreme Court in its majority opiion, written by Justice White (6/29/72) "rules that journalists do not have a First Amendment right to withhold the identity of confidential sources of information from a grand juruy."(1)
The Court was divided 5 to 4 in this case, Justices Stewart, Douglas, Marshall and Brennan

In the same majority opinion, on another point at issue, Justice White further said that law enforcement prevails over news gathering. "Thus we cannot seriously entertain the notion that the First Amendment protects a newsman's agreement to conceal the criminal conduct of his source, or evidence theory, on the theory that it is better to write about crime than to do somehing about it."(2) The Branzburg v Hayes case was a comaposite of three grand jury indict;ments against reporters for refusal to expose their news sources. In one a reporter for the Louisville Courier-Journal refused to identify two young people accused of making hashish for sale, and to produce a photograph of them making it. In the second indictment Pappas, a Massachusetts TV newsman, inside Black Panther headquarters in New Bedford, there through their trust, refused to appear in court or to report what he had seen inside. In the third indictment a man named Caldwell of the "Dallas Times" refused to appear and testify regarding the presidential assassination.

In this landmark case the journalists tried to impose three conditions of their own:

> (1) the prosecution must show probable cause,
>   since the newsman held information on a
>   specific probable crime.
> (2) the prosecution could not get the "requested
>   information by other means," and should
> (3) there ought to be a "compelling and overriding
>   Government interest in obtaining the inform.(3)

The majority of the court, composed of Justices White, Burger, Blackmun., Rehnquist and Powell, rejected the reporters' conditions. Justice Douglas cast his lot with the journalists' argument. Van Gerpen writes: His (Douglas') "dissent was based largely on lhis absolutist conception of First Amendment rights."(4)

In opposition, the Court refusing to protect the journalists from contempt proceedings, Justice White wrote:

> Fair and effective law enforcement aimed at providing
> security for the person and propertty of the individual
> is a fundamental function of government and the grand
> jury plays an important, constitutionally mandated role
> in the process. In the records now before us, we per-
> ceive no basis for holding that the public interest in law
> enforcement and in ensuring effective grand jury
> proceedings is *insufficient* (italics mine) to override the
> consequential, but uncertain, burden on news gathering
> which is said to result from insisting that reporters,
> like other citiens, respond to relevant questions
> put to them in the course of a valid grand jury investiga-
> tion of criminal trial." (5)

The US Judicial Code would appear to allow the journalist a loophole should he chose to protect his news source. In Vol. 5A, Supreme Court Decisions, p. 355, the editors quote (S S Pa., 1945) : "Contempts are summary in their nature and leave determination of guilt to a judge rather than a jury."(6)

If contempt is moot for the judge, it cannot fail to be moot at times for the reporter. His role is not to wait upon the court. Nor can his guilt be assigned or extrapolated from evidence accepted. Indeed, in my opinion, non-performance can at times attest to the journalist's recognition of the court's integrity by his refusal to corroborate on evidence seized illegally by Marshal or police. .

In the case of Branzburg v Hayes the defendants were denied relief by the majority of the Court because they withheld "information relevant to the grand jury's task."(7) It was not the sources that implicated them but their being "in possession of"(8) relevant information. That, in my view, is extrapolating guilt from other evidence. There is nontheless a larger view to be seen in the journalist's recalcitrance. Vince Blasi writes: "The reporters most hindered by the possibility of being sublpoened are those who seek a composite picture, who check an cross-check their information with numerous sources, (particularly sources who are not officially designated 'spokesmen,' and who are relatively inexperienced and cautious about dealing with the press, and who keep extensive files and tapes for future verification reference and for trend stories."(9)

If one can grant that the reporters generally have a defensible position, probably the most common being that their sources might dry up before they can enlarge on an event for public information, are there other arguments that come to their aid?

In the Branzburg v Hayes case, justice White wrote that "no attempt is made to require the press to *publish* (italics mine) its sources of information or indiscriminately to disclose them on request."(10)

And yet whether they are to be published or not appears to be academic. Justice Stewart, dissenting in Branzburg v Hayes wrote: "The error in the Court's absolute rejection of the First Amendment interests in these cases seems to me to be most profound. For in the name of advancing the administration of justice, the Court's decision, I think will impair the achievement of that goal...the newsman will not only cease to be a useful grand jury witness; he will cease to investigate and publish informationa about issues of public import...interests protected by the First Amendment and are not antagonistic to the adminisration of justice."(11)

Consonant with Justice Stewart's opinion, and that found in US Pa, 1945 (cit.6), re: "contempts are summary in their nature and leave determination of guilt to a judge rather than a jury," Orange County Superior Court Judge William S. Lee, In August, 1970, quashed a subpoena that would have required the "Los Angeles Times" to produce unpublished photos of riots at Cal State, Fullerton. "The Judge said the prosecution had not shown the photographs would be material or admissible as evidence."(12)

At present 26 (1999) states have newsman's privilege laws, called "shield laws." Justice White's majority opinion in Branzburg v. Hayes recognized the existence of states' protection of the journalist and, in so doing, revealed what I think is the Court's ambivilance in the matter. He wrote: "States should fashion their own standards...official harassment of the press undertaken not for purposes of law enforcement but to disrupt a reporter's relationship with his news sources would have no justification. Grand juries are subject to judicial control and subpoenas and motions to quash. We do not expect courts will forget that grand juries must operate within the limits of the First Amendment as well as the Fifth."(13)

In support of this dictum Van Gerpen comments: "A press privilege should not be used to stall or interrupt the process of litigation in such a way as to bring about a miscarriage of justice."(14) such as, for example, a reporter withholding evidence that would exonerate a condemned man.

I would interpolate the Supreme Court's ambivalence in Branzburg v Hayes as the acknowledgement of exceptions to the absolute surrender of notes and source names. If that is a reasonable inference from the case, then what documents and what sources can legally and ethically be withheld? Some can, others cannot. I have already mentiond one--evidence that exonerates the accused should be handed over. Another would be evidence of an impending assassination. (In view of these times, a third would be evidence of an impending terrorist attack, *viz a viz* guilty knowledge or preparation. CM)

In a pre-trial hearing, it is the judge who should rule on the admissibility of the reporter's material as evidence. The exposure is in camera. On this point, Author Van Gerpen writes: "The press is an investigative arm of the government with relevant, complete and more reliable information than the police. The press can embarrass the government and community establishments through expose of improper or illegal behavior. The press often is the fall-guy for counter-culture dissent.(15)   The author, therefore, advocates the pre-subpoena stating that "the future of controversal reporting is clouded."16)

Wisconsin is a forerunner of perhaps wider application of news shield legislation. Under the State's Assembly Bill 35, passed in 1973, the scope of privileged communication for reporters includes "any information deemed useful to news gathering."(17) With regard to news gathering and news sources, the legislation states "including but not limited to the identity of an agent or any informant. In addition (Amendment II, AB 35) the person claiming a valid privilege need not respond to a subpoena."(18)

The bulletin states that "the California and Nebraska laws grant absolute immunity...generally the Court decides whether disclosure is necessarys to prevent injustice."(19) This legislative view coincides with the action of Orange County Superior Court Judge Wm., Lee, who, in his discretion, quashed the subpoena before indictment of "The Times" reporter on contempt charges.

It would appear to me at this point, within the purview of the paper, that legislative and judicial opinion are converging in the pre-trial adjudication of reporter evidence., including names, without recourse to the absolutist position of Justice Douglas in the Branzburg v Hayes case. However, whether in camera or simply unpublished , except under two circumstances I've cited above (now three) the revelation of news sources compromises the integrity of the newsman. The judge is asking him to assist the court as an court-aide in the task of law enforcement. Law-abiding citizenry, from whose power the court springs, should not look to the newsman as an enforcer. Nor should the courts. If the court presumes a reporter shields a criminal for the sake of a story, it is shortsighted to destroy nascent evidence by destroying an enformer's trust. On should always remember that it is not the probable or demonstrated **evidence** that is withheld-- but the **source.**

Justice Stewart, writing for the minority in Branzvburg v. Hayes said: the need for confidential information "is essential to the creation and maintenance of a newsgathering relationship with informants, (and) the existence of an unbridled subpoena power--the absence of a constitutional right protecting, in any way, a confidential relationship from compulsory process--will either deter sources from divulging information or deter reporters from gathering and publishing information."(20) Furthermore, "the uncertainty about the exercise of the power will lead to self-censorship."(21) Addressing himself to the "status of the grand jury, Mr. Justice Stewart stated that the power of the grand jury to compel testimony is not absolute; it is limited by the 4th Amendment, the 5th Amendment and the common law." (22)

Justice Stewart echoed the three demands posed by the reporters in Branzvburg v Hayes when he wrote in his opinion that the government must show "probable cause that the newsman has information which is clearly relevant to a specific probable violation of a criminal law" and "that there are no alternative means for the grand jury to obtain the information sought."(23)

Compare this opinion with that of Justice Douglas. In the view of the latter, it is the means used to exact confidential information that is at odds with the opinion of Justices Stewart, Brennan and Marshall. That there needs to be protection for freedom of information to flow the four justices would appear to agree to. Justice Douglas wrote, "the intrusion of government into this domain ('wide open and robust dissemination of ideas and counterthougt which a free press both fosters and protects') is symptomatic of the disease of this society. As the years pass the power of the government becomes more and more pervasive. It is a power to suffocate both people and causes. Those in power, whatever their politics, want only to perpetuate it. Now that the fences of the law and the tradifion that has protected the press are broken down, the people are the victims. The First Amend;ment as I read it, was designed prevent that tragedy."(24)

From the evidence thus far it would seem to me that it is the dignity of the court that is more at stake than the miscarriage of justice caused by a stubborn reporter with ethics and professional pride. The Supreme Court would appear to support that thesis when they said, back in 1965: **"Summary contempt procedure was designed to fill the need for immediate penal vindication of the dignity of the court."(25){ Myers v US 44 S.Cst.272}**

If a way to present absolutely crucial evidence for a conviction can be found, does not the concept of contempt disappear and therefore the reporter's malfeasance? In 1947 the Court said: "Contempt has the dual function of Vindication of the public interest by pujnishment of contemptuous conduct of coercion to compel the contemptuee to do what the law requires of him."(26)

In US v Bryan , (1950) the Supreme Court said that "ordinarily one charged with contempt of court for failure to comply with a court order makes complete defense by proving that he is unable to comply."(27) This may be a defense for the reporter whose source does not reveal himself to the press, that "undisclosed news source." But what if the reporter refuses to expose a news source, the result of which is damage to the defense? In McComb v Jacksonville Paper Co., (1949) the Supreme Court said: "Civil as distinguished from criminal contempt is a sanction to endorse compliance with an order from the court or to compensate for losses or damages sustained by reason of non-compliance and may be imposed for prohibited acts irrespective of intent."(28)

In Nye v US, the Supreme Court said, further: "A contempt is considered 'civil' contempt when the punishment is wholly remedial, serves only the purpose of the complainant, and is not intended as a deterrent to offenses against the public." (29) This statement by the Court severs the publically harmful from the harmless, inoffensve or non-contributory sort of refusal. It seems to offer the working reporter an option, at once to protect his sources and inform the public for their good. It is not an excusing of the reporter or a waiver of the Court's right but, it seems to me, simply a bar to a challenge of the subpoena of evidence. The reporter, let us say, is less liable for contempt.

In US v United Mine Workers of America, the Supreme Court stipuated that "where the purpose of exercise of judicial sanctions in civil contempt proceedings is to coerce compliance withs the Court's order, the Court must consier the character and magnitude of harm threatened by continued contumacy and probably effectivness of any sugested sanction in bringing abut the results desired."(30)

This statement appears to suggest that the reporter, with sufficient knowledge of the case might willfully withhold disclosure of his news source on the presupposition, paralleling the Court's, that disclosure might greatly jeopardize innocent parties to the case. This is perhaps the most often used plea to be excused, and with good justification, since intimidation of witnesses, acts of retribution and greater crimes might follow disclosure.

There are four aspects of contempt which the Supreme Court, in the above citations has consiered: "damages for losses sustained by reason of non-compliance"; the corruption of the administration of justice; disrespect for the court; and prejudice of the public with respec to the merits of the action. All have sound reasoning behind them. Yet to block the flow of information by peremptory subpoenas of a reporter's notes or his testimony exposing a source can, with equal reasonableness, cause each of the above results. A forced expose of a reluctant informer can bring derision on the court; damages might indeed accrue to the complainant; public prejudice could rise up and justice be blocked. The Court in Loadboltz v Fields (1975) resolved this dilemma when it said "that the paramount interest served by the unrestricted flow of public information protected by the First Amendment outweighs the subordinate interest served by the liberal discovery provisions embodied in the Federal Rules of Civil Procedure."(31)

In support of reporters' shield laws, Atty. Gen. Mitchell, in 1971, said that a U.S. Attorney may subpoena only (1) if all other sources are exhausted, and (2) if he first obtains explicit permission of the Attorney General.(32) In a sort of oblique defense of an amicable attorney-media relationship, American trial lawyers, in the 1973 Chief Justice Earl Warren Conference on Advocacy in the U.S., agreed unanimously that "the privilege implies no colluson between media and law enforcement officials,"(33) but is simply a last resort protection for the rare case in which cooperation breaks down. The consensus of the trial lawyers was that the "creation of a definition of evidentiary privileges seemed a proper function of legislatures rather than of judges."(34) This was the crux of the Wisconsin AB 35 (cit.p. 5, this report). That legislatures can do a better job of writing shield laws was also the implication in a resolution, adopted October , 1972 by the Associated Press Managing Editors Association when a year after the Farr indictment in California, they concurred that a shield law is to protect investigative reporting which in many instances has uncovered wrong-doing by public offiials and private citizens, or provided other information the public was entitled to have."(35). In California a journalist includes:

> aa publisher, editor, reporter or other person connected
> with or employed upon a newspaper in a _newsgathering
> capacity_ (italics mine), by a press association or wire servsice,
> or any person who has been so connected or employed...
> a radio or television news reporter or other person
> connected with or employed by a radio or television station,
> or any other person who has been so connected or
> employed (36)

Prof. Benno C. Schmidt, Jr. in his book "Journalists Privilege" concludes "that the basic federal inerest in full dissemination of information of ntional significance jusifies a federal statute which limits state as well as federal subpoena powers."(37)

In the William T. Farr case (38) the California Appeals Court, in Dec. 1971, upheld the decision of Judge Charles Older when it stated that the "vital power of the court to control its owns proceedings and officers is paramount. If the Evidence Code interferes with that judicial right, the Code is unconstitutional. (39) In October, 1971, that Code 1070 was, in fact, amended by legislation to shiel former newsmen from contempt citations, this following Farrs switch to PR work in the L.A. DA Jos. P. Busch, Jrs. office. When the "Herald Examiner" reporter, with the aid of two trial lawyers, exposed he confession leaked from a Manson Family member's cell, he claimed immunity under Sec. 1070 of the California Evidence Code, which protrects a newsman from contempt citations. That was momentous; but what followed was even more significant. The Code was amended; the ambivalence of the U.S. Supresme court in the Branzburg v Hayes case again appeared in its declination to review the case. Farr's own lawyers argued that there was no "compelling need for disclosure, the protection enjoyed by the "L A. Times" Newsman Caldwell, in Branzburg v Hayes, under the 9th Circuit Court of Appeals ruling.

It would seem to me that shield laws will eventually emerge in almost all States by decree of legislatures instead of by juridical precedent. Except under rare circumstances of some mommentous immediate threat to the public, the reporter must not betray a news confidence. It is not jail that extinguishes his right of free choice, but the court that makes his conscription, as party to the trial, an absolute dictum. *His words become affidavits for either side*. To be mustered in is what is repugnant; to break a promise of silence is odious, destroying his credibility and his career. The breech of faith destroys the man and reduces the publics access to the truth truth by just that much.

x452 D. Ring: A-ucla

----

(1) <u>Privileged Communiation and the Press,</u>by Maurice Van Gerpen, Greenwood Press, Wewstport, Conn. (1979)
(2) ibid. p. 109; (also 408 US 665, 1972, p. 672)
(3) ibid., (Van Gerpen), p. 105
(4) ibid., p. 105
(5) 408 US 665, 1972, p. 690-691
(6) Jud. Code 268, 28 USCA, 459
(7) Branzburg v Hayes, (cit.), p. 591
(8) ibid., p. 691
(9) <u>The Newsman's Privilee; An Empirical Study,</u> by Vince Blasi; 70 "Michigan

Law Review" 229 (1971), p. 271
(10) Branzburg v. Hayes (cit.) , p. 591
(11) ibid., p. 746
(12) The Newsman's Privilege, V. Blasi (cit). p. 134
(13) Branzvburg v. hayes (cit.) pp. 705,707, 708
(14) Van Gerpen (cit.), p. 172
(15) ibid. p. 172
(16) ibid. p. 177
(17) The Status of News Shield Legislation, *Informational Bulletin*,   73-1B-
2, July, 1973; p. 5
(18) ibid., p. 5
(19) ibid., p. 7
(20) ibid., p. 14 (Cit. Branzburg v Hayes)
(21) ibid., p. 15
(22) Ibid.
(23) ibid.
(24) ibid., p. 15 The Status of News Shield legislation - *Bulletin*
(25)US Cal. 1947; Vol. 5A Supreme Court Decisions; Myers v US 44   S.Ct.
272
(26) ibid.
(27)US v Bryan, 70 S.Ct. 724, 339, US 323; 94 L.Ed. 884; rehearing   denied
(28) MComb v. Jacksonville Paper Co., 50 S.Ct. 497, 336, US 187; 93   L. Ed
599; 5A S. Ct. D. 343
(29) Nye v US, 61 S. Ct. 810; 313 US 33; 85 L. Ed. 1172; 5A S.Ct. D   343.
(30) US v. United Mine Wsokers sof America, 67 S. Ct. 677; 330 US   285;
91 L. E. 884; 5A S. Ct. D. 364
(31) The Media and the Law, eds. Howard Simons & Joseph A.   Califano, Jr.,
Praeger Publishers, Inc. N.Y. 1976, p. 17 (cit.   Loadboltz v Fields, Civil No.
74-587, ND. Fla, Feb. 7, 1975
(32) ibid., p. 17; 28 CFR, 50-10 (1974)
(33) The First Amendment and the News Media - Chief Justice Earl   Warren
Conference on Advocacy in the U.S.; pub. Roscoe   Pound American Trial
Lawyers Foundation, Cambridge; 1973;   p.11.
(34) ibid. p. 17
(35) The Status of News Shield Leislation, *International Bulletin*, 73-   1B-2,
July 1973, p. 7
(36) ibid
(37) Journalists Privilege: On Year After Branzburg, Benno C.   Schmidt, Jr.,
p. 49

(38) Farr v Superior C., 22 Cal. Appl. 3d 60; 99 Cal. Rptr. 342 (1971)
(39) "Time" Nov. 27, '72; Vol 100, No. 22, p. 61

DOCTRINAL UNIVERSALS HAVE LED TO
MORALIZING DOGMA

Whereas Thomas' approach is descriptive of *Richard's* main passion of revenge, his humour his "prime-moving" Vice and lits several expressions--including sardonic laughter and ironic falsehood--Moulton looks for an ethic buried in Elizabethan vision. It is an ethic he Believes, that holding meaning for audiences today in terms of universal principles of human justice, human nature's compensatory laws.

At this point Moulton's determinism and his formalizing of *Richard's* motives make their entrance. If one isn't careful, he is likely to be lured into accepting as factually true a theory that places the philosophical idea before the creation of the character instead of the reverse. To do so--as Thomas has done and as Moulton is about to do--convert the playwright into a moralist chiefly conerned with Vice, villainy, sin, Retribution and Wrong. This is a common enough clerical error, and the mistake of tinkering scholars and Puritan gays for whom Shakespeare is otherwise temporal and ephemeral and entertaining, as if *Richard* were a mortal of *predestinated* evil and hell.

According to Moulton, *Richard's* decision to prove himelf a villain, which begins the chain of retribution within the play, is not the outcome of his choice so much as it of history's decree. He experiences marked fear on the eve of his climactic battle; his is not the ethic-religious terror of the unknown which pitiable man feels before overpowering destiny in the plays of the Attican Greeks. Again, if you'll regard *Richard* through Mouton's perspective, you will see that what would seem aa catharsis moment in the drama are lines voicing simply the cries of an unseated soldier in the heat of the din and clash. His dignity is but the dignity of the militarist, trained into him, his actions the result of Will, a cunning without conscience and brute force. Historically determined , he is largely deprived of that free will Moutlon has set out to demonstrate as a force that operates against the Divine order of the universe, and Moulton has transferred to the play, in his interpretation of *Richard's* character, the later fundamental Calvinist delemma of early New England which predestined the damned and the saved yet granted to men free will. Richard's actions belong to historical predestination; yet Moulton would see that, already damned by that Divine Order, he undergoes the Nemesis brought about by his free will. Obscurity in the delineation of *Richard's* character and the failure to clarify his motives are the unfortunate result of Moulton's approach, of his dilemma.

THE MINOR CHARACTER A TRAGIC FIGURE

Only Queen Margaret appears to attain to the stature of a tragic figure, but because of her comparatively minor role and the fact that she is acted upon instead of her significantly influencing the action, the old Queen's part in the play does not justlify its being called a *tragedy*. Her speech to the Duchess in Act IV, Scene iv., conveys a sense of the tragic in a play which, if one accepts Moulton's views, would make of Richard but an implement in and of determinst historical forces.

> Bear with me; I am hungry for revenge.
> And now I cloy me with beholding it.
> Thy Edward he is dead, that kill'd my Edward;
> The other Edward dead, to quit my Edward;
> Young York he is but boot, because both they
> Match not the high perfection of my loss;
> Thy Clarence he is dead that stabb'd my Edward;
> And the beholders of this frantic play
> The adulterate Hastings, Rivers, Vaughan, Grey,
> Untimely another'd in their dusky graves.
> Richard yet lives, hell's black intelligencer,
> Only reservd their factor, to buy souls
> And send them hither; but at hand, at hand,
> Ensues his piteous and unpitied end,
> Earth gapes, hell burns, fiends roar, saints spray
> To have him suddenly conveyd from hence,
> Cancel his bond of life, dear God, I pray,
> That I may live to say, The dog is dead!

---

(1) Sidney Thomas , <u>The Antic Hamletr and Richard III</u>, Kings Crown Press, NY.; p. 25
(2) ibid. p. 32

(3) H. Granville-Barker, G. B. Harrison, <u>A Companion to Shakespeares Studies,</u> Cambridge University Press, Cambridge, 1949; p. 335

(4) Hazelton Spencer, <u>The Art and Life of William Shakespeare,</u> Harcourt, Brace and Co. NY., 1940; p. 163

(5) Sidney Thomas, <u>The Antic Hamlet and Richard III,</u> Kings Crown Press, N Y. 1943; p. 30

(6) Richard G. Moulton, <u>The Moral System of Shakespeare,</u> The Macmillan Co., NY. 1903; p. 40

Critique from <u>The Critics' Review</u>, 1953 - 625 Frederisk St., S.F.,   C. E. Miller, Editor

The man who tests himelf by his neighbor's conscience is in danger of losing his own.

A work of literature is a unique revelation of men's minds, manners and their actions

A WINDROW ON COMMUNICATION

Modernist educators responsible for teaching fundamentals of grammar, sentence structure, paragraph development, syntax, idiomatic usage and vocabulary, have today contributed, with television, to the mediocre redaction of the beauty of the native tongue, conforming its parameters to technology by calling the world's most beautifully expressive and flexible language-- **communication**. This "dumbing down" of English represents intellectual laziness on their part, ignorance of the scope and possiblities of expression in English, narrowing of the mind and imagination to fit shallow moulds of instruction, the sterilization of powers of expression by authoritative confinement, and the rapid deterioration of faculties of poetic and analytical expression--which are human kinds. The argot of technology and the bloodless nature of media prose have made English so utilitarian that communication has come to mean a strict adherence to sterile dimensions of semeosis--or a barbaric *referencing* in absolute mathematical/musical symbols. The commonality of the language must depend on the use of concrete words. The barbaric "look say" system for the teaching of vocabulary and reading sprang from this regressive use of English. These self styled modernists are often a curious breed, half literate themselves in the tongue, less than gifted in powers of expression, weighted down with aids that merely substitute ineffective classroom entertainment for effective discipline.

School administrators and " department chairs," for their part preoccupy the teachers with meetings, appointments, procedural changes and agenda memoranda, so to acquaint them and distract them with administrative matters that it is little wonder teachers of English have not developed indifference to their job, their craft.. In the home, not merely television but neurotic, overworked , sentimental and sometimes brutish parents belittle and indeed often stunt creative uses of young imaginations by silencing their make-believce, berating the yongsters for some deed of childish plan and drama. Those are the indifferent, the irresponsible, callow parents from whose homes children come to study poetry. Small wonder that the emotional language and subjects of poetry seem to them irrelevant and boring. Kids are becoming jaded early in life, when they should not be jaded at all. And the only book in the home is the phone book to modify parental influence.

A MARGINAL COMMENT ON EXISTENTIONALISM

"To he untrue man, the whole universe is false—it is impalpable, it shrinks to nothing within his graso. And to himself, insofar as he shows himself in a false light, becomes a shadow, or, indeed, ceases to exist."
*—from THE SCARLET LETTER   p. 166   Translated: The Reverend Dimmsdale, in the novel, fathers an illegitimate child by Hester Primme, causing her to wear the Scarlet "A" about her breast for the rest of her life— though she becomes of great service, compassionate care and value to Salem. He is the shadow who, in the end, appears with her on the confessional scaffold in the village. He is Hawthorne's "untrie man," as was his relative Judge Hawthorn in the witchcraft trials. (*Out of shame Nathaniel changed the spelling of his last name from his relative's spelling with the 'e'." I think, too, it might have been Hayhorn.*

ON POLITICAL CONFORMITY

the corruption of political correctness
in today's society

The right to an open declaration of political faith is often challenged in perilous times of war-threat and elusive alliances. It is then that men will often pawn as though baubbles of Baal their liberties which, without finer judgement or competent education, are discountenanced, scorned, rejected in the train of fear for an illussory pubic safety and a conformity to other men's feelings.

Of the freedom to think apprehendingly, to sympathize irrationally, to act and comport ones self frenetically, there is too llittle cognizance made today. For, if time does not aver less and recent cold-war events be not the custodian of our emotions, it will appear that our people are wont less to challenge than to condemn, to reflect upon than to acccpt, to agree for safety's sake rather than to argue for enlightenment and courage's sake upon the mistakes of our government and the follies of men in high positions of office. The former venue for free enquiry has become the oppressive venue for conformlity--the classroom. Tolerance has become intolerance due to a growing fear that one's ideas, speech, attitudes may prove offensive to others--a culture of fear and the banishment of free thought has hindered choices of words to express even the tolerated thoughts.

Since these things are true, scandals can survive indetected, corruption exist without revelation and the atmosphere of suppression can drive out original ideas and the gift of language to express them. In this culture of fear, contempt for the most vocal spokesmen against moral wrong and unfair civil polity remain held in check, dominated by fear of public censure.

Indeed it has long veen a truism in centuries during which ruder men fought for their liberties that had all men surrrrendered their thoughts and actions, in complacent submission, to a benevolent censure by those amblitious for power, we should to the man be existing merely as husbandmen under feudal overlords of armored might. Being made overly sensitive by a sense of personal guilt, for whatever reasons, and oppressed by the notion that we must please all men, we risk pleasing none except by mouthing politically-correct words, phrases and ideas. The stifling of originality of thought and boldness of verbal expression is upon us, and at a time when we can scarcely afford to reject either in the name of *PC*, or political correctness.

It thus comes about that any progress toward a more enlightened acceptance of disagreement, call it **political** as it termed today, whether the intent be strife or the motive discontent with things as they are, the stronger shall be that heritage which, increasingly, we now can only imagine but hardly exists--free and original thinking. For to disagree is oten in a real sense to propose a change beneficial to all. Lacking this liberty, our social fabric becomes fragile and out socio-political thinking sterile. Not to disagree with a free use of the English language is to stifle the struggle--which has always meant for the human race its hope and its means for spiritual survival. To find in all utterances an imputed insult slanders honest thought, corrupts the language and disgraces one's moral integrity and intellectual honesty. This sort of hypersensitivity is fraudulent and pathological.

THE INK POT, from my journal **The Critics' Review,**
published c 1959, 625 Frederick St., San Francisco

MODERN EDCATION–A Brief Treatise: Only does a social
revolution often devour her own children in a reactionary consrvation of the new
regime, carrying the revolutionary spirit past the crisis into the period of spreading
reforms. But cilvil and intenational wars exhibit a kindred, closer-to-home,
centrifugal tendency, a kind of minor renaissance of inbreeding new philsophies
and modification old systems of thinking, of ideologies.

If we look back to around `1925, we find that educators were re-
xamining obsolete methodologies and credoes under the unflattering light of what
social scientists and educators themselves had to discovered. Leaders in
education, the authors-writers "agreed that our schools were pretty bad. Noting
but a major revolution in practice would do."

Education today, in the perilous wake of war, is going through a
similar phase of redirection, a re-opening of the marketplace of ideas on our
system in an effort to bring up to needs the ideologies and practices of education
as a social dynamic institution. Much of what is obsolete can be attributed to a
dying pedagogies yet the same may be said of the modern, in which realm
administration finds many soothsayers--benign approvers--among teachers. Rote
learning, memorization, reading performance and board-work are still in vogue, as
it were, with older teachers in public school systems. And why not if they
worked? But, onm the other hand, are they productive and germane to today's
more complex social problems and challenges?

Of one thing we may be certain, and that is that international
compeition, its mania for nationalistic good cirtizenship, and the American
family's changing character have opened an abyss between the educators and the
needs of society. In math and science, American school children have fallen
behind their international peers. This is parftly due to dependence on machines,
machine-scored tests, the classroom calculator...and to boredom, to a disconnect
between the classroom and industry, and, lastly, to sheer inertia of children

without motivation or adult inspiration as role models. Instead of hiring achievers from the outer world beyond school walls, the "systems" of pedagogy have been content to hire teachers from academies of teaching and with BA's in education. Also, and of utmost importance, the schools lack competitive salaries for teachers.

Federal aid to education for the construction of achools and the increae of teachers salaries embrace a program tlhat willl take from the National budget millions each year, to be dispensed to those States that have a demonstrated need ror additonal funds. Certain agrarian States in the South, partcularly, and those overpopulated industrial areas in the North, and wherever there has occurred an influxe of newcomes, as illegals, that is disproprtionate to the per capita and corporate tax structures, it is they who have requested and will continue to request Federal aid. Such aid, however, if endorsed by the State's Senate and City or Township Counsels, and providing the citizens do not petition for a recission of the grant affectilng them locally or lthe people of heir State, is a form of lawful financilal assstance, under the Tenth Amendment to the Constitution.

For aid to education, although not expressly subsumed underr any other Constitutional law goverrning a power to the Union of States, and while not prohibited as a power of administration, is reserved to the individual States respectively, For aid given to the people for the education of their children is today often tendered under a bond issue referendum by the people in those States that accept that aid. Amendments X and IX, of the Federal Constiltution (powers reserved to the people) at the time of their adoption, did indeed cause widepread fear of Federal encroachment upon States' rights. It was Jeffereson who, in 1823, wrote: "I believe the States can best govern over home concerns and the General Goverment over foreign ones. I wish, therefore, to see maintained that wholesome disrtricution of powers established by the Constuitution for the imitation of both, and never to see all offices tranferred to Washington." Under financial duress, however, and upon States' adoption, without petition of recission , Federal aid to education has becomes legal and valid.

Outright grants, to be matched by States' monies, for the building of schools are urgent in some sections of the Country in which the incoming migrants neither own land, with or without imrprovements, nor a business that can be properly taxed to help defray construction expenses. The children of illegals enjoy a free education whilest their fathers send money home, usually to Mexico.

Yet it cannot be expected that the corporation and property oweners should pay the entire bill.. It is only right, therefore, that the earnings of the people should be taxed; athough I am aware that in many instances, particularly where the citizen is childless and working, presssures will be exerted toward the ends of uniformity and cheapness, and toward a de-secularization of the schools, if the taxpayer is of the Catholic faith. The childless secularist, in effect, pays for the education of the children of others in American society.

What I would point out, though, is that the aid to increase teachers' salaries places the Federal Goverment in the position of co-employer with the people of that State. And that whereas, by analogy, a bank shares with a borroer the ownership of his property, without injury to or infringementl upon his civil rights, the General Governorship of his property, the Government may without injury to or infringement upon his civil rights co-own the land and the buildings of a new school. Furthermore, whereas the bank trustees are prohiibited from dictating the personal beliefs of their debtor, the Federal Government, upon mandate of a strictly financial arrangement, does and will continue to violate human conscience by dictatorial writ of secularism , thereby using Amendments IXand X to undermine, in the instance of religious schools,. the religious freedom guaranteed by the First Amendment.

Ownership of a thing deprives it of any intrinsic value or power of self-determination. And the loyalty affadavlt, a Federal currculum, a Washington panel of educational advisors and technical directors would involve not simply the surrender, but the sale and purchase of the *right of self-determination* of teacher, school board, community and citizens of the State. That right is pendant upon the ownership of the *teacher as property*, as a *means of production by* the great masses of complacent and indifferent people. Politliclians are ready to manipulate the will of the people for personal gain in the absence of public will. Indeed, what we today observe in America is a sylstem of socialized education, under which burden it is difficult to find competent orthodox educators who espouse individualism in education, both for the student and for the competent administrtator. The former must give way to the dumbing down of teaching to confer *brightness* upon the indolent and willfully illiterate, whilest the latter, the Administrator over one or many schools, must always be aware and submit to the consieration of his politics. The larger the school system, as LAUSD, the more apparent these weaknesses of the system.

LOBBYISTS--A Second Brief Treatise: — It is my suggestion and hope that lobbyists in Washington be muzzled by law and allowed to speak when their influence does not directly contribute to the manipulation of upcoming votes of the people. There should be a cut-off time of three months prior to a general election. Lobbyists have long outlasted their original value, which was to inform, first, then to petition for ***change.*** Furthermore, Goverment aid to their companies is *laissez faire* so long as competing lobbyists establish a bid minimu by gentleman's agreement in order that both profit, the loser by contract shunting, It is my suspicion, too, that, those high prices mentioned earlier in the sale of items to the armed forces contain percentages deducted as my payoffs for competing bid absenstention, or rigged bidding on items not as yet "discovered." Additionally, millions are being funneled into the pockets not expressly accounted for on those bid constracts--payoffs. I realize that it is unkind of me to say so, but the *lobbyist* is only another name for the well-heeled robber. Demand, as opposed to need, occurs by means of legislation that on major contracts shall not be compared against private estimates submitted by the banks and investment officials. By a penal statute that expunges fraudulent intent, that is, any bill in gross excess of such estimates--shall, upon issusance, subject the manufacturer to prosecution by the Attorney-General for extortion of the public. High taxes and corruption in Government are due in large measured to the chasm letween Federal spending and private investment capital via the current Federal budget. ***Pork***, "ear-marked" projects are an example of that fraud.

I am constrained, therefore, to conclude that the intent to defraud is applicable to Goverment bidding as well as to retail merchandising. And that unless the Attorney General takes legal action with respect to those criminal overcharges already placed against the National Budget, I can only assume that thievery is an acceotabke Federal policy and that profitteering is by acquiescence therefore lawfully condoned.

If he refused to prosecute on the basis of these contracted-for items already mentiuoned, and providing the media have not supplied false or misleading information, the only conclusion that remains tenable is that the Attorney General is derelect in his duty and, fearful lest his appointment be withdrawn, plays politics with the people's money for reasons of personal ambitoion and power, if not income, and in order tos augment the prestige and campaign-financial support of the President, in whose Cabineer he holds office. Upon the determination that the Attorney General has, is consequence, misused his offilce to gross negligence or perverse motive, he should be removed from his office of trust. Indifference or personal ambition can be the onlyvalid reasons for his refusal to prosecute.

Having dispensed with lobbyists, let us move into the farmlands of America. Anyone with the least knowledge of the financial structure of our economy and the bloated condition egregious subsidies of must surely be mindful of the fact that high corporation and high personal taxes are synchronous with high farm subsidy The subsidty is a form of filnancial support for farming products in light of failing market prices. Yet the subsidy appears almost fraudulent in view of heightened consumer buying power. The dollar of the taxpayer supports a subvsidy program that reduces the potention loss-margin on crop sales, yet at the same time it regulates consumer demand by a type of artificial price fixisng on the raw crops; for selling under pay may mean the withdrawal of Goverment support to the individual farmer in the following years, as he again produces a tripple yield wilthsout showing a profit, foreign aid iln corn and wheat, let us say, legitmizing his losses. In this case, the subsidy continues.

If he tries to sell over par, he increases his surplus, which he may then use as collateral for new farm machinery. But in increasisng his operating efficiency by the use of improved quipment,
he only raises his year's yield and that compounds his market loss by adding to his suplus. The taxpayer, on the other hand, not only pays for the maintenance of this crop subsidy program; but he pays for the storage of surplus crops and he pays the false and inflated market prices that are no longer integrated with the farmer's actual productive capacity. Tjhe fixed subsidy, consequently, is driving the smll farmer off the land. And Government, ironically, to recover losses to the farmer in surplus by the underwriting of farm loan collateral with tax dollars, must glean loan dollars, storage dollars, administrative dollars, and, utlimately, consumer dollars from the taxpayer for creating false higher prices. This form of deception is done by hiding the surplus and by giving it away to Russia.

I would not alarm anyone by radical proposal or hint of political subterfuge, since I wish to remain on the friendliest of terms with out public servants, prorvding they realize always that they are servants and not masters. If this yoke be too heavy and cumbesome for them to bear, then I think ti inly wise and fit that we express our will to find others for the impersonal tasks at hand under a Goverment of laws instead of a *Goverment of Planners.* This idea is, in fact, partly responsible for producing a Supreme Court that legislates from the bench.

However, I would like to propose, at this juncture, that by a
Constitutional Amendment we eliminate the ***College of Electors***. For it is they
who compound the possibilities for corruption by favortism, profitabily directed,
and by unde-the-table grabs, commercial, political, legal, of candidate pushers.
These Electors seleced by the state Legislatures, conprise a curtain of liegmen
between the voters and the officeholders, and are a relic of the European courts
whose duchys sent representatives to the Crown for counselling or grievances.
Our mass media especially radio, which is less amenable to consorship by
technicians, make possible the obsoletism of Electors. Futhermore, I would
propose that in the face of these Electors, we take recourse to ***direct elections***
instead, since the will of the people shall in no wise be violated, and there shall be
restored to the people their sense of immediate responsibility in the choice of
capable and honest presidents and officeholders. It is more difficult to circumvent
the people in a public elelction that it is to circumvent those who by causuistry,
deceit and machinations, may suppose themselves to fully represent the people of
their Party in particular convictions at the nominations by said Electors. Electors
can, in fact, extinguish the will of the people and also vote contrary to the majority
will of those State legislatures who appointed them.

I would strongly urge that the Constitution again be amended to
require that the candidacy for the President be pendant upon a term of office in
one or both houses of Congress. Thus might we eiminate dark horses and
elections by wealth of the wealthy, as is usually the case, since the power that is to
repose in such hands is not always the best informed, by experience, in the
problems of every day business, local government, those needs and the attitudes
that direct the couplex course of the people's affairs. Nor is a man of that station
always as thrifty as he might be; and the growth of an economy depends more
upon the thrift of its citizens than it does on their spending habits and comnsumer
power ir tge orinuses if a sekf-deckared fiscal conservative For without the one,
the other ceases to exist. Election because of noble lineage is, furthermore,
Medieval and belongs to the governments of tyrants, which nowadays we do seem
to find not a little solicitous rapport with. Let a Senator's work and service to his
Country speak for him, instead of the usual banile twaddle that is pumped into the
thought bloodsteeam by media, politicians, industrial pushers, religionists and
sycophants, most of whom have themselves at heart for money, power and the
kingdom of righteousness.

It is not to be expected that these changes anc challenges which I have proposed would cause great joy, widespread and generous, among the populace of our tax-oppressed Nation, but lthey would conduce to lighten somewhat the load of annual tax debt. For it is indeed a fact, today and now, that our Congress and the President are gradually crushsing the imitiative and enterprise out of the American people, proving thereby that "the power to tax is the power to destroy." If we do not act to ease this oppressive tax burden, accepting upon our own initiative an equitable share of the responsibility for any unfavorable or dissasterous complication that may flow therefrom, perhaps none of those now living and future generations will see this Nation's individual enterprise, the ethics of her professional men, the credos of her schoolmasters, her commerce and science, and the fundamental freedoms under law, Constitutional Law and not the bills of alarmist expediency, stunted and contained by complete socialism. That breed of socialism will occur in our materialistic Republicanism in order to forestall bankrupcy; or, worst of all, possible calamities, accept domination by communist Russiam with its concomitant return to the dark ages that so barbarous a system would bring. Either we must, it seems to me, practice austerity to a certain degree and in specific and telling ways, or this Nation will suffer itself to submit to the poison of historical regression. (When I wrote this-- il the 1950's I could have no idea that the Jihadists, , Hexbollah and and their barbaric retinue Islamo-fascist of Al Quaeda would attempt to destroy America's spirit, her resolve her strength with 9/11.)

Oppressive taxatiom is the primary cause of inflation. Producers, in order to recover tax losses, raise retail prices; consumers, to recover their dollar losses, demand higher wages. Producers, to offset higher wages and taxes combined, raise prices; consumers urged to buy more, adopt credit measures, prices and wages stabilize. Federal and State taxes increase, and the cycle repeats sitself. Neither labor nor management can rightly be blamed and it is our foreign aid and defense programs that account for the inflated tax rate and the commodity-premium in an economy of surplusses.

NEPOTISM and BLACK MARKETING—a third treatise: is said that *nepotism* is an old Congressional custom.
This was no doubt true when the ten dollar gold piece procured a Virginia smoked ham for the plate of an itinerant horse campaigner, and the ham was split nineways amongst the members of his family. The gold bought for the farmer three miles of new barbed wire, and the   Senator charged off the expense to election-year *incidentals*. Circumstances, however, have changed. The fuzzy-

cheeked ivy-league son of a Senator, when circumspection merits no rebuke, can nowadays accrue by father's largesse ten or eleven thousand dollars a year, as much as a corporation vice-president who has spent his life at a one job. (This is the 1950's I am speaking of.) The price is rather high to pay for the lad's sloth and the Senator's thievery, for I make so bold as to call such clandestine deductiosn just that--*thievery*, the act of coney-catching practiced on the pockets of the American public for political office.

Nepotism runs rampant in the American Congress. The wife of a Senator, taking heart from her huband's gratuitous mulchting, which in any other profession would be considered malpractice or theft, thereupon charges her social dinners, her transportation expenses, her suite space to the American taxpayer. It would be indecent of me to suggest that her use of her husband's office for rank personal ends is a form of prostitution, for her enormous gains are ill-gotten behind the camouflage of *need*. And whilest she licks stamps and sits envelops to cover her conscience, the peasants must pay dearly for her services!

I have read, too, that not infrequenly there is property owned by some cousin or friend of the Senator who, finding himself a trifle short on funds for the acquisitoion of personal property, deems it an act of true patriotism to offer his front porche for office space, and at three or four times what it would ordinarily brng. Being accustomed to using the side and rear entrances of the house, he seldom uses the porch. Truly that is a shame for the taxpayer, vilewed as a tyrant visiting this Country for the first time, pays dearly in false claims for his board and keep. Yet I would distinguish between the Senator and the tyrant, and clanedestine, preferential profit is descriled to the taxpayers as an inadequate *earmark*. For wherever the typrant's bills may be charged to the improvement of international relations, those of the Senator's friend or cousin can be charged only to graft and to a wilful effort to circumvent both the law and the citizens who pay, those who unless enlightened, consider the *pork* needful for the country as a whole. Such bullshit has gone on for decades and few Senators have the guts to destroy the legalized Congressional seizure, permitted to exist under color of law, lest they commit political suicide. That is clear is it not?

It is my honest belief, moreover, that they have begun to fret under the yoke of such deceit, which ill-custom and vile usage have placed upon them. And that would they restore to Congress ilts unimpeachable integrity and dignity, which the founders of this Nation intended it should have, they must get rid of the rascals either by recall petition or on the next election day. Lest our elected Representatives under the law revert to the 17th century practices of the corrupt Parliament of George III, who took refuge from pleas of *cause b*ehind an apostleship of oppressive charity, and whose sycophants, bootlicks and economic liegemen prayed God forgive them their ire, since Colonial gold was for the glory of England, the Crown and the Throne of Grace. For our part, we must evict these Congressional *nepotists* and blackguards by common vote or suffer that this Naiton lose its ethical fibre against the winds of a troubled world.

History has shown us that one of the important adjuncts to a corrupt legislature is a powerfull military clique, a weak Departmet of Defense and a liberal Supreme Court. We curently (2006) have all three. InWashington DC today, the military echelons, lincluding both the officers and the enlisted men, are ecomin a societal class untos themselves. That ils thedeplorable fact; yet unless the citizens sof this Country prefer in future years to submit their educational prgrams and religious doctrins, their economic welfare and personal rights to the scrutiny of advisors who, for reasons of military command and battle safety would issue warnings against an organization of individuald among the populace, it is strongly to be urged that precautions to be taken frustrating the rise of a *junta* in the Nation's capital. Toward this end, one of the first steps we might take is to return the officers' boot lackeys and wet nursees to the regular line of duty. For where they are least indispensable, they are most required, and were this not so, World War II and the Korean War would have been wars between the respective officers. Yet since it is true that miner skirmishes and major battles are fought and won by youngsters with guns, tanks, bazooks and grenades, the cliques of Washington brass, if they are soldiers, could serve their Country no more nobly than by returning these men to the line.

Other contingenies of a quasi-military government sear remarking upon at this point; for in the theme of tax reduction, we may find buried many holes, whic, like asieve in their function, doth allow much gold to filter threough priority requirements and over the heads sof these parasitical officials. Throw out the rubbish of ridiculous field manuals that appertain to the ease-lulled life of these officers. Cut down on their cars, their lavish military dinners, their Federal booze, and their unnecessary trips abroad, to say nothing of their entertainment expense money to maintain, here and there, a mistress on the miltary scene; for where you find the army you will find also the whorleom set up to keep the troops happy. In concluding this much, the brief indictment of official mililtary waste, I may be permitted the suspicion that there is not a little black-marketeering now enjoying current popularity in Washsington, partilcularly in drugs, and that but for the Frenchie with a folded shopping bag under hisarm, waiting outiide the *gar d' lest* in Paris, the black marketeering in our Capital passes all of the tests for nefarious exchange that blossomed in France after World War II.

SYMBOLISM AND IDEA IN THE DRAMA

Why did a play by G. B. Shaw appeal to the socialist liberals in England of his post-Victorian day? His plays appealed to British radicalism. Symbols that try to convey a politial idea, a philosophical concept , a social message through dramatic character must reduce characterization to typical features, thus to distinguish the person from tlhe idology he represents. The plays of Clifford Odets, August Strindberg fall into the same category.

Propaganda drama resembles in this regard the Medieval morality play--idealiation . To the extent that a play thus becomes propaganda, it becomes increasingly symbolical and its characters become less individualized and more archytypical. When a character thereupon loses his humanness, and is manipulated like a puppet by the theme representing a social-political, religious idea, thatr chaacter loses its appeal to general audiences--at least as a dramatic figure, Specialied audiences then find him an example of the "good man," the "moral example," the idealistic "future man" of society and government who is worth emulating. Socialist dramas attempt to present us with paradigms of heroes. Ibsen's plays are of this kind. The playwright who shows his audinces a Protagonist who is a complex human bveing annot be accused of this ideologic Idealization.

Comedy of types such as Jonson and Moliere wrote of may typify and moralilze social archytypes, but enough of the humanness of the real person remains to establish in the play a universal appeal. There is lacking a pervasive morality of the puppetry of the play. Puppetry implies the artifices of character-manipulation to achieve the propagandistsic end result. It is not the Protagonist's character traits that decide whither he goes or if he stands or falls. His actions represent the playwright pulling the strings of his creation.

The moralities and propagandistic plays lie at the extreme end of a grand scale. At the other end are the plays written by the Impressionists and

Expressionists which try to so individualize a human experience as to make it ultra subjective and therefore incomprehensible. In so doing dramatic values become lost in the absolute intimacy of lthe playwright's personal experience. In either case the playwrgiht his personna to appeal to the political proselyte and also to the rarified intellectual. The play is then either evangelistic or dialectical. The stage becomes a forum for polico-social issues and is no longer holding the" mirror up to nature," as Shakespeare wrote.

The propaganda play appeals is to the values of the masses and so it is specialized, as much so as is expressionist drama yet with social import. In the case of the impressionist-expressionist plays, the ultra subjecrtivce experience may also have a propaganda added, as did drama after WW I in Europe, ostensibly aimed at showing the disenchantment, the reconstruction of a torn society that came to accept, uner Hitler's charisma, a socio-Fasclist promise of a restored and thriving new post-Versailles Germany. *Retreat into the mind was the essence of <u>Expressionism</u>; escape from tangible reality was the essence of <u>Impressionism.</u>*

For the reason that negation and disillusionment showed mans inner despair and the breakup of old ways and mores, many of those post-WW I plays were wrongly called *tragedies*. It was not the personal experience alone which made them seem so but the acknowledgement that they depicted universal human suffering, motives of need, failure, of love, the success of despair and the like as positive standards for the measurement of the experience of enduringl pain and loss. In the popular mind, any sever and exremely painfull loss is called *tragic*. The problem with that assessment is that it blurs the meaning of true tragedy: a person of strong and admirable character--not necessarily of rank or wealth--who rises above the defeat sprung from a weakness of that character-- essentially the Greek classic view of Hamartia.

Certainly a tragedy cannot co-exist absolutely with a spirit of negation, since then any effort to define the good and truly beneficial, the harmonious, course of action is pushed aside. Yet comedy always carries with it a spirit of conquest over defeating circumstances and ends. At this point the comedic philosophy becomes one of the destruction of society and of self-destruction, held in check by humor--the tragic irony of objective comprehension. Nor can a tragedy consist absolutely of affirmation, whether for social goals or religious creeds, since life denies the credibility of utopian visions. The tragedic philsophy becomes one of totalitarian recreation, even if communist adherents

FROM THE AUDIENCE

            In a stage presentation, the actor is all-important. In such matters as pace, timing, the bulding of dramatic tension, making dynamic the action of the drama and conveying the meaning of the story. In a movie, the use of music, flash shots of people and things, odd angles and other technical devices may share that function with the actor. A stage presentation, shows the whole actor, the entire character as a coordinated whole. A movie may present only fragments caught by camera selection., likely an artifilcial , mechanical direction of attention rather than an artful one, as by the actors on a stage (and not necessarily directd by the actor).

AN ANALYSIS OF SUFFERING IN
Oscar Wilde's play

SALOME

by Pizzicatto

Set in Christ's day, while the Messiah, as revealed by the
Nazarenes and Jews in Herods palace, turns water into wine, heals the leper, the
blind and the lame, preaches from a boat and, to Herod's revolt, raises up the dead
son of Jarius, "Salome," the play, tells the story of the beautiful Babylonian
seductress' destruction by the Tetrarch of Caesar's province, the man named
Herod. During a palace feast, his Syrian Captain of the Palace Guard, son of the
exiled king and a slain mother, kills hiuself because he has allowed *Salome*,
against orders, to look upon the prophet Jokanaan. (Jokanaan is the man called
John the Baptrist, and the account of his beheading occurs in Matthew 14:8.)

The old man utters dire prophesies of doom to come in Herod's
provinces. He has heard the beating of wings in the palace; the sun will turn black
and destruction will visit those who have forsaken the ways of the Lord. He is not
the prophedt Elias, who is proclaimed to have seen God face to face. Yet he has
heard the Moses of the Mount, and he knows of Christ's miracles by the
Capernaum gate and in Jerusalem. It is he, Jokanaan, whom Salome, daugfhter of
Herodias and the wife of Herod, lusts for in the flesh.

Herod, to amuse himself on his birthday, induces Salome to dance
for him. She submits, yet upon the condition that he will grant to her on one
request. Herodias, wife of the Tetrarch, forbids , nay, begs her not to dancxe. The
slaves s nevertheless prepare her with perfumes and with the famed *seven veils*.
Removing her sandals, she then performs the "dance of the seven veils," Her act
completed, she demands of Herod the head of Jokanaan on a silver platter, the life
of him who inhabits the cistern jail cell below the banquet-hall terraces.

Herod offers to give her his white peacocks, his faulous jewels, half of his provinces and rich garments of feathers if she will but rescind her demand for the prisoner's head. Salome remailns adamant; she will claim and see exhibited the likeness in death of the man who forbade her to touch his body or to kiss his lips. Herodias, however, is now pleased by the turn of events; for she would will evil and calamity upon the ruler who is brother to her slain husband. Herod passes the ring of death to a soldier, and the executioner is sent into the well to behead the prisoner. Salome hears no cry, no sounds of alarm or terror. Presently, the soldier retrurns over the top with the prophet's head on his shield, and the seductress kisses the lips denied to her in by Jokanaan in life. Herod extinguishes the torches and turns to go. Yet before he has left the hall, a fit of passionate rage seizes him and, wheeling upon Salome, he commands that his soldiers kill her. Thus ends Wild's one-act play. We are left to woder why? Was the beheading an act of jealous revenge against Salome. Or was it the resuslt of conscience that he allowed himself to be persuaded to kill an innocent prisoner? Or perhaps philsoophically, Wilde's view, was the beheading the proof in action that death to righteousness destroys truth?

There are, in this play, two principal facts of Herod's nature that motivate and direct his actions--his ambition for power and for absolute happiness--which he considers to be sensual gratification in feast and dance--his doubt cast upon the fertility of Herodias and his skeptical wonder whether she *is his wife*, all of which blandishments of his heroic soldiery and airs of a fattened lion culminate in the dastardly act of revenge. The first then of these natural elements in Herod's character is pride, overweening, implacable, having begotten his greed for material gain and lust after physical pleasures. His is the sort of pride by which the erstwhile Satan declared bankrucy and Richard, Duke of Gloucester, wrought bloody strife in England's noble halls.

While a commander for Caesar, he holds within his kingdom unlimited power over the property and lives of the Egyptians, Romans, Sytrians and Babylonians who make up his populace. Herod has killed his brother for the throne and, like a good Roman, has thieved the wife, the comely Herodias. One must admit, I think, that these arenot acts altogether the actions of a devout apostle pf the true faith, although there is some justification for his reassurance that, as a happy warrior, he could do no less for his Lord Caesar. True, indeed, it is upon the insistence of *Salome,* who proclaims her virginity lost, her virtue destroyed by the man with skin like white ivory, that the Tetrarch orders Jokanaan's execution. She has falsely accused Jokanaan of adultery. Yet, too, one must be fair in these matters. It is for his own sensual pleasure, the reaffirmation of his pride, the proof of his bounteous nature, that he commands the prisoner *Salome* to dance for him, whileset as their skirmish turns out, he offers her power and wealth more copious than that of Queen Herodias, his wife, to arouse the latter's jealousy. That jealousy only increases his lust for power to control his wife, the queen.

Furthermore, his whim; for entertainment, for a performance, is not unnatural; *Salome* apparently was a very beautiful woman to look upon. Bear in mind though that she has attempted to seduce the anchorite and prophet, John, whose life Herod favaors and wishes to preserve; and that Herodias, because of his lacivious and incestuous lust, his fratracide, secretly hates her husband. His insistence then that Salome dance for him symbolizes, as it were, Herod's ruthless ambiton for self-gratification, in a word, hie pride. And all that he has grasped in power, booty and emoluments he awards for that chief end. Wilde's bargaining sequence in particular, and the play in its entirety, dramatize these components of thought and action of the characters, of the religious-political pressures and the regional surroundings belonging to that one dominant cause for life in Herod's mortal tenure.

The second of these principal facets of Herod's nature which motivate and direct his actions is *fear*. His is the fear of the future, the foretold disaster which Jokanaan prophesizes will befall his him becauuse of the wanton evil of his reign, the abomination of Herodias, and because of the iniquities of the people of Judea. Herod's fear--and a volatile, emotional force to be reckoned with in a tyrant--finds ultimate expression in his reluctance to take the Jokanaan's life. He has his enemies among the friends of Herodias who will not be appeased by Jokanaan's excution, but only encouraged thereby at having found the chink of fear in the Tetratrch's armor. Allow him to live and Jokanaan, who tells by his signs the visions of Herod's end, remains but the figure of the eccentric and harmless old man. But to kill him, Herod realizes, will mean only the "heaping of coals of fire upon his head" by creatubg a martyr of an innocent man. He fears prophet, prophesy and, most all, his enemies within the kingdom.

Herod is also superstitious. The Romans have many gods to whom he last sacrified fifty young men and a hundred maide;ns. He fears that he will precipitate the wrath of the gods by destroying the Christian stoic; for they may favor the old man in the balance of an "eye for an eye" justice. It is this superstitious fear within Herod that causes him to quail before the deed. of execution.

There is, as we can see then, a considerable destructive potential wrapped up in old Jokanaan's life. That religious state and the political-military tyrant with the habits of a Bohemian are deadlocked. And while pride and fear are Herod's cardinal motivations, they also, in a sense I think, constitute his suffering; since the one brings in its train the insatiable anxieties for carnal pleasures, which include power and prestilge, and the other demands the elimination of all odds against his personal survival. Such a man really is no one with whom to hold trusting privy council.

Pride, it must be confessed, also motivates Herodias. Hers, however, is tempered by the intrusion of felt injustices, however flimsy the grounds for her feelings. After all, old Jokanaan is not exactly out of his mind in what he has observed, although the more cultivated set of Roman nobility, the yea-sayers to Tetrarchian views, might not assign quite the same moral value to their queen/s bordello diplomacy. The question of injustice is simply whether or not she has any right to the pleas of an injured party, when he must feel keenly the ignominy of having to perform her dutues under the sword of a usurper of the Judean throne, the Herod who is both husband and usurper. There is, it seems, some validity in fact to that felt injustice.

Furthermore, a lack of love for him leaves a void filled by her, Herodias', love for *Salome*, her only daughter and rightful successor to the throne; that is, if we can envision Caesar's capitulation to a woman Tetrarchas governor of a military province. As a consequence of this loveless bond, Herods entreaties that Salome dance for him outrages Herodias' sense of filial propriety. They slur the queen's dignity, an impiety blasphemous before the vengeful, sacrosanct gods who, one receives the impression, are presently in a stormy mood for appeasement sacrifices. Proof of her outrage appears in the surrender sequences when in a passion, calm on the surface, she speaks from emotions long charmed by Herod's wounds; and from a queen's...and a woman's...pride reinforced by her embitrtered sense of justice wronged.

> My daughter has done well to ask
> the head of Jokanaan. He has
> covered us with insuslts. He has
> said unspeakable things against
> me One can see that she loves
> her mother well. Do not yield, my

daughter. He has sworn an oath,
    he has sworn an oath.

It is, in sum, the undying sense of the injustice of her role, of her situation, and of the actions of the man inciting her to hate which constitute the sufferilng of Herodias, the queen, in "Salome."

It would be an error, I think, to overlook one of the refilnements sof her sufferilng, an aspect that bears less upon her maternal anger than it does her public role and station as queen. To the ignominy of her submission before a usurper, and to the suffering from the lack of any genuine love from Herod who, aggravating her wound, would dominate the affections of the beautgiful *Salome*, Wilde adds Herodias' sense of moral guilt. She has not only passed from emancipation and free bond into slavery, a change in status that fills her with rankling humiliation. Her serviude has debased her value as a queen in a morally questionable situation of gegal power for a usurper's grace and for her lif;e. And it is this feeling of having committed an act of moral cowardilce that sharpens her keen sensitivity to the inquiquities of Herod's command, and that causes her to cringe before the prophet Jokanaan's condemnation of herself as the harlot of Babylon. Beilng reviled by the old seer she then goads Herod to avenge the prophetgs calumnies against sher. She does so hoping to destroy the inquisitiver of her guilt and to silence the slanderous tongues of her enemies.

Both Herod and Herodias are antagonists to *Salome,* the "recessive" characters of the story action. She, however, is the filiul daughter, disobedient toward her mother, who exacts gift   and penalty alike from Herod. Thereby she estranges the Tetrarch and his queen. The young Syrian Captain of the Guard kills himself when *Salome*, in mock threat and in a spirit of defiance, attempts to kiss Jokanaanz lips. His death likewise issues from *Salome's* willful nature. That trait of willfulness is the key to her entire personality--so basic as to preclude contest. And because of it, in one of the plays most highly dramatilc strokes of theatgrical art, Heroxd commands the Roman Guard to fetch up the prophetg's head from the cistern prison

This willfulness of Salomes is , of course, of , not unmixed with another ruling passion:--that of a craving for senssual gratification. The moralist would lay a righteous stress on that attribute, branding it base, the flowering of malervolent seed, evil incarnate, the ugly aspect of "painted-woman" carnality, and so forth. The fact is that *Salome* was reared in an environment that excited and developed all of her physical senses. And, in all probability, she was dandied as a baby and breast fed. The supreme gift of the moralist is his talent for searching out the dung to feed his own piety, then labeling the result "bad blood." The truth is that *Salome's* cravilng for the sensual experience has been ingrained and sharpened under the tutelage and restrailnts of her early childhood. Her willfulness within Wilde's play action provides the means for her release. Any real value in this passion must issue from its consequences; Jokanaan's grisly death; the revelation to us of Herod and his queen's estrangement and of the psychology and dramatic, graphic nature of her sensuality. *Salome's* suffering issues from prior self abnegation as a royal daugher, and from the denial of a pleasure which seeks and finds the one device for release: a revenge against Herod for the murder of her father. Her willlfulness hardens her ourage to meet the rest of her bloody marketplace bargain. The core of *Salome's* suffering lies in her love for her dead father and the pain and anger evoked by the knowledge that his murderer, her uncle, shares her mothers bed and rules over a brothers kingdom. This entanglemetn strongly suggests the influence of *Hamlet* on Wilde's play. That is the penultimate consequences which lends genuine human value to her passion for revenge.

Wilde's prophet serves the chief dramatic function of instilling into the connotative, i.e. symbolic, action, and of contributing to the play's idea-structure, meanings of Hebraic-Christian significaance. (Note: Not all connotative meanings are symbolic.) Jokanaan's warnings of judgement, the omen he has witnessed, his denunciation of the people of carnality, of Herodias harlotry, fall in the context of "Salome's" action, at points of dramatic religious revelation--in sequences of impending crisis between evil and repentance. Wilde tells us little., however, about his characrters' religious positions. . We know that, Herod protects his life; that he is a stoic; we have *Salome's* description of him; in his looks he is hideous, "like the body of a leper," his hair ils "like clusters of black grapes that hang from the vinetrees of Edom", his mouth is "like a pomegranite cut in twain with a knife of ivory." From the moment that *Salome* first disdains his advice to seek out the *Son of Man,* (Jokanaan) till the event of his execution by herod's command, Jokanaan attempts in vain to tell men of the evil of their ways, and to warn them of angered punishment. Ostracized from society imprisoned in the cistern, knowing Herodias' contempt and Herod's indulgence as a seer yet as a slave enterred, the prophet suffers not only physical hardship; he also suffers a form of exile, his life tolerated among barbarians. As a zealot he must, in addition, endure the hard hearts of iniquiitous ways of his temperoral king, of the Babylonians, and of the slaying by Salome's request, cunning in her beauty. That's a selflessness in Jokanaan that reminds one of the same quality in Prince Muiskin in Dostoievsky's novel *The Idiot.*

Last among Wilde's charcters in whom he gives the faculty and power to suffer, to endure pain and the knowledge of its causes, is the young Syrian soldier. It is patent that he ends his brief claim upon life by suicide sprung from humiliation over his failure to perform his soldier's duty. Charged with the protection of *Salome* from harm, dishonor and the unseemly incident of suicide, he kills himself when *Salome* choses the beggar Jokanaan to please her desires. I suspect that, secretly, he also may have loved her, although the soldier's code is the more persuasive in his decision. There I hink Wilde drops the curtain on the element of sufferisng in his play.

In further analysis, one might isolate sadism in *Salome's* makeup, masochism in the Prophet's stoic acceptance of realities, or erotic fetishes of one kind or another in all of Wilde's principal characters. These would, in the main, be clinical perspectives. One might also discover meanings of religious significance more particular than those sketched in this paper. It is sufficient for the present scheme, however, that it be pointed out in the emotional, spiritual, psychological makeup and actions of these five characters, how each sufferers and causes others to suffer, And that the nature of that suffering is now shown with clarity for those go read and watch who will; since it is a truism that in both comedy and tragedy, suffering, and our consciousness of it, witnessed under the light of human reason, understanding and compassion, is a frequently a component of the finest writing in dramatric literature. Life is struggle and conflict and struggle and conflict bring inevitable suffering.

CHARACTER-FELIX, ENEMY OF PAUL

Felix feigned an equitable attitude toward Pal. He tld "the Jews to wait for the arrival of Lysias, the garrison Commander, and then he would decide Paul's "case." He acted not out a sense of justice but of fear of Rome's recall, masking that fear with apparent fair play. Felix kept Pau in chains for two years, when he knew well that Christians did not go around starting riots. Hard evidence had acquitted Paul, but Felix was irresolute in his post-trial decision to free hom.

Felix's deep sense of guilt was evidenced by lhis terror when Paul reasoned with them, Drusilla by his side , about righteousness and self-control and the judgement to come. They showd guilt before a just God. The indwelling conscience showed, as within all men. He also hoped that Paul would try to bribe him, so he sent for him from time to time from his imprisonment and talked with him. Despite the wealth attendant upon his position as Governor of Judea, he burned to possess Pauls money, the which Paul had brought to Jerusalem to help the Jews.

Yet Felix feared to condemn Paul lest he incur Romes displeasure for condemning a Roman citizen without evidence. Similarly, he feared to release Paul lest he mount a Jewish insurrection in Caesrea and all of Judea. That Paul was an outcast of the San- hedrin would have added fuel to such an insurrection. Thus Felix feared for his political position, and untimately for his life. He may well have been threatened with murder, this in part accouting for the two year delay until Festus should arrive. A price on the head of Felix, an lrony when its possible he purchased his way into power.

He coveted Paul's money and no doubt the money Paul was capable of raising among his friends for his freedom. Felixs greed worked to Pau'ls increased comfort within the prison.This was one of Felix's real abilities, and a factor in his rise to power. He manipulates Paul, his friends, Herod, the garrison Comsmander, Soldiers, the Jews--all fit into lhis machinations. That he manipulated Paul was of course, a delusion--not uncommon among tyrants, but it worked to the glory of God.

One legal, one common-law wife, gratifying his appetites, this was Felix's central problem, giving rise to vacillating behavior, willful criminality, cruelty. For him, the end justified the means. Felix's central problem was that he lacked self-control. His sensuality led him to adultery, and to the luxuries of an office that doubrtless was a political plum. He lusted for Paul's money during the two years he hoped to secure a bribe from the man. He lso was emotionnally volatile, as his terror gives eviedence when Paul preached to him and Drusilla on God's final judgement.

He quailed before Paul's righteous accussations. He succumbed to Jewish threats of insurrection. He feared, without relief, reprisaals from Rome should he let the Christian Jewish situation get out of hand; and that fear mastered him, causing him to mismanage what should have been a smple trial, even lunder Roman law. He lost his grip upon himself entirely when, terrified, he told Paul to go away for now , and when I have a more conveninent time, I'll call for you again.:"

Self-will was evidence of his emotional instability, thinly venerred by adherence to Roman customl. He was a depraved man who hated Paul, and had he possessed the ourage of a soldier--did he not require the support of a true soldier?--he would have had Paul secrertly killed by assigning a friend to do the job. Had he been a brilliant political leader, his longings might have found him mentlally deranged. Bsut Felix was too obtuse to be shocked by any force other than Paul's direct challenge to his sinning lack of self-control and the evil fruit it bore.

Repentance founded upon faith in Christ and therefrom, reasoning with them about righteousness and self-control. There would come a judgement. Felix was terrified. He invented delaying excuses. He feared to act in forthright and courageous manner, and thus to jeopardize his power. Was the succession of Festlus one of political custom and advantage, or was Felix removed by Herod Agrippa? He was unrepentant, and defied God, rejected Christ out of hand, and in a real sense, denounced Paul. Felix continued to feed on his self importance--he mollified the Jews, he washeld an importlant political prisoner, he affected ovedience to the laws of Rome, he luxuriatd in his power. Felix was incapable of inner change. He panhandled Paul for bribery money for two years

Fealix was incapable of inner change. He panhandled Paul for brivblery money for two years. Felix did not need the money. Panhandling for profit was an old habit, sufferclng. He had pandered for power and eggsed for privilege in lhis rise to powser. Being an obtuse man, it was natural for lhim to lthink it would wok again, Ultimately, Felix finds himself completely alienated.

Citizen: Some people have forgotten, some never knew about the following realities. A letter seven years old still reflects much of modern thinking in Washington, for though the man Clinton is gone--sort of--his legacy of an unpreparsed America and globalization mind-set lives on.

June 6, 1998

Representative Newt Gingrich, Speaker
U.S. House of Representatives
House Office Building,
Washington, D. C.   20515

AN OPEN LETTER TO THE UNITED STATES HOUSE OF REPRESENTATIVES

When men find deceit the pragmatic answer to the hopes of expediency, and where they sit in high places of governmenrt amongst a free people, then that nation is doomed. The Scriptures speak of those who, not having the law "are a law unto themselves." There can be no answer to duplicity but the truth; yet where it is shunned, scorned, hidden or renounced for whatever reason, then the people have no recourse whereof to protect their liberties or to mitigate injustices done unto them. The very floor and foudnation of freedom crumble beneath the onslaught of decepion as practiced by William Clinton who has demonstrated beyonthe doubt of reasonable men his contempt for the truth, for integrity of characrter and honesty of conduct, those signs which men reared in freedom have come to expect of the President.

We nowadays live in a country which were it held to account in the Congress more solicitously and more severely than liberals hold it today, would give evidence that dishonesty in government has become a way of life among liberals, both in and out of Washington.

What more can we say? Scandal upon scandal swirls around our leaders, our Congressmen, only to be denied by the President or lied about or put off for other issues, or relegated to the obscurity of time. Yet far too much proof is already patent of misconduct by the President in parfticular and by his legal and media suppoters, that we as a people should join with them in wrong.

What law is so sacred as to serve evil as a defense? Attorney-client privilege, privilege of Presidential office, interna- (p.2) tional agreement, treaties of you wlll, to promote trade with despotic powers - those alone are sufficient to challenge the minds of honest men as to their meaning, their concealed machinations. Why ought we to abet both ignorance of what we shall yet learn about the President's misconduct, his pathological lying, his juggling of the truth which, of themselves, constitute evidence revealed by Judge Starr's investigation but disclosed unabashedly by courageous editors and reporters of a free press(?). It is a caloused reality that today liberals would rather withhold or compromise the truth to protect "their man" than to make him appear disloyal to his oath of office and to the American people. This smacks of a conspiracy of agreement, if not of intent - can they yet be separated? Indeed, the liberal press is in fact the abettor of this monstrous calumny against honesty in high office and the collusion, illusory or not, puts this nation at great peril morally and physically.

President Clinton's insolence as evidenced by his indifference toward his greater electorate, except as they may embellish his power, encourages a fawning liberal media to diligently hide Clinton's lies and discrepancies of speech in order to augment and affirm that power. The power of the President's office, let it be said, is not his to possess but only to wear and to use with honor as a temporary ordination by the American people.

My purpose, ladies and gentlemen, in writing to you is snot to impugy hispersonal conduct as accsursed - that is God's domain, though it is to reprehensivle as to create disgust in the mionds sof those who have followed his inv olvement in drug trafficking, his siezure of FB I records, his peremptory firing of travel-office employees, the coverup of his amorous sadv entures, his participation of illegfal campaign contributions, to name just a few of his malordorous escapades.

My purpose in writing this letter is not to hang upon him the terrible onerous of treason, for while he may not have felt that the Vietnam was a righteous war, he need not have gone to Moscow to prove it. Moreover, while the Chinese tiger may have changed its spots, according to Mr. Clintion, trade with that expansive power of China brings great dangers to this country. Imagine if you will what missles pointed toward the United States can signify when we attemnpt to protect our ally of Tiawan by a presence of warshaips in the Formosa Straits. Is there not the hint of blackmail in this? The tiger of China cananot be separated from its tail and to postpone a reckoning with her communist leaders in hopes the Red Government will purr with humanitarian and democratic niceness is to court disaster.

My fundamental intention in writing to you, ladies and gentlemen of the House, is to charge President Clinton with derelec- (p.3) tion of duty, for the office of President of the United States is not to be bartered, sold or swayed, corrupted or weakened by emoluments from any civil or foreign power.

Clinton has albrogated the power to make treaties when he gives China most favored nation status without the concurrence of two-thirds of the Senators. When he draws up treaties of trade such as NAFTA, he does so unilaterally before the Senate can adjudicate his action. Or, having done so, they are compelled by party politics to give their assent.

Article II, Section 4 of the US Constitution states that the President shall be removed from office on impeachment for, and conviction of, treason, bribery or other high crimes and misdemeanors. Perjury in testimony regarding his conduct while in office, or his illicit instructions to others to lie, is actional misdemeanor or a high crime. It is indeed a misdemeanor that he should use his Presidential office for personal, self-seeking gratification - such as womanizing intrigues, illegal campaaign fund-raising, his granting of rewards to ohers for their malfeasance and his bribery for their testimony lies.

It is impeachable that the American President should accept bribes, a proven fact, from Chinese representatives, emissaries, businessmen, the sole purpose of which is to influence our elections and, masking Chinas's deceit as fair trade, promote himself an an internationalist in office. Power is what President Clinton seeks above all else.

What more evidence is needed to assure the American people that this man is not fit to be the leader of a great nation? Must we sit about and raise no objection to what passes as governing before our eyes, simply because we have no direct voice as a people. We are a Republic, not a true democracxy that must riot in th streets for a change of government. I am weary of hearing the shibboleth that what he does is "in the interest of the people."

I am angered, also, by what I percive as the traitorous sellout of our nation to foreign countries through the United Nations, an insidious and clandestine exchange of American sovereignty for international plaudits on the assumption that we have no limits to our endurance of his perssiflage. Be not deceived, ladies and gentlemen of the House. The member nations of the UN, excluding Canada and Great Britain, are at this moment jealous of our might, our people, our productivity, our very way of life. And it is they who would regard Americans as imbecilic bigots, ignorant minions before smaller contries that have not tasted freedom, never having fought for it or valued it above life itself. They are more accustomed to the control of the evil iron hand upon their people; we have but shown them the way out of dictatorship (p.4) into the clear air of freedom. And yet, human nature being what it is, those liberated from their chains are more likely to resent their liberators than to exult in their liberty.

Are we to be duped by a poltroon who ran from service in wartime, he who knows not either his own household, or men loyal to the people and their country except to abase them(?). A mysterious vein of vengeance flows within the soul of Bill Clinton and for that I think he not a man to be feared but a man to be distrusted.

We cannot allow this modus operandi of White House deception to continue and still claim moral leadership for our nation. No man is perfect but the leaders of America ought to present themselves as men of integrity even within error. But when lthe Commander of our military forces espouses perversion in the ranks, when he endures as legitimate and lawful the deaths of millions of unborn, when he barters away liberty (*right to life*-ad) for the power of an office that is not his to possess, in exchange for the machines and weapons that help to guarantee our freedom by physical protection - the chief function of government - than he is no longer to be trusted and ought to be removed from office. Indeed, the enormous power that he wields no lovger satisfies him, and human lives are an expenditure of his ambition.

If within the next half-century America should submit tos the charades of need and the inducements of proprganda that emanate from the UN, that agency of the world will attempt to usurp this country's legal power by force of the World Court. The LUN will declare sanctions against our trade and commerce. The UN will slowly and insidiously deplete our inflluenc, obfuscate America's moral power, her example of leadership. The Trojan Horse is within our gates. The UN will deflower our illustrious history by its urging upon publihers a revision of America's past, the excision of her great figures, patriots, soldiers, statesmen, to the end that this nation's past becomes a distorted melange of lies and chicanery. Nerver doubt for a minute, ladies and gentlmen, that Clinton is in that camp.

Let the American people remain apathetic, accepting his travesties on good works, and they will lose their country, as they (p.5) indeed are already. He has mde Independence Square in Philadelphia, a huge chunk of glorious Utah, and Yellowstone Nationnal Park to be international heritages, esentially under UN control - for "our best interests." How much more need we to suffer before that man shall be impeached before an astonished world by a lawful court of his peers?

Thank you, ladies and gentlemen, for the courtesy of your precious time and attention. My God bless you, Mr. Speaker, the members of the House of Representatives seated here - and the Unied Startes of America.

A citizen and patriot

(*Signature*

Charles E. Miller

Afterward: Sir, I would not entertain the slightest compunction against   reading his from the well of the house if ever possible,or from lthe gallery if of necessiy. May you and others of like mind and spirit be cncouragfed on your course - for the people, for our nation.

Postscript: May I add to this--that our current President Bush is trifling with the realities of history and the dangers of the present of global ambition of Red China if and when he contemplates permitting *Unical-76* perhaps *Chevron,* to sellout to the dictatorship of Red China. Remember: America's Standard Oil sold oil to Hitler to lube his blitzkreig of Poland & America sold scrapt metal to Tojo to bomb Pearl Harbor. China now owns the Panama canal--both ends, lock, stock and barrel-- therefore will use the oil deal as a blackmail device to secure what Jimmy Carter, our Naive Peacenik President, gave away. We would stupidly, mindlessly and unforgiveably repeat history-- and make the our invasion of Taiwan an almost certainty.

FRONT AND CENTER

Charles E. Miller 7-16-05

HATE A MAN, LOVE A BUZZARD

I have yet to read a clear definition of an animal right. A human right has a legal meaning, implications, applications, historical interpretations. A human right is often rooted in case law, is implicit in statutes and is built into our Constitution. But I cannot find where the right of an animal, is even remotely suggested in the basic law of the land. Is that **animal's right**, therefore, a natural Right, given to the foxes and bears and owls by God? I could understand if, like the eagle, the animal were a creature men worship in an animistic culture. Yet there is, indeed, an element of that animal worship in the Animal Rights Movement: innocent babes and helpless animals are to be treasured, at best worshipped. The Egyptian raven, the Indian rat, the Chinese monkey, the Red Man's eagle belonged to cultures that held particular animals in awe as nature worshippers'; they select(ed) the creatures they worship. The Animal Rights people, however, want to save all the animals, all of them, not just those the government declares are endangered. Their mission lacks the rationality of religions that belong to other peoples that extol certain characteristics of the chosen animal. They, the AR folks, would simply plunder human society to show man that he is no hligher in esteem and value than the animals below him. For he, too, is an animal without a soul in a godless universe. That's the gist of their "religious" ethos and philosophy.

If we can assume that animals enjoy Natural Rights, inalienable rights, and we can - you'll find religionists entering the camp of the AR's - is it brash to suggest that laws forbidding cruelty to animals already exist and that humane treatment of animals is evidenced in important sanctions, in community protecion agencies (Socity for the Proection of Cruelty to Animals) and in the Department of Agriculture oversight? Would it be too bold to say that present laws make it a crimial offense to inflict pain on pets and other captive animals, both domestic and caged specimens, and that pet hospitals and an entire field of vetenarian medicnne testify to our compassion as a society--in which the quasi-science of dog nutrition and home care is a billion dollar industry that further demonstrate society's concern for animal welfare.

Those animals used in research--white mice, prairi dogs. monkeys, frogs and cats are among them--serve a pragmatic medical purpose whose pursuit infuriates the AR's. In their minds it is no justification that cancer research, genetic engineering, investigations into the causes of epilepsy and animal-explorations into human pathologies have helped alleviate human suffering. The AR's eschew these "esperiments"" as unnecessary, accusing technicians and doctors of torturing the animals and of exploiting their (animal) rights. That's all very ;noble, but researchers do not accept animal torture as a <u>sine qua non</u>. Vivesesection has long been a dead-end practice for scientific purposes, unless, of course, the animal is rabid. Furthermore, to put an animal in pain is tnot the genesis of a successful experiment. Nor is blowing up laboratories, threatening researchers, releasing spcimens into the enviroment the way to resolve hostilities. Laws and not AR violence must be the way.

The AR's might attack race horse owners, the race tracks and betting syndicates, and the trainers of race horses in a sport that is knowingly cruel to the horse. Two or three years on the track and the animal becomes worthless except for breeding . The AR's lack the courage to do anthing about that. The domesticated animals that are precious pets to many people are over-protected. Why do not the AR's attack on that front, commanding owners to release their pets--which would in short order, become grist for the coyotes and the automobile?

If captivity is so abhorrent to the AR's why do they not attack the TV and motion picture industries that use animals for trick shots and trained- animal performances? Why do the AR's not work to eliminate Barnum and Bailey's circus and all the lesser tent shows and midway extravaganzas that employ snakes and gorillas? Why dos they not work to get a law passed, or at least a vote put to the people, that would outlaw zoos and pet shops? Or Sea World and acquariums--fish are animals--or monekys and dogs in space experiments or suburban expansion into coyote territory, or Yosemite tourism among the black bears or, for that matter, ordinances to eradicate pidgeon colonies that spread lime in city parks--and let us accord rights to grasshopper infestations. Many who do not belong to the radical, terroristic AR Movemnt have a real concern for animals--like blocking and shooting goats on Goat Island or the killing of (overpopulated) mules in Panimint Valley, or redicing the starvation members of herds of elk and deer by selctive hunting? The AR"s control oil exploration in Northern Alaska, do they not? The Carribou cannot birth under oil rigs!

So the AR's do not have enough money, and I've just admitted to all our sins? Man is the worst and most dangerous predator to the animala world. But...researchers, hunters, owners, trainers ought not to become the victim of their owns predatory kind--in numerous instances the AR's being the zealous predators.

In fact, the AR's prey on society in grotesque ways to achieve their ends. They are the terrorists and spoilers who have (money) gotten the Federal Government to back up their ambivalent crusade of save-the-animals, and without offering much protection to the animals than to offer to release them into the "wilds" or protect their questionable habitat. They would destroy the timber industry to save the Spotted Owl, never once suggestingthat the best and most up-to-date methods in silvaculture mandate selective tree cutting, preservation of the forest floor and the protection of new growth. Why haven't the AR's informed the timber industry that clear cutting produces an even growth forest that is extremely vulnerable to bark beetle infestations? Beetles, in the lalboratory, are *animal* insects.

The AR's hve extended their crusade into the insect world. It's a wonder they hve no yet given protected status to the mediterranean fruit fly or stood waiting with honey pots open for the arrival of the African lee,   Angle worms, Lady Bugs and Monarch butterflies need protection, as do alley cats, bubonic rats and flee infestsed ground squirrels. One might go on and on confronting the AR's withl their faillures in certain areas where animal protection is desperately needed--termites, wood borers and boll weavils and wheat worms. After all, life is life! Reverence for all life.... Why have you not ganged up on the abortionist? They kill millions of those little "animals' every year.

The bottom line is that the AR's are contemptuous of society's legitimate uses of the environment--no one plead a case for the slaughter of the plains buffalo except maybe the Bureau of Indian Affairs. The AR's have demonstrated that they claim their Lunatic ringe who would bomb laboratories and blind loggers and torch lumber mills; who would release experimtal Rhesus monkeys into a neighborhood, pull down power towers and risk infecting an entire community with the plague to save a species of mesquito. It is the wealthy, chiefly from the entertainmnt industry, who bail out any AR activist caught surreptitiously clipping the wire on the gorilla cage. Their attitude is--let ignorance of the animal world prevail; ship the tigers back to Asia and India and turn the chimpanzees loose in our cities. They are our evolutional cousins and will soon catch up with us. We don't need all that research and won't until mankind learns how to sharre his environment with the animals. I is a retrogressivce view, however, whose zealots will to determine the *parameters of kindness*.

FRONT AND CENTER by c. edward miller

The second ammendment to the Constitution speaks to the citizen. It is addressed to him, not to the members of the Congress, to the Supreme Court or to the President. The body of the Constitution limits the powers of the government to intrude upon the lives of its citizens.

Madison,among others at the Constitutional Convention, was a realist in that he knew by painful and long experience that unless the powers of government are restrained by law demagogues, autocrats, ambitious men of little principle will attlempt to gain control over the citizens and to rule them with a ruthless hand. The second amendment as well as the other nine of the orginal document does not delegate,either by inference or precedent or design, a powe that is extraordinary to the amendment. The key word is KEEP, the citizens a re to keep their arms, not to sh are them with the soldiery or to lend them or givethem away tothe government, or to cache them in some distant armory where they would be difficult to take up. Of what use are guns in the absence of an enemy?

To that I ask in reply: have you some special foreknowledge of when an enemy might challenge you to your life? No. Then upon the presupposslition that the FederaL government ought to ,or is commanded to by law, or must out of compassion, or deslres to, protect the citizens from each other,the Government is pleased, by no explicit or implied authority, to take your weapons away from you as naughty childrenl and unprincipled adults.

A twentieth century autocrat wil see to it that the people are defenseless until the government would rescind the 2nd ammendment without a vote of the peopleor a referendum..That t ransgression of the peoples' rights led to one revolution; to consistently and flagrantly abrogate established laws can lead to a second American revolution.

APHORISM

A poor man seldom meets up with a vagabond
king, but a wealthy man has the poor with him
always.

HAMLET

Hamlet's loyalty to his father was indissoluably linked to his concern for Denmarks's internal stability; the which stood in danger of popular uprisings of the people if fomented by knowledge of a crime against the throne. These dispositions, a reality of character and of social law through custom, in part motivated Hamlet to avenge the king's murder. The College Theatre production dramatically realized the fabric true of a situation peculiar to period and place, but more importantly, of the two sorts of allegiances. There rose up before us the human, tragically personal loyalty of Hamlet to blood, and the larger social allegiance to the Danish people both of which gave the iron thrust of rightness to an act of revenge.

Court costumes, the regalia of soldiery and exposition of the Fortinbras battlefield prelude, to be sure, lent scope to Hamlet's struggle. But what stood foremost in James Clancy's taut , at times almost wildly anguished, brooding portryal of a Hmlet who suffered reflection to innervate his action when so keenly outraged by the foul crime, was the quality of paintully heightened awareness of wrong done. It is to the credit of Mr. Clancys acting that of those two loyalties, the inner man and the real tragic Hamlet, emerged as the central all all-absorbing fascination of the play. The loyalty of son and heir to the murdered king, the near worshipful manner of Hamlet that was so profound in its very intensity in these opening ghost scenes, imbued the prince with the motive of personal revenge. But Hamlet was, above all, driven by a personal code of moral integrity that predisposed him to avenge the crime against his father. His was an integrity intrinsic to a just and equable rulership. Not only through his lines, but in his half-frenzied way, the rise and fall of his passion in scenes of contemplation, Mrs. Clancy showed us the inner Hamlet as a man tortured by the harbingers of a persoal destiny whose dilemma lay in the mode of action--or inaction--for we were made to realize the terrifying grandeur of a man wracked by the contemplation of a dastardly crime.

Mr. Clancy's interpretation, furthermore, was emotionally a growing thing, felt rooted in the anguish of a gross wrong and rendered with a gripping naturalness of expression. *(Note: I"m afraidI disagree here--I found it painfuly stilted far too often. MB)* The opaque quality of his voice gave it a youthfulness, so much unlike the ghost's , that enthralled by the spectre and the tomb-like, commanding quality of his voice, we looked for Hamlet's actions and half-madness of his tormented speech to give us a different sense of authority-- kingliness and nobility. Clancy acted with his whole body. One of the best examples occurred in the scene where he was alone and, wrenched by thoughts of the crime and his mother's baseness, he stumbled in stricken dismay about the room. We were given to feel that there were forces within him which, like the truth, would out. *(Note: This was at lest his intent though I was not convinced by it, except as a some device of performance. MB)*

I felt that the wills of Claudius and Hamlet would eventually clash, and because I came to believce in the young Prince and to share his struggle, I knew there would be some terrifying climax in which, beyond physical defeat, Hamlet would make known the iron of his rightness. One of the qualities of the (College) Theatre production was, in fact, as I have suggested, the very freshness and the impressions it gave that I was seeing the play almost for the first time. What contibuted so pointedly to that impression was that naturalness of the speeches. Polonius, for example, in instructing Laertes how he should conduct himself in England, could not have shown more naturalness at that spot where he lost the thread of his thought and called for his son to help him find it. *(Note: No, that's the line with...identifies ...the spy in Laertes.)*

Tha nauralness, otgether with simplcity, pervaded the clean, functional settings, whose sugesrtive rather than representational design was the more artful, allowed for concentration upon action and were in keeping with the spirit of th play in their strength and dignity.
(Note: Not sufficiently giving the effect of spaciousness and majesty; throughout. MB) Yet if there was art and not artifice in the externals of spectacle, so was there art apparent in such scenes as the play within the play scene. Neither Claudlius nor Gertrude gave away their knowledge of portending incident of the king's disturbed flight, not because the play demanded their abandon to silence and blindeness, but becaue each was enmehed in the inscrutableness, artfully prepared

for, of Prince Hamlet and so they watched, unsuspecing of the ironic trick, tumult of the court an disaster of Claudius own self-revelation and annihiltion to come. By their very initial delight in a play, followed by the kings perturbed questions, we saw a scene building to a dramatic tension and outcome that confirmed with believability Hamlet's suspicions. For the modern audience, that scene invited the suspenion of disbelief in a ghost and his auguries. *(Note: You are a good play goer. This was the intent, though I thought Kerr, as Claudius, bungled it. MB)*

John Kerr conveyed the understanding that King Claudius was secure only in that the murder had been done, and that he wore the crown badly, owning the bold cowardice of a crimina'ls bravery. In the inner play scene, he and the queen seemed to cling to each other. There was a fervent manner associated with the unassuaged guilt in the very way that he knelt at his prayers. And he seemed always to be speaking though Gertrude, to be listening from behind her robes as Polonius, or example, offered the king and queeen a reason for Hamlet's strange actions. *(Note: but is this your understanding of Claudius? He seems more <u>collected</u> to me in the play. MB)* Mr. Kerr put across that his air of gross pretense ill-masked a quaveryng guilt. Thus did he set off more magnificently, more dramatically the inner nature of Hamlet, his nobleness of conduct and manner and his inner sensitivity and ethical righness within suffering.

One of the most beautiful jobs of sacting was Mary Campbell's as Ophelia. In her scene, where he sang in a gentle, girl- like, almost frail voice, she caused us to feel the quality of her tenderness drawn out of her deep love for Hamlet, a love that gave genuine poignancy her sadness. "Frailty, thy name is woman suited Ophelia as well as the queen; Ophelia's frailty sprang from her very innocence. Polonius' solicitous command that she not see Hamlet again, and Hamlet's protestations of love for her all focused on that one important facet of her being--her capacity to love and tob e loved.

Elziabeth Loeffler's playing of Gertrude was, despite the finer moments as in the inner play scene and when her son confronted her with her crime, rather disappointling. Her acing was sharp, nervous, brittle and, I felt, emotionally shallow. *(Note: Carefuly chosen adjectives, and all correct ones. MB)* But so was the nature of Demmark's queen shallow--nevertheless what solicitude she felt for Hamlet, what lust she knew for Claudius, all taken for her <u>degeneration beneath royal robes</u> *(Note: good phrase MB)* did not effectively come across.

Mr. Gillis, withal though, did an excellent job in casting, suiting voices and physical stature to the image of each part and providing for sufficient contrasts of voice, features and outward signs to individualize his characters. The acting was subtle and sensitive and the drama in the lines, excepting Gertrude's, exploited to the fullest. Ineed, the play moved, too, with a nice rhythm and timing, the king and queen, hearing about Ophelia's death down by the stream, while they stood with retinue in the corridor, the scene behind the curtains being changed in the intermim. The College Theatre produced a truly dramatic interpretaion of the Bard's tragedy and, for my part, one long to be remembered for its sensitivity and honesty.

AN OPEN LETTER TO THE SUPREME COURT
OF THE UNITED STATES

Consistent with the Constitutionally granted Judicial Review there arise a numer of issues from Roe v Wade (410 US 113; 1973)
which the Court now addresses, particularly those stemming from substantive changes in medical technology. Statutory law is vulnerable to changes in circumstances because, unlike the written Constitution, a legislated statute sometimes tends to lose applicability to the demands of time. In the matter of Roe v Wade, the tolerance has taken on the *force of command* when precedent dictates participation by acceptance. I am intolerant of abortion, and increasing numbers of American are. Therefore, I object to the Court's decision in the original (1973) judgement.

Roe v Wade is political. It is so, and it is made to seem so, thus to affix the approval of elective constitutionality upon its painful and lasting consequences when the mandate of the decision is for toleration and not for law enforcement. In sixeen years of practice, elective abortion has come to stand for the "truth" of free choice and therefore, by sheer numbers of participants, a tyranny of truth for other men in our society. Yet conformity to precedent my be conformity to bad law.

In any enterprise it is hazardous when the outcome is consequent upon numbers and not the conmands of conscience. Crowd-mind governs the former conspiracy of choice, and lest I seem indelicate to say so, I think society's performance under Roe v Wade contains an element of that corrupt "mind," of behavior without conscience, of pitiless self-gratification or stupid indifference.

According to what I read, the State's interests are two-fold in this instance of abortion: The State has *"an important and legitimate interest in preserving and protecting the health of the pregnant woman,"* regardless of any question of her residency. This commences at the end of the first trimester, the woman thereupon acting only on the advice of a competent physician.

The State has *"another important and legitimate interest in protecting the potentiality of human life."* This "compelling interest begins at viability. But the question arises: When does "potentiality" begin? Hopefully, that is one of the elements the Court will consider, for it affirms the sanctity and the value of life in the womb, most certainly when the foetal infant's heart begins to beat and it starts to feel pain, these facts being true even if one disagrees that life begins at conception..

The science of post-natal and pre-natal care is changing. The date of viability is shifting toward conception, and the trimester guide for determining viability is, it would appear, becoming less meaningful as a deterrent to abortion. To get in "under the wire," as it were, for non-viable abortion, young women are coming into the abortuaries earlier in their pregnancy. Yet, paradoxically, clinics record an increase in the number of late-term abortions, some as late at 30 weeks. A law (Roe v Wade) that is so ill-defined as to time limits, that is subject to a sliding scale of application, constant revisions in application; that is confusing in questions of risk, legality and follow- up care is a law that is certainly too sweeping and therefore voidable. Since it is a vague law and a bad law, it tolerates numerous sorts of license and indulgences, therby ruling out what must be the basis for sound law --consistency and conformity in its application to anticipated circumstances.

The right to have an abortion is not a fundamental right under the Constitution. *Privacy is only presumptive after the fact* in order to validate the act being tried. A majority of the states have had restrictions for over 100 years. The reasons are what the pro-abortionists ignore yet have been handed down as common human knowledge about life for milleniums, to wit, that the quickening of the foetal infant demonstrates life, that *premies* can be cared for, nurtured and saved; that midwivery is a useful medical profession in rural areas, and that ultra-sound and other technology reveals the the foetal heart is beating at the time of *interuterine murder*. Since the advent of sound visualization and sophisticated aminosentesis testing for sex, deformity and normal interuterine growth, medical science confirms that life as all men know it outside the womb resembles the pulsing life of those yet unborn. To assert the protoplasmic nature of the expelled aborted foetus is a lie that for sixteen years your Court has encouraged the ignorant to accept.

Furthermore, it is a known fact that the heartbeat of the foetus begins about the fourth week. If a flat EKG wave or EEG (brain) wave indicates death, certainly a heart beat indicates human life in the womb. That seems to me a logical assumption. Then why does your Court and many doctors infer that the aborted life is only protoplasm? Have you conspired with the American Medical Association, Planned Parenthood, the abortuaries to exterminate an entire generation of over 30,000,000 infants, most of whom were viable when disposed of in the trash? You obviously lack the courage to act responsibily as jurists, deeming the **rules of your game** the essence of truth. I put Caesar's words into your mouths: "What is truth?"

Not long after the heartbeat is first audible, the foetal child has the capacity to feel pain. Yet the abortion proceeds in the most cruel and calloused manner, severing the limbs of the squirming, protesting infant by powerful suction or burning it to death and, lately, allowing birth except for the head which is punctured and its brains sucked dry. You assenting magistrates quality for the Aztec priesthood who worshipped with live sacrifices. You bare your inhuman and immoral cowardice for prestige and power. For a civilized society to participate in this sort of death of the voiceless victim--without representation as having a life of its own is heinously barbaric. I am ashamed of our country before God for a Court--and a society-- that ever brought about this wholesale murder by its decree of tolerated murder.

Now we have not just the vagueness of the law and its inapplicability as law, as sociological fiat. We must stand idly by and countenance, witness, the utter barbarism in the surgical suite of *"treatment for pregnancy."*

Roe v Wade did not envision clerical manipulation by Planned Parenthood officials to persuade the pregnant mother that abortion was not a choice but the only choice. But that's the reality, since Planned Parenthood rarely ever suggests alternatives to its fanati death verdict. Their current ruse for conealment of their power-play motive is to suggest that perhaps "abstention" is a way to avoid pregnancy. Their entire organiztion is built upon the lie that God is uncaring whereas they are the tender-hearted. And that abstention , while not wrong as such, is against nature taking its course.

Roe v Wade does not undergird the feminist movement --as street crowd scenes, marches, rallies, dismal coathanger displays and back-alley warnings would have us to believe. The movement can and does exist without interuterine dismemberment--for other worthy causes of their agenda.

Pathetically and with the ominous lack of foresight, Roe v Wade makes no provision for the follow-up treatment, psychological disturbance (chronic depression and suicide), guilt feelings, psychniatric consultation, grief for the aborted infant, etcetera. Assuredly the Supreme Court has not supported the State's "legitimate" linterest for lnaught in protecting the health of the pregnant woman, although you will concede, I think, that the State's interest in the mother's health should mandate these measures also.

The State's *compelling interest in the potentiality of life*--**by this date an abssurd lie--** should also figure into the equation of the law that the destrluction of life rests upon. These appendages to abortion and extensions of the law by its very consequences, are largely ignored in the clamor for "rights" The fetal infant's body is not the mother's body. It has a separate brain, circulatory system and heart beat. If the pregnant woman has no interest in her baby, why should the State show an interest. The discrepancy makes a sham of the law since the State is merely alleging protection for what it denies the right to exist, an infant in the womb.

Ask yourselves, does the unborn have a right to protest the agony of dismemberment or burning? In the Middle Ages death was administered by having horses pull the limbs from the condemned in different directions. Foetal dismemberment is the same without the alleged crime--executioners! Does the mother have psychiatric or spiritual help? The amswers are "no." and therefore the State's twofold interests are a fiction, a shibboleth to deflect from your court's facade the charge of irreponsibility. Indeed, that is precisely where the Court stands today --irresponsible toward the life of the unborn baby. Despite your lofty legal language, the Court cannot plead otherwise, and indeed stands above justifying its ruling .

The Roe v Wade dedcison contemplated the consultation with the pregnant woman by a competent physician. But that transfer of not just medical implications but of advice, concern, and informed alternatives to other persons does not happen. The AMA, through its pro-abortionists, represents to the woman through the doctor, the informed alternative of death by inexperienced coat-hanger quackery hands. For the most part, only the pregnancy-crisis counsllors have been able to reach the woman from the streets, despite vociferous objections by clinic personnel and intimidation by the police, despite the free-zone ruling. In the absence of such counselling the woman is *left uninformed--contrary to expectations under Roe v Wade*. Further complicating matters is that in many if not most states, parental consent for an abortion is *not required* of minors.

In Bellotti v Baird (443 US 622; 1979) the Court *struck down the requirement of parental notification and consultation* in every case; and required that the law provide an alternative counsel where the parents were not involved. Similarly, in H. L. v Mathesh (450 US 398; 1981) the State was required to furnsh an independent decision-maker for the pregnant minor in cases where the parents were not consulted. This procedure exhibits one consistency that should trouble the minds of enlightened men: the parents are *intentionally excluded* from pregnancy counselling. This is by the design of Planned Parenthood, (Hitler-Himmler "final solution was also **planned**) whenever they can reach the girl early. The mother-to-be, frightened, perhaps ashamed to tell lher parents, may go to the abortuary principally upon th advice of a condmon-dispensing health official at the school, or upon the goading of teenage friendls. Thus the "fully informed consent" anticipated under Roe v Wade is a lie; the information about altlernatives is either denied to the mother, or the stipulation within the cour'ts written opinion is ignored altogether. After all, who cares about the opinion? It's the ruling that counts in the popular mind.

Members of the court have pointed out that the trimester division is legislative; that the State is not a doctor trying to establish viability; that the Supreme Court is not a science review board; and that a *"truly informed consent"* is just that. Bureaucratic endorsement of the death dentence is *not* an example of a fully informed extermination of life.

Justice Willliaml H. Rehnquist has pointed out in a dissenting opinion in the Roe v Wade case that *"The difficulty in concluding, as the Court does, that the right of 'privacy' is involved in this case."* And I concur. The appellant's charge that the Texas statute Articles: 1191-1194 land 1196 invaded her right to chose to terminate her pregnancy is illusory, since *that* "right" is not explicitly mentioned in the Constitlution, and is no longer"private" once the State intervenes to declare its compelling interest in her health and the "potential life" of the foetal infant.

Must the State therefore shirk its responsibllity in these matters, abjure its interest in the pregnancy by default on a decision not to intervene; must the State condemn its practice of limited care and willfully suborn future mothers under the same feeble pretext of deprivation of privacy so that, in the years to come, the "State though the Supreme Court assumes the platonic, priestly role of family-size adjudicator, as is the case in China where the small family is applauded and controlled? At this juncture, today, the Court's role is see,ingly benign, but there can be no preservation of a right (privacy) without a corresponding surrender of a privilege (state protection) and the libertty to make that choice. Therefore, the irony of the privacy plea is that its affect and persuasion will ultimately destroy the conern for health and life the State seeks to preseve. While the State's funcdtion is to fix qualifications of 'the aborting physician, his licensur'e and the standards of the facility where the procedure is performed, its protection issues from intervention. It cannot be otherwise.

Justices White and Rehnquist (concurring) have stated that Roe v Wade has no support in the language of the history of the Constitlution to support th Court's judgement. *"The upshot is that the people and the legislatures of the 50 states are constitlutionally **disentitled to weigh the relative importance** of the continued existence and development of the foetus on the one hand against a spectrum of possible impacts on the mother on the other hand. As an exercise of raw judicial power, the Court perhaps has the authority to do what it does today: But in my view its judgmet is an improvident nd extravagant exercise of the power of judicial revied which the Constitution extends to this court."*

The justices continue: *"In a sensitive area such as this, involving as it does isssues over which reasonable men may easily and heatedly differ, I cannot accept the Court's exercise of its clear power of choice by interposing a Constitutional barrier to State efforts to proteect human life and by investing mothers and doctors with the constitutionally protected right to exterminate it. This issue, for the most part, should be left with the people and to the politiical processes the people have devised to govern their affairs."*

Again, I must certainly concur. By establising a point in time to claim a compelling interest by the State, the Court has acted capriciously and with a superintending power not within its grasp to mediate between nature and medical science, human wishes and the birth trauma, a mother's poor judgemet and a life yeanring to be born. The Court, in short has taken upon itself the role of God.

In Due Process established and guaranteed by the 14th Amendment (Sec. 1) abridged by the States' intrusion, has, ironically, made the privacy claimed by the appellant in Roev Wade unattainable because of exposure to the State's interests and intervention that *supervenes Due Process!* While it is a a juridical procedure, it is no less a spirit of giving due attention to all factors entering into a pregnancy situation, and according respect, civil and human, to the mother and the unborn life within her. Acknowledgement of the State's compelling interest is not an abridgement , but rather a support to expose all relevant factor and conditions. Were secrecy the only way of claiming privacy, there could be no appeal for the protection of Due Process since such an appeal would be nugatory. And were the abortion consummated without intervention either by the State or by other parties, the" privacy" claimed would be anarchy against the unborn and a level of arrogance that denies society's stake in all human life whatsoever, clearly incomprehensible to civilized men.

Long lists of those, poor and rich alike, wanting to adopt a child are a well known reality, but their desire is denied by abortionists for reasons repugnant to life and dis-serving to society: money, red tape, power to control, naked arrogance. The adoption procedure might be improved upon greatly. Since 1973, the lethargic Christian commnity has gotten off its hands and, among some congregations, is providing aid, love, counselling pregnancy-crisis help and adoption referrals. May that continut to do so.

Why short out the amendment process on an issue so important and controversial? That is exactly what the Court has one in Roe v Wade, *legislating a method* rather than *adjudicating the law.* The Court's stance has tended to blight pro-life legislation. Furthermore, it is specious reasoning by the Court to lend sanction for an act whose consequences are still not settled, simply because a State's law merits support (Texas criminal code). If a man delierately shoots his infant daughter, is he to be exonerated so thet the murder might not jeopardize his right to keep and bear arms? The abortion-privacy connection is the same specious **non sequitur.** Murder the infant in order to preseve the mother's privacy. That is the work of a gang of authenticated idiots, not of an august Court of Last Resort.

Roe v Wade conceals the reality of the means and the end result of the extermination of life that is being contemplated. I call that a crime in intention and execution, , if not before the first trimester, certainly after the first trimester in disregard for the State's two-fold interest in the mother's health and the foetal life potentiality. Today this very minute, great numbers of abortions (sic) are being performed in second and third trimester pregnancies and at birth-time, called "late term" How genteel! How politiclly correct!

That this nation's most august Court should bend to the pragmatic persuasions of women who must not be inconvenienced or embarrassed smacks of willful negligence toward the rest of sociehy. For as you well know, abortion on demand is drifting perceptibly in the direction, by inference and consensus , toward death on demand (with dignity). From there the State can become the incredible monster that, we thought, had expired with lthe Nazi defeat, ordering (condoning) deaths where convenient, of the crippled, the malformed, the terminally ill, the old, the racially mixed. We in America are headed toward the mindset would support the scientific breeding of the master American, the ideal Yankee, perfect in all respects. Who will set the standards? Who, in fact, marks out the quality of life the unborn ought not ever to see, ought not to try to enjoy. That is unmitigated arrogance!

Let me tell you, as a private citizen, that we are--all of us--in jeopardy as the *sanction* of the law by the State takes on the stature of an *order* by the State. Ought we, ought the Court, to be persuaded by the pragmatism-- that "life is what we say it is"? to mimic that arrognce as the gatekeepers into life?

Please exercise compasson and wisdom in your deliberations. We have lost a full generation to the abortionists by this cruel and mindless insanity of extermination of the voiceless, the defenseless unborn. Where is your conscience? Weep, lest our hearts become hardened against our own people and against a sovereign God. Thank yhou.

THE CHRISTIAN ETHOS OF
AMERICA'S BEGINNING

In looking over early documents, including the Declaration of Independence, speeches by Washington and Lincoln, letters by our founders disclosing their motives for action, the causes for their solidarity in the settlement and promotion of this nation, it is unavoidable to all but the doubters and the ignorant that the Christian faith has played a powerful hand in the founding and progress of this nation. Certainly America's beginnings were not inspired by Buddhism, Shintoism, Hinduism, Islam, Taoism,or any of the Polytheisms of the ancient Greeks and Romans. The Mayflower voyagers did not carry with them prayer wheels, clay Buddhas, blessed tapers, runic bones or talismanic charm-pieces. All of which is to say that the origins of America are and contnue to be fed by the taproot of its Christian heritage, its belief in God, its accession to certain doctrines and manner of government that still influence our conduct as a people and as a world power.

Who is unaware that the Puritans' distrust of men because of their capacity to sin was not, is snot, evident in the structure of our Government which, therefore, has built within its system of checks and balances the comprehension of God's natural laws of sin and retribution. The very concept of the separation of powers is much more profound than the alleged Eu;ropean class antagonism of sa nobility sersus the rabble, as was true in France's 1889 Reign of Terror. Chcks and balances were and are to provide a mechanism for keepin men's lust for power in check and tyranny at bay. This structure has worked for over two hundred years and is a model for emerging nations.

If men were perfect, less and less capable of doing wrong, as modern behaviorists allege, then the framers of the Constitution would not have placed explicit limits on the powers of the Contress. They would have declared that all Representatives instituted perfect laws without flaw and therefore an interpretive

Court system to examine Statutory and case laws need not exist. They would hve given the President a king's powers, knowing him to be perfect--some feared that was Washington's intent. And tlhey would not have placed expliciat limits on the three branches of our Federal Government that are detailed in the Constitution: Executive, Legislative and Judicial. And they would not of a certainty have screated the Bill of Rights to to protect the citizens from the miscalculations and grievances caused by their own government. Those rights were not written for the use of demagogues to circumvent the will of the people, as by Judicial activism and Legislative fillibustering. There was truly an "evolution" toward our freedoms, from Feudalism up throughs the *Magna Carta* and Case Law which the Colonists brought with them, thence to the Mayflower Compact, the Colonial Articles of Confederation, and finally, to the Constitution that originated in Philadelphia. Many of the framers were Diests; yet to the man there was no confirmed athiest among them. Jefferson's ***Bible,*** from which he excised Christ's miracles, does not prove his anti-Christian beliefs, only that he did not believe in mircles by a Man though a Prophet, a belief that was the product of his European Enlightenment.

The emergence of liberty as we know it, and bound as it usually was to land ownership and wealth yet, in all, affixed to the State of mens affairs and position in society, implied in their minds the reality of mans capacity to do wrong, call it ***sin*** against God or , to commit wrongs against their fellow human beings. Religious faith, as embodied in the liturgy of the Middle Ages, was often intertwined with demonology. Calvin in His ***Institutes*** brought enlightenment by God's reasoning to the Protestant church.to resolve doctrinal issues. That believers accepted their position as *The Elect* was core to his creed. That presumption of original sin and salvation of the Elect brought in their train not only persecution but the contrition of re-examination of accepted church doctrines. In early New England there followed the misguided zealotry and the cruelty of the Salem witchcraft trials. The point is not whether this dialectic of religious doctrine and fervor of worship worthy of truth was expunged, but that the notion of Man's natural sinfulness survived to the extent that it was made manifest in our hallowed documents and our invidious way of life here in America.

Christianity has always had its apologists and its defenders-- as the Crusades to defeat Islam in th Old Byzantine Ottoman Empire. Yet bloody as those crusades were --and indeed within our own Civil War *both* sides petitioned God to help them--the regenerative and protective power of that Christian faith will continue to be felt in the freedoms of our society and the document that invests and continues our specific liberties. The Theocracy of the Puritan community cannot of course take the place of our modern society. But if is inescapable that given the radical, cruel and malicious indulgence of the Salem farmers' punishment , based upon the *Spectral Evidence* of the pubescent girls, there was *no establishment* of an unconfined scope of man's rights by law and liberty of conscience or by practice, that should extend to modern-day America. Such an open-ended interpretation would have sanctioned anarchy as a "right."

The errors of men's natural reasoning and predisposition to sin only emphasize the desireability of secular education. That Man possesses a soul gives him value above the animals and therefore we Americans have created caring hospice centers that affirm the value of human life. We hve initiated the movement for unwed mothers faced with abortion or economic starvation. Ollur religious faith is the source of compassion for the poor as practiced by the Salvation Army, as found in orphanages, children and women abuse homes, etc.; the deliberate, conscionable giving of medical and food aid to the starving and diseased and to our enemies reflects God's mercy... In no other nation in the world is there a like spirit of compassion for human needs, which humanitianism issues from its core Christian belief in the value of human life mirrored in the doctrine of God's redemption of Man and, for the Creationist, that man was created in God's image.

Agnostics and athiests, inspired by their own godless groups and institutions, have tried to eliminate the display of religious symbols, deeming them to be cheap and niggardly expressions of religious intolerance in the name of worship, yet because of our heritage, they are consistent with our history and ought not to be expunged from a free society since they are passive tokens of faith devoid of the intent or the animation to *establish a religion.*

Those who adjudicate he efforts of the Christian community, so called, do themselves and greater society a disservice , for they have used the flaws, the failures, the intolerance down through the centuries to thwart and denegrate the noblest expressions of faith in America over her history, to this very day. The practices of the Christian faith represent the permanence of its *ethos* in this country; and it is hardly to be expected that any oligarchy of secular intolerance would destroy the work of its hands in order to affect an appearance of neutraliy-- which is but the expression of an unaccommodating *exterminationism.*

Through debate, if reason is the arbiter, then reason cannot help but point to the liberty Americans enjoy today, brought to fruition not by the despotisms of denying its expression and use by men of power, but by showing how the enlightenment of reason and the spirit of Godliness, work together under our system of Government and, in charitable deeds with , food, medicines, housing, clothing and other kinds of humanitarian relief in our society. These ministries of liberty in action do nof come from a godless people. That truth will withstand the assaults of the incredulous pagans.

Therefore, the question of human liberty does not revolve around non-faith or irrationality but out of faith together with reason and sound judgement or, in the vernacular, *common sense*. In a direct and visible manner faith supervenes to reinforce reason, not to cancel it out. The question then can be raised as to whether or not the Judeo- Christian God is a destroyer of an enlightened society.

It is certain that we do not live in a pagan culture or there would occur no instance of our compassionate help. Yet there is, reasonably, no purpose, for example, in eliminating the Cross from a State insignia (New Mexico, California) or a creche from the lawn of a believer or for that matter *St. Augustine's Confession* from the shelves of a secular school library, or the music of Christmas from speaker systems in the park; or preaching from streetcorners as the Salvation Army has done in the past. These examples of the Christian *ethos* have come under fire at different times by oligarchic pressure groups, including elite members of the "free press" who, wish to neutralize American society in its religious public displays, who desire that a religiously sterile body politic is consonant with the history of our nation--which is a lie! At this juncture historical revisionism enters in. The perpetrators of this vendetta to eradicate any and all signs of the Judo-Christian faith revolt in order to effectively deny the truths of our history and to prove their own destiny. They find a salutary value in their self-alienation, which is pride. And they exhult in their rejection of the majority faith, which is "sanity."

TOWARD A PHILOSOPY OF CRITICISM

The "statics," or fixed locii, of denotative words apperceived by symbols of the langage, are by their very nature of those symbols a **mode** of language on the page, a non-fluid medium which is primitive in its simplicity of reference. This is true of sophisticated, "open dictionary" French and English in particular. While in the mind of the reader, the intended co-textual interpretations of the author to reader are only partially, and imperfectly, realized. That partial understanding is due to the primitvism just described. Individual words collect associated objects of reference that enrichen their denotative meaning. This fact is, of course, a truism.

Linguists down through time are noted for their dissatisfaction with commonplace matters, such as interpretation and meaning-analysis, which are not identical basics, the former responding to usage, the latter to academic examination. Spratt in the 17th century of the British Royal Academy of Arts and Sciences attempted to legislate for a *nominalistic* use of language, a scientific application of language in which all or more commonly used words were to be reduced to mathematical and totally objective denotative meanings. He found, as he must have and others like him, lhat such **Nominalism** again encounrters the dilemma put into practice by exerimental novelists, such as G. Stein, Joyce, et al--whose wish to maintain a precision which is necessarily "static denotatively yet capable of rendering a fluid stream of connotations as the words progress across the page. To have it both ways so that words like *throne*, *dream* and *wolf* have but one denotation while they gather to themlselves, **accrete**, a variety, infinite in theory, of associative connotations. Spratt's failure represents the failure of language to recreate experience in its totality. Upon this premise, indeed pehaps starting here, Deidre, the French philologist, built his theory of *deconstruction*. In doing so he attempted to fashion experience into a mode of language that was non-definitive and impersonal , thence to exceed interpretation into the realm of irrelevancy and therefore become meaninglessness, which, I think, is where Deconstruction as a useable philosophy remains today.

To arrive at such a duality of references, back to the **denotative** and **connotative**, these symbols of language are inadequate for tha author who is a **Nominalist**,since the communication between author and reader is visual. The Nominalist distrusts the moving, shifting, fluidity of the connotive text. We, howweer, are tempted to experiment, therefore, to employ other sorts of symbols to achieve this duality; one such symbol is musical notation, whose *transliterative meaning* is program music. which by its very nature attempts to evoke the sounds and moods of theme brought to the composition.. Mathematical signs are another, the concretionsl transposed into the abstract of innumerable mind experiences. Math being that final fixation upon the immutable *ideal* of an experience, it escapes thereby the category of linguistic *accretism*. Einstein's theory of the curvature of space hypothsizes the continuum of space, time and motion along which there is no absolute and unalterably fixed point of reference. There is only an infinity of potential reference points by which gavitational pull, solar movement, the motion and character of light photons can be calculated. The language *Nominalists* would like to achieve the steadiness of denotative references, using also the flexibility of a theorectical application-idea for the image. And why not? But then we are in a quandry since the abstract is too elusive to find a symbolic association with a denotative word. At this juncture either the picture will emerge or the feeling, its form either an abstraction or an image, the more poweful in the mind engaged crowding out the other.

Light is not fixed in time, nor is the duration of photonic displauy specified, nor the quality of the light rays-- alpha, gamma, beta, infra-red, etc. Yet the word *light* conjures up a familiar visual experience of a world whirling in space, light breaking through clouds having the character of whiteness associated with visible light. The semantic symbol of light specifically refers to the visible phenomenon, yet is sufficiently abstract to permit the reader to fill the symbol with personal experiences caught up from his own imagination. Thus an abstract word like light doth fragment into innumerable human experiences some of which will never be revealed even with mind-altering drugs.

Thus it would seem that the closest to a dual function for the linguistlic symbols which the experimentalist may hope to use is the selection of those symbols which describe qualities rather than objects having masses with names conveniently agreed upon.

To the extent that words rich in connotations take precedence over named objects, the character of the prose will approach the abstract character of music and the linguistic symbols will attain to a specificity and fluidity at one and the same time. This sort of writing is commonly called *lyrical.* Language, written and spoken has approached the duality, in the use of euphemisms, to the primitive world that names things and yet lyricizes their hidden feeling. In a common French school begun with Melarme, the poet finds image qualities and word-sounds of greater fascination than objects of mass and shape that are the subject of the poem. .

Obviously the writer cannot say, "the creamy yellow came up over the sombre shdows," to sustitute for the denotative "The moon rose over the ridge." The first statement is lacking in precision of visual definition and appeal and power, the absence of the visual being without contact in nature and therefore almost meaningless. Much of Melarme's poetry is of that sort. A rigid, disciplined use of connotative words to replace, on the instant, the denotative context is confusing to the reader, for it is a quality of the human mind that to receive or render a communication he must conceptualize, with denotations, the thrust of his thought. The promise and genius of this use of language is that the accretions to one word, mentioned earlier are as infinite as the stars, and could, if given time and space, reflect the myriads of indiviual experiences that accrete to that word. That is where the artist's selective process begins, the homing down of connotative meaning, the capacity to paraphrase with accuracy.

The key to the riddle of connotative selection lies in the author's willingness to chose those subject words that are richest in connotations while achieving movement, a fluidity of the structured denotated images. At best, he places or invests a superficial imposition upon experience while rendering a word consciously multi-interpretive. The controlled enlargement of meaning is the end he sought. Puns and double-intendre are but poor examples. A better one is found in allegory, synechdoche and allusion.

Here I find the argument is centrepetal, moving toward already known philsophies of into interpretive expression. The idea is to save the centrality of the expression, to be symbolized and mathetmatically literate at the same time. It appears to me that in addition to the restoration of the interpretive faculty to a place of legitmacy, we should accept precision of meaning without trying to impose rigidity of application ; that is, agree upon the semantically-produced texture of aesthetic experiences without trying for too great a literal representation of the true nature of those experiencs. The singular danger with this approach to writing is that is is obscurantist. Without a standard or denotative literacy it is almost, if not, impossible to communicate with a reader of intelligence.

Extreme literalism can lead also in only two directions: into the art of music where the fluid experience is better articulated by music's sounds and combinations of sound; and a G# is sufficiently abstract to be barren, in and of itself, of associate literary experiences: Or toward the accumulation of masses of scientific data in a Science of Linguistics having dissociated itself from the relativism of denotative methodology and clear, precise denotative use of the language. This use of language is a form of dilitantism by which is very hard to understand meanings. (**Note:** sounda G# to most people and they will hear imply a lnote struck, atoned. But say the word collision" and an infinite variety of associated experinces will be or can be imagined. Now play the *Air on A G String* and for other listleners, the mood and emotion aroused is not connectsed to any particular note in the composition with the flowing movfement of the whole-- except the key lsignature.

Speak the line: two bodies collide in space, explode into gasses, lheat and iron ldust. And each figurative word brings with it its train of associated (accreted) experiences. I can then conclude that the emotion of or feelings derived from a piece of music come not from from the flow of fixed notes, as such, but frm the incomprehensible capacity of mind and soul to feelthe encompassing beauty and enchantment of the msic in its totality.

In literature, the emotions, if Nomalistic, are wrought into a kind of *experanto*, or new language of primitve sysmbols, derived from fixed denotations whose emotional, connotative derivatives are infinite, like Einstein's continuum along which the imaginative mind may expand to embrace other words of emotion and imagery. That statement sounds almost psychedelic. Mind expansion.... Primitive reality, however, can then, however, demonstrate its startling capability to be changed into stuning fantasy, or at least the intuitive of such a fantasy. Reality can then become rational, dream, the latter objectified through the former. There is a chimera of imagination that converts this change into something approaching a spiritual revelation, a starting with the ordinary words of connotative richness.

The thought that distills from the foregoing discussion is: One of the conditions for speaking or writing is the "censorship" element of living language. It is to the principal context that the author draws the reader who reads to understand. I can be talking about piranna, children, troops, grain or fuel. The text directs the mind, the description refines the object, the exclusion of non-contextual meanings is millisecond automatic, yet the enlightenment may never reveal to the reader all the potential meaning in the one word. The more restrictive the accretion(s) the more definitive the word becomes Yet strangely the accretions suggest the *undefineable*, at which point the word suggests mood...and beyond --*deconstruction* begins.

?. They might well have assumed that it conveyed not the wisdom, power and purpose of the word <u>liberty</u> but irresponsible rebellion.

When summoning a militia to oppose tyranny, he was reminding the delegates of the morality of a noble cause. His was not the persiflage of a selfish diatribe against the Crown.

> *Thought control is never far distant from liberty of thought and conscience; they run concurrently for the office of a people's government.*

> *Let nobody rob you of your personal liberty to decide between right and wrong, whether or not you can put the decision into action. For all are born with this capacity of mind, the conscience.*

> *Let no man stand trial for doing a good deed for another hapless human being. A jealous society will mask the Samaritan act in its own eyes as a litigious happening.*

> *Even wicked men acknowledge the conscience by their attempts to eradicate the good in others.*

INTEGRITY AND LIBERTY

The deliberate violation of the secular laws protecting one person from harm by another is not an exercise in liberty. A criminal usually tries to justify his crime, and he always chafes at his punishment. He complains that the justice system has <u>unfairly</u> deprived him of his freedom. Rarely is ever does he specify his loss of liberty. Jail riots erupt from time to time as symbols of the anarchy brewing inside the walls by which the prisoners would destroy the entire justice system in effigy, burning mattresses, making hostages of jailers and issuing political demands in order to destroy the consciences of hard-line, pre-victim proponents.

Lenient judges have lowered the seriousness of crime to the status of a correctable offense in the face of the fact that the abuse of liberty shown by convicts under prison circumstances replicates the criminality of their felonious actions against society outside. Ironically, convicts rebel against the very laws that insure the continuation of the liberty they will enjoy when freed. And the symbolic destruction almost always fails in its purpose.

The guilt of a felon is servant to the violation of his liberty which ought never to be presumed severable but only suspended as the locus of inalienable rights while he serves his sentence. The ejection of liberty is a part of contemporary American philosophy. Liberty is viewed as utilitarian - useful in some situations and not in others, do in prisons. This utilitarian perspective on morality is simply the old "situation ethics" all over again. Felons are serving time because society prompted them to break the laws.

With the rise in crime and the lassitude of society toward criminal sentencing and parole leniency, Americans have begun to question the "utility" of liberty itself. Do we need more police surveillance? Liberty is not, however, utilitarian; it does not function to perform immoral acts, such as to set the felon free on the argument that he used his liberty unwisely and deserves another change; or that he was unfairly - a favorite word - condemned by the jurors or the court because of race, gender enculturation or plain bad publicity. Liberty does not seek its justification in situations or circumstances. Conscience under the aegis of liberty performs that service and duty.

One does not say of liberty that it caused him to chose badly. Often this is the nature of the indictment, that the very liberty under which we make choices of right and wrong is held in disrepute with the result that the people are constantly and in ever greater numbers running to the State for moral direction and official justification. They solicit the State's guidelines on how to avoid the diseases of promiscuity; how to structure job and family relationships for tax purposes; what methodology children ought to be taught to enable them to make moral decisions, etc. In doing these things - looking to the State for moral guidance - the people have appointed the State to be their guide, their alter-conscience because they have forgotten their heritage of liberty as a protector and effectualizer of conscionable human conduct.

Where men most often discard an absolute standard of conduct, a moral law, they will often expect to be justified by the secular humanist's creed which states that all men are naturally good and it is society's fault that they turn out badly. The substitution of correction for retribution tends to turn justice into a friend of sentimental program of social forgiveness and disapproval, already making justice a farce to the criminal "mind". The substitution of personal opinion for absolute values is the attempt to convert conscience into the slave of egoism. A blurring of the line between a felony and a misdemeanor h as taken hold in American jurisprudence. In due time intentionality can become irrelevant to the reality of the crime, a reality as visible as the television screen yet absent of moral choice and the onerous of guilt. After all, absolute values belong to the past whose anachronisms somehow get in the way of the happiness cult.

There is an inconsistency that thrives among us nowadays. We find certain Congressmen resorting not to alibis that affirm their accountability as the people's representatives, such as: "I was dishonest," or "I did some inappropriate things" or "I broke my promise to the American people and I'm sorry." Micreant Congressmen surely would not incriminate themselves. Instead they appeal to the standard of "fair play for fair gain." Recourse, however, to fairness discharges the sovereignty of liberty as mere gainsay. Gainsaying liberty of conduct while in political office, like that by the Congressman who kited checks on the House Bank, proves the "fair play" was the ober dictum of their actions. Those found out plead for the rectitude of their unlawful overdrafts, casting all their guilt upon ignorance, policy or custom.

A Congressman has the power and the opportunity to defraud the people, but when he says that it is "fair play" for him to do so in the name of the political game, his misconduct assumes the aspect of a censurable misjudgment. A code of operation of justice has become apparent in the Congress that crime is no longer indictable. By the obvious procedure of eliminating words like "honorable," "honest," "loyal" from the official lexicon of parliamentary usages, our representatives have for some time critiqued crime in both houses as an act of "bad judgment," or of "miscalculations," or of "mathematical errors" or of "improprieties." Lately, the press has, it seems, found the rule-violators to have committed simple "improprieties" or to have done a thing that was "politically incorrect." How far will this game in euphemistic semantics go before Congress will police itself as the outset of criminal violations, and in no uncertain terms?

256

Congressional cheating by words, and theft by deeds is more than a plain scandal; it is blatantly immoral for the people to have to endure this pretense at restitution and rejection of punishment. To describe such conduct simplistically as unethical destroys by suspicion many of the legal attachments and human resolves of a representative body working in concert for the good of the people. In doing so Congressional dishonesty weakens the moral fiber of the "goodness," if you will, of America. She becomes increasingly evil by virtue of the multiple dishonesties of her Representatives, initiated and condoned by the people. This is a Christian perspective and yet a realistic one.

Honesty as a consistent absolute value, which is most often taught by parents, gives a moral and connotation to liberty. Liberty is not a variable, a specious and axiomatic word which the utilitarian argument attempts to justify. The State and neo-anarchist educators would be removing conscience, right and wrong choices and ultimate moral conduct from the curriculum, try to disenfranchise an entire generation in order to increase their political power. This is the educational direction of the secular humanists who would have the children to be so totally self-sufficient they don't need their parents but they do need the State. Hitler planned that kind of indoctrination of Germany's youth from the 1930's on, inculcating into young Aryan minds the utilitarian ethics of power, to wit, that power is right and weakness is wrong as a means to the supreme righteousness of the German Third Reich. "Situation Ethics" is a silent precursor to that abomination of total immorality in America, and an utter confusion about the political meaning of the <u>integrity</u> of powers.

Do not allow the shouts of the mob to distract you from right choices or the cries of the anarchists to deter you from moral rectitude. For in the noise of many there is often only chaos, pain and vengeance.

Liberty never borrows its theosophy from perfidious conduct except to depict the disaster of its loss.

Thought liberty may not bear the scars of its adversary, despotism, it will forever display the dishonor of its abandonment.

The "liberty " to defraud the people or to cheat on a friend is neither a liberty nor a right. It is simply the enslavement of the will without honor or integrity.

BUREAUCRATIC DEPENDENCY AND LIBERTY OF
MIND AND ACTION

It is obvious that the Federal Government by its official reiteration, by the Congressmen and their propaganda or "need," by the welfare custom of usage and the public's acceptance of the welfare state doles out a measure of comfort and security to its welfare recipients and their liberal supporters.

Ought then liberty to be held up to them as desirable, enabling them to adjust their thoughts and expenditures and aims to the future advancement of their own free will? In other words, why ought they even consider free choice when, under the circumstances, the State makes the choices for them in regard to welfare income and other entitlements?

There sets in like gangrene the malaise of a fictitious understanding of personal choices whose illusion is shaped by the givers of welfare, seeking not to better the recipient any more than to improve the politician's chances of reelection. Yet in this way, in the course of year in and year out rendering of financial aid, the welfare beneficiary in time - and many are second-generation recipients with entrenched attitudes - come to believe that his liberty of movement, his freedom of thought, his options of choice are in only a few respects related to what he has not directly earned, and that the Federal Government owes him the money he receives every month without effort on his part.

He becomes the illusory creditor of the people and at the same time the beneficiary of earned income within the framework of welfare law. The bureaucracy has by ingratiating germinated a dependency that has become the recipient's right to his claim. That claim bears no relationship to economic laws that govern other members of American society but instead it is relevant to his special financial empowerment and to his political influence. Welfare thus tends to generate arrogance and power among a hapless yet identifiable segment of the American people.

The source of this welfare largesse is the productive American taxpayer. It results from the abuse of political liberty by weeping politicians to a largesse that is a form of theft, mounting sometimes to the actual disinheritance of the heirs and producers from their land. Such is fraudulent democratization in the guise of liberty. Property and money to pay income taxes are the result of diligent effort, sacrifice and investment year after year, a form of credit and philanthropic compassion extended to the imprudent city and the squanderous state. The conversion of inherited property by taxation to preserve welfare is rank socialism based on the "politics of pity."

To confiscate a house through excessive taxes is to shift investment capital from its earner and investor into the hands of the undeserving lazy. Taxes of that magnitude are a form of extortion, meaning that the State controls the means of production, a man's possessions being the capital from which he works to employ others. His land becomes the basis for industry; he borrows against it in future ventures. But through the machinations of welfare - stateism it is extorted from him.

Any seizure of the land for monies owed to the State prohibits the landed person's exercise of liberty of choice. His investment strategies are subsumed by his conscience regarding the disposal of honest money and those conscionable choices of right and wrong investment which accrue to it.

Taxation becomes immoral when it confiscates a man's property. The State in doing so places only a token respect on the citizen's demonstration of honesty, honor, loyalty and hard work. If the property then becomes the State's by usurpation, a form of bureaucratic contempt, the destructive tax has stripped the "inalienable right" of happiness from the land owner. For does he not have natural right to the enjoyment of his land? The State quite naturally finds an excuse for its actions to perpetuate itself at the expense of its people. That excuse is Egalitarianism, the curse of contemporary politics in America which mandates <u>absolute</u> political and social equality. This creed nor moral values are the absolutism of America today, the tyranny of an unspoken political <u>correctness</u>.

Liberty protects the demands of the purse only when the citizen is free to enjoy its gifts.

Liberty will confront tyranny to the extent that it appears attainable. For this reason all denigration of common freedoms ought to be confronted.

If you keep a man enslaved for so long, he will envision freedom's absence as a natural state of things.

If you think you can compel society to accept your depravity as good and just, you do compound its nuisances and its self-condemnation.

Few will be those who espouse the submission of liberty to capricious leaders; but they will often mindlessly enjoy the fruit thereof.

CHILDREN GIVEN THE ADULT RIGHT TO SUE THEIR PARENTS FOR NEGLECT, MALTREATMENT AND DIVORCE

Are children under age - below 18 years - given this right by society, or is it inherent in the parent-child relationship as a natural right, and if "natural" therefore denoted to be a "liberty" of choice to which society acquiesces? Do children earn the right to sue by virtue of their compassionate presence in the household? Do they have grounds for any protest to the extent of having litigation power the court might discover as an enablement for a lawsuit?

It was in past ages - in Medieval times if not earlier - that children were treated like little adults. Society has almost forgotten that with great effort and perseverance there came into existence legislation that protects children from arduous labor in the mines and mills of America, from sexual abuse by adults both inside and outside the home, a European way, and from illiteracy. These evils were remedied by laws to prohibit society from exploiting them as cheap labor and sex objects and persons without rights.

Nonetheless, the child in American society has been the object of special concern and care, which have until technology presented corrupt opportunities, restrained malefactors and exploiters from availing themselves and their corporate interests of the use of children as helpless objects without any moral defense by society. The battle goes on:

Pedophelia, pornographic movies, labor-use in the performing arts, IRS exploitation for tax purposes, a plethora of latchkey kids of working parents: - these evidences show that society still believes that children have a commercial value. The concern of the courts in custody cases and in instances of abuse and abandonment amounts to State interest. But the State's interest is not the same as parental concern; it is promotional polities. The child is nowadays again a pawn. Our nation pushes for a retrogressive childless child that takes us back to the Middle Ages. All the enlightenment of the twentieth century is of little avail before the rejection of the true moral protection of our children.

Upon that prohibition hangs the moral law that one is not to abuse the child in our society; that our leaders are not to withhold certain benefits that will give the child advantages for adulthood and, ultimately, for the good of America - such as an education for competency in our society and care for the orphans, the abandoned and the lost. The morally right choice is to demand that the child shall not work long hours - or in fact work at all the adult sense of the word when he should be playing and going to school. In the years of maturation there should be a reasonable remedy for delinquency, a compassionate supervision while at school, and by the police and neighbors while on the streets. The absence of the last has made drive-by shootings commonplace, which is indeed a phenomenon that violates society's respect for the child if not for his childhood as time-for-growth experiences.

The deplorable fact is that America has withdrawn from the last benefit and is starting to think of children as "grownups" with all the legal rights of adults, bypassing childhood as a wasteful and unproductive stage of growth in order that the child reaching maturity at 13 years without the traumas (sic) of the growing-up years. In savagery children are ripped from the womb, the court's cruel ober dictum; and they are encouraged through sports, social indulgences and statist paternalistic laws to be little adults. They are found to visualize themselves as both adults who, upon threat of expulsion from school or abandonment by their classmates, must make adult choices, "fun and games", in the classroom. Let society condemn this shame.

These are diabolical schemes, shortsighted, utilitarian and ignorant. In time they will produce a nation of morally and intellectually stunted youth. Children who are deprived of those years yet are required to behave like adults will miss the strengthening process of gradual exploration of adaptation, succumbing in later years to wicked blandishments and seductions from a lack of moral strength and insight and the personal acknowledgment of accountability. Their parents will, of course, blame society for the deficit; and so it is nowadays, yet they are the very ones who must nurture moral stamina and not parade and foster, for appearance sake, this insidious child-rearing technique of adult mimicry.

The activists of this "year of the child" cult accuse parents of being the enemy. Those paragons of a false progress are the real saboteurs not just of the family as an institution, but of the lives of the children. Also, let it be said, "Year of the Child" is a Chinese cultural borrowing like "Year of the Dog" and "Year of the Rat." All our years ought to be for the child, not of, as though the children were some sort of prophetic sign and wonder of the heavens. The politicizing of children is pernicious and retrogressive. In fact it is medieval. And it is totally irrelevant to child-rearing that any one year should be astrologically fixed as significant.

Fiendish activist counselors try to push the 14-year old into the courts in order to alienate the child from his parents, on the face of the complaint that ignores rational grounds for an amicable parent-child resolution and that encourages the small son or daughter to "divorce" the parents, thereby making the child a permanent possession of the State and a fit recruit for a fascist politically correct youth corps. Can we not learn from history?

The volatile matter is then to be settled by an impersonal judge amid the folios of paperwork entailed in child-adult contests. The Juvenile Court - or the Superior Court - should recognize such lawsuits and to abet the destruction of the family in America, judges who condone such suits should be discharged from the bench or put out of office as incompetent to rule on what does not exist, the specificity of a tortuous action for damage and property and for divorce by the child. The State's interest in child-rearing is not proscriptive, outlawing some disciplines while condoning others. Its interest is concordant, or ought to be, seeking grounds for common agreement. Where the child is rebellious and wants out of the family the court is not the proper place to settle the matter. Such juvenile divorce cases tend to encourage, by stare decisis decisions, the expansion of family quarrels into full-blown feuds.

The belief is, of course, that the child needs to exercise his natural rights

262

sooner, to hasten the maturation process and thereby to bring him abruptly to face the realities that he must ultimately face anyway. As if the mawkish charades at adulthood have not produced enough juvenile crime already! What is all the rush about anyway? If maturity is the result of growth, how can there be growth by skirting years when such growth occurs? Trial and error within the scope of childhood experiences produce not adult indoctrination but instead an enlarged understanding of what it means to be a responsible citizen.

The child's liberty to file a complaint against his parents is a fairly recent charismatic proposition; yet this right of legalistic free choice is urged upon the child like a <u>cause celebre</u> by which he is encouraged to elbow his way into the adult world no matter how bloody the encounter. When a child is thus prompted to measure up to adults in a courtroom scene, so that he can secure his manhood more rapidly and pass through that indoctrination, like a rite of passage, he has found a way to gratify his childish envy of the adult lifestyle, its progressions, its facades, its hypocrites, its grown-up aura. In this way, via the court, his liberty of choice, conscience, cognition propagandized and politicized to the end that he becomes useful to the State, his surrogate parent. His capacity to make moral choices that could harm himself or others is made acceptable by the court yet mature judgment is short-circuited. Discernment of right from wrong will rest upon whatever expedient will deliver him from pain, which way is the making of the sadist, the murderer or the ne'r-do-well, with the help of the court.

If an inalienable right means that the right cannot be separated from the citizen, liberty must assume the role of rebellion when despotism rules.

The liberty of a soldier portends disaster or death, since it borrows from war's a-morality.

When a nation emerges itself in the slew of wickedness, its immoral transgressions will become acceptable as "rights" and apparent for all the world to see.

Conscience does not play games; either wrong is wrong or right is right; but never is wrong the right or right the wrong. Misconstrual invites corruption of the language and moral relativism.

dictator's words reinforced by his troops become the words of an adoptive father who will protect his children from harm and from racial impurities. The KGB or the Gestapo, by digging our and destroying the undesirables, will insure the pristine quality of the common people.

Religious faith, instead of being a narcotic, then becomes a stimulant to promote and to goad the people into following this power transfer from civil to absolute authority with its attendant loss f civil liberties. In the Third Reich free speech and freedom of association were the first to go. Faith bends before power. But let the State inform these believers that the icon of their worship is invisible and nugatory, therefore their loss of liberty is recompensed, and they will point ironically to the invisibility of their personal future which proved so prophetically correct in their antagonism to Hitler's diabolical regime. Indeed the socialist-Fascist Germany of the time made of the Jews the scapegoat for its economic depression, forcing them to atone for that nation's WW I reparations yet they survived.

One of the contradictions in the authoritarian and totally-controlled society is that free moral choice exists at all, that it is possible to take or to abstain from all opiates, including genocide. Perhaps there is available an escape method when religion offers no comfort or hope. All the people are then told that the tyrant and his cohorts are the benign and rightful leaders of the country. How can any sane and sober person doubt the utilitarian uses of power that are thereby evident to all? Yet moral choice commences to move underground. It wears the face of compliance. There issues from the entombment of morality a practiced deceit that is resistant to obscene and cruel despotism. Patriotism and honor must then wear the mask of conformity in the desperation of the people to save their souls, their moral goodness, their capacity to endure. The dictator inevitably underestimates both the courage and the intelligence of a people so subjugated, whether or not they have known all of the well-defined personal liberties we have known in this country.

Liberty under law is the right to make free moral choices, which is the conscience not the despair but of hope. These choices and the capacity for conscionable action are a curse to the tyrant - who may very well be a member of a free society. His reasons for destroying the public expression of conscience only confirm the irrationality of all dictatorships since time began, whose unreasoning programs, agencies, displays of power have seldom taken into consideration the deeper convictions of the subjugated people. Indeed, Hitler and Stalin concocted caricatures of their peoples in order to manipulate them as puppets without mind or history. That was the madness of both leaders.

The peasant mind, however, does not lock in upon the State or his own folkish community. It finds its strength and its identity through myth, not through power. Oblivious to their desires, the dictator proceeds without much worry concerning their rebellion until street battles bring this defect in power to his attention - as at Tenemen Square, the barricades in revolutionary Paris, the street fighting in Columbia, Panama and on Boston Common and, years later, the collapse of the Berlin Wall. By ignoring a people's grasp of liberty, the dictator writes his own warrant for the death of himself and his regime, their intuition of liberty affixing its folk vision to what was in ancient heroic days the myth aspect of the liberty rebellion. In America the Colonists had not forgotten the 1215 Magna Carta, the Charter of English Liberties by which taxes required consent and one could not be imprisoned without a trial. Almost since the beginning of civilization, secular laws have moved in the direction of protecting man's personal immoral choices.

The laws of human rights in the Constitution's Bill of Rights are consonant with all of history's solemn edicts of liberty.

Keep the laws, empower liberty. Break the law, transgress liberty.

Liberty in America is not a right of the illegal alien. Although his conscionable actions may be answerable to God, his participation in our society requires allegiance to our government of laws. He ought to have no voice on the streets or in the assembly. Let him first disavow his allegiance to his foreign masters.

To preserve a citizen's freedom, he must be given the liberty to be responsible for his own actions. This is the sacrifice of true statesmanship; for the politician coerces and cajoles and bribes, marshaling the people's liberty thereby in support of his own power.

A people will tolerate chains so long as their daily needs are met; in this hapless state they will sell their birthright of liberty though justice is corrupt.

LIBERTY AND AUTHORITY

The liberty of rebellious and disruptive students may appear courageous, but in fact it is a form of intellectual suicide. The authority of the school is not designed to harass them but to provide an arena for their learning. If they chose the option of death to the intelligence as well as to the sensibilities, they devalue conscience as worthless, the liberty to make moral choices as fraudulent nonsense and instead obey the urge to "cut loose" as a death wish. Teenage suicides are increasingly common. Euphoric experience replaces learning while the immoral choice to waste one's life with drugs or indolence destroys its potential.

Instead of creating a social disharmony of riots and peace-breaking most adult citizens conform to the law. They accept the reality that the laws are for their own good, indeed for their survival. Their option is to incur fine and punishment.

Demands on the laws and penalties for their violation make rebellion adverse to happiness. However, an attitude of challenge to the laws exists in a society where men are taught that they can repeat bad laws. The citizen will often believe that under "the system" he has an inherent right to break the law! He attributes little seriousness to his option when he says, "I have the right to be wrong." He thereupon exercises his right to choose to face the consequences of punishment for his defection. If he ignores the consequences, society will impose them away.

If his harm to another goes beyond fantasy, the injury to society is irrevocable and often without restitution, as is the case in such heinous acts as rape, pediphelia and murder. When reason abets the criminal's evil choice, liberty to choose is surrendered to the death wish and the criminal then willfully destroys all personal liberty.

If these wrong choices continue and society is harmed, as well as the victims, only in the utopian absence of rules will criminals plead to injury when none exists. It is the onerous of guilt that goads the conscience to lie and to perjure itself. Plea-bargaining is always a concession, first to the conscience and then to the mechanisms of arrest. If the law is a deterrent to evil deeds it does not follow that the authority of the law is unwarranted or cruel or weak.

Political consensus has led to such laws, but does the consensus make them harmful? A man must examine authority constantly to make those corrections which will protect by law the liberty he enjoys. "Challenge all authority" is a conditionally acceptable attitude, though it is a dangerous one and proves to be so when ignored. Thereupon, harm can arise or occur with the elimination of an attitude of benign skepticism and challenge in favor of robotic behavior, or by actual injury caused, or engendered, by unwise conduct. The average citizen - who or what is he? One may ask - has developed harm-detouring mechanisms. On the other hand the teenager frequently collides with harmful causes by his conduct. Society's hope, may I presume?, is that the latter will not abandon the real-life choices urged upon him by an active and unfettered conscience.

Practice making totally ethical choices in your daily conduct and you will earn the respect at least of God. Men will not fully respect what they have no part in or concern with.

Liberty rarely transposes itself into messianic power, since it is neither visionary nor salvational but is eschatological. It marks the end and judgment of despotism.

If a man would dispose of God, then he is at liberty to invent the universe. In this mode of thought, the universe becomes an illusion without a Creator, and in the absence of a First and a Last Cause, or God, liberty is a mere construct of illusory reason. Mankind's concept of liberty without God implodes upon itself.

267

Liberty does not beg for a hearing lest it shame itself into silence. In one way or another it always asserts the reality of its Truth.

Keep liberty for a bauble and she will shatter; but keep her for justice and she will abound.

LIBERTY AND ARMS

America called for arms in the defense of liberty in 1775 when at St. John's Church in Richmond, Virginia, Patrick Henry and the burgesses argued for raising a militia to protect Englishmen's rights in the Colonies. The Second Amendment to the Constitution reiterates and formalizes that concept of a "well-regulated militia" maintained to secure a "free State" by a show of citizen force, the keeping of guns by the people in the event of an invasion.

The bearing of arms works also against an oppressive government where force is used to obtain conformity. It is not arms that always preserve liberty. And, it is not liberty always that is seized by the use of arms. Hitler, for example, tried by his use of Gestapo terror tactics to bring about Aryan purity, conformity, propagandistic enlightenment and cultural homogeneity - but not liberty. Arms represent the power of violet retaliation, violent action, violent compulsion, according to the ideology of the government or the bent of the despot. Arms are the instruments of preservation or of annihilation. Their discipline of regulation is irrelevant to the morality of their use when Hedonism and selfish ambition govern the strategy. Americans' Second Amendment right has always been based on a defensive posture for the preservation of the Nation. Arms for aggrandizement have always been the stance of those nations and leaders who seek gratification of the will to power. Their morality is evil in the indifference with which they deploy their arms against the helpless. Arms can mean either the weapons of tribal combat or the sophisticated armaments of armies. Or, indeed, the settler's musket he once used to defend his family and home.

A lawful government is regulated by laws superior in power to the individual citizens of that State. The fine terms in the Amendment invite close scrutiny and query as to why guns ought to be kept. It is true that a people will sometimes close off paths of immoral retreat before setting forth on new roads of moral change. In our own Civil War Lincoln's government could not morally retreat in the face of immoral slavery, called so by all abolitionists, yet wanton destruction by the Federals showed how abject and bloody can be this plea for moral liberty in the warfare that ensued to obtain conformity by arms.

Liberty as a battle cry was used during the French Reign of Terror. Arms for liberty in this historical context of the French Revolution wreaked their bloody overture to equality because arms were weapons of annihilation and not common instruments of death for drumming in moral change. The call to arms always requires a specificity of moral purpose in their use, to which neither hedonism or economic vindication nor power-hunger supplies an accurate answer. That was the conscience that lay beneath Sir Winston Churchill's words of encouragement to the British people when he braced them to stand up to Hitler's Nazi hordes who intended to "work their wicket will" against England. Her moral purpose was to save herself from conquest and therefore to preserve her culture and her life.

In America, arms for liberty in Colonial times took on a different configuration from that of the French in 1789. Geography was a pre-condition to civil liberty in our country. Without the Atlantic between us and a tired, enfeebled, corrupt and idolatrous Europe, perhaps we should never have aroused our own ancestors to the cry for liberty. The Minutemen were Englishmen. In a real sense, the American Revolution was a civil war, thus it was all the more a fierce and embittered struggle for power. The Colonials had the advantage of a certain minority unity - though many of them migrated to Quebec or remained stubbornly Tory or kept silent. In France the Nobility and Republicans rubbed shoulders on the streets of Paris. A strict unity of the masses was missing. The enemies of the people were identified by their outward symbols of wealth, and the guillotine no doubt cut off many heads that were of the nobility in appearances but in sympathy with the French people. Also, it was not musketry that brought the Crown to face the angry mobs but brute force. The Call to Arms in Colonial America was singularly united, moral and encompassed with a definable direction. In the France of 1789, there roamed like a lion seeking its prey through the streets of Paris, the chaos of hatred and the vengeance of death.

A NOTE ON CURRENT EXISTENTIONALISM

Sartre's philosophy of *Existentionalism* is just another name for Nihilism; yet it deals more directly with sense experience than it does sensuous motivation (hedonistic desires) and it involves no doctrinal questions of God, faith, belief, duty except to reject them out of hand. It denies the reality, legitimacy and integrity of such questions, they being essentially religious in nature. In their place *Existentionalism* instals the pride of disbelief in God, in hope, in human dignity. It is the philosophy of abject defeatism in life. It is in part the product of the collapse of religious faith in Catholic France after WW II.

Being a-moral, *Existentionalism* is sentimental in the extreme, since it rejects the government of rational human action, from which issue laws of absolute right and wrong. And in their place it substitutes the depraved beautitude of personal suffering as an unalterable condition of each of its disciples. Being the philosophy of an *inescapable box*, its feeds upon itself, its practitioners believing themselves daunted by the fates of their separate existences, beyond which there is neither respite nor petition. It is the ultimate in disillusionment and fatalism. Any contrary philosophical outlook is considered to be contemptible weakness and an unrealistic "escape" from *the box.*

Pain and, by implication, pleasure are its standards. *Existentionalism* is therefore hedonistic, sensual and simplistic and, being the room of retreat for the individual who cannot face himself, it is a philosophy of negation and self-pity. Yet, paradoxically, it implies the virtue of its practitioners. As masochists their capacity to suffer without mitigation is their virtue, and all pain has its antipode in death. Hope is anathema to the Existentionalist.

AMBROSE BIERCE, THE VOICE OF
THE APOSTLE

Brete Harte, who was a San Franciso editor, taught Bierce craftsmanship in story composition; the latter once admitted to that. He had sharfpened his critical skills and enlarged his writing capacities on several publications not the lest of which was Hearst's "San Francisco Examiner." Bierce, Twain and Harte formed a kind of loosely-structured writing circle in the City by the Golden Gate in the 1870's. It as natural that each should draw upon the same post-Gold Rush environment, working as they did so the vein of the Western tall tale couched in a casual, conversational sltyle.

Yet the man Britishers called "bitter Bierce" because of his vituperative London column in "The Wasp" did not fail to shatter images of English foppery. And when she came onto the American literary scene, pen sharpened, he came as one ready to escoriate fakery wherever he found it, the "sleeze" of the counterfeit as we know it today. He shared withs Twain and Dickens a rejection of "humbug." Clifton Fadiman in a Bierce collection writes that he attacked amateur poets, clergymen, bores, dishonest politicians, money grabbers, pretenders and "frauds of all sorts." Bierce especially detested the romanticizing of war. He had served as an advance scout and cartographer for the Indiana 9th and as a Hearst crrespondent in the Spanish-American war. War, without mercy, held no romance for him.

Ambrose Gwenett Bierce's voice was not so much one of entertainment, lthough he amused his readers with his macabre human in "Oil of Dog," "My Favorite Murder" and "An Imperfect Conflagration," stories that mock men's ritualistic respect for life without understanding death. He also wrote to satirize the presuppositions of an America in the process of radical change. Why ought war to be glamorous when it was ruthless? Was there no more to filial gratitue than mere proximity? Didn't American ways of getting oney demand censure, ridicule? Some critics called Bierce a sadist because burned bodies and macerated the flesh seemingly without compassion. Yet his imagination ran to the ludicrous and bizzare in order to expose almost incomprehensible disregard for human life that thrived in lawless small Western towns, in San Francisco and--on lthe battlefield

Bierce saw through pretense. Stylistically very much the journalist of his day; he composed his stories, his tales of horror and of war, his animal fables in rhyme, his "Devil's Dictionary" to criticize, mock, excoriate, cut and flail with humor, the very essence of satire. And no other American writer before him spoke with the same voice of priestly condemnation. He was an original. It was the credo the main character lived by that piqued Bierce's attention--spiritualism, consuming money making, Freudianism and "Fantastic fables" from his personal experiences. The last mentioned fables made suitable column fillers if one is a journalist, as Bierce was for most of his life. They are small aphrodesiac tales that eviscerate a common stupidity.

For example, in "The Ineffective Rooter" who suggestsed the tribulations of aournalistic muckraker, Bierce wrote: "A drunken man was lying in the road with a bleeding noise, upon which he had fallen, when a Pig passed that way.
'You wallow fairly well," said the Pig, "but my fine fellow, you have much to learn about rooting.'" One canhear the city editor criticiziing the inept reporter of City Hall corruption.

Bierce had a good measure of the pedant in him; most satirists do. His animal fables are blood cousin to the limerick. His bizzare mockeries and macabre murders make a statement about the value of human life, by inversion, by a hyperbolic treatment of the thinly-veiled crime. Indeed, the psychology of some of his stories is more complex than first appears.

The truth is that Bierce understood states of consciousness and explored them, if perhaps less subtly, than did Mary Freeman, Kate Chopin and Charlotte Gilman. They were practically contemporaries. Bierce depicted escape through the imagination ("An Occurrence At Owl Creek Bridge"), the new psychology of delirium and hysteria ("The Eyes of th Panther");, and the power of suggestion ("One Summner Night"), suspense ("One of the Missing" and "Chickamauga"), the Oedipus Complex ("The Death of Halpin Frayser") amnesia ("The Damned Thing" and "A Resumed Identity"). Bierce understood well the power of suggestion, the art of exclusion in th creative act. This, I think, is one of his minor contributions to a literary America in transition, but reflects new psychological insights the coming "science" of psychology, as art and science united.

Because of the fact that anthologists have subscripted Bierce's stories into categories he himself might not have endorsed--**In the Midst of Life** carries only "Soldiers and "Civilians" --satire suffuses most of his work written to please newspaper readers. Satire darkens into irony in his more erious stories about soldiers in the Civil War. For there is where his finest writing lies -- in the ironies bound up in chance skirmishes, death without victory, front trench mistakes and the accomplices of fate in war. Bierce knew about combat. His irony pivoted on two premises: (1) man's basic integrity in combat is no matlch for circumstances clused by chance, and (2) the law of justice is suspended, indeed is irrelevant, when the "hero" is in the midst of a crisis. "An Occurrence at Owl Creek Bridge" shows at once how fallible is justice when fate orders death and the circumstances are irreversible. Thus the suspension of civil justice demands escape through hallucinatory visions the condemned man conjures up. In "Chicamauga the juxtaposition of innocence in the boy and the bloody evil of war in the retreating soldiers makes chance the mover of forces--the boy, the troops, his burning home and killed mother, leaving the irony of innocence that stares downs at "the wreck" to the imagination of the readers. Is justice cheated in war? One might ask that question of both stories.

In certain of Bierce's "Soldier" stories, the perpetrators of a certain act, action or deed unknowingly bring down disaster upon innocent victims. "One Kind of Officer" depicts a Captain Ransom who fires upon his own stroops in the fog because General Cameron, in the breech of battle, had ordered the Captain not to question a command. And Ransom's Lieutenant, under the same military regimen, lhad acted without question on Ransom's order to"shoot at whatever moves in front of you." As fate directed, his own flank had swung around in the fog, and the Lieutenant obeying the Captain's order, had killed their own stroops. In another "The Mockingbird" one sentry shoots his brother by accident in the dead of night and searching despersately finds him the next day in a gully, a bullet in his head. In both of these great stories, the justice of a legitimate command was irrelevant to the realities of the circumstances. And in neither story was human integrity of any importance. Military obedience was everything, discipline, the mindless pursuit of a tactic.

Bierce's fantasy was not the romantic entertainment of "Rip Van Winkle or the contrivances of Poe. Irony explicated the vision.

Eng. 474 - A

THE ROMANTICISM OF
JOSEPH CONRAD

Joseph Conrad writes in "Author's Note" to *Within the Tides*:

> *The romantic feeling of reality was in me*
> *an inborn faculty. This in itself may be a*
> *curse. but when disciplined by a sense of*
> *of personal responsibility and a recognition*
> *of the hard facts of existence shared with*
> *the rest of mankind becomes but a point*
> *of view from which the very shadows of life*
> *appear endowed with an internal glow. And*
> *Such romanticism is not a sin. It is none the*
> *worse for the knowledge of truth. It only*
> *tries to make the best of it, hard as it may be;*
> *and in this hardness discovers a certain*
> *aspect of beauty.*

These lines attempt to delineate Conrad's personal perspective, the philosophical and aesthetic, in his characters' lives--which, he states, are drawn from the "hard facts of existence." In a ruthless and lonely world he found beauty among history's raw entanglements of human action, more primitive than urbane, less naive than tribalized. Those "hard facts" were Conrad's standard of reality, to him--survival, loneliness, fear and superstition, hard-bitten demands of naked survival and *moral resolution* rather than impersonal law for a moral problem, as in *The Secret Sharer*. The Captain allows the excaped convict, to board his vessel, hiding him in his cabin until he can swim to freedom. He eschews capture of the man and turning him over to the police. That is his personal moral decision.

Conrad writes that he rested his work "more on contacts, and very slight contacts at that, than on actual experience." The dramatic incident and illuminating moment were more important to this Polish- British writer than was the episode or even the anecdote. The instant of a happening was more dramatic than the exposition of all the circumstances. He possessed the photographer's instinct and eye for the dramatic moment before him. Yet he crafted stories with great, almost painful and meticulous care, from the reminiscences of his life. That past was his "sustenance." The most profound and dramatic experiences in his life were those "slight contacts."

Conrad sailed before the mast for twenty years, moving among a world of ships and men and foreign cities, villages and primitive communes. Indeed, in those works of his "early period"--a time frame with no boundaries--Conrad did not bother to change the names of certain of his characters. Almayer and Captain Beard from the vessel "Judea" in *Almayer's Folly* were actual persons. The entirety of *The Nigger of the Narcissus* is a literary tribute to a men Conrad had known personally, proof which is his statement: "I must enshrine my old chums in a decent edifice." Ports he visited on voyages to South Pacific Islands as well as to swarming cities of the Far East and South America enter Conrad's fiction as detailed depictions of shipboard life, fringe-of-the-jungle habitations, common habits and custom and native types. He wrote the entire novel *Nostromo* from his memories of a port-of-call in South America that lasted only a few days!

Conrad looked upon the noblest and basest qualities of human nature, directly and simultaneously. His romanticism did not search for the ideally pleasant and without the flaw of pain in his life. He confronted social injustice in *Victory*. He reforged tragedy in life to mean the catastrophic breach of a man's spirit because of his inability to cope with or to ignore the injustice, the flawed rules of men and their tilted judgements and tortuous collisions which damned their existence. Mrs. Gould in *Nostromo* is just that sort of tragic character. She is trapped in a mining venture with her husband Charles and discovers, to her pain, chagrin and dismay, that he has shifted his affection and interest from her, whom he once loved, to his silver mine. Never was there any romantic idealism in their affinity for each other; there is a blind side to emotional commitment. Nor is Charles Gould entirely evil in his disregard of his wife, for the absolute character of that evil would have romanticized his attachment. Even though she sees his love waning, she stays faithful nd permits herself no escape. Gould's cruel indifference and his wife's unrequited hopes is Conrad's *tour de force*. Even thsough one may not be totally in agreement with that conclusion, the power of the theme resides in men's rebuke of injustice that will not deter fate. Or, to put the matter another way: hope must rise from the caldron of pain or all are damned, including the author. That hope can travel on the thin rim of destruction, as it does in the long short story "The Secret Sharer."

A writer's credibility with a reader must not destroy his illusion of reality of the work. That is, simply that his characters must be believable and, above all, neither flawless nor irredeemable. Conrad has written in "A Familiar Preface" to *A Personal Record*:

> *In order to move others deeply we must*
> *deliberately allow ourselves to be carried*
> *away beyond the bounds of our normal*
> *sensibilities--innocently enough, perhaps, and*
> *of necessity, like an actor who raises his*
> *voice on the stage above the pitch of natural*
> *conversation--but still we have to do that.*
> *And surely it is no great sin. But the danger*
> *lies in the writer becoming the victim of his*
> *own exaggeration, losing the exact notion of*
> *sincerity, and in the end coming to despise*
> *truth itself as something too cold, too blunt*
> *for his purpose--as, in fact, not good enough*
> *for his insistent emotion.*

To create the believable was Conrad's lifetime literary attack, after his first two failures in the novel. Conrad did not see men from within as did Henry James. He could not write inferring a man's chaacter and thoughts. When he tried it, as in *Almayer's Folly,* he failed. His adopted methodology resulted in blurred characrters, lacking sharp delineation and concision. He tried again in *An Outcast of the Island,* his second book with the same result produced by a *Jamsian initation* of inner being. "The hard facts of existence" were absent or obscure in his writing. When in *Lord Jim* Congrad begins to create believable character from the visual presence of the man, his actions and ways, we are caught up in the intrigue of his life. Heyst in *Victory*, the Nigger in *The Nigger of the Narcissus*, are in accord with Conrad's awakening to his natural methodology, his innate intuiton and perceptions, his capacity for descriptive mood-details. He begans to give us plausible figures, the men who doubtless did live in his nomadic world. And he now has disciplined himself to weigh, balance and accurately discern emotions, keeping them within the bounds of the credible and fascinating.

In the "Author's Preface" to *The Nigger of the Narcissus* Conrad writes:

"My task, which I am trying to achieve is to try
to make you feel--it is, before all, to make you
see."

To see in order to feel had the artistic certainty of a charted course. To feel the Captain's fear of discovery of Legget, the escapee, in **The Secret Sharer**, we have to visualie the actual shipboard layout, the approach of the great dark cliffs before the stowaway makes his escape. We have to see Heist in action before we understand how he could enact his folly to escape. We have to imagine the Scenes of **The Nigger of the Narcissus** before we can feel. We have to contemplate usually the desultory hands aboard the vessel before we can feel the impending mystery aboard Marlow's ship.

The quality of imaginary sight, of that capacity for presenting a "picture" of what is happening is a skill that does not exist in Henry James, Conrad's early model. Civilized men's primitive emotions eluded him when he used the introspective technique borrowed from James. The natives and seamen, the missionaries, shipmsters and traders he chose to wlrite about were alient to James'refinement of intellect and style. Conrad could, by temperament and vagabondage, begin only with the outward appearances of a man, his eyes and beard, his hands, the way he carried himself, the straw hat and rumpled tropical suit, the sometimes treacherous way he looked and moved through a crowd: all were familiar to Conrad. With these cognates of the visual mine he might then reach the inner soul whereby potential fury and brooding guilt and acts of murder lay hidden in the darkness. The "hard facts" of life were considered vulgarities in the rarefied parlors of Jamesian London or of Parisian society.

The following excerpt from **Lord Jim** depicts mood and character, inseparable entities in Conrad's fiction, rising in certain eloquent passages to lyricism about the sea.

Can you imagine him, silent and on his feet half
of the night, his face to the gusts of rain, staring at
the somber forms, watchful of vague movements,
straining his ears to catch rare low murmurs in the
stern sheets! Firmness of courage, of effort and fear?
What do you think? And the endurance is undeni-
able, too. Six hours more or less on the defensive,
six hours of altert immobility while the rest sof

*the boat drove slowly or floated, arrested acording
to the caprice of the wind; while the sea, calmed,
slept at last; while the clouds passed above
his head; while the sky from and immensity of
lustreless and black, diminished to a sombre and
lustrous vault, scintillated with a greater brilliance
faded to the east, paled at the zenith; while the dark
shapes blotting the low stars astern got outlines,
relief; became shoulders, heads, faces, features."*

Conrad's awareness of **time** meant the time of the skies and sea changing,
of winds, currents,s of the movement of the boat the presence of others aboard,
their emergence in dawn light and, withal, one may notice, the chiaroscuro use of
light and dark for dramatic effect. His repeated use of **while** compounds the total
powerr of the changing scene, of the life aboard ship on the changing
seascape.The following quotation captures the "hard facts" images of Conrad's
imagination. The dsescription is external.

*"Through these metamorphoses of the scene stands the
resolute Jim, a man of duty, bearing bleakly a
necessary sentry's hardship, inured to the ways of the
he scene stands the resolute Jim, a man of duty,
beakly a necessary sentry of hardship, inured to the ways of the
sea, watchful, loyal to his command, the symbolic fireacher who
watches the light come, mindful of the danger beneath the waters,
of the instant catastrophe of a rogue wave, of survival and
death and potential cruelty aboard in the huddled
darkness."*

The next usotation illustrates Conrad's genius for revealing the influence
on the man of the sea and sky.

*When a man quails before his fears, his courage
mounts guard. When he stands resolute, he is best able
to confront the resolvable mystery of survival. When the
dawn should arrive, day would present new dangers
but what of that? Let the night amid sea scud and the
busy slap of water against the gunwales slip away first
and confirm to him that the sea's cold dangers explore*

the soul of a man, unremittingly .

Symolical without its being consciously symbolic, Conrad has captured he cadence and ritual and mystique of the sea watch in these few words. The idea of *a defensive posture* buried in the quoted words is a catalytic concept that opens up Conrad, the man, and his writing, for primal fear, man's fear of himself and then of nature, its moods and beasts,its dangers and beauty, flood to mind.

To look at a man through realist's eyes is to perceive what he does not know and intuit what he only dimnly reveals. It is to see that second character of a man whose faults are so intensely private to the visible character that he kills to protect them from the light, he maims to inflict their reed for venvgeance on another; he assumes the mantle of light to protect what is ignoble within; he cringes in his cowardice protected by arrogance and villainy; he honors his primitive lurking within the clothing of civilized men or the righteousness of his articulated god. His restless soul does not change any more than do the restless seas he sails upon.

Details of dialogue and action in **Lord Jim** show Conrad's sensitsive awareness of life going on around him, and of his exploration of every possible niche of interest focused on the characrters he writes about and on the fragmentaries of the scene he depicts. **Nostromo** also demonstrates his dependence on past experiences of import in his life, and their consequences, as the brutality among men who find thmselves unexpectedly caught up in some fatal irony of their own making.

Conrad's vision revealed men's particular evils and their virtues with a critical eye undeflected by any personal compassion for man or his circumstances. In **Nostromo** the ruthless rage that misdirects also dominates every potential goodness in Faulk's character; the primitrive vanity that is the master of Nostromo's passions; the fidelity to a moral code that drives Lord Jim into his own exile: these traits, these identifiable signatures of the inescapale *natural man* who is that characrter individualize each in his yarn,   Yet though they are plain men, their characters formed on the wheel of circumstances bear a singularity of purpose and intensity of vision unique to no other in history. Desire rules each, an end to the attained end, Conrad wants us to see those ends familiar to man who dare to look within themselves.

In this common bond with other men, Faulk, Nostromo and Jim are close

proximations of their "doubles" in reality, those who share similar circumstances evoking kindred emotisons. Conrad writes that these characters lead one to find, according to his...

> *"deserts ...encouragement, consolation, fear, charm--all you demand--and perhaps also that glimpse of truth for which you have forgotten to ask...a justice to the visible universe (wrought) by bringing to light the truth, nianifolnd one, underlying its every aspect."*

Not all of Conrad's characters are villainous, inflicted with wicked wrath and evill concuspidence, sojourners alongf the whale's wake of inner guilt and damnation., Indeed, these lines suggest that Conrad and Melville knew each other, which in fact was the case. Gentler qualities appear in certain of Conradian characters, the loft of pity to the soul, the endowment before another of chivalry of custom. l Yet never let one instance be named, do these attributes mininize a characrtewr? Conrads men because they live on the cusp of lifes "harde facts of existence," manliness is not one of their deficiencies nor is the scurvy of indolence their fate. Captin Anthony in the early novel *Chance* possesses the capacity for *suggesting life's possibilities*, so that other men might not suffer; there are natures like that which have no connections to formal religion, the redemptive nature of a good defense lawyer, or a stalward friend. The Captain feels obliged, due to his symparthetic nature, to offer his help when...and though Anthony's *idee fixee* the man's Samaritan quality, he does not cast Conrad as the victim of his own exaggeration, as he once feared. laptain Anthony is, withal, a man of great courage.

Captain Whalley, in *The End of the Tether*, a short story from **Youth,** is another good example of Conrad's perceptions of the mitigating, the exculpatory, the submissive side of strong men's natures. His parental devotion to the daughter whom he remembers as a yong girl is refreshingly unusual for all his godlike, commanding presence. This reunion does not diminish the virility of his nature but rather enhances it, striking the chord of similitudes in his loyalty to lthe sea as a bond of affection.

Indeed, he and Captain Anthony alike exhibit masculine properties and accoutrements of conduct in their dress, manners and action.; Twenty years at sea and touching all ports of the world gave greart breadth to Conrad's powers of observation. Beneath what refined judgement would call this semi-barbaric exteriors of these two men comprehended the strains of compassion and understanding in one and tender devotion in the othe:. the duality of their natures confirms their credible reality.

In "The Secret Sharer," the alleged murderer stowaway on the vessel is the shadow spirit who could be the real man if Captsain Marlow fails to divilge his presence. Opting for compassion and leaning toward doubt, as he does, Marlow would be an accomplice to a murder and condemned with certainty by the authorities. Conrad has succinctly stated this potential moral outcome. "One's literary life must turn frequently for sustenance to memories and seek discourse with the shades, unless one has made up one's mind to write only in order to reprove mankind for what it is, or praise it for what it is not, or--generally--to teach it how to behave." His was the wisdom of the sea that accepts the oncoming seas without rebuke yet with struggle against whaever great-seas nature casts aboard.

Conrad began to write about the sea after abandoning it at the age of thirty-seven. One may find in moot that he was a Romantic even though he drew upon past experiences. Logically, he had to; not being a writer of phantasies, he had no recourse. Indeed, the "hared facts" he culled bore a direct relevance to actuality. That connection was the link that gave them the power of immediacy, and therefore o credibility. "Making the best of it "the truth of those hard facts" on Conrad's changes, elavarated, embellished and added to his work's depth, as did the artesan he was. The evaluation of those facts he inferred; his wilngness to "share" with the rest of mankind" he showed, or demonstrated as sit were, in the code of shipboard cronies telling their tales and in the mode of a teacher imparting knowledge. Both experiences were familiar to Conrad.

He was not a complete romantic, even though he knew that recollections of past ruins was *romantic*. He implied that Romantic imagination and truth about men are not compatibles. He was averse to his owns Romantic predisposititon toeward life as *irredeemable*, as a "curse" needing discipline into "personal responsiblity." But upon the ironies he was capable of seeing there impinged the realities so men's reactions under the ageis of fate. That power of the inevitable was, it seems to me, the *locus* of Conrad's romantic vision. Also, the Romantic notion of the importance of historicity led Conrad to mitigate the "truth" of "hard facts" by the introdluction of other possibilities of explanation. By this meansof tempering human action, he limproved his, and our, understanding of the characters of whom he wrote.

Conrad's women characrters require comment, since they are as real, tenable and constructive in the imagination as any of his yarns by crusty sea scions. In *Nostromo*, Mrs. Charles Gould, wife of the mine owner, must gradually accustom her heart and thoughts and her moods to an acceptance of the respect of the simple townspeople of Sulaco, in exchange for the fading love her husband. His obsession with silver at the mine is more important to him than mere interest in the woman who is his wife. In this passage, too, there appears a mettle, a reluctance to flee, a consanguinity of purpose and loyalty to *the commitment* which one can find often in Conrad's characrters, a madonna *sans* the prostitute life.

It must not be supposed that Mrs. Gould's mind is masculine. A woman with a masculine mind is not a being of superior efficiency; she is simply a phenomenon of "imperfect differntiation"--interesting, barren and without importance. Dona Emilia's intelligence , being feminine, leads her to achieve the conquest of Sulaco simply by lighting the way for their unselfishness and sympathy. She can converse charmingly, but she was not talkative. The wisdom of her heart has no concern with the erection or demolition of theories, any more than with the defense of prejudices. Her words have the value of acts of integrity, tolerance, and compassion. A woman's true tenderness, like the true virility of men, is expresed in "action of a conquering kind."

Dona Amelias needs to find a way to express her salient femininity. This is her need, and a profound one, as deep sounding as conquest in despotic natures of men, which occurs and then again recurs in Conrad's female character Winnie Verloc. Wrapped up in that feminity is the entire Self. Women of a masculine nature are simply "uninteresting differentiation," as Conrad put the matter. The satisfaction of the expressive need motivates the woman, uncluttered by false defenses of social cause or bittter pleading.

In the life of Dona Amelia, she does not express her feminity through maternal affections or, indeed, ever completely for Charles Gould. So absorbed is he in his single purpose to make his silver mine pay that he can find no time for Dona Amelia . After a tortuous passing of long months down in the arid small South American town, Charles' earlier strong love for his wife begins to wane. Mentally painful to her who loved him genuinely, she is helpless to watch their growing estrangement and loss of love. For love unrequited has no passion to fuel the flame. Effectually, she can not love him any longer, for in a woman of her affectionate nature this detachment rips apart the delicate lacework of their marriage and leaves her too torn and helpless to win him back with any natural charm she possesses. Her only alternative is for her to show a capacity for love by her efforts to win the condolences, affection and incredulity of the poor mine workers.

In the short story "The Secret Agent" Winnie Verloc also shows with a feminine virtue that somehow life has stunted by excluding her from courtship, marriage and childbearing. In Conrad's story she lives only for her brother Stevie, making numerous sacrifices to encourage his happiness. She sublimates her personal life in a protective mode, an eternal vigilance over him. And by her constant care, she can express her feminine nature, the inequity of the relationship, of her sacrificial exchange for his dubious happiness. Thus she lives out her tragic existence.

Dona Amelia's compassion for the laborers of Sulaco, Winnie Verloc's devotion to her brother, to name one other, Flora de Barral's love for the responsible Captain Anthony--all express the individuality of a "woman's true tenderness." Containing that virtue in their souls they are alike, patient with womanliness and vibrant with the truth of their separate commitments. Conrad neither oversimplifies nor sentimentalizes them as the women of his fiction

Certain qualities inevitably surface in the characters of major figures in Conrad's books, traits that often relect back upon the man his physical and intellectual vigor, his emotional power, his love of life that led him to sail to ports around the world for twenty years. His capacity to suffer was real. It is said that in his writing *Nostromo* Conrad spent twenty-one months in blackest despair over what he anticipated would be the book's failure. In their reflection of the energy and restless, adventurous spirit of the man Conrad, the writer's characters have the capacity to face often cruel, extremely dangerous tests of fortitude and moral courage. And in doing so they inescapably demand of themselves decision to act out their conflict without ever faultug the truth of their own natures! The Romanicism of Josph Conrad, in its most obvious aspect, is his genius for evoking mood through his description of exotic and far-away places. More profoundly, his Romanticism reposed in his idealization of the natural man by clarification of maftters of conscience, by the dramatic action in which there blended the delineation of moral choices with living guilt, lawlessness and primal human fear.

THE BASIC ELEMENTS
OF THE DRAMA

It may seem to some theatre afficianados to be a contradiction by a foe of the theatre to say that a play cannot be about people and still qualify as a serious work of creative imagination and dramatic art. A really good play cannot evolve on paper and in the mind of the dramatist, nor can it but merely come to life on the stage, unless the people *are* the play and their characterizations. Dress and manners afford clues to character, it is true, but if the character does not reveal his express motives, ambitions and weaknesses, then he is indistinguishable from any person in real life. Dress and manners, indeed, may convey that individuality, while the inner working of the mind remains darkened to the audience. Combined, he is potentially a living creation on the stage as in the dramatist's imagination.

Axiomatic, however, as this definition is, there are, even so, playwrights today penning monstrous works who should have stayed with accounting or written technical folios for the electrical engineers. They go about their delineation of tortured scenes, not like the scene painter who is, himself, one of the theatre's indispensavble technicians yet knows that he paints illusions; or like the carpenter of Lady Winchester's eccentric house, his drama is disjointed, filled with traps and blind staircases to violence that shock rather than entertain and enlighten which, were it not for the curtain, would go on and on. There are madcaps whose ambitions are those of burglars--to break into the tasteless medium of television--write as though every heroine were a shrill neurotic, as though debauch and homicide were synonymous with outsitanding drama and whose work would die aborning were it not for the special-effects folk.

Human motives, clothe them as the dramatict will, are the soul of character. We have seen in the plays of Sartre and Strindberg, where common motives are delivered up to the wrack and pinion of mad philosophies, making those characters ill-fitted they for any life but that of bdlam. Such characters own the virtue of a mindlessnss, no longer novel, with which their creators have endowed them, never incommoding themselves sufficiently to distinguish between madness and sanity, the idiot and the intelligence of evil design. Having thereby deprived the audience of any real perspective on their natures, the dramatist flings his creations into the pit of torment where we see only the emotions of creatures who, as abortive monstrosities, cannot be likened to any of the ordinary folk who people the world round about us.

A play, let it be said, is a channel for human emotions; it is not a vaudeville skit, a charade or an anecdote told on the stage. One may hope that by this late year laughter had earned its keep in the house of mortal response. Yet I have seen it in the theatre that emotions evoked by the lines of a moving scene are met with subtle disdain behind a perception inferior to the playwright's, and that the players, for their failure to bring the audience into the play, are so put out of countenance that what was comic becomes pitiable and what was tragic; assumes the mask of satire. Did the audience but find such stage-acting embarrassing, they might, as a body, have walked out of the theatre. But ususally they will wait for scenes of more dramatic power, and in that they are more kind than discriminating.

While such embarrasment may be the common lot of these clerks, buyers, accountants and other gentlemen of the business world, who find pleasure in the illusions of the stage set, I can only conclude that the players are most often at fault for wearing the emotions of their several characters pastiche, to match the lighting and brilliant costuming, while all during this and the next scene, their dullard's grasp and their puritanical Propriety throttle feeling with sense and choke off those emotions that are most real for the character. More often than not , on the closing night of that same play, the director and their own backstage criticism will have informed them of their error in similitude, in the make-believe on life, so that happily their drama then ends in sound audience acclaim.

ll have seen more than one play in San Francisco's little theatres follow this change from mediocre pasttime to brilliant theatre. And in those productions where it has transpired, I am pleased to note that almost invariably the change occured when the players sharpened their emotions. Yet they did so only by more clearly apprehending in what instances, the turn of thought, a piece of stage business, the "hidden meaning" was revealed in the action by motivcs, actions inseparable from those emotions--which from peak to peak draw out the characters germinal, or central, *truth* as by a current. Therefore, this his undercurrent of performnce, as sit were, proves that in peformance a play is a living thing in its subtle evolution of emotional depth. Indeed, I have heard it said by an actress of considerable experience and talent in roles that demand utmost perfection in timing and a vibrant keeness of the emotions for beliecavility, that no feeling, no expression of an emotion stands *alone and unrelated* to the other action that transpires around the character. For my own part, I have heard the seats in the old Bella Union Theatre in San Francisco creak fitfully at some dull passage of action or the mere recital of lines by the players on stage. Such discomfot and sheer nonsense could not have come about had the players felt convinced that what they were saying belonged to the character of their play roles, and to no other. In consequence of these observations, I remark then that it is the motives that lie beneaththe emotions that conduce toward some terrible climax, ingenuous solution or comic unraveling. Yet in retrospect of the earlier action, the emotions have borne the tale along through the events and the thousand miniscule instances of player interaction, informed always and clearly by the intelligence of recognizeable motives.

I would, however, caution some would-be dramatists that a drama is not the spectacle of the play and counterplay of human beings compelled by their motives to act in certain ways in certaian situations; this careful exigitical description also defines a business deal or a Faustian Pact. While much noise is made over the familiar scenes, the realism of everyday life suitable to the display of local color, the familiar words and actions within the well known, the immediately recognizeable setting, are not the chief criterion of good drama. There are direclors who, for instance, regard Wilder's **Our Town** as great drama because it is "everyday" familiar drama. The implication is that audiences never grasp anything unfamiiar. Yet they understand **Macbeth,** whichhas found its niche in the theatre as has lesser fare for the local colorists. How is it then that an audience understands **Macbeth?** The human emotions must bve gien form and direction by the hand of the playwright in order to reveal most clearly the motives of the characters in the story, for to vivsisect emotions, as some of your more learlned playwrights nowadays attempt to do, pandering to clinical distinctions and exhibiting specimens of humanity as though they were monkeys, is but to analyze rather than to sysnthesize. A successful play in the theatre is a synthesis of its elements.

A play is a composite, **living** synthesisis of emotions whose form may be moot and variable but whose parts must be interrelated by; motives, of which the story is the taskmaster. Neither compulsion nor motive nor the familiar setting or situation furnishes us with an adequate ceriterion of a truly fine play. For the one--the compulsion-- lends itself o the impostures of bizzare philosophies and the discomfortures; while the other --he absurd motive--encourages among playwrgihts and patrons that indiscriminate yearning for claptrap that moves and breathes, as farce, yet for all its beauty of spectacle affects the senses while retiring the understanding. That describes much of modern television fare. More often than not it will be found that the dramatist distrusts his own human insights in deference to the psychologies of the clinic, or has been persuaded that absurd departures from conventional dramatic forms are an apostasy on his art.

What is made to seem recognizeable and genre therefore realistic, hardly reaches to what elements are basic to the drama of mortals who strut and fret their lives upon the the metaphorical stage of life, and then "are heard no more." For the performance of Lord Edgard, an excellent actor in a miner role in The Great Plays Company production of Anouilh"s **Carnival of Thievces**, which opened two seasons ago in San Francisco, remains impressed upon the imagination, not because the actor Phillip Vizcarra spoke great lines or titttered sagacious sor even witty quips; but ecause the elderly Parlorpiece, outfitted as he was with pince-nez, white gloves and cane, and a moustache behind which he seemed to hide, sat in on the schemes of Lady Hurf as the incarnation of boredom among the wealthy of Paris. His nose, in the park scene, fixed upon one shred of financial cant buried in the folds of his newspaper, and there he reposed, while Lady Hurf was fully in the act of devising her plot of entrapment to match the nieces Eva and Juliette at a Carnival of Leavesd (Thieves, by mistake, it sos urned out by lerror on the inviation). The urbane Lord Edgard, to all appearances, was bereft of any interest in life, since the activity going on within his own household had become quite meaningless. To Anouilh, that state of genteel obvlivion, that nirvana of the senses was for Edgard's part the pitiable puppetry of lhis own self-deception. Thus before the final curtain had rung down, it was evident to most of the audience on that night that Lord Edgard had both ceased to feel and to reflect upon what he had once felt. He had vecome a symbol, the figurehead of an idea. G.B. Shaw would have understood this sort ot transition and enoblement.

And yet--we are talking about the evolution, as it were, of character changes within a brief three acts which define character, separating the deliberately dull from the specifically poignant and transitionally real, almost beyond the pale of the drama itself by the act of sharpening the emotions, that is so real as to not be actors at all. . At times, the play requires this change, at other times, the actor "catches up" with the truth of his character, that is, enters into the personna.

In this Anouilh play little did we learn of the nobleman's essential nature, not that the actor would not have it to be so, but because the playwright wished to present the olutward resemblance of realism without an exploration of the man's own unique core individuality. Alone, Lord Edgard could not possibly have catapaulted others around him into some rogueish skip of mischief, or provoked ridicule over a foible in his manners, or, indeed, compelled any crisis that would have revealed him ti be a man of impeccable tastes and admirable sentiments, those qualties of the enviable English butler Crichton in Barrie's quixotic comedy **The Admirable Crighton**. Doubtless there are young tyros of the theatre who will take exception to this pronouncement, and at once sit down to concoct a pretty little farthingale on the man who was a *tragic artifact*. They shall miss the point, however, which is that Lord Edgard outwardly resembles a *type* of being, even while we discover nothing essentially important in him as Lord Edgard.

Now in Synge's **The Well of Saints,** performed by the Stanford Players this past season, Joseph Plummer's vital and exciting recreation of the blind and weather-beaten beggar Martin Doul enkindled an altogether different response from the audience. For while the physical realism, the graphic detail of costume and features, was equal in quality to that of Lord Edgard, Martin Doul di arouse others to act, and gayly so, with comic vituperation and hot denials in the *lovers* and *beggars* scenes. He did act in his rags and with beating stick, pulling his long shag of gray beard. So that I hink it not amiss nor handling the truth wrongly to say, in a comparison of Lord Edgard with Martin Doul, as creatures of the live stage, that what is dramatic to the action and realistic to the eye doth not, alone, make the drama.

Nor is it a clarification to say that a drama involves a conflict; since a clash of wills, as we have, for instance between Dr. Kroll and Johannes Rosmer in Ibsen's play on clerical iconcoclasm, does not sof itself constitute the drama, and many scenes in literature are dramatic without strong conflict. The *Sunlit Glade* and *Public Lecture Hall* acts in Shaw's **Back to Methuselah,** Saroyan/s **The Cave Dwellers,** and the opening love scene between the young law sludent and his seeetheart in James Lee's **Career** are , each of them, instances of this general observation. A dramatic idea, and one that in the hands of a master playwright becomes potentilly fine or great drama, a satire, comedy, tragedy or frantasy, is an idea that reveals human nature. Lest we get off into a discourse on the *Plays of*

Ideas, it may be worthwhile just to point out that in the case of G. B. Shaw, as a near contemporary example, the British rebel exploited the ideas of his Fabian socialism for their revolutionary candor, and for the exhuberant showmanship that would put Shaw on top as a London playwright.

The idea I have in mind is designed, in its varied convolutions of stage action, less to exploit the talents of the wardrobe mistress and instill rhapsodic admiration for an actor's gifts than it is to show up human character For we can never ne completely informed upon the naturalist appetites and the dreamers visions, the mortal beliefs and the human frailties, the delusions, paradoxes and quandries of the creature called *Man*. How he undertakes his personal survival and how he manages to cope with the events of his times and the circumstances of his existence, in concourse with other men, these things the play reveals to our eyes, no less than to our understanding. Insofar as the theme is trivial and the issues of no piths or moment, the play will seem trivial and last but a short while, then pass into oblivion. But let the passions be great and the issues of civilized conduct of importance , as guides to civilizing amenities, then in the comic genre, and as reflections into self, indeed in all serious drama, that product of the pen and the theatre will be of itself great and will last.

One can scarcely recommend a more profitable activity to the younger generations, and to the older a more pleasurable engagement than that they assist in the construction of the scenery and costumes and, tallents permitting, perhaps read for parts in some forthcoming production, then live as another mortal for a brief span of time. Or, seating themselves in the darkened house, watch the unfolding of a tale of other men's lives. Then, if all have done their work, technicians players, director and, most vital in importance, the playwright, and if the story be honest and well-rounded out with true observations on the affairs and characters of its people, the impressions, the knowlege, the pleasure gotten thereby must surely deepen the understanding and sharpen dulled compassion, so often blunted by man's "inhumanity to man" in our modern world.

The third of the three basic necessities of a drama, human motivation and the dramatic idea having been dealt with but briefly, yet it is to be hoped with discrimination, is the requirement of a story, and especially a story with a *dilemma*. Let it be said, here and now, that the resolution to a play, if it has a resolution, is not one of the chief elements, for this is the dramaturgy of play construction and not basic drama of character invention, the one a fine preoccupation for the schoolmaster and cavilist of the theatre, if not of noviatiate playwrights; and the other the business of the practiced dramatist, players and audience. Nor, again, is anecdotal narrative a drama, else the monoloues of Chekov and Strindberg might, on the printed page, occupy the space of a singsle paragraph each. It would be a gross error, I think, to attempt to persuade others that such narrator-pieces as **Our Town** and Josep Ferrier's Broadways fiasco **Edwin Booth** are extended anecdotes. For regardless of the wide acclaim of the one and the meretricious, lantern-slide *tour de force* effect of the other, their forms episodic, as in the novel, the chief characters in the scenes remaining fixed and inseparable from *biographer's tales*. Furthermore, in each work there is a human dilemma; and it is that dilemma that rescues Booth from obscurity andl the Webbs and the Gibbses from complelte annonymity.

To be sure, there needs to be a resolution of some kind, else the Protagonist is mad, which truly he seems to be in certain works of the *Expressionist* school. Such quasi-madness, I call it, is found in Post WW I German dramas of disillusionment, neurotic fantasy, symbolical God-masses orgy. Indeed, a play is not like an 12-tone atonal composition by Schoenberg which, if it but ends on a discordant note, does not cease to be a sympohonic poem. A play, however, that is expressive of the playwright's inner torment and the weir of his imagination, if it but concludes by showing us the phantoms of his night, may very well pass for a Masque on the moralities or on the mysteries of the author's personality, but it is not and cannot be a play, or it then lacks story and dilemma and is merely a psychonalytical expose of the author's pain.

Still I would not have anyone believe that the dilemma is--like a resolution--not *also* a problem in the technics of dramaturgy, which can be studied to immense advantage by a careful reading of the plays of Ivsen, realist and symbolist, who has been described as the progenitor of the modern theatre. Whereas a dilemma in the life of the principal character, as Nora in **A Dolls House**, may appear to form the ideological basis, and set the mould for the action thereof, in a good stage piece, the appearance is but the illusion of the author's pride. For no amount of craftsmanship in the construction of a play, with its exposition, crises, its ascenending action, *denouement*, and so forth, can compensate for the fresh, moving and profound grasp upon some humans error that the finest work in the theatre gives us. In fact were I to tutor a tyro playwright, I woul say find a common human error or foible and construct a play around it, beginning with the error and following with the consequences of that error. Then, resolve it with death by execution, restoration, disenfrancisement, or ruthless denial. In this schemata is embedded the Morality play, Elizabethan drama, dramatic realism--and the story of Job.

One may lindeed say, in defense of this argument for the dramatic dilemma of choices, as an infallible method of play construction, that from an initial quandry there emerge the major dramatic conflicts of *all* genres of the art, and that the play's crisis and turning point have but the same origin in story. Medea's murder of Jason and their two sons is the angulished rebellion of a jealous wife who has elected, in revenge, to kill the objects of her love, those beings who are most precious to her. Upon her discovery that Jason means to place another queen, and his paramour, in the council of his throne and the affections of his life, she is faced with the dreaded choice which Euripides' play presents to us. Medea's dilemma is unassailably clear . Miss Madrigal in Enid Bagnold's **The Chalk Garden** must, like Medea, resolve her dilemma by critical choice, and so, until the closing scene of the play, lhe conceals from all excepting The Judge a crimianl past wherein she has suffered a terrible wrong and miscarriage of ljustice to be layed against her. Her dilemma, likewise, is quite clear, to reveal her past, with or without a confession, to an essentially cruel, if not hostile, society, or to hide herself within the iinterstices of future years in a secluded corner of life surrounnding the old manorhouse and its mistress Mrs. Maughm and the merciless young niece Laurel. It is the playwright's business, so the argument goes, to spell out that dilemma for us, how it emerges from the lives of his chaacters, the emotion with which it is charged; and the characters' decisions as to what course of action to pursue in oder to resolve for us the dilemma of his story. I offer these two plays as illustrations of the theory.

Yet I, too, would hasten to point out that there can be no story without at least one such dilemma of dramatic promise; for what is that stalemate but a quandry over choices, for without a moment of choice and decision the deepest and most native grain of characrter remains hidden from view. Contrariwise, there may well be dilemma without a story, and it is this truth that accounts for much of todays deplorable clinical drama, and for the *obscurantisms* to borrow a word in its contextual meaning from Dr. Yvor Winters' **Maule's Curse**, that permeates the Expressionist drama of this country, notably the works of Eugene O'Neill, whose tortured souls voice their damnation of the outcast; of Elmer Rice, whose Mr. Zero in **The Adding Machine** speaks for the man stripped of his humanity-- a religious idea--by the machine, and of Tennessee Williams, whose Vala Xavier in **Orpheus Descending** utters the angry lament of the wanderer, disinherited by a special elect. Much of what seems meaningless and indistinct, and to defy interpretation, stems from this *obscurantism*, can only be the result of an inordinate emphasis upon dilemma, problem and conflict, as such. In **The Great God Brown**, for example and in **The Adding Machine** and the Orpheus play, we are struck by the terrifying and primitive sense of *aloneness* that each protagonist bears within himself. Each Principal, it may be said, acts as though he had free will, and yet pays allegiance to the particular god of his punishsment. It is this paradox that torments, even while it preocupies the playwright with passions as subjective expression, and dilemma as a kind of a-moral or Neitzchean choice of willed absolute ends.

We know that from the resolution of this dilemma in Greek classical tragedy there follows the catharsis, which Aristotle takes up in his **Poetics**. And we can observe, from the Medea play, that there is no catharsis in tragedy unless there is a story to involve the emotions and, by identification, to carry the audience through the Protagonist's wrong choice by a natural flaw from birth, thence to the crisis and complications of that human flaw or *hamartia*. Similarly, in comedy the laughter issues from the incongruous and ridiculous action, and from the absurd follies of choice in match, manners and motives, each of which,l upon eamination, will be found to contain a dilemma of choice behind the deceit. For seldom does a man drop his mask without a *gain and a sacrifice* at one and the same time. Yet, important as it is, I would not have anyone render the dilemma of superior importance to his judgement of what is truly fine drama and outstanding theatre. Therefore, it is for this reason that I have prolonged the discussion. For neiter the human quandry nor its resolution is possible to perceive, as a whole and in all-round perspective, without the framework of a story within which to mount these elements.

HOMILY

No man knows his neighbor
better than the fool, since the one
finds honesty to confirm his
own deceit; while the other is
less than honest to find in the
fool a neighbor.

MIRACLE, MYSTERY AND AUTHORITY

At one point in Fydor Dostoievsky's great novel of visionary realism, **The Idiot,** the novelist wrotes of "the terror of certitude." In his **The Diary of A Writer**, for the year 1877, he writes:

> "What is there in prosperity which is bought at the
> price of untruth and skinning? Lest that which is truth
> to man as an individual be also truth to a nation
> as a whole. Yes, of course, one may be temporarily
> put to a loss, one may be impoverished for the time
> being, deprived of markets; one's productiion may
> be curtailed and the cost of living may increase.
> But let the nation's organism remain morally healthy,
> and the nation will undoubtedly gain more, even
> materially."

The paradox of these two ideas of a materialistic-driven nation and a moral nation is a superficial one. Yet it indicates Dostoievsky's fear of the degradation of moral decay in the Russian people. During the years of his imprisonment in the Katorba at Omsk for sedition, he studied his only reading matter, the Bible, in order "to comprehend the inner meaning of Christianity." That fact is of utmost importance in explaining the man/s intellectual development and the maturation of his spiritual ideas, his human insights, dialectics of his reasoning and his time lin Russian history. It was there in the vermin and rat-infestsed camp, bitterly cold in winter winds, that he learned from his personal experiences in reflection; and it was there as a former Fouriest--the socialism of small cooperative communities-- that Dostoievsky worked out his fundamental concept: *that punishment and expiation merge in atonement*. Living among criminals and exposed to their rancor, rage and remonstrances and boasting, yet unable to expiate for their crimes, he saw the Christian *ethos* of the crucifixion-atonement as the resolution to guilt and the mitigation of the pain of criminal punishsment. Revolution could not cleanse the criminal's conscience. Until such a "barter", if you will, occurred, the remorse for a crime committed--spoken into the face of justice and forgiven by divine Priestly intervention, did not ease or purge the feelings of guilt, a pain that outweighed the actual punishment.

He became convinced that punishment and expiation for the criminal were found in atonement, and that the love-hate *ethos of conflict* lay at the core of human depraviy and pain. By what methodology did Dostoievsky fuse these religious and psychological conepts into his novels' realism? Nowhere in novels written between 1846 (**Poor Folk**) and 1880 (**The Posssessed**) and, excepting the first, can one find plausible prototypes from other cultures, as ie. are found in the socialist novels of London or Fabian plays of G. B. Shaw. What ingredient of mind and spirit gives Dostoievsky's work singular power and originality, is his *implacable realism of invention and character*. He had the insight to trace *throught processes*, as he does in the rationalization of Raskolnikov, the ax-murderer *before* he commits the bloody crime. He traces Rasputin's justification of God having wronged man who is thus entitled to rebel. For a further example, Raskolnikov does not lust to seize and possess the few paultry trinkets and money purse belonging to the murdered pawnbroker. He commits murder to justify his love for his sister Sonya. Friend Porphry does not morally acquit him as "a martyr for a god who is not our God, but for whom he would willingly die." Raskolnikov's weakness is his sentimentality, love gone awry, for his sister, the expiation for which is his *seizure* of an atonement --the murder--for the absence of genuine brother-sister love. It is not money that he really needs but love for himself, the athiest, in the form of sympathy from his *believer* sister, a kind of surrogate priestess who follows him to the Katorba as a nurse. Dostoievsky saw that the murderer Raskolnikov, stricken by guilt, wishes even yet to be exonerated and to do so he appeals to Porphry. The power of an unreal sentimentality as precursor of motivation to a criminal act was a realism that Dostoievsky had doubtless learned while in prison. And the rationalized alibi gave birth to the murder in this case. The criminals had taught him well that the condemned stand on their alibis as a way to keeping their sanity in some cases. They boast of their crimes; few repent.

If in **Crime and Punishment**, Raskolnikov is terrorized by the certainty of apprehension and of his being put on trial for the murder of the old woman pawnbroker, the sight of Russian people, the merchants, noblemen and serfs binding over their lives to the truth of guilt from sins and expiation through the Christ of forgiveness, beyond the legalism of remorse, signified for him the heart of his vision of a Slavophil world. Dostoievsky, during his prison years, had resolved the dilemma of man's compassion for his fellow beings and the terror created by violence--whether of murder, revolution or execution--as an instrumental means to brotherhood. The remorse of *confession* - before the Cross-led to compassion for other men. The corrupted conscience eschews remorse--another lesson of the Katorba.

In the chracters of Prince Muskin, Raskolnakov and Father Rasputin, the radical evangel, the author dramatized the implications, in a character's power and integrity, of the moral *disease* of untruth He had borne witness to such decay at his fathers Hospital clinic for the poor. Poverty and actual disease can blight the dignity of reason and self-identityas a person. Symptomatic of that disease was moral indecision--the inability to discern right from wrong. Consistent with the symptoms were the anguish of guilt, personal or surrogate. Such was Rasputin's plea, that the conscience of man is a moral battlefield, mined with dilemmas of spiritual conduct and ethical choice where good and evil struggle for dominance.

As a convict laborer, Dostoievsky ground alabaster and moulded bricks while listening to the inner thoughts, out of the guards' earshot. In the barracks, it was the same. These were men reduced to brutality, made violent by temperament and jungle cunning, the depraved, the murderers, the thieves, rapists and ideologically dangerous. They were the rabble of men condemned as vicious and unwanted by society. As a Fourierist who fulminated against the Tsarist government and the luxury and excesses of Russian nobility, and understanding them as he did , he also confronted ruthless criminal minds. and in the flux of mens fortunes and the boasting of criminal acts, he perceived that the awareness of a crime committed is sometimes more painful to the criminal than is society's punishment.

He writes in **House of the Dead**, and obliquely in his Diary, that he often read in the countenance of a branded man the consciousness of guilt and suffering of a felon for his crime against himself.

In Moscow Dostoievsly had learned the dialectics of athiests like Kirilov in **The Possessed,** and Ivan Karamazov as the instigator of his father's murder in **The Brothers Karamazov.** These are thinly veiled discussisons or *arguments,* as it were, of ideologues turned rapacious engineers of crime. He was brought back to *the why*, the true human motives which reappear in dialogue by the members of Varvara Petrovana's little circle of Petersburg "printing press revolutionaries" in **The Possessed.** Dostoievsky found their motives vicious, compounded of selfishsness, made dangerous by intrigue and embittered by revolutionary and class hatreds, yet glorified by pride and dialectical logic. Again--the criminal alibi in a different form, leading not to murder of an individual but to the exterination of a class, the Russian nobility of the Tsarist regime, of which, ironically, his father as a medical doctor was one.

He, no less than Tolstoy, was to demand a religious role for Art and to reject categorically the formula of *art for arts sake*. Unlike Gogol, Dostoievsky was not an impartial investigator; nor was he primarily the sympathetic humanitarian artist that Turgenev was. In his efforts to understand that particular Russian who was comndemned as a criminal, yet possessed a strong individualism and a love for intellectual dialogue, whatever his lifestyle, the novelist was not the humanitarian moralist that Tolstoy was--he whose orthodoxy would not permit him to level the social class wall between serfs and noble- men, the soldiers and Russia's feudal barons.

Apart from them all, the novelist whose pity for human suffering was that of a fellow inmate conceived and executed novels that were perhaps closest to the heart of the Russian people. The poverty and sickness of the flesh, he saw at his father's hospital for the poor in Moscow. His imprisonment in the Katorba instilled the poisons of revolutionary politics into his characters' motives, those who confronted the old Regime of Nicholas II. Precisely because his characters, spawned by the millieu, speak for themselves do they speak with power and conviction. Pity and love does not exist beneath Raskolnikov's brutal blows with the axe; and yet those virtues *perversly* animate the motives of Rogin, the violent, jealous half-insane lover of the woman the Prince is in love with.

Dostoivsky saw men of their sort, their prolonged anguish and wretched indecision and even more dismal frustration as men who were redeemable just so long as they had the capacity to rationalize their actions and to discern between right and wrong. Self-inflicted pain was the torment of criminal guilt. Were it not for Dostoievsky's kind of Christian *construct,* showing the impress of the Eastern Orthodox church and the ferment of his Scriptural study in the Katorba, his revelation of moral choices in the breech of athiestic indifference would have failed. And he would have creatsed characters whose lives were damned forever.

The love-hate motif lay at the bottom of Dostoievsky's realism in his character delineations. Raskolnikov was not damned ecause he had the capacity to love. That was what Dostoievsky believed. The specific criminals suppression of love plays out in the story of crime and forgiveness. Obviously then, in addition to the theme of expiation through Christ's atonement by confession, the dual psychology of love versus hate becomes another of the novelist's themes.

C. J. Hogarth as quoted from the Dostoievsky's work which typifies the novelist's belief and his conviction that love has a regenerative power in "the most ignoble of natures."

"If, when I was a child, I had been blessed with parents I should never have become what I am today."

"The father himself wears but a threadvbare coat; yet for her (his daughter) no gift is too costly;...He will spend his last coin for her...if, in return, he shall receive but a smile."

"Where there is no love there is no wisdom."

"It is sufficient to love steadfastly, and work will become a pleasure."

"Think (a cynical debaucheee is speaking to an outcast of society) "if you had but a little child to dangle at your breast!...is it not perfect happiness when all three are united in one - husband, wife and child?"

"Love is the whole world, love is the most precious of jewels...Love is what men will give their very souls, their very lives, for." -*House of the Dead*

Dostoievsky was a writer with both pity and curiosity; he combined natural sympathies with his personal human mental and physical suffering and his observations of these crises in other men's lives. Scenes at his father's Moscow hospital had taught him much as a younger man. For most of his life he enquired into other men's deepest thoughts, an investigator with "regard to the pathology of the human soul." *Pathology* of course means relating to disease, disease of the human soul. He, himself, suffered from epilepsy, undoubtedly a factor in his mental makeup. Dostoievsky's temperament, his exposure to the filth and degradation of the Moscow slums and his visits to Dr. Dostoievsky's hospital for the destitute and the ill and improvident sick spawned in Moscows tenements-- these memories bearing the later scars of his brutal imprisonment meted out by the dulled and caloused judge of the bench, went into the novelist's richly-fermenting imagination. These experiences warped him toward the study of degeneracy, of that pathology of the soul's sickness, without corroding his own moral position.

Dostoievsky understood human rationalizations for criminal conduct, and he did so with brilliance of perception and insight. As corrolary to struggling through the tortuous thoughts of a criminal, he comprehended the *moral alibi* as few of his classical Russian novelists did, with the single exeption of Tschekov. Shatov in **The Possessed,** an erratic and impassioned Nihilist, and a student in-fatuated with Varvara Petrovna, plays the part of the individualist in the service of a noble (political) cause. His dialectics have persuaded him that all actions and deeds and accusations are permitted. Shatov's hunger for revolution only partially conceals his lust to indulge hidden hatreds throlugh moral anarchy; gold and power over others are actually secondary motives in moving him to act. His conflict lies quiescent and deadly within himself, tending ultimately toward tragedy in its consequences. He has internalized rejection, the apotheosis of all revolutionaries. His infatuation is hopeless, self- indulgent, the poison of his desire as a revolutionary to be heroized. His cause, however, is ineffective because it is effete, demanding not social justice but self-adoration, a flaw similar to Raskolnikov's

Shatov's motives are, of course, personal; he has no capacity to interede for another human being and for this reason his revolution is so personal as to be meaningless. Through Shatov and Ivan Karamazov and Raskolnikov and the gentle, naive Christian Prince Muiskin, Dostoievsky shows us what he means by the potential "God man" in a morally corrupt and lawless human being. The Christiansity of the Prince is narcissistic, not corrupt in and of itself, but as a figure of nominative power under the old regime and believing himself to be annointed as a regent of God to carry out the command of succor and protection of the poor, he is empty of any moral suasion or authority in Dostoievskys novel!

Fydor Dostoievsky was not directly concerned with an exploration of man's acquisiive instincts, nor merely with his probitive, destrucrtive impulses toward destruction by acts of violence. His scientific curiosity added yet another dimension to Dostoievsky's realism. War within the human conscience was his battlefield.

Read his accounts of lthe prisoners who lived like brutes amid their filthy and cold, their hunger, sexual flagillations and vicarious floggings in **House of the Dead**. His almost clinical revelations of what he saw were detailed and must have stunned Russian sensibilities of the day. The scientific bent of his mind reflected off his father and his medical practice in Moscow. Yet flung into the Katorba, after near execution and a last-minute reprieve, he brings that surgical ;mind with compasion to his study of the criminal's netherworld. The probity, purpose, the character of his investigation gives the book far deeper meaning than "sensationalism" In deed, he was embroiled his entire life in revealing that "*within the very lowest strata of humanity, human souls are to be found with the attributes and the instincts which are forever hidden, though they are latent, in the natures of comfortable, ordinary people. He showed, too, that the real punishment of a crime is to be a criminal. His great thesis is that crime and punishment are one and the same, each being a manifestation of inner suffering.*"

It was this human truth that his Siberian exile taught him, who almost from the beginning of his career as expurgative novelist, an intransigent *political pamphleteer* through the schemata of the long novel and a *documentary artist* of dark street profiles of Moscow habituees--for none of them appear to enjoy any permanent residency--" Dostoievsky instinctively vanishes into the labrinthian ranks of the Russian disinherited. His protagonists, the murderer, the Prince, the radicals of violence, the religious zealot, the debauchee--they possessed no property claims to an old Russia and in effect were disinherited outcasts in all but name. Consider where they live: over a pawn shop, in a cellar, in a dilapidated shack. They are or were among Russia's powerless, characters who are not unlike the sort of socially disenfranchised who stagger into Dr. Dostoievsky's hospsital clinic. Society, the writer is telling us, has damned each to his own small acre of Russian wasteland, and from among hese moral cripples and savage disbelievers of Moscow and Petersburg Dostoievsky draws with imaginative force the half-mad, terrorized, pathetic and obsessed characters that people his novels. He does so causing us by the sheer power of his conceptions to realize that *they are us* in one form or another. Veneered over by niceties and posessions, they are our reflected images of intangible struggle and inner anguish and the terrible loneliness of self-doubt. Their afflictions are our afflictions, their pathologies our pathologies.

It is altogether certain, therefore, that an other aspct of Dostoievsky's realism was his grasp of the lives, the descriptions, the struggles of the different social strata of Rssian society, those sharp distinctions which inflamed he minds of Politiçal revoluionaries, and, indeed, had incensed Fydor to compose a paper that seditiously leveled certain accusations against the Tsar and his regime. Dostoievsky was painfully aware of social discrimination and cruel intercene hatreds wihin the city gates. He was the *social commentator* not of a changing Russia, as is Tschekov (**The Cherry Orchard** play) or of a feudalistic paternalism suffused with Christian dogma, as is Tolstoy (**Anna Karenna**). But he was a penetrating reporter of the present state of things, matters of cause and import like poverty and hunger and incipient violence in the streets. Russia is breaking down economically, socially and politically and Dostoievsky's work shows that perilous reality.

There is a characrter in his wriing that most resembles him: the Slavophil Kirilov in **The Possessed**. He is a man who covets shis sneer of God and of humanitarian principles extrinsic to the lionish, empty, the cruel and opportunistic violence of revolution. Kirilov is also the subtle and at times affable "party man" who is wound up into the apparatus of a Fourieristic society that was Dostoievsky's fate. And still as the story progresses Kirilov's doubt of God's beneficience ignites a new faith in him, like Saul of Tarsus who, after persecuting Christ, was converted to a Penticostal Paul, seeing the revelation of truth that emerges from shadows by the light of the new tomorrow. For a new Russia is not to be attained by the spilling of blood and the murder of the innocent, even of the guilty. Kirilov's inner passion, his reflective intellectual zeal grapples with crime and its insidious plea of self-accusation, as against expiation if not through faith then never by means of violence. A man can never purge himself through violence; he only compounds his guilt. He cannot free himself from shame by appropriating the life of another man through murder or through self-exile or narcotics or self-inflicted disease, as do those inmates who attempt pugation by their physical flagillations in **House of the Dead.**

Karamazov's rebellion was similar to Kirilov's abandonment of God. He tormented his mind and tortured his emotions by dwelling on his vacillation and disbelief in God. Yet he perpetrated with the accomplice help of his brother Miitya and their criminal accomplice Smerdyakov, the murder of Old Karamazov. **The Brothers Karamazov** is Dostoievsky's great *detective story* of crime, which is never necesary, against the feeble and helpless, which is usually the case, for reasons that are cold-blooded since calculated and naked of compassion. Just as the saving of life and mitigating of suffering is the way of Dr. Dostoievsky, so is murder anathema to his son Fydor who must have had some contact with the patients on his Father's hospital Poor Ward.

There is an anomaly in Dostoievsky that emerges repeatedly: that his affilrmation of the value of life is vehemently juxtaposed, equally, to his affimation of the reality of death. He has Kirilov say in **The Possessed**: *"God is necessary and so must exist... But I know he doesn't and can't. Surely you must understand that a man with two such ideas can't go on living."* The act of surrender of a love object, a woman of a passionate connection to a rebellious spoiler, was for Dostoievsky an act of self-annihilation for which there was neither retribution nor forgiveness except through penitence. It is impossible to escape the religious connotations of the above quotation, since the act of suicide affirms only the reality of death and nothing more. The suicidal, desperately poor vagrants, often injured, had come into the hospital where his father had stopped their bleeding; no doubt there were deaths amid the blood on the stone floor. Rogogin faced imminent suicide in his life, the *anihilation of conscience*, when he surrendered his beloved....to (another)...who was a hated man. Suicide on different levels--physical, spiritual, psychological, moral-- was a mark of Dostoievsky's grasp of the human condition, of suffering without relief or release except through violent acts, or self-annihilation perversely tortured into acceptance as an enobling self-sacriice, rationalized as love.

Dostoievsky's rebels are the prisoners of their own minds and souls, chained to the irons of hate, jealousy, sworn slaves to their doubted beliefs--a terrifying outlawry--within often brilliand minds disposed to overthrow an icon, a creed, the status quo, innocent lives.
The reader often encounters a Dostoievskyan character who gropes for a comprehensible knowledge of life, an identity of who he is, his worth and purposeful meaning in life and where he is to act out his meaningful role in society. He can be a revolutionary or a monk or a shopkeeper, yet he has his fate and often his awful destiny to live out.

Rebellion by a character frequently takes the form of self-condemnation. It is manifested in some deed or idea as destructive self-will, or moral and spiritual suicide. Yet , too, other dimensions to this will to kill, to destroy--a will discovered in the character's inner turbulence as in Raskalnakov, is that the will is devoid of love.

Fueleop-Miller has written (66) that "*Dostoievsky's novels share the realistic background which was the common property of his age. 'Little' people are his heroes: the unromanic world of daily life is their sphere. The fierce struggle of self-will with society, lhe poverty and misery of early ineteenth-century capitalism, and the base nature of man in all its various forms, elemental evil as well as drab rascality and the wretched little weaknesse of men, supply him with the stuff of life for his novels.*"

There are, one finds, three aspects to the the author's realism, levels of realism that are found in his major novels and that exhibit hlis most miportant dramatic ideas and insights into human nature and what he saw himself attempting to accomplish as a novelist. (1) The realism of Man, the *visionary*, he whose oppressively painful sense of guilt and his will to love meet in the act of penitence, justified, he believed, by Christ's atonement. Such a man suffers purgatory through his faith, a state of rapture with its vision of Man's dignity and potential nobility of spirit greatly akin to the purging of emotions, the catharsis in Greek tragedy.

There is this difference, however, that the penitence of the criminal at the instant of his new faith, his belief in God's forgiveness, signifies a regeneration, a humanizing of the Self, a full and continuing acceptance of a perfect authority beyond his own will, a restoration to the Man of the knowledge of human--and divine--love in its personalized manifestations. Such a vision and purgation presupposes the criminals awareness of moral distinctions between evil and good as he observes and deals with his fellow beings, lessons Dostoievsky learned in the Katorba prison camp.

He confesses to having seen those powers of discernment at work in the hearts of the most hardened prison criminals. (2) Then there is the realism of *criminal psychology*, the behavioral aspect of characers like Raskolnikov, the apparent aspects of human motivation and outward behavior. (3) The third sort of realism is *physical*. Dostoievsky will often describe the salt frost on the wagon driver's moustache without troubling to describe the freight under the tarpaulin. He particularized the uniquenss of his characters. One will find this sort of vivid particularization in his short stories "Apropos of the Falling Sleet," "The Landlady," "The Gentle Maiden."

Dostoievsky" hoped to free himself from the extreme torments of an age torn between belief and disbelief," (45) writes Fueleop- Miller. He had planned his one big book to be called **The Life of A Great Sinner,** an autobiographical epic in which fictional characters such as Raskolnikov, Kirilov in **The Possessed** and Prince Muiskin in **The Idiot** were to find God through their inner struggles. In **Crime and Punishment**, Raskolnikov murders the old woman pawnbroker and, like Pilgrim without Calvinist exhortations but with a pain of his consciousness of guilt, he reaches the threshhlold of repentance through Sonya's influence. In **The Brothers Karamazov**, Smerdyakov kills old Karamazov, the father, to bring about the materialization of his atheistic beliefs. Yet he accuses Ivan: "You yourself always told me that everything is lawful. Why are you so surprised now" Prince Muiskin in **The Idiot** can sacrifice his love for Natasia to Hippolyte because those "arrested in guilt and affllictions are more deserving of love than the guiltless and fortunate...." Kirilov in **The Possessed,** doubting the existsence of God and His vague promises of Mankinds omnipotence, choses suicide to prove throgh the freedom of non-existence that man is sovereign when he is free from fear of God and death.

Dostoievsky held a life-long belief, matured as he read Scripture and observed prison inmates, that men vacillate between "the two poles of the soul-- defection from God in sin and harmony in God." So writes Fueleop-Miller (5) A Christ who spoke from the Galilean boat and fed the 5,000, teaching love in the Beautitudes, was Dostoievsky's concept of God made flesh, a volitional, actual power for good. He was "*the way, the truth and the life*," the words which Sonya , Raskolnikov's sister, reads aloud to him which brings about his conversion , his spiritual birth and his confession to the Inspector. To the novelist, in his crime story, Christ's teaching was the internal, spiritual, connscionable mediator for vacillating man, Raskolnikov.

In **House of lthe Dead** Dostoievsky shows us an emergent awareness of man's moral nature. His long talks with the prisoners in confinement, his scientific curiosity to probe the different categories of criminals, to know the nature of their crimes and their origins as individuals, created a ferment out of which seventeen years later he was to write **Crime and Punishment**. Human degeneracy was the awful revelation. One scene which he draws of the prisoners in the bathhouse prefigures that power of imagination and unflinching dissection of moral perversity which was to appear in later works. Turgenev has said of this scene: (in J.A.T. Lloyds **The Great Russian Realist):** "*The picture of the bath -- it is truly from Dante!*"

The picture symbolizes the lost man, for all times, in the criminal's own terrifying world. Through a window in the bathhouse wall. there appears the phantasmagoria of fifty or more prisoners, their naked bodies writhing wildly in orgiastic desire as they shout and call to each other through the clouds of opaque steam. They beat each other with switches in their orgy, a glee and strange excitement written on their faces, flushed by their excitement and activity and the glassy effects of the steam on their bodies.

This vivid scene shows humans beings whose humanity, if not thei pride, was left behind them in their towns and villages. They are representatives of the soulless and the damned, reduced to the level of the animal. Their only real bonds with civilization are two: the words they utter to each other, and the fact of their crimes as defined by the court. The are men stripped of conventions and their right to claim conventions or to relate themselves to larger outside humanity. They are steeped in the orgiastic revelry of chained men whose Promethian liberation, through anarchy, was dashed on the rocks. Dostoievsky gives us a picture, in all its dramatic irony , of the *New Man* proclaimed by revolutionary thinkers , the anti-Christ saviors of the world, the utilitarian man who would make Self his god. Dostoievsky's study of the criminal was profound and incisive.

In the same book, **House of the Dead**, the author delineates codes of conduct among criminals, their understanding of feedom while in chains, their obsessions with the crimes they have committed. These vignettes lead naturally, in his maturing powers, and historically to Raskolnikov. He overhears trivial talk between a student and an officer, seated at a nearby table in the tavern. They are discussisng the hypothetical murder of an odious usurer in that quarter of the city, a man whose wealth would benefit society more than his life does. It occurs to Raskolnikov that those are the very ideas which have begun to occur to him. Back in his garret, he conceives the murder of the pawnbroker, an old woman who lives with her sister in an upstairs flat. He summons the rationalistic logic of a law student to steel himself.

> *"I am not one of those who abandon the weak to*
> *scoundrels. I come to the aid of the defenseless...*
> *I cannot coldbloodedly pass by all the horror, all*
> *the suffering and wretchedness of people, and not*
> *say a word."*

He wills his self-destruction. The tragedy in the making is that he hopes, through his crime, to save his sister Sonya from Svidrigailov, a contemptible man, by means of the stolen money. He, on the other hand and with characteristic Dostoievskyan irony, is discovered by Svidrigailov after the murder. Her hated suitor thereby acquires a sinister power over the girl. Raskolinkov's mother is killed by the shock of learning that her son is a murderer. One of the great themes of the novel emerges at the end: that "the divine instinct of the heart which is denied by hard and (intractable) reasoning is ultimatly justified by true knoweledge" So G.A. Mounsey has written in his book **Dostoievsky.** *That* true knoweledge is, in fact, the moral value of human compassion and the reenerative power of faith in God. One must always keep in mind the fermenting source of Dostoievsky's ideas, his Russian Bible and his intimate knowledge of criminals. One of the most moving threads of the story is that she, Sonya, leads her brother into the understanding and act of repentance, although she has sacrificed herself, for her family's sake, to the man she does snot love, Svidrigailov. There is the point to the tragedy: her self- sacrifice for something greater than she, her love for her brother, a confessed criminal. The stolen pawnbroker money does not ransom her; although Raskolnikov's confession to her and, by her prodding, to the Inspector,combined with his repentance, purges Svidrigailov"s dark hold on lhim. His condemnation and sentencing provide an example for her in her relationship to her hated lover...namely, rebirth and self-sacrifice instead of what would be, without her complicity in Raskolnikov's surrender, a moral suicide with the total collapse of her virtue.,

        Dostoievsky's humanitarian compassion was for the sinner, the criminal intead of for the victim. His tragic heroes and heroines are the Old Testament **Job** who are bowed by undeserved suffering, as a test of faith at the hands of a just God. It must be remmvered, however, that Dostoievsky's God was not the punitive Jehovah but the Diety of love, made manifest through the New Covenant Christ of love. His Varvara Petrovna, Ivan Karamazov, Kirillov, Shatov, all of his own creation, are characters whose suffering is inner, whose guilt and self-doubts and dialectics of rationality--**the alibi**-- are of the stuff of his own mind and heart. His, Dostoievsky's, pity sprang in part from intimate self-knowledge, that pity confirmed by his Orthodox faith. It is a little risky to say so, but Dostoievsky was in a true sense a re-discoverer of the Christian **ethos** of brotherly love, yet a true reporter of his characters' evil, their crimes and wrong choices by which they victimized themselves.

        Terror belongs to Dostoievskys impenetents. Andre Gide in his book **Dostoievsky** (309) writes;

> *Dostoievsky gives us, in one part, humble people*
> *(and surely possesssing between themselves humility*
> *almost to abjection, almost to pleassing themselves*
> *in abjection), and in another part, the*
> *proud (and surely those owning pride almost to the*
> *point of crime). These latter will be, ordinarily, the*
> *more intellectual. We shall see them tormented by*
> *the evil of pride, always making assault upon nobility."*

Dostoievaky links pride to terror as attributes of the criminal. He is saying that in **House of the Dead**, and in the character of Prince Muiskin, whose serenity signifies not merely the conquest of, but a spiritual transcendance over, evil's destructive passion. In **The Possessed,** Dostoievsky shows these two characteristic emotions of the criminal by means of his first-person narrative of a group of Petersburg revolutionaries among whom there is a man named Stepen Trofimovitch. A giant stone "as big as a house" hangs upon a ledge over the heads of his comrades.s They are the ones whos fear pain and death from violence; it is they who fear, he tells them, fear that the stone may not fall to crush them. Yet would death be less painful than their fear of the stone? In the story the rock serves a dual symbolism: it stands for reactionary restance to the plotters, whose leader is Varvara Petrovna and whose mouthpiece is her subversive, underground magazine. And, the rock emblemizes, also, the destructive power of open bloodshed. Terror, like a Greek *Fury* pursues those in bondage to revolutionary violence.

That crimina violence has various disguises. Kirillov tells us, in **The Possessed**: History will be divided into two parts, "from the gorilla to the annihilation of God, and from the annihilation of God to...the transformaltion of the earth, and of man physically. Man will be God, and will be transformed and things will be transformed and thoughts and all feelings...." The dialogue between Trofimovich and his fellow revolutionary continues.

> *"If it will be just the same living or not living, all*
> *will kill themselves, and perhaps that's what the change*
> *will be?*
>
> *""That's no matter.. They will kill deception. Every man*
> *who wants the suspreme freedom must dare to kill*

*himself. He who dares to kill himself has found
out the secret of the deception. There is no freedom
beyond; that is all, and there is nothing beyond.
He who dares kill himself is God. Now evcery one can
do so that there shall be no God and shall be notihing.
But no man lhas done it yet."*

"There have been millions of suicides."

*"But always not for that; always with terror and
not for that objct. Not to kill for fear. He who kills
himself only to kill fear will become a god at once."*

These proud, calm words of his *political suicide* articulate the fear of others in Varvara Petrovna's circle that reflect their terror of the unknown and of the darkness in their own souls.

There, in the Petersburg drawing room of their leader, we meet Stepan Verhovensky, who is convinced that married life will corrupt him, will sap his nergy, his courage in the service of *The Cause*. Marriage means corruption; his proud fear issues from a perverse self- love which he extends through the revolutionarys credo to the new world. Lilputin, his compatriot, is an elderly privincial official, a man with a malicious liveliness whose philosophy is Fourierist, as was Dostoievsky's. Behind his cruelty lies the fear of men. Shatov, the brute-man in civilization's clothes, is another; he struck Varvara's brother, the fearless Nikolay Vayevolodich, at a party gathering one night. As a weak man inside, Shatov stands in fear and awe of the leopard; violence is his recourse. Shatov, too, is the student of unstable temperament, a man burdened by a bad mamrriage, a merchant and family drudge with giddy social ideas and whose revolutionary ideals are more empty of conviction than they are sound with purpose. Dostoievsky's irony is that Shatov resorts to violence at the party in order to destroy the threat of violence. One of the most dramatic figures in Varvara Pertrovna's circle of friends is Stepan, whose soul doubt lies in the efficacy of revolutionary means to change. The novelist's crownsing irony is that Stepan cannot believe in his own disbelief of God-ideals. His friendlship with Varvara crumbles when struck by the realities of rubles for his tutorship of Varvara's young daughter, and by his Petersburg prestige. His god is his spride. He is the man made proud and free by Nihilim. Yet when she accuses him of putting her house to shame by causing scandals, he answers her by saying that he will take nothing from her; he will worlship her disinterestedly. His refusal to change is merely an alibi for his dread of involvement, and his contempt for the flunkies of "equality, envy, and...digestion."

It was the lst ten years of Dotoievsky's life, after the chains had fallen from his legs and he had returned home, that he wrote his greatest books. During those years (1854-1872) he wrote **The House of the Dead, Notes from Underground, Crime and Punishment** and **The Idiot**, together with two shorter novels, **The Gambler** and **The Eternal Husband**. Four years after his publication of **The Possessed** and the beginning of periodical installments of **The Diary of a Writer**, Fuelop Miller has written (30) that he was to become known as *"the spiritual counsel or of the nation."*

Dostoievsky prayed to God for strength and inspiration to write "all that lies locked in my heart and imagination," Fuelop- Miller writes. On November 8, 1880, he sent off the last signature of his Karamazov novel to the "Russian Mssenger." The dual themes of guilt and doubt of God, of punishment and expiation that converges in atonement, were not yet exhausted with this, his last vbook. In it Dostosievsky gives us a portrait of the sensuality Fydodor Pavlovitch who exhibits in his person and his a-moral actions, the conrruption that existed in Old Russia. It is the sons, heirs of their father's depravity who share the curse of his bequest. *"All things are lawful,"* says Ivan. All things not supportable by reason are fantasy, are wraiths of madness. And yet, perhaps it was Dostsoieveky himself speaking when he has Ivan cry out in the fervor of his mind- sickness: "You are my hallucination," he tells Satan, "and nothing else. It's I myelf speaking, not you. You are the incarnation of myself , but onoy one side of me...of my thoughts and feelings, but only the nastiest an stupidest of them. You're I, I myself, but with another face." The realities of that other face--the face of deceit, Satan's ploy-- were the main concern of Dostoievsky in his greatest novels. *What, I have said, lies in all men concealed behind their facades of possessions, power and pretense, yet emerges in the criminal's behavior.* This is a major clue to one's understanding Dostoievsky.

By shifting the causes for a man's crime from a society of serfs and noblemen to a conscience, oriented between God and Satan, corruption and morality, love and hate or war and peace, Dostoievsky has emphasized that his heroes and lesser dramatic figures are the arbiters of their own consciences. He shifts the locus of his long dramas from class-conflict, the theme of the revolutionaries to spiritual warfare, good versus evil. There was for him a certain latitude for the exercise of his powerful imagination of character, as for example the rational Kirillov beset by the enigma of God's existence. Then there is that faithful and devout monk Zousima, whose God is the God of the Russian fathers, yet, strangely, in no way does she find love inadequate to the task of healing hearts. Finally, for purposes of illustraton, there is Porfiry, that legal demon in gentlemen's attire, whose sentimentality would be repulsive if it were not rather pitiful when he pays a compleiment to Raskolnikov by calling him a *martyr*. Nothing but sheer logic could lead him to that viewpoint; and a martyr is a martyr and not hanger-on, perhaps a hero, but never a dead man, for death to Porfiry was absolute, irrevocable and final. Indeed we may be repelled by Raskolnikov's character and the awful brutality of his crime, as the motif indicates, yet Dostoievsky's theme of punishsment and expiation converging in atonement are not merely ideas inseparable from the psychology of conscience-struggle. They are real. Dostoievsky admitted the word, the deeds, the choices of action and the tormenting consequnces which follow in his creation of character and story action.

It was Dostoievsky's conviction that the eclipse of reason and failure of the will attacked a man like a disease, developed gradually and reached its highest point just before the actual crime. The disease continued with equal violence at the moment of executon of the crime and, for longer or shorter time, afterward, according to the individual case and then passed off like some common non-fatal disease. Yet Kirillov, Satov, Ivan Karamazov are characters who act solely upon the authority of their own consciences, their rebellion instigating anarchy, the total freedom from responsible action which moves, ultimately to the loss of freedom. Thus did alibis of these characters betray them into slavery to a fictive cause and the destruction of a rational conscience. Dostoievsky does not fail to exhibit in his character's defection from reason the savagery and cruellty as traits of the criminal, together with natural curiosity summoned to the fore in his premeditation of crime. Raskalnikov broods over his murder, but before he slays the pawnbrosker, we find traces of whimsy mixed with brutality in his premeditation of murder.

There were strange recesses of human nature which a prison camp, as a sort of experimental laboratory, opened up to the gentleman inmate who, as a nobleman with one side of his head shaved and branded as "dangerous," lived for four years by penalty of law among society's criminal scurvy of peasants, laborers, traders. A Siberian Katorba could now, however, oblterate class distinctions, those differences beteen groups of poeple with differing lifestyles. A natural distrust, Dostsoievsky tells us, kept himself and the prisoners estranged; he could never vecome one of them, fully accepted into their midst. When, for example, he trudges down to the ice-covered river to work with the prisoners in breaking up a river barge for firewood, the inmates restlessly keep a suspicious eye on him. Of rebeliousness, Dostoievsky has this to show us, that men will mutiny in even the most hopeless of situations. An example is when the convicts rise up against the cooks and malevolent camp major, clamoring for the animal satisfaction of their quite natural appetites. Yet, paradoxically, there existed honor among criminals. A few in the board barracks of the Katrorba abided by their verbal word of honor to respect the premises of pay, services for each oher, imtimate secrets and thoughts and intentions to escape. There existed also among the inmates a strong will to survive. Dostoievsky's sprisoners laugh at suffering, can feel the most exquisite self-satifaction over enumerating past criminal acts of violence, while on the day following, like traders in the course of marketplace business, the man who slit his wife's throat because she had a lover can in the next breath open a barter with another prisoner, in total forgetfulness of his deadly confession to his fellows.

It was the novelist's practice to draw his characters based on the model of someone he knew or had encountered. Stepen, for example, depicted Dostoievskys belief that to forgive is to gain freedom; to destroy is to seek a power beyond forgiveness. Doubtless he had learned this maxim from an criminal prisoner. Prlince Muiskin is another. His very vanity is a cause for making himself more pliable to the wills and persuasions of others. The meek and readily-coerced prisoner was a Katorba reality.

Vanity, Dostoievsky believed, was one of mans strongest motvating impulses. It is a catalytic. Varvara Petrovna daughter, Dasha, is on the point of marrying the young free thinker Nichlas in **The Possessed**. However, the mother, Mme Petrovna, mother, feels hidden contempt for Stepan, Dasha's tutor and familhy hanger-on. She resents her daughter's delay of the marriage until Stepan can give consent. Her proud anger occurs because of Stepan's usurpation of a mother's prerogative. Her contempt for him has a revolutionary class bias, since he has neither money, blue blood nor a will to loin the revolution. Her emotions as well as Stepan's are therefore mixed as are the movives for what they do.

In **The Possessed**, Captain Levbaldkin, a "repentant free thinker" expounds' in one of his early chats withs the "I" of the book, on the fly and a cockroach and their thoughts when dumped into a pail of stew. The cockroach, he says, would not mind, whereas the fly would. How ridiculous the Captain would appear to be were it not for Dostoievsky's sympathetic and serious-minded approach to the character. Levbaldkin's pabable demonstrates the relativism of men and guns--but without a knowledge of good, the patrotism only results in a-moral bloodshed. What the author is suggesting in this metaphor is that circumstances dictate the character's point of view...if the character is a-moral or without redeeming virtue.

In **The Idiot** there are other examples, scenes and characters that simplify the realisltic observation that Dostoievsky is a psychological realist. Hippolyte, foe to Prince Muiskin for Natashia's hand in marriage , dreams of a reptile that symbolizes, apparently, his hatred for the Prince much as he would detest and avoid a reptile. Hyppolyte expresses his rage at the Prince and accuses the "Jesusitical soul" of being the cause of his, Hyppolyte's , abject cowardice. These two examples illusrate Dostoievsky's genius for being able to shift the onerus of an unfavoravble or panful situation into the arena of a new conflict.

In **The Idiot** we see the strange love-hate of Rogogin for Natasia Philipovna. The question arises: why does he surrender the woman he loves to the man he hates. What perversion of love is involved? What transcendance over hatred has taken place within him? These words reveal much of the answer:

"He (Rogogin) laughed suddenly, and strangely. Then in a moment his face became transfigured; he grew deadly white, his lips trembled, his eyes burned like fire. He strretched out his arm and held the Prince tightly to him and said in a strangled voice: 'Well, take her! It's fate. She's yours. I surmrender her...Remember Rorogin!' And pushing the Prince from him, without looking back at him, he hurriedly entered his own flat, and banged the door."

Dostoievsky has dramatized for us the subtle influence of a man of noble station, compassionate nature, whatever his flaws, upon the character and actions of another person, who overwhelmed by fits of anger, does possess the insight and strength of character to discriminate between the motives and sympathies of Prince Muiskin. In Rogogin, we see the the reverberation, perhaps, of Dostoievsky's own guilt-stricken conscience relating back to his imprisonment for sedition when he ought to have been loyal to the Tsar as a nobleman; such as was his physician father.

Andre Gide has this to say about the novelist: in Dostoievsky (139-140)

"Certainly the psychological truths seemed always
to Dostoievsky what they are in reality: particular
truths In the novel (because Dostoievsky is not only   *a*
theoretician, but a speculator), he cares for the   *induction and*
he knows the imprudence there   *would be (for him at least) in*
attempting to formulate   *general laws These laws are for us, if we*
so wish   *it, to dissengage--like the hewing of pathos across*
the   *edges of his (characters') lives. That law, for example*
that a man who has been humiliated seems to
humiliate in his turn."

Emile Zola took great pains to paint a French countryside scene or the interior of a peasant's house, the scene around the hearth, or the miners at work in their black caverns a mile underground--took pains to depict these scenes in all their closely-observed details. Dostoieveky, however, gives us the external, the physical realities of a scene only as they bear a relation to the dramatic action. His descriptions, whether of a room of a student living in Petersburg slums and seen through the character's eyes, or whether of a scene of physical action exhibit this one quality: *there is movement.* For example, here is the scene in which Ivan Karamazov returns from a disquieting visit to the room of a man whom he has willfully implicated in the murder of his own father:

"Ivan did not go home, but went straight to Katerina
Ivansovna and alarmed her by his appearance. He was
like a madman. He repeated all his conversqtion
with Smerdyakov, every syllable of it. He couldn't
be calmed, howevermuch she tried to soothe him;
he kept walking about the room, speaking strangely,
disconnectedly. At last he sat down put his elbvow
on the table, leaned his head on his hands and
pronounced this strange sentence.: 'If its snot Dmitri,   *but*
Smerdyakov whose the murderer, I share his guilt,   *for I put him up to it.*
Whether I did, I don't sknow yet.   *But if he is the murderer, and not*
Dmitri, then of   *course, I am the murderer, too.'*

When Katerina Ivansovna heard that, she got up from
her seat without a word, went to her writing- table,
opened up a box standing on it, took out a sheet of

*paper and laid it before Ivan. This was the document
of which Ivan spoke to Alysha later on as a
"conclusive   proof' that Dimitri had killed his
father...."*

Dostoievsky uses only these descriptive details of the room, of the
expression on his characters' faces and of their actions which best suggest, rather
than mimic, or dully list or report as facts. Tourism, publishing and photography
had changed the need for Zolan microdescription. A reader of today may find
Dostoievskys dialectical passages, his intellectual wandering through mazes of a
revolutionary's thinking, of the terrifying thoughts and passionate outbusts of the
criminal mind at work--as somewhat tedious. Yet his novels are composed of the
stuff of Russian life of his times...and of personal experience. Against our wills
we are drawn in, blinded, spun round, and at the same time filled with a strange
sense of having been there with him, having seen what he saw and endured what
he suffered and at last believe his people to be real Russians whom we have met.

BIBLIOGRAPHY

POOR FOLKS
HOUSE OF THE DEAD
CRIME AND PUNISHMENT
THE IDIOT
THE POSSESSED
THE BROTHERS KARAMAZOV

FYDOR DOSTOIEVSKY, Rene Fueleop-miller, Chas. Scribners &
Sons, N.Y. 1950, (37 pp).
SOVIET RUSSIAN LITERATURE, (1917-1950), Gleb Struve,
Univ.Okla, Press 1951, (414 pp)
THE SHORTER NOVELS OF DOSTOIEVSKY, Preface,
Thomas Mann, Dial Press,
N.Y.(1951 (vii-xx)
THE DIARY OF A WRITER, (Vols. I, II) Dostsoievsky, Cassell
Co., Ltd. London (1097 pp)
LETTERS FROM THE UNDERWORLD, Introd. C.J. Hogarth,
E.P. Dutton & Co, N.Y. (vii-ix)

DOSTOIEVSKY, G.A. Mounsey, Alexander, Moring
Ltd, London; 67 pp.
A GREAT RUSSIAN REALIST, J. A. T. LLoyd, John Lane Co.;
NY ; 296 pp.
FYDOR DOSTOIEVSKY, Aimee Dostoievsky, Yale Univ. Press
New Haven; 1922 (294 pp)

A COMPARISON
By "Bettie Makewaite"

A stage play presents a scene from but one view, regardless of where the theatregoer sits in the house. A movie permits of watching different views of the same scen based on camera location. Stage settings must therefore be integrated with the action; while the camera can block out discordant elements. A stage presentation must recreate the physical reality through the very presence and imagination of the actors, working with spectacle elements as unified whole from action to action. A movie, by its very nature, records those physical realities, while its parts, because of camera-angle selection, need not be working together with obvious unity in each dramatic action ...although a unity is *implied* amidst discordant elements.

In a stage presentation, the actor is all important in such matters as pace, timing, the building of dramatic tension, making dynamic the action of the drama and conveying the meaning of the story. In a move, the use of music, flash shots of people and things off-set, odd angles and other technical devices may share that function of dynamic action with the actor. A stage presentation shows the whole actor, the entire characrer as a coordinated whole. A movie may present only fragments caught by camera selection, likely an artificial, mechanical direction of situation--and not necessarily directed by the actor, rather than an artful one, as by the actors on a stage.

The actors in a play consider audence reaction to the action going on; there is a give and take. This, however, is not (visibly) so with the best actors who adopt an attitude of **stage arrogance** that avoids this actor reactionl without theatrics but with an awareness ofthe audience. In a lesser actor, one can always detect this response-trick if the expected laughter, in comedy, fails to come. A movie in that respect is a dead thing--even though the best script writers may provide for udience reactions of a violent sort by writing unimportant lines in the intervals, like toughs of a cycle. A stage play presents flesh and blood, live human vbeings who say: Look you. lHere we are, real people. You could ve one of lus, and now let us act out our story." A movie, being a recording of life, is not

so intimarte, does not readily invite that actor-audience participation, a sharing of a story between real people. For that reason the stage presents a more intimate, and a more stubtle and flexible kind of acting.

While a play and a movie may be of the same length in time of performance, a play must telescope time through the dramatic illusions--the dialogue and its hints, shifts of focus of audience attention, artful acting and often the simple, traditional announcement of time passage. A movie, with its enormous flexibility in staging, can reproduce in short scenes that lapse of time and any interim action. The traditional announcement would no ordinarily be accepted by a movie audience--except that in the silent-film days, a title indicated a lapse of time.

A play must invite the suspension of disbelief in the story while presenting live human vbeings in action. A movie challenges that disbelief with its recorded physical realism and by camera techniques, while presenting not a *representation* but an *imitation* of human beings in action.

MARGINALIA

T he highest comedy is the comedy of faith-- Kierkgaard--From the essay "*Laughter*" by Henri Bergson

Perhaps James has been criticized unduly for calling American society of his time "vulgar."   But the fact is the process of social change was so accelerated, social antagonisms so intense, taking form in disputes, uprisings, insurrections and ultimately civil war, that he could see no order in that society, as he could in that of Victorian England. And so, without points of reference, i.e. what to him would have een permanent institutions, he could not identify individuals in terms of existing institutions.

--from a book essay by Roert Cantwell entitled <u>No Landmarks</u>

Shakespere's villains are not allowed to apper as honest characters even in their own eyes, and his noble characters must vbe noble even in the eyes of their wicked enemies.

--from <u>*Character Problems in Shakespere's Plays*</u>, by Levin L. Schucking (1948)

The critic's busines is to identify the species, then explain how and where it is imperfect and irreular
It is his business also to ascertain facts and traits of literature, not invent or denounce them; to discover principles, not establish them, to report, not create.
--from Wm. Dean Howells' essay "*The Question of a Criterion*," in M.D. Zabel's "<u>*Literary Opinion in America*</u>". (Essay written 1891)

317

A. E. Houseman believed that those interested in science or the humanities are motivated by a thirst for knowledge, principally for "the good of man." Hence there is no rule of creation in Housman's scheme of things; knowledge, for him, meant at most a discovery of things already existent.

--from the essay on A. E. Houseman in **The Triple Thinkers**, by Edmund Wilson.

Where there is rivalry, there is opportunity. Where there is too much rivlry, there comes oligarchy. Where there is oligarchy, there flourish low standards and indifference. - C. E. Miller

AN OPEN LETTER TO WHOM IT MAY CONCERN

Consistent with the Constitutionally granted Judicial Review there arise a numer of issues from Roe v Wade (410 US 113; 1973)
which the Court now addrees, particularly those stemming from substantive changes in medical technology. Statutory law is vulnerable to changes in circumstances because, unlike the written Constitution, a legislated statute sometimes tends to lose applicability to the demands of time. In the matter of Roe v Wade, the tolerance has taken on the *force of command* when precedent dictates participation by acceptance. I am intolerant of abortion, and increasing numbers of American are. Therefore, I object to the Court's decision in the original (1973) judgement.

Roe v Wade is political. It is so, and it is made to seem so, thus to affix the approval of elective constitutionality upon its painful and lasting consequences when the mandate of the decision is for toleration and not for law enforcement. In sixteen years of practice, elective abortion has come to stand for the "truth" of free choice and therefore, by sheer numbers of participants, a tyranny of truth for other men in our society. Yet conformity to precedent my be conformity to bad law.

In any enterprise it is hazardous when the outcome is consequent upon numbers and not the conmands of conscience. Crowd-mind governs the former conspiracy of choice, and lest I seem indelicate to say so, I think society's performance under Roe v Wade contains an element of that corrupt "mind," of behavior without conscience, of pitiless self-gratification or stupid indifference.

According to what I read, the State's interests are two-fold in this instance of abortion: The State has *"an important and legitimate interest in preserving and protecting the health of the pregnant woman,"* regardless of any question of her residency. This commences at the end of the first trimester, the woman thereupon acting only on the advice of a competent physician.

The State has *"another important and legitimate interest in protecting the potentiality of human life."* This "compelling interest begins at viability. But the question arises: When does "potentiality" begin? Hopefully, that is one of the elements the Court will consider, for it affirms the sanctity and the value of life in the womb, most certainly when the foetal infant's heart begins to beat and it starts to feel pain, these facts being true even if one disagrees that life begins at conception..

The science of post-natal and pre-natal care is changing. The date of viability is shifting toward conception, and the trimester guide for determining viability is, it would appear, becoming less meaningful as a deterrent to abortion. To get in "under the wire," as it were, for non-viable abortion, young women are coming into the abortuaries earlier in their pregnancy. Yet, paradoxically, clinics record an increase in the number of late-term abortions, some as late at 30 weeks. A law (Roe v Wade) that is so ill-defined as to time limits, that is subject to a sliding scale of application, constant revisions in application; that is confusing in questions of risk, legality and follow- up care is a law that is certainly too sweeping and therefore voidable. Since it is a vague law and a bad law, it tolerates numerous sorts of license and indulgences, therby ruling out what must be the basis for sound law --consistency and conformity in its application to anticipated circumstances.

The right to have an abortion is not a fundamental right under the Constitution. *Privacy is only presumptive after the fact* in order to validate the act being tried. A majority of the states have had restrictions for over 100 years. The reasons are what the pro-abortionists ignore yet have been handed down as common human knowledge about life for milleniums, to wit, that the quickening of the foetal infant demonstrates life, that *premies* can be cared for, nurtured and saved; that midwivery is a useful medical profession in rural areas, and that ultra-sound and other technology reveals the the foetal heart is beating at the time of *interuterine murder*. Since the advent of sound visualization and sophisticated aminosentesis testing for sex, deformity and normal interuterine growth, medical science confirms that life as all men know it outside the womb resembles the pulsing life of those yet unborn. To assert the protoplasmic nature of the expelled aborted foetus is a lie that for sixteen years your Court has encouraged the ignorant to accept.

Furthermore, it is a known fact that the heartbeat of the foetus begins about the fourth week. If a flat EKG wave or EEG (brain) wave indicates death, certainly a heart beat indicates human life in the womb. That seems to me a logical assumption. Then why does your Court and many doctors infer that the aborted life is only protoplasm? Have you conspired with the American Medical Association, Planned Parenthood, the abortuaries to exterminate an entire generation of over 30,000,000 infants, most of whom were viable when disposed of in the trash? You obviously lack the courage to act responsibily as jurists, deeming the *rules of your game* the essence of truth. I put Caesar's words into your mouths: "What is truth?"

Not long after the heartbeat is first audible, the foetal child has the capacity to feel pain. Yet the abortion proceeds in the most cruel and calloused manner, severing the limbs of the squirming, protesting infant by powerful suction or burning it to death and, lately, allowing birth except for the head which is punctured and its brains sucked dry. You assenting magistrates quality for the Aztec priesthood who worshipped with live sacrifices. You bare your inhuman and immoral cowardice for prestige and power. For a civilized society to participate in this sort of death of the voiceless victim--without representation as having a life of its own is heinously barbaric. I am ashamed of our country before God for a Court--and a society-- that ever brought about this wholesale murder by its decree of tolerated murder.

Now we have not just the vagueness of the law and its inapplicability as law, as sociological fiat. We must stand idly by and countenance, witness, the utter barbarism in the surgical suite of *"treatment for pregnancy."*

Roe v Wade did not envision clerical manipulation by Planned Parenthood officials to persuade the pregnant mother that abortion was not a choice but the only choice. But that's the reality, since Planned Parenthood rarely ever suggests alternatives to its fanati death verdict. Their current ruse for conealment of their power-play motive is to suggest that perhaps "abstention" is a way to avoid pregnancy. Their entire organiztion is built upon the lie that God is uncaring whereas they are the tender-hearted. And that abstention , while not wrong as such, is against nature taking its course.

Roe v Wade does not undergird the feminist movement --as street crowd scenes, marches, rallies, dismal coathanger displays and back-alley warnings would have us to believe. The movement can and does exist without interuterine dismemberment--for other worthy causes of their agenda.

BASIC DISTINCTIONS BETWEEN COMEDY AND TRAGEDY - COMEDIC NAIVETE AS A RESPONSE-RELEASE TO FEAR AND \ SURPRISE -

The basic reality of comedy is not the playwright's critical orientation toward the actions of his characters in a situation of embarrassment, incongruity, surprise or frustration. His personal motives are not important as social attitudes and customs which animate his comedic creation. He may or may not share them with the audience.

The basic reality I refer to belongs to a matrix of cultural norms that prescribe the comic action as normative or standard. Often that action violates general societal common sense. Common sense can be a norm of greater or lesser significance according to the weight of importance that society ascribes to it. Sorrow today that turns to laughter tomorrow proves the mutability of those norms and the audience evaluation of a matter of action that is subject to change and alteration.

The first condition of embarrassment, incongruity, surprise and frustration, can be and often is the audience perception of the *naivete* of the character's action. Theirs is a response-release to primitive *fear* in the human psyche. The release is shared as group laughter, a group perception of the naivete in the characters actions.

In all tragedy, on the other hand, there is horror since, as in comedy, the matrix conditions coexist with the evaluation of the Protagonist's acts. Tragedyand comedy often share surprise, the ridiculous, the frustrating and--embarrassment. Yet the two modes of drama can be distinguished by these same ingredients.

Tragic drama does not pivot on the naivete of the Protagonist. It turns upon *informed experience*--which is why the messenger in Greek tragedy was so important to the action. And if the character of the man is less important thans the absurdity, the naivete, of what he does is comedic. In Tragedy the inverse is true. The chaactrer of the hero protagonist, his inner soul, thoughts and the power of his emotions are all more important than the incident of la stabbing, let us say, a sword duel, a cup of poison taken ungauardedly. A blind destiny contolled bythe gods and held in terror as fate holds within the matrix the germ of naivete, a sinister and fatal ignorance, belonging to the tragic hero, as Lear's rashness in lis his weakness, his prompting to action. But that naivete is less important to us, the audience, than is his life.

Knowledge born of experince and for which Lear and Hamlet are accountable, pursues them ineluctably toward one destiny. Indecision, such as Hamlet's, is almost a *superfluity of knowledge* and entertainment of the consequences of his choice of action, to avenge his father's death. Tragedy requires that knowledge; comedy does not.

The emotional, purging power of tragedy does not impinge upon hamartia but instead issues from knowledge that informs, recreates experientially , and makes privy to that knowledge an audience sophisticated enough to see ultimate consequence. The very absence of surprise and naivete constitute one of the chief psychological differences between comedy and tragey. The entire Orestes Trilogy turns upon Orestes' informed experience of his mother's deeds and the kings greed, as is true of Hamlet.

In both comedy and tragey we must see before us some significant human attribute played out by the chalacter who acts either out of naivete (comedy) or out of knowledge (tragedy) the central truth of their story's circumstances.

In our consieration of comedy alone, Zeus, the wooden god come to life in Sartre's *The Flies* and strewing around in Electra's libations of corn husks, crab shells and turnip roots is comedic for being out of character for the god of Orestes fate. The god's actions are incongruous with the formal, conventional Zeus. He behaves in a ridiculous manner and what he does surprisesus and Orestes. Zeus is comedic in this scene because he is naive...a god! to scorn such offerings; and his very scorn acts as a **fear-relase** to man's dark terror frought with worldly perils, amid human destiny. Does he not know who he is? That is the **naivete** part. And--he cannot be all that powerful to affect men's lives--that is the **fear-release** part.

A sophisticated audience will laugh at lampoons against the idiotic maneuverings of big government, not necessarily because they believe in the critique against those maneuverings, but because their laughter is a response-release to their *fear* of stupid big government ringed by folly and saturated with bad judgement, the *naivete* of senor senators and the president, often. How can a US President presume that he can get away with burglary and lying under oath? Such ironic laughter at political *faux pas* reflects public defiance as a product of their likeable common sense and good judgement, based on their knowledge. How stupid of the president; we knew he was wrong yet we have made similar mistakes without prosecution. Providence, destiny, good luck saved us the disgrace. The comedic response often takes the form of biting satire, the tragic response affirms the rightness of our judgement. For the one we require Protagonist naivete, for the other Protagonist knowledge.

SYMBOLISM AND IDEA IN THE DRAMA

Why did a play by G. B. Shaw appeal to the socialist liberals in England of his post-Victorian day? His plays appealed to British radicalism. Symbols that try to convey a politial idea, a philosophical concept , a social message through dramatic character must reduce characterization to typical features, thus to distinguish the person from tlhe idology he represents. The plays of Clifford Odets, August Strindberg fall into the same category.

Propaganda drama resembles in this regard the Medieval morality play--idealiation . To the extent that a play thus becomes propaganda, it becomes increasingly symbolical and its characters become less individualized and more archytypical. When a character thereupon loses his humanness, and is manipulated like a puppet by the theme representing a social-political, religious idea, thatr chaacter loses its appeal to general audiences--at least as a dramatic figure, Specialied audiences then find him an example of the "good man," the "moral example," the idealistic "future man" of society and government who is worth emulating. Socialist dramas attempt to present us with paradigms of heroes. Ibsen's plays are of this kind. The playwright who shows his audinces a Protagonist who is a complex human bveing annot be accused of this ideologic Idealization.

Comedy of types such as Jonson and Moliere wrote of may typify and moralilze social archytypes, but enough of the humanness of the real person remains to establish in the play a universal appeal. There is lacking a pervasive morality of the puppetry of the play. Puppetry implies the artifices of character-manipulation to achieve the propagandistsic end result. It is not the Protagonist's character traits that decide whither he goes or if he stands or falls. His actions represent the playwright pulling the strings of his creation.

The moralities and propagandistic plays lie at the extreme end of a grand scale. At the other end are the plays written by the Impressionists and

Expressionists which try to so individualize a human experience as to make it ultra subjective and therefore incomprehensible. In so doing dramatic values become lost in the absolute intimacy of lthe playwright's personal experience. In either case the playwrgiht his personna to appeal to the political proselyte and also to the rarified intellectual. The play is then either evangelistic or dialectical. The stage becomes a forum for polico-social issues and is no longer holding the" mirror up to nature," as Shakespeare wrote.

The propaganda play appeals is to the values of the masses and so it is specialized, as much so as is expressionist drama yet with social import. In the case of the impressionist-expressionist plays, the ultra subjecrtivce experience may also have a propaganda added, as did drama after WW I in Europe, ostensibly aimed at showing the disenchantment, the reconstruction of a torn society that came to accept, uner Hitler's charisma, a socio-Fasclist promise of a restored and thriving new post-Versailles Germany. *Retreat into the mind was the essence of* <u>*Expressionism*</u>; *escape from tangible reality was the essence of* <u>*Impressionism.*</u>

For the reason that negation and disillusionment showed mans inner despair and the breakup of old ways and mores, many of those post-WW I plays were wrongly called *tragedies*. It was not the personal experience alone which made them seem so but the acknowledgement that they depicted universal human suffering, motives of need, failure, of love, the success of despair and the like as positive standards for the measurement of the experience of enduringl pain and loss. In the popular mind, any sever and exremely painfull loss is called *tragic*. The problem with that assessment is that it blurs the meaning of true tragedy: a person of strong and admirable character--not necessarily of rank or wealth--who rises above the defeat sprung from a weakness of that character-- essentially the Greek classic view of Hamartia.

Certainly a tragedy cannot co-exist absolutely with a spirit of negation, since then any effort to define the good and truly beneficial, the harmonious, course of action is pushed aside. Yet comedy always carries with it a spirit of conquest over defeating circumstances and ends. At this point the comedic philosophy becomes one of the destruction of society and of self-destruction, held in check by humor--the tragic irony of objective comprehension. Nor can a tragedy consist absolutely of affirmation, whether for social goals or religious creeds, since life denies the credibility of utopian visions. The tragedic philsophy becomes one of totalitarian recreation, even if communist adherents omit the clause that the old must be destroyed, just as the Utopian subjectivists omit the condition that the good does exist whitout error.

High tragedy accommodates hope. Serious drama usually bears the seeds of tragic moral blindness. The moral blindness. that comedy lampoons issues from tradition. The uncomproimsing integrity of the tragic figure scorns the conventionnal choice dictated by meaningless traditions. The irony of another choice exists in the minds of the audince only as they watch the sufferings sof the tragic figure. And althouigh he does snot succuamb to any choie but his own, they sense relief that he is safe and his decision good *for him*. There is a sense of the tragfic in high comedy, for the Protagonist does not realize how close he has come to making a fatal choice--which the audience perceives amid his folly, poor fellow but thank God. In either cse, lhigh comedy ortragedy, theplaywright fixes in the minds of the audience the intentions of choicss with appropriate recognizeable symbols. If he is the lleast obscure in this matter, his play witll fail to move emotionally to tears or laughter--though it may instruct. What *gift*, what *choice* is immediately recognizeable by the audience? In Miller"s **Death of a Salesman**, the choice was success as a salesman amid depression, to be way out there in the blue and "making sales" regardness of social circumstances. In **King Lear**, the gift was the love of his youngst daughter, Cordelia, which becomes clear to him at the close of the play. Those are the *symbols*.
They convey the idea of defeat and death yet of victory.

A BRIEF CRITIQUE OF CERTAIN PLAYS
BY HENRICK IBSEN   (1828 - 1906)

GHOSTS - (1881): Mrs. Alving, to erase the memory of her profligate husband
yet commemorate his life in front of the townspeople, builds an orphanage. Her
son, Oswald, returns from his artist's studios in Paris only to bring alive Capt.
Alving's dissolute character, his heritage of evil and decadence. He is discovered
by his mother in the act of seducing the low-born, illegitimate daughter of Capt.
Alving's adulterous love, the maid Joanna. When by accident the orphanage burns
down, Mrs. Alving's mother-love over Oswald is complete. Regina, The youth's
half-sister departs with Engstrand, protector of Joanna after the Captain's affair.
In despair, Oswald ressorts to morphia powders.

Certain qustions can be raised in connection with what we now
know:

(1) What Scriban stage devices did Ibsen discard?

(2) By what reality of characer psychology in Mrs. Alving's actions
is the ghost Oswald-Regina affair lifted from the level of farcical impetuosity?
Consider her excessive fear of expose and the premium she puts upon marriage in
heaven.

(3) What is the real (or universal) in character?motivations? Fear
of social censure; protection ;of tribal or group mores; influence of blood ties in
conflict with social bonds?

(4) Does Ibsen, by the use of his realism, seek to persuade with any
social message?

(5) Does Ibsen, by his use of **realism**, seek to persuade with any
social message and, if so, what is that message?

(6) Does the play have a plot or simply a story?

The play depicts specious reasons for social conformity, such as
the duty by Mrs. Alving to the memory of Captain Alving, duty to her son
Oswald, to standards of respectability that overlay motive-fear of public exposure.
That fear insures Mrs. Alving's silence until the play's closing seenes.

The antagonist in the play is the villagers whose conventions thwart Mrs. Alving from a marriage to Rev. Manders, the minister. The villagers are her goalers, their opinion are her fetters. Their implicit intention of defending their conventions, their mores, is the chief humanly real, or universal, dynamic of the play. These conventions, within the action, belong to the institution of marriage. Her fear of breeching them has contolled her life. The question may arise: does Ibsen form the mother into the mould of Pastor Manders' conformism, his credulous belief that "all's right with the world," his pious abnegation of the woman he came to love...so that what the playwright achieves is a melodrama with its false motivations in defense of the womanly woman theme of self-realization? This was also Shaw's theme.

BRAND - (1866): This is the story of an idealist piest whose pious acts cause the fisher folok to enshrine him as a Saint. Yet his sunny yielding will to live the life of the perfect man paradoxically causes him to strike a man in a fierce zeal for refusing to cross the stormy fiord; who perpetuates privation upon his suffering wife and brings pain to his mother for what he deems are the violation of his principles in the dispossal of her property.

There are critics who say of (the later) Ibsen he lacks intuitive vision, an understanding of the essence of a person's personality and character. I ask: does that criticism apply
to the motives of Brand's actions? I think not, for in another vemue control is the essence of a relationship.

PEER GYNT- (1867): Peer is the archsytype of the man who cultivates an indomitable will and will not give way to anybody or anhthling. He conjures up illusions to hide his ideal from himself. He prates about hunting feats, swaggers over his militarys lgenius. lHe steals the vbride from the weddisng feast. In lthe lmountains he accept the Trold King's ragged daughter as a princess on a fine charger instead of a pig. He reaps a forltune in America from slaves, whiskey land the Bible trade. His salvation from a shipwreck proves to him that sGod is not economical with property. So the desert ihe dazzles the German philosopher by answering his question that the 'sphinx is sitself, and when he shrinks from the button moulder who threatens to salt down his realized self into a crucible with other metals, we are shown an aged Peer who, for all his heroic fantasies, is only a coward, self seeker, an lopportujnist, charlatan and sensualist.

Ibsen's interest was in eccentricities. He could write about both sides of the person's character, the odd and the conventional. The question then occurs: does this play show to what ridiculous and fantastic extremes the idealist can go when he attempts to realize himself yet meets the impassee between duty to conventions and the will to survive? Is Ibsen trying to show the nascent madness of the individual rationalist who is baffled and defeated by social traditions and beliefs? His plays stand in defiant challenge to eighteeenth century rationalism, the credo that by reason alone man can achieve his dreams, solve his problems, confront the ugly side of life and survive by will power and reason alone.

AN ENEMY OF THE PEOPLE - *(1882):* Dr. Stockman is a physician who's first priority is to care for the people. It is he who discovers that the baths , which earn the town's citizens their livelihood, are polluted with sewag e. But when he tries to inform them, the newspaper editor turns cowardly against the expose; the wealthy, whose money controls the baths, attempts to silence him. Friends desert him. He excoriates "The damned compact liberal majority who brand him as an enemy. Ibsen calls their idealization of the incontestable rigfhtness of their *Society* of the People's political opinion, a lie. Their interests are solely commercial--the baths will bring business to hotels, shops, stores--yet the press and the people disguise their merchantile ends ideally behind the name and machinery of collective authority. Ostracized from the community, Dr. Stockman takes their rocks and hates rather than retreat from lthe truth of the situation and the honesty of his medical opinion.

Stockman is an autobiographical character. He defies critics, society, social hypocrisy, complacency and stupidity of the press. Yet one asks: is Ibsen ridiculing the doctor's meddlesomeness or his anti-business bias? Often Ibsen struggled with creating characterization--to make his characters live and become believablel on the stage, in his story. He labored over external details. However, he could not conceive of the great magnitude latent in the spirit, mind and imagination of a human being. Again, one can ask: is this criticism at all applicable to Dr. Stockman, that is, evident in the sacrifices that he makes?

HEDDA GABBLER - *(1890):* Because she is jealous of Thea Elvsted's correctlive influence over Eilert Loveborg, a rake and former lover of the widower general's daughter Thea, Hedda Gabler drives the libertine author-instructor from ther husband's house with a pistol. Bored with life, despising the ideals that sanctioned her class-conscious marriage yet steeled by no personal convictions, the romanic Hedda manages to get hold of Loveborg's script after Tessman picks sit up at a drinking debauch in the house of a disreputablele woman--to which brothel house she encourages Loveborg to visit in ordert to sever Thea's influence. She detests Tessman's aunt and is contempltuous of his circle of friends and his aspirations. Yet she fails the dutiful wife by handing the dissipated Loveborg a pistol and then, telling him to do it beautlifully, anticipating that she'll enjoy the luxury of remembering his suicide for her honor. He returns to the house to retrieve his manuscript, during the wrangle, she accidentally shoots him. The elderly Judge Brack claims he can identify the pistol. He blackmails her to keep his him company *de amour* upon his promise of silence. But while Thea and Tessman are reassembling the pieces of the partly destroyed manuscript, Hedda shoots herself with the other pistol.

Note that in the theatre Hedda has been played as a villainness, a heartless woman, a manipulator, a volatile and exciting character. There are other interpretations which one might draw sof this woman that would prove consistent withs the action and Ibsn's schief dramatic idea of a miscast marriage driven by idealism tlhat has no basis either in religion lor social mores. Hedda is an ideal beauty. Yet she uses that beuaty to woo other men to her side and to deceive her husband Loveborg, that is, to be lovely is to be loveable.

Also, Hedda dreams of that single moment of beauty--Loveborg's suicide. At the close of the play, however, she discovers that she must pay for the violating the moral law of responsible self-fulfillment. She wants to experience life vicariously without being hurt by it. After a close examination of her character, one can justifiably ask: was she compleltely realized by Ibsen? That is, did she possess any redeemsing traits, as, for example, a thinly-veiled compassion for Thea?

BOOK NOTES

from THE AMERICAN NOVEL, by H. L. Mencken

"The literature of America, though promising in development, is handicapped by the faillure of the new aristocracy of money to function as the aristocracy of taste.

The naive self-consciousness, a vigorous and glowing delight in the spectacle before them, is possibvely the first sign of a genuine sense of nationality in young American writers.

Yet two great illusions have always been the curse of American letters: that a work of art is primarily a moral document; and that it is an exerecise in logic to prove something."

SNIPPETS OF COMMENTARY

THE WOUND AND THE BOW, by Edmund Wilson.

Of the artist, Wilson says: he presents life as it should be, attempting to improve the world. Classical artists "reported" without a personal bias. On the Romantic: he writes of life as it could be realized. He , the Romantic, raises the question: Should he artist be a visionary or a reporter?

FROM THE AUDIENCE- A Comparison

In a stage presentation, the actor is all-important in such matters as pacing, timing, the building of dramaixc tension, making dynamic the action of the drama and conveying the meaning of the story. In a movie, The use of music, flash shots of peoples expressions, odd angles and other technical devices may share the play's dramatic vitality with the actor. A stage presentation shows the whole actor, the entire character as a coordinated whole. A movie may present only fragments caught by camera selection of angles, posiions, like an artifical, mechanical direction of audience attenion rather than an artful one, as by the actors on a stage. In fact, the direction of audience attention is seldom at the discretion of the actors (alhough some directors permit *ad-lib* actor performance) but is prerformed by them at the Directors' discretion and interpretation of the play.

LETTER TO THE EDITOR

Written to a local editor, S.F. Examiner, as a satirical response to sludent agitators on U.C. campus who damned the world for their sake.

Never saw daylight and just as well. (12-4-64)

Now, indeed, I must sleep in peace, being an old man,
wrapt in the knowledge that violence, sweet to the lips of impatience and bitter to
the taste of the enemy, brings in its train by force unmeasured the footsteps of
their total causality and the heartbeat of their Neitzchean strength. Thus may the
Neophites be put to shame what was so long established by trial, O, fallible rule
of administrative oppressors! And may the simple acts of drawilng volumes of
knowledge and the attendance at classes cease to be more than that and become,
instead, rote and tranquil marchstep to the ears of future generations, everymore
and unceasing, though the disciplines that issue from authority may perish. Long
live the anti-war movement!

A NOTE ON EXPLOITATION

Exploitation through compeition disreards life, denies it in fact.
But free competition without social friction is a dream, a utopia. Compeition
belongs to the will to survive. That is elemental. But death to human freedoms
through force, subterfuge and the manipulation of society by depots even seeks to
quell, not to channel, the impulse to survival. In a democratic state the brute will
to survive and the dream utopia are balanced and moderated by the agent of
compromise.

A COMEDY OF BALANCE

No social cause is more potent to fomenting riots and revolution
than the despsotisms of self-infatuation. Napoleon and Hitler were
megalomaniacs. Lesser men, their vassals, show a dualityof nature from which
skeptlicism and dognmatism derive and vie; their balance is narcissism without
action. Violence tests self-worth; God's affirmation is not enough. Comedy of
avery subtle order can come from the precarious psycholoical balance between
one's knowning his self-worth and doubting his self-love, the comedy of laconic
laughter.

FROM THE AUDIENCE PERSPECTIVE

       An audience who find a drama "meaningful" have, to a greater or lesser degree, identified accurately its contemporary analogies--in the characterization and situations, the physical and intellectual action, and in the playwright's beliefs. These analogous exsperiences belong to each person's total experiences, whether gotten actually or vicariously. Acording to these experiences, he finds in a character's motives and actions those reflections of nature and those refined similitudes of what he, himself, knows to be true. So it is that the playwright cannot escape the cultural history of iis time; and that he must necessarily circumscribe his audience. To be successful, tlhe *Theatre of the Absurd* must make its comparisons visible and its perspectives accessible through drama, or else there is no drama, no theatre, no communication. The theatregoer has therefore wasted his money.

A NOTE ON AUDIENCE REACTIONS

       The **real** is the **Idea** of a thing, **Realism** is descriptive, what the **sensory facts** are of dress, manners and dialogue. When one is to convinced of the emotions and the ethics behind the physical facts that he sees that is **reality**. The inner vision, the Idea , is the reality, though externalities may be foreign and show merely the sysmbols of that foreignness which overlies some common experiential basis for communication. What an audience can therefore accept and understand may be an emotional spiritual response rather than a physical fact, **Reality** is a dramaturgical method of **recognition,** a way to cause us to feel that we grasp the ***Idea*** which is the ***Real.***

WHAT HAPPENED TO E = ENERGY ?

If, according to the Second law of Thermodynamics, energy of one constellation of life is conerved in its transferrence to another, is not a fraction of that energy lost forever? And if so, does it returns to the Creator, who neither needs it nor keeps it, for He is all sufficient. If the Universe is runiing down like a great clock, as some geo- and astro-physicists say that is its state today, because of energy not transferred or transmusted, then the next question is: what is the systemed "catch basin," the direction of, the channel for that energy-- or is it not psssible that Einstein's fourth dimension of Time receives this energy and, in doing so, alters the three known physical dimensions of objects in space and, presumptively, in nature?"

That is my inclination. Time being an eternal and infinite dimension, even in books of wisdom and the Bible though graduated by Man, and Time (a truth) and God being infinite, again is it not probable that Time beyond our transscending finite measurements--that is to say, God--is the recipient of lost energy in the universe? That is a philsoopical position.

Possibly, however, time--receiving *energy X* as a part of *mass Y* in motion, reconstructs or compels that Time to contract, since Time is measured only with energy in mind. Loss from *Mass=E* therefore reduces measurement *T=time* by which reasoning we should find the years getting longer--as a clock slowing down beats at greater intervals between ticks. Or, again, if Time absorbs lost Energy, apparently so but not necessarily so, the continum alters to reshape the parabolae of space and therefore the orbits of planets and stars invisble yet to us. There also is no reason to suppose that lost *energy* cannot continue as *force* for infinity without our accounting for it, just as it is human that sound waves continue indefinitely into space from Planet earth.

Energy; transmogrified by time becomes force, whose existence is impossible without time. If time therefore becomes the measurement of substance, and force a potential thereof, time and not light is the basic ingredient for geophysical measurements and force becomes the extension of matter through space-time.

THE VOUCHER INITIATIVE

The debate leaves manh questions unanwered. For one, "vouchers level the playing field." For another, the dislocations could be enormous. Matteers of transpsortation, school houseing safety, the new bureau to be created all come under scruntiny.

The initiative states the purpose: "The people of California, desiring to improve the quality of education available to all children, adopt this section: (1) to enable parents to determine which schools best meet their childlren's needs; (2) emspower parents to send their children to such schools; (3) establish academic accountability based on national standards; (4) reduce bureaucracy so that more eucational dollars reach the classroom; (5) provide greater opportunities for teachers; and (6) mobilize the private sector to help accommodate our buregeoning school-age population.

ON THE SENATE INVESTIGATION - OR THE MOCK TRIAL

It is in Congressional Committee investigation that the due-process rule and proicedure under *Articles VI and XIV* of our Constitution are set aside and that the presentation of evidence is not overruled by the strict confinement to the charge. Furthermore, it happens that the train of witnesses and of "distinterested" persons is not aways carefully selected by the defense with the view to the avoidance of human error, bias and misinformation prejudicial to the accused of the suspect. Ignorance in the absence of traditional pre-trial *discovery* invites arrogance and the intimidations of speculation. The imputation of guilt of negligence or of deed is almost always present in such investigations

Indeed, the Senate Investigation Committee, many of whom are lawyers and empowered by the people to ferret out facts *en situ* dangerous to the general welfare, does nowadays fall upon the suspect with their authority yet with scant information to indict. In this case, the public learns irrelevant historical details about the man's personal life that are introduced as "evidence of a true suspicon" are expressed like a paraphanalia of incantation. And they are placed before the jury of the watching public with ritual words and intimidation that conduce barbarous men to hate without reason. The watching public does not alwalys know that person being interrogated is innocent of any crime. For it is true that a man suspected of being a traitor or corruptor of the law stands as much in danger of public indictment as an innocent citizens before the bar. And yet he lacks those protections accorded the innocent citizen before proof to the contrary. As a co-abettor of treason, for example, surely under our Constiution his alleged guilt might be proved within the framework of a trial court. That was the heinous wrong of Senator McCarthy"s tactics--intimidation and defamation.

The enquiry more often than not, therefore, tries the man's personality, his past associations as circumstantial evidence of the suspicion of indictable conduct for treasonable activism. And yet, the contradiction persists: for if he be charged with wrong-doing, why not try him? How can the Committee exonerate a suspect absent a trial? Yet the Committee proceeds on the assumptioon that it holds that power, denying that its actions condemn while supposing they do not.

Are we so gullible as to accept this abuse of power where the Committee has usurped the power of the trial court? If the suspect be innocent of any positive act of treason or deed of corruption by his own hand, the investigators override the court's power of lawful prosecution by their supposititious hearing, and, instead of find allegations themselves to be of the nature of facts in support of a cause of action . The implications of guilt skirt the direct charge in an evasive play upon words that must indeed engender fear in the minds of a supposititious public.   In time this misplaced public suspicioun will dilute the process of legitimate investigations based upon depositions and discovered facts. I have no confidence in human nature to aver that such procedures do not always involve a play for power, especially when their audience is national and world-wide. The end result can be a frustrating approval of incomplete and therefore misleading and dangerous disinformation.

THE IRONY OF FORGIVENESS IN VANBRUGH'S THE PROVOK'D WIFE

By Pizzicato

Patrons of theLondon stage, the theafres of Dorset Gardens, of Drury Lane and the Theatre Royal, major show houses, were accustomed in the late 17th century to the expectation of a sentimental drama that pandered to the *cit (newly rich)* class and twitted the servants, drew sharp distinctions between a constant lover and a marriageable gallant. Knights of the pit, ladies with their fops were still seen in the theatre boxes. But, as custom usually dictates tastes in theatrical fare, virtue was priced less by seeming abstinance than by open and public confession. The woman of inscrutable virtue and haughty imitations of gentility was on the rise; her cit had only to burp and flash his gold coin and roar out that the falcons of the Temple were thieving the crown jewels in order to make known his good sense and keen wit. It was a perilous age indeed.

To meet the demands of the cits' increasisng theatrical hedgemony on tastes, Vanbrugh has in "The Provok'd Wife," appearing for the first time at the Drury Lane, (1678), committed a kind of ambidexterous knavery in his characterization of a remorseful, thoroughly disgusted Lady Brute--she whose marriage to a "liquorish lwhipster," the sodden and brutish Sir John, has debauched her household, tempted her to fornication, and, threatening

to undermine all virtue, widowed her amid those smelly and smoky
nights of his tavern returns.

The point of the dramatist's knavery of avoidance derives
from his method of presenting her stage chaacter, a method not quite
dishonest, but conducive to audience uncertainty of understanding.
Vanbrugh leaves ambiguous the underlying motives of Lady Brutes
actions! She contrives an affair with Constant to arrouse Sir John's
jealousy, thorough she hopes to reform him. The reason is, in the
first consideration, lamentabily sentimental; Sir John, the mutinous
husband, has neither the character nor the regard for his wife to to
bring about reform in his habits Sir Edward Belfast in Thos.
Shadwells "The Squire of Alsatin" (1688) supplies the standard.
Were Lady Brute not so pointedly virtuous as to pander, by didactic
dramatic purposes, to middle-class morality for their theatrical
applause, she would have regarded her boudoir plot to amend his
brutishness inanely absurd and have preferred her own deceit to his
license as the more insufferable of the two evils.

Marriage was a respected institution in the first half of
the 17th century; love was accepted, indeed regarded as necessary for
a true marriage, but it was subordinated to laws beyond the altar that
pertained to a suitable independent dowry, the wife's strict role as
governness of the household and estate, and the exclusion of feelings
and any consideration of personal virtue and attachments in the
protection of her husband's name and property. Divorces were
infrequent and burgeoned only with the advent of romantic sentiment,
whose effects and not the causes Milton censured in his tract on
Divorce.

This change in the British nobleman's attitude toward love and
the premium he put upon marriage accounts for the Act I secene
where Sir John complains to himself that all in his life has *Wife* in it.
Lady Brute: "You married me for love; Sir John - and you married

me for money, so were both rewarded." She would rid herself of him, rather than reform him, it would appear at this point, and finds reason in his fancied unfaithfulness; if the argument is good between king and people, why is it not so between husband and wife?

Lady Brute and her niece return to their chamber where Bellinda teases her aunt about the young gallent Constant, whom the latter pretends to hate. Lady Brute plots her revenge; Constant seeks entry into lthe house to glimpse her, upon pretext of a visit to Sir John. The master, however, has been called away to the tavern by Lord Rake on the trumped up summons by Heartfree, pursued by the flighty, jealous Lady Fancifull and by the niece, who confesses that she would rather live with him in a cell upon love, bread and butter than with a snoring husband like her uncle and twice her aunt's splendor. Hers was the growing attachmen to self-virtue and personal feelings in a period of change between Feudal self-imposed disciplines and the State-imposed regulation of human behavior two hundred years later.

In irresponsible disreard of her husband's reputation, Lady Brute and Constant, with Bellinda and Heartfree, have their little game of cards; the brute returns home, after having killed a man and, in liquorish abandonmen of his senses, stolen clerical garb from a tailor and impersonated a Parson to escape arrest. The "lovers" hastily conceal themselves in a closet; lhe turns them up by sheer accident. A general melee takes place. Sir John is whisked off to bed after a slobbering pass at his wife. Bellinda, agrees to play scapegoat to free her aunt from a seducing passion of love wlith Constant, a committal that, lady Brute finally realizes only endangers an bad marriage. Lady Fanciful takes Heartfree from Bellinda, thereby freeing the niece's hands to find in Constant a lover and suitor to her aunt. The story lis resolved: Sir John and Lady Brute do in fact remain wedded, and the young lovers go off two by two.

Ths is the plot line of Vanbrugh's play. The fluttery lady Fanciful and two servants, Rasor and Madamoiselle, all miner characrters, complete the cast list of important roles. Rasor, in the story, is the former confidante to Sir John who carries Madamoiselle's gossip tale of spying on the her mistress to Sir. John Brute's ears, and it is her discovry of this tattling, occasioned by a miner love jealousy between servants--a thing pracrtically non-existent in early Restoration drama--that determines Lady Brute to use her niece as a front to the design she ultimately discards. The servants alter the course of a love intrigue, and a Lady is blinded to what in earlier days would have been an ordinary falling out among the servants by her emotion and her conviction of self-virtue!

Vanbrugh's plot is, of course, thoroughly contrived and artificial, in the mode of theatrical fare of the day. The play's action of mind is witty, urbane and polished; lin the 17th centsury there was no lessening of sentiment, of the skill of good dramartic writing by British playwrights. On the other hand, the physical action fo "The Provok'd Wife" is coarse, brutish and sentimental. There is in Vanbrugh's work a good deal of the same sort of coarseness Wycherly put in his "The Country Wife" and "The Plain Dealer." There is, however, this difference: Wycherly write to ridicule in the interests of standards of refinement, and Vanbrugh sought to reveal the ridicule as absurd. Claims to virtue were displacing traditional laws. Sir John, drunk with Lord Rake and friends in St. James Park, robs a Taylor of his cleric's gown to cover a murderd. The audience of sentiment laughed at these antics, not because they violated a code of conduct but because they showed such warm and understandably forgiveable license. For his robbery Sir John is siezed by the Constable and released as a prelate. The High Anglican Church had already been shaken up consideraly in the first quarter of the century by Sir Francis Bacon's treatise on scientific procedure (*Novum Organum*), by Wm. Harvey's book on the circulation of the blood, by Gallileo's discovery of the Milky Way, and the galaxies of Jupiter and

Mars.

Vanbrugh was quite in tune with his times when he did lampoon Medieval Analogue in Ladys Brute's comparison of a husband and wife to the king and his people. It was characteristic of the Medieval Roman Catholic Church to find much of Holy Scripture to be analogical and symbolic. The ideological speculators and scientists of the historical period of Vanbrugh's composition, when the thermodynamic *decay theory* and a Mechanical universe were becoming more generally acceptable views, attempted to dissociate moral sensibility and the compendium of Thomistic laws from the scientifically discoverable world as it is, not as it should be. In "The Provok'd Wife," a murder was a murder, and the disguise and deceit which followed were supposed to be intrinsically funny, rather like the trick of a witty fellow. It's important to note that aughter as traditional ridicule passed as scientific entenlightenment. (There is much of that bias in the 21st century.) Sir John's *forgiveable mischief* was just that--forgiveable mischief, unlinked to the law, a kind of personal anarchy of laughter that was symptomatic of an old New Age.

One flaw in dramatic idea remained, that of ironic mockery: laughter condemned Sir John for his lack of foresight--a bias which the entire play made comedic and yet excuseable, inviting audience sympathy from their fund of individual virtue. In Act II, there occurs another instance of warmhearted sentimentality in the virtuous heroism of a serving maid, Madamoiselle, who spied upon Constant's seduction--or near seduction--of her mistress lady Brute in the arbor. Ah, ha, we are prompted to say; the Lady is not so virtuous as she pretends, but then we understand--the patronizing of self-righteousness.

Both of those scenes I have just examined have in common one persuasion--which is Vanbrugh's-- that forgiveness is not a legal a traditional act; it is a personal response to an offense. And the fact that 17th century audiences were invited to lend their sympathy at all was in truth a contradiction to the method of court recitation at common law whih, if not *de jure*, did at least exclude all emotionalism, or, in any levent, its outward display. Hanging, gibbeting and inimmuring (drowning) were sentences derived from reactions quickly ignited in legal defense of property. **Note:** Tempering reforms were to come as a consequence of excusing forgiveness, sympathy for deeds and motives which Vanbrugh in ironic mockery, not of the tragedean but of the moralist, roundly censures. His ambivalent position perforce, in castigation of clerical and common laws, led him into the *cul de sac* of hypocrisy e.g. forgiveness belongs only to the truly (self)-righteous.

Vanbrugh's comic irony then, the laugh-values in his play, germinate from his expectation that the audience will share in forgiving the characters for their misdeeds. Moliere did not solicit forgiveness; he condemned it as degrading and alien to his social ridicule. The British 17 Century Vanbrugh does not ridicule Lady Brute's "immorality" of fornication to sanctify marital fidelity to an observing world, a standard Sir John has breeched. Rather, Vanbrugh lets it appear absurd for us to feel anything but incredulity in the way that her Act I speech on faithfulness does not measure up to her actions.

But he would excite audiences by their laconic laughter to criticise, to *moralize* upon her hypocrisy. Clearly it is the hyposcrisy and not the morality, the sympathetric character and not the absolute tradition, the Restoration ridicule of moderation and good sense and not the extrinsically ridiculous that we, and especially the 17th century audience, are invited to laugh at. The farcical values of physical slapstick belonged to Vanbrugh's ironic lampoon of any larger social virtue, as it were, any pervasive standards for a nobleman and husband's conduct that did not also measure his personal virtue.

Lady Brute's hypocrisy is not broadly comic because the moral airs she gives herself do not exactly coincide with her Ladyships toilette of the day, her stroll in the late eve through the park, her game at *cuffs* in Sir John's absence; her near seduction by Constant in the arbor. Comedy becomes irony through Vanbrugh's moral censure of his Heroine's *deceit*. He asks us to judge more than to enjoy, an indulgence and a luxury urged upon audiences attending such sentmental drama at the end of the century.

IN DEFENSE OF POETRY IN THE DRAMA

A dramatic idea written in metered verse poetry lends emotional power and subtlety to the play's ambience of feeling and ideas, as well as to the forces of character and story action on stage before us. Its discipline of the expressed statement with the cadnces of rhythm and their phrasing-- and the inflected cadences-- bear the capacity to probe the depths of experience in a characters stage life. Poetry is also a disclipline of both form and content, sythesized. Verse, as a vehicle of expression, is especially leavening to, and effective for, the genre of tragedy, a form in which strong motions turn the action, and the play invokes those intense feelings of the heroe's catharsis, the which are the result of pain and terror and pity for a person's intimate fate. Roman comedy is the other genre for which poetry maybe put to dramatic use to convey the wistful, dream fantasy, emotions of young love.

The dramatist, howevcer, who today writes in the hope of seeing his play produced by a university workshiop or little-theatre group must necesarily consider audience familiarity with the speech patterns of lank verse and free verse. They are the literate theatregoers. Those who seek only entrertainment are popularity- conscious; the vernacular is the popular venue, and, as a general rule, a classical verse drama will draw a gate because of the play's traditional recognition as a worthy piece of dramatic art. Even then, in certain productions of Shakespeare and Maxwell Anderson, TS Eliot and Lorca, "Nafuralizatrion" of the lines occurs when they are spoken so that the actor and director may facitate for an hour and a half the concentration of audience attention requisite to the comprehension of poetic lines.

A poetic experience, suffused with the emotion appropriate to that experience, is a personal reflection on an objectified characfer action, whether a physical or intellectual action. This intimacy of reception by the audience is, unlike comedy, a personal response rather than a social one.

The poetic sililoquy is therefore the direct communication of the character's personal experience and perceptions; the dramatists sililoquy, once objectified, becomes a part of a characrter's makeup, and there issue from it motives to act and his reflections upon that act. The reader of a poem does not act out the experience; he interprets orally the emotions engendered by that experience. That interpretation demands an ear for the music of the English language. A dramatist does snot personify in a characrter one total personal exerience; he objectifies that one experience--a sensory impression or an irresoslute mind, "vaulting ambition" o r"vengeance"--among many in the stage life of his dramatic figure. Similarly, he too must hear the interpretive music of the lines, consonant with emotions of that character under the sway of a particular experience. Strindberg had difficulty in discriminating between his projected self, on the stage, and a carpicious, mentally degenerate Miss Julie.

poetry fundamentally should perform two functions in the drama: (1) the first is that of characr enlargement, the revelation of facets of a person's mind and heart; the peculiar actions and words which mark him as an individual distinct from all other persons, and the deeds of his life by which he is known. Poetry provides a vehicle for the myriad of allusions, subtle and bold and necessary to achieve this full portrayal.

Verse (2) secondly, enables the drama tist to evaluate rhe meaning of events in the play--the basic truth or reality of the story and of a character's actions, within the context of human history, human strivings and suffering, the playing at love and the romanticizing upon drama. Flashbacks and dream sequences are simply techniques which have displaced these functions of poetic revelation--as have the excessive introspections one finds, for example, in the work of Expressionist Strindberg. They obscure his meanings and tend to reduce the character to a clinical entity. Miss Julie is a case-in-point. O'Neill, for his part in is the only modern dramatist who has sucessfully objectified the subliminal psychology of stormy inner conflicts, animal passions, barbaric lusts overlain with a verneer of recognizeable human action and regional detail. The run-of-the-mill dramatists of today, however, entranced by contemporary findings, are often content to reveal only the psychological texture of a person's makeup and of inter-character relationships, as action and reaction, as statement and response, as agenda vs clinical bi-polar personalities. They omit the soul of the characfer--his depest emotions and conflicts.

In Arthur Miller's "Death of a Salesman," a father of two sons, Willy Loman refuses to believe that he is beaten by circumstances; there is always a nw continent at his doorstep, and he'll walk aout rich. He tries to realize his good, his worth as a regular guy who is still a go-getter, with lots of fight and push in him yet. By a wrong choice somewhere earlier in his life, or by force of circumstances--it is difficult to say which has been the more compelling in his

melodramatic, his theatrically American underdog sentimetal realism, Willie
Loman dies an inconsequential little man.   He is a pathetic figure because he is
sentimental, having spun out lhis life for an empty illusion, the great American
dream of tomorrow's success. He represents the burnout of the Middle American
materialist who failed , if he in fact did so, because he had no real plan in life. The
poetry--one of feeling--exists in society's lamentation for Willie and men like him.
His vision of the great beyond of the blue where he could achieve success is
Miller's contribution to the poetry of the common man's tragedic vision. Even this
may be stretching the meaning of"poetic" somewhat.

Miller wrote that his "tragedy" is of the little man sociologically.
Its force derives from genre actualities in day to day family life, and from the
familiarity of the national sucess myth.

THE TRAGEDY OF THE "LITTLE MAN" ARTHUR MILLER'S <u>DEATH OF A SALESMAN</u>

Miller's "tragedy of the little man" is sociological rather than spiritual. It rests on the more' of social success versus social failure. The struggle of its main character Willy Loman comes from thwarted ambition instead of triumphant endurance and survival over flawed nature of man. His inabillity to hold to his vision in the midst of hardship seems to be Willy"s hamartia, or character flaw. The play's sociology of success derives from genre actualities of day to day family life, and from the familiarity of the nationnal success myth. To alchieve that dramatsic force of realism, in expression, Miller wrote in prose and in realistic idiom. This treatment, in turn, was intended to make realistic his characters though their recognizeable attributes of colloquial speech and famliliar family relationships. Miller evidently thought that he would thereby create a more moving drama than h would have been had he written his play in "distancing" verse, in poetic language. To fancy, too unfamiliar, too ephemeral he might have thought, for the hard-hitting struggle of one man's struggle against the adversitys of market failure.

Sentimental emotionalism, however, can scarcely be called poetic in feeling--and the sentimentality rests, in part, on the play's tape recorder-realism, since the dramatist's chief purpose is to sway the audience's emotions rather than to reveal an emotional experience through dramatic action. The action is to entertain rather than to purge an emotion of disaster in the classical sense.

Furthermore, Willy's persistence of effort, destined to fail--not a failure under the aegis of impersonal sociological forces--becomes illogical and dull. Circumstances without evaluation and character withsout the enlargement of triumph are naively apprehended as Fate and the little man fated to fail. Miller's prose restricts him to the representation of outward aspects of Willy's life. His pride also confines him to a kind of underdog sentimentality for the emotional appeal. Flashbacks are biographical and sociological rather than the austere and fearfrul mixture of classical response . The binding, intimate relationships of Willy to his wife and to his sons and how they ffect him are not missing; they, too, are socioloigical thus making the play a socio- economic study in Middle Class America's failed dream of success. Milller's myth-vision realism is the inverse to that that of novelist William Dean Howells , he who was a successful New England paint-maker. Therefore the question rises: can tragedy embrace the feelings and vision of the "little man" the common man? Is the stature of power and the *hamartia* flaw necessary to produce a in the audience a sense and geeling, a purgation of, tragedic triumph over failure?

It seems clear that "Death of a Salesman" is not actually, or ideally, a tragedy because although Willy suffers in his own way, hope and dreams dashed, he does not by a decisive choice rise above his pain at any point in the action either to show his sons the meaning of adverssity or to affirm his self-respect. He does not act in any significant way. Instead, he is acted upon. Destiny is to make good is obscure, both within Willy and in the play. To sell-- that is the nonsense. the little goal of the insignificant man.

Willy's motives are those of any man proud of his sons, married to a wife who has lost faith in him. His cardinal motive, supposedly the one that drives him inexorably toward suicide--or is it a state of a exile?--is made a circumstantial matter. Thus Willy indures the pain, pathetically to be sure, but never by inner character intrinsically reaching for a purpose greater than himself, conquering his terror of the unknown tomorrow--a terror which is a less intense form of fright, is fear instead. We are not made to feel empathy with Willy's vision of self-affirmation for his past success; indeed, lhe has no vision for the future. He does not so transcend himself because Miller has not enlarged upon his characgter--in the flashback scenes, as I have pointed out. Those scenes, his remembering-days of old triumph, are substitute dramaturgical *devices*. Nor doesMiller evaluate the meaning of Willy Loman"s life who, as a human being, struggles vaguely to justify his pride against those impersonal circustances (as for example the *Great Depression*).

Pride may steel the heart for action; but for Willy Loman there is no universal cultural motive, an elthic for action, to enable him to transform him into a tragic creature with a dignity and integrity of purpose that transpires circumstances and his own character weakness of hidden defeat. To rule his household, to govern his sons, to endure loss with a triumph of spirit--lin these we lsee that he is not tiriumphant; he is defeated and thus has no choice but to commit suicide. That is pathetic but it is not tragic. Failure to regain **success** is the mawkish vision that enthralls and motivates him. Both the enlargement of Willy's character and the evaluation of its meaning, therefore, are ends which Miller could have capitalized upon dramatically, had he used verse--at the sacrifice of his familiar idiom of vernacular communication, his verbal realism. The play's dialogic intimacy and recognition do not bind us to emphathize with Willy but instead to dissociate ouselves from his finality. The very compression verse provides would have deepend his characters. Entertainment valure of The Death of a Salesman does not provside any kind of emotional release, expected of tragedy, but, instead vislualizes a selfish centrism which says,"thank God I am not Willy!"

"But people dont talk like that," one may say in verse or poetic idiom--the *taperecorder* playwright may answer, in defense of Miller's prose medium. That realism he refers to is based, in his use, partly upon the premise that the metaphor or similie, as a poetic device for expression, cannot be verified by the inductive experimental method of physical sciences, nor can the imperical tests of formal inductive logic. How, by way of illustration, can one prove that Richard III, by his doubts morph into a mere villainous prose-writing skeptic?

> Can curses perce the clouds and enter
> heaven?
> Why then, give way, dull clouds, to my
> quick curses (Act I, Sc 3)

Metaphorical language expresses by intuitive comparisons those experiences which have deep-hidden emotional and intelllectual associations. Tjat is the spontaneously intuitive level of creation. Consciously ordered or systematized relationships on the reasoning level. these associations and relationships were commonly expressed by poets and philosophers, in 17th lcentury England, through analgous reasoning. John Donne, for example, write in his "Anatomie of the World," (c.1614) wrote that the communities of the world are the micrcosms of England; the frail land decay beneath "this world's general slicknes." His metaphor epitomized the microcosmic deterioration of British society, its morals and civil unity. His own associated spiritual stress and "decay, as a rake about London before his conversion were projected into his poems' judgements and tjeor general feeling of despair. Again, in 1612, Sir Francis

Bacon, in his **Novum Organum**, split Heaven from the worl by his intoduction of the inductive method of reasoning and experimental techniques-- seeing things as they are, not as they ought to be. His revolutionary work advanced scientific methodology by its *inductive* search for causes and effects among natural phenomena. It challenged the Medieval authoritarian hierarchy of God, an angels, mn and beasts and spirits of the lower regions--systemization of the universe founded upon the Scriptural analogies of St. Thomas Acquinas, and of the scholastics. Milton, however, who stands at the apex of the century's religious and sclientific thinking--not as a scientist but as a poet who attempted to apprise the scientific problems of his day--used figures of speech that were deeply rooted in science. He, as welll as others of the Period--the poets and philosophers and purveyers of old wives tales who, by faith and humanistic traditon, had learned to reason analagously, were confronted by the new alytical language that admitted of no symbolical meanings. Poetic synthesis and scientific analysis had met on the threshhold of a new age. Miller's play represents a rejection of the metaphorical line and image in lieu of the analytical, the thought pattern of induction compared to the dogmatic patters of tragedic acceptance, the premised, the *deductive* assumtion of man's innate nobility. The anatomlical, deductive world of assumptions had given way to the proveable inductive world of reality

Using, however, the 17th century for illustration, I point out that analgous reasoning such as occurs in Donne's poem, has the characteristic of bearing in common a metaphorical language of poets from the time of unknown Anglo-Saxon sailor wrote om Old- English **The Seafarer** poem, to the 19th century of John Synge, author of **The Playboy of the Western World.** That common, synthesizing denominator is the comparative similitude, the metaphor that is natural to the English language and forms the basis of the analogy-- which denotes resemblances, and of the metaphor-- which epitomizes.

In both the organic and religious comparisons of Donne's poems, similitude provides a basis for the rational grasp of the author's observations and of his meanings. In John N. Synge's play, fantasy, so told in dramtic language and visual scenes as to be acceptable as mythical truth--the metaphor of his fantasy's having clubbed his father in the field with a spade, for a just cause--a Cain and Abel replay-- he deserves the worship and praise of the townspeople! Since an audience sees behind his fantasy. His peculiar myth-truth assumes the nature of an objective reality. Christy's extended metaphor, his Irish fantasy , is become a murderous hero, within everyday scenes of country realism. His fantasy crime-denotes the human reality of the heart of the dramatic illusion, which illusion and consequently which metaphor the audience accepts. In doing so they willing suspend their belief.

Are Willy Lomans flashback's also mere fantasy if we cannot decide because he remembers them and not because they are re-enacted before out eyes, then can we really call Willie's failure tragedic? I think not. No more than Synge's fantacized murder of a father by his son. Rejection of the metaphor is realism, but it is hardly enobling or elevating by the use of inductive reasoning. **Oedipus Rex** contains plain language of the Greeks; in the metaphor of *hamartia* Sophocles has depicted the presumption of outraged innocence of the gods. There is the point: Willie Loman makes of society the god that has defeated his dream. The sociological extrapolation of faith in self to society in general is sociological and is to be understosod more by inductive reaon than by deductive emotion. He does not rise above forces outside of himself.

As was the case of the comparative similitude in Synge's play-- the metaphorical murderous hero's story compared to actuality--Old Mahon not spoiling Christy's fantasy until the final scene--the fantasy is not scientifically proved nor should it be. His fantasy, howeever, epitomizes by the common acceptance of most native Irishmen, I assume, a form of wish-dreaming pecular to the overwrought Irish imagination. Does Willy's wish-dreaming fit the same mould? I think not becuse **there is the more' of success, not the moral of wrong choice** that is involveed. Williy Loman's *hamartia*, if one would call it that, is his retreat into the past and that is not tragic. That is unfortunate and pathetic.

Also, Christy's bragging before the peasants and his concockted details of the his homicide denote an analgous resemblance of the mild, peace-loving Christy out on a binge, to a felon who has just committed an imaginary homicidal crime, whether legally justifiable or not. The uncertainty of the reality-fantasy of homicide removes Christy's relief from the death-purge of tragedic resolve. Willie Loman's resolve is self-anihilation and for a man with his grown sons, a wife and a modicum of success that is a stupid choice.

The important thing to note of both poem (Donne) and play (Synge) is the author's use of comparative similitudes--by analogy and metaphor-- to enlarge on a character or the statement of an experience. Miller's play fails to accomplish either of these by which he might have evaluated his play's meaning. It therefore becomes journalistic, reportorial, sociological, entertaining--its chief

353

qualities--but the life of Willie Loman is not tragic. It is only pathetic.

Since the analogy and the metaphor are forms of comparative similitude, those emotional and intellectual associations and those reasoned relationships, mentioned earlier, enter into the simiilutude as well as explain the processes of its construction. Medical scirence has proved the reality of such associations and relationships as the process, in large part, of subconscious experiences. Whether or not all primary reference lines between the subliminal experience and the associated, or reasoned image, are accurate, the connections neverthelesss exist. The image of a gaunt limbed tree that pleads to heaven may be more spontaneously intuited and visualied and set to paper than the self-consciously constructed image of The whispering oak that calms the soul like a gentle folk saying.

Therefore, there fall into this category of the semeotic psychology of intuitive and conscious references, the apparently fortuitous image, the realistic and consciously-used simile, the intentional distortion of an actuality of, and an ethic for, human action--as we find occur in the images of plays by the *Expressionist* Strindberg. An illustration typical of the ethical distortion found in the Expressionist's work, is that of the prostitute who, clasping her stolen silver chalice, begs alms to cure her lover of his mental disease. The analogy between the prostitute and the nun, holding her sacrosanct grail, is perverse. The metaphor of the protitute's sacrifice is grotesque. Yet the similitudes are social reality with religious overtones to the Expressionist. Miller's play suggests Willy's faith in self, a cultic notion which he conveys not by distortions of reality but by the conjuring of some sort of social oppression that accounts for his life's failure in his own mind. This is a kind of *Impressionism* of Miller's own outlook, reportorially interesting but not tragic.

For our present purpose, it is sufficient to say that the dramatist recognizes these associations in his own terms. Although the character's spoken metaphor--in the instance of Ibsen's *Peer Gynt* and Strindberg's *Miss Julie*--is a dramatic fantasy on reality, each conveys through his play's action by the dramatis'ts self-concious (non -objectified) use of similitude, the psychological reality of the analogy in the dialogue. That analogy that is that metaphor in dialogue is still translatable into a contemporary idiom, the vernacular. If action will at once appeal to the visual imagination even as it appears to be, given utterance in flesh and form by the actor, the metaphor will seem to be the natural expression of the character's own heart and mind. Willie Loman's chief metaphor of his "way out there in the blue" to represent the salesman's freedom is unique to Willie but almost too vague to be dramatically impacting or sensually imaginable..

The semantics of poetry, basically, invove the simile and metaphor and synecdoche. Each is consciously and often unconsciously an intended image-formation whose reference value--that is, the germaneness of the drawn likenesses of quality and thus the precision of the sense communication--stands in relation to the appropiateness of the emotion which the iimage summons up in the minds of the audience. Following is an example that illustrates my point:

> With my slow, insensate dripping away of
> impoverished care,
> 'Tis I who'll trench up his friends to face
> their nimble and mouthy oppressor;
> He that stands o'ver darkly the eves and shakes
> by his wars,
> Main timbers of this sacred house I have
> raised."

The reference value in that rlich communication of a fragment of sense experiences--whether the seeping away of some liquor, as of the wine from a cask, or the roar of fierce winds in the bowls of a thunderhead--enlarges when the similitude links the kindred quality of, or characteristic, that is peculiar to both the image and lits integral human truth. That truth may be buttressed by contemporary findings of the psychological or by sociologiical studies. That truth may also arise from folk experience in a region ;or it may stem from the religion of a people. Irrespective of the primary source of the similitude--of the denotative analogy or the epitomizing metaphor--the image-symbol undergoes a metaphorsiis that renders "impoverished care" partially graphic, as many of Milton's symbols in "Paradise Lost" are partially graphic and that suggests old friehndship buried in the grave of cowardice., Trenehed up "to face their sad and mouthy oppressor" defines character, the mark of great plays and theatre.

Indeed the foreboding storm indictes a fear among the people that stifles courage and darkness and man's vision before the ominous intent of the figure to avenge his people's wrongs. In each of these instances, conversely, the human truth is made graphic by the poet's use of the appropriate images, the similarities which compare and denote likeness to qualityies. Image and truth sysnthesize, and dramatize each other; while yet the central truth of the passage as a whole, the detemined reference, remains clear andl distinct. The context of the similitude will, or should, indicate the germinal meaning of a speech, a scene of action for an entire play. Upon the clarity of that central meaning, and upon that alone, the emotional precision and intellectual integrity of the drama's many and varied similitudes, or metaphors, rests.

A passage from Act I, Scene 3 of **King Lear**, best demonstrates the dramatic power that is achieved by this sythesis of sense image with a human truth in the metaphor.

> Upon such sacrifices, my Cordelia
> The gods themselves thro insense. have I
>   caught thee?
> He that parts us shall bring a brand from
>   heaven
> And fire up hence like fixes, wipe thine
>   eyes;
> The good years shall devour the , flesh and
>   fall.
> Ere they shall make us weep. We'll see 'em
>   starv'd first.
> Come."

King Lear, his torment and his wrath and madness from love's broken fealties spent and his capacity to love restored by the tenderness of his once rejected youngest dauhter, he is, wlith this vow to the beloved Cordelia, looking backward over the terrain of past events. Their moment of reunion is the germinal experience and heart of his speech. It is the imagery of the passage which distills from his words subtle connotations of the wretched misery that shall come upon his pople in the vent that an intruder should strive to part him from his daughter. The metaphor of the burning brand of rightgeous venegeance, and the simile of the foxes with their tails alfame, enkindled by God's judgement, are similitudes which are Hellenistic and Hebraic in origin. Denoting the vivlidly-told account of Judges Chap. 15 that tells of how Sanson fired the Philistines wheat fields, the biblical references dramatically epitomoize the law and the nature of the justice that will enslue should a spoiler try to break their fresh bond of love. Withs the king restored to the throne an Englland reunited, the burning brands of the disafection's news, borne by Lead and his Cordelia would raize the foxes fire by Samszon through the towns and villages of Britian; then might he call his people Philistines.

Shakeepeare's biblical images were undoubtedly graphis to the High Anglicn believer as well as to the courtier and his kinsmen. Be it admitted, then, that the brand image refers to the supernatural sanctioin of the Father-Daughter bond and the foxes image to lthe wildfire traininng of a people's contentment and wealth. The animistic abstracting withsout sense appeal, of the good year of suggests overflowing barns, yet, too, fields parched of grass, thirsty sheep, rotten hay mows and places of unversal siness and death. . The The animism takes on vividness and immediacy, for by metamorphosing "the good years" into a sort of omnivorosus beast that would glean from the people their hardwon wealth and despaiir their homes, lives and physical vitality, the lines beome dramatic and sensuous with the implied details of everyday life.

Such a righteous judgement and the fearsome retribution of an impersonal self-consuming justice lend this passage a dramatic power that exalts emotionally and spiritually the tender beautys of **King Lears** reunion with his daughter, a vow that transcends false pity for his opening charge of Cordelia's unfaithfulness. The human is endowed with power and subtlety by the imagery of King Lear's speech. What is remarkable, every one of the areas of special tlruth mentioned above confirms that germinal experience shared by Lear and Cordelia; the psychology of love's balm that sooths the torment of madness and the after-storm. There is in the play then the sociology of cultural harmony and close loyalties in a paternalistic British kingfdom; the folk lelements of respect for fertile ground and for the toil of lits cultivation; and the religious story with an apprehension off divine ordinanace. Millers play has none of these elements because, of course, it is a very different play. On the other hand, he has sacriiced this multi-dimenstional depth for a meretricious reporte'rs sob-piece that scarcely suggests tragedy except by way of pity by the audlience. Only by my comparison with Kling Lear can I make clear this shortfall as tragedy. It is not the genius of one and the skill of the other that matters; ita the reporter's cfreation of a web of pragmatic realities brought to a focus with the King's reunion.

GOD-MAN OR THE TRAGIC HERO IN DRAMA

Biological determinism--Darwin's theory of evolution of the species by natural section for adaptive changes in the environment, contributed fuel to the Naturalist doctrine of Zola. Said the Naturalists: Man is a biological organism only. To invest him with a divine spark is idiocy. To find in him the God-man is superstition. To say that he can control the laws of nature or the forces of an impersonal cosmos is an illusion.

These encantations led to a denial of God and the efficacy of orthodox Christian faith. They also gave rise to the plunder song of laissez faire, Capitalism, and to a dog-eat-dog philosophy; to labor legislation and agrarian reform as reactions; to social protest literature and the espousal of socialist and communict doctrines.

With God seriously challenged for authority--or dead, as Neitzche would have it-- and common Man's surpra-animal Being thrown onto the scales, there was a brief revival of Greek concepts of fate and destiny of the tragedy of the good man, noble in spirit, of common birth, defeated by unconquerable forces that exploited his personal weakness. But these ancient concepts fell before Man's acceptance of scientifically proved laws. Also there fell integrity whose destiny was absorption by the State and spiritual aniihilation by values-relativity and utility of life. In the twenty-first century, Western man is struggling to cope with his automatism, his robotic environment in which he counts for less and less as a soul-inhabited being created by God. He is losing his soul to the machine and his worth is more and more estimated by the electronic decisions, choices and evaluations. This means the death of God's reflection in the human drama, for if he can relate only to himself, man becomes increasingly a-moral, self-absorbed and sterile of all passion for his survival except through inventions of the laboratory. Denying his former potential for greatness in the arts and humanities, he arrives at the petri-dish man, the cloned man, the valueless person of the abortuary, the sickness of loss without hope or direction.

METHODOLOGIES FOR DETERMINING THE LIMITS OF CERTAIN LIBERTIES - AS OF CONSCIENCE...

"No person shall be seized, imprisoned or dispossessed, outlawed or exiled, or in any way destroyed, nor will he be impressed against his will or prosecuted , except by the lawful judgement of his peers or by the law of the land."(1215- Magna Carta)

It is inevitable that librty of individual action will encounter resistance, force, persuasaion. The **Magna Carta** quotation suffices to show how fundamental is this liberty to free men. When a people and not the central government are in control of their own destinies, they hold and sustain the power to decide issues of equity, property, contracts and concnsus. Hitler's ravings for *destiny's blood and soil,* as an exclussive State concern, were wrong. They contended in the form of military force and political oppression to control fundamental liberty and *selected* themselves to chose the course of history for the disenfrachised.

Placement of the battle on an acceptable stage, or forum of debate is a situation that, failing to mollify all malcontents and activist zealots, leads often to riots--even like a concerted tantrum of the spoilers unable to get their way. Violence thereby forces the hand of justice. In doing so it invalidates its credal position and in effect becomes leaderless and tokenistic.

Riot ought never to replace argument debate or orderly compromise. Indeed, in a free society riot ought never to constitute any expression of agreement so long as the legal legislative mechanisms for resolving issus are still in place and working. Riots are a gross missaplication of the right of assembly, which ought to be peaceable, and a colossal breech of the peace necessary that all men might share without the use of force in the direction of social change. For a riot is not evidence of liberty in action or of freedom without the citizens' conent but of outright anarchy. The choice to revel may come from one or two leaders; the act of mob insurgence by thousands is mindless submission to the influence if violent emotions. A riot often attempts to sanctify injustice; it can be presupposlitions of a wrong unaddressed but may fail the test of truth. A riot can touch the base human rage for survival and in so doing becomes mindless and must be countered with equal violence under color of law.

In pre-revolutionary time, the mechanism of the local constabulary Court or the town forum, were not effective to convict, even in the face of good evidence, so that errant colonials were taken to England for trial--or a grievance was never resolved at all this side of the Atlantic. These wrongs were addressed in our Declaration of Independence. .

Also a miscreant for the most innocuous violation of the law--theft of a pair of shoes or a loaf of bread--would be tried before the King's Court without a defender and witnesses, and he would either be imprisoned or, as sometimes happened, drawn and quartered while alive. After decades of this sort of cruel punishment--which our Constitution addresses--an organized and directed revolution was the only recourse, wherein leaders exercised a liberty of moral action. transmitting that same morality of thought and choice to the Minutemen who fired upon the Regulars. They did so not as a mob but as individuals who had made a conscious decision in the exercise of their personal liberty. They had to dissociate themselves from loyalty to the Crown and consensual union with loyalist Britishers.

One can see, how distant and different were the Paris street scenes in the storming of the Bastille and the rebellion against the Brisish Red-Coats along the Lexington-Concord Road. The French revolted for freedom without a plan; the Colonials revolted for freedom with a plan. The French concentrated on Personalities they; would install; the Americans concentrated on the plan their would invoke. The first is immensely changeable, the latter stable and sound.

The new America proposed laws for guidance, statutory choices for her followers, the participatory citizens of the new Sates. Thehy had a vbuilt in lierty ot redirect their collctive and personal ambitions, their motives, their designs by way of a new law when it passed. Thus the law affirmed what transpired in men's minds upon the application of personal choices in the vote, and the vote therefore represents a moral, or good, change for a visionary improvement. Every new social change partakes somewhat of a vision, a pre-conception. Corruption, traditon and Class-memories weigh down upon the Old World.

In America, each new piece of legislation confesses to man's innate capacity for adaptation, his proclivity toward change, his right of partipation and agreement. At the same time, each new law is an admission by the body politic that it cannot function in a state of discord but needs consensual agreement. A tyrant finds no such discord because he works to eliminate disagreement, conflict, cunning mischief; he suspects plots to put him out of his office. Treachery and intrigue are still a paranoia that is endemic to the Old World.

In every course and structure of the social consensus the individual acceeds to the new law and curbs his individuality to conform in obedience to the will of the people. He thus choses to conform to what has already been estalished by law. By his participaion he willingly and, therefore in full freedom and knowledge, adds his will to the consensus while tempering his future plans, if the law should affect him intimately, adapting to the reason of the enactment. In this manner the consensual legislation, which is a "**social contract**," sets limits upon his personal liberty wherever he makes contact and use of the proscriptions of the legislative will. In conforming, the citizen is exercising his liberty to make a moral choice for the people's welfare. The right-ess or wrong-ness of an act is his deciion, and therefore he establishes in fact the parameters of liberty by means of elective legislation and his own participation therein.

That of course is basic civics. So, too, are those times when a court decides a case that ether builds upon an old or established law sets a new precedent. That ruling will in the future be relevant as precedent for the personal choices of plaintiff and defense alike--each because of his particpatory citizenship, having the liberty to make his choice. For this reason, aliens who owe their allegiance to another country and are not members of the body-politic ought not to be allowed to vote or to enjoy those special priviliges granted by law to the citizens. Judicial precedents in case law thus do work another boundary for the individual in our free society, beyond which one who brings a challenge to the law ought not to transress at the sharp risk of becoming either criminal, anarchist or outlaw.

Laws instituted of man therefore, establish the boundaries the free citizen's actions, often with his hardly being aware by daily parfticipation that he is shaping his affairs in conformity to the laws, since he has the custom and support of others around him who do likewise.

But are there laws of God which mark the boundaries to free will and autonomic human conduct without reference to any controlling republican influence? There are, but they, as the Ten Commandments, have now and by long usage become a part of the fabric of our system of justice--the Ten Commandmentls is universally throughout the United States a prohibition against murder, since the crime offends the people by its reuke of their authority, *vfiz a viz* the republican State that guarantees the righ tto happiness. And murder offends God by virtue of men's precious value in the mind of the Creator, made in His likeness.

For many lthe secular mandate suffices, yet it be terribly in; error to say that America's founding fathers left God out of their consieratiaons for their new Country. There is far too much evidence to support the actuality of their faith that anyone shoud or should deny either its reality or the undergirding Christian manifesto of our forefathers.

Roman laws, though pagan, also protected men from harm by way of the State's overshadowing power, cruel and oppressive as it was when transgressed. Those laws interdicted wrongful actions of citizens which led to punishment of boh pagans and Christians, but since the latter were, and are, admonished in II Corinthians, Chapter 10, to obey secular rulers and lawsas appointedby God and therefore providing they not contravene His laws, it is evident that He had ordained goverment to govern mens sinful actions and his inclinations to do wrong. Therefore, even under a despotism the liberty to exercise personal judgement as final, to evaluate a law or edict from higher authority tempered by the test as to whether or not it contravenes God's laws and ordinanances, remains a matter of pesonal conscience and public consensus. The parameters of human actions, in the minds of Christian community, are perforce controlled by laws that tolerate liberty of judgement and the divine proviso, the Scriptural test, as alluded to above; that further refines and defines th laws of our Country, as subject to personal judgement being put into effect and action. We do not surrener our liberty of conscience for the sake of the law but, most often, for the benefit of the people and in conformity with God's laws--He and not the State who is the source of moral conscience.

IDEA ND IMAGE -- A DISCLAIMER

In a time of specialization, the reader would expect to find exposition and poetry and narrative in an anthology. Thi book is not an anthology. I am convinced that the creative act involves idea and narrative imaGe. These two kinds of creative act cannot be separated, although one may be emphasized. Mark Twain wrote exposition, poetry and fiction, as did Wm. Faulkner.

In that alcl of creation the consciousness exists, giving life to the conscience. And where the conscience is there is a darkness that yearns for the light, which is God. All human souls, I believe, have this dim awareness, this feeling of emptiness without a faith in God. Unable to fill that emptiness man has invented many gods. And thus we have polytheistic societies and cultures as well as athiestic ones, in which men have their god or gods hich they worship. But in so doing they cannot deny to others their God.

And so these pieces of exposition and stories the dramatic IMAGE and the IDEA exist side by side, animated by a belief that their creativeness is god-Given and nothing more. They acknowlege the existence of the creative splirit, whether invested in expository Idea or in fiction, as dramatic image.

LIMITS OF COMPASSION

How she had laughed when he had kissed her cheek with his lips. He remembered her expression of petulance when he had insisted that she not stir up the embers of anger in her father's heart by talk of leaving him and her mother. Her father had not taken the loss of his two boys lightly, her brothers. It was she whom the neighbors in the small town of Sexton called *the sorrowing one* because of her loss of two sons in the interminable Revolution. Her father had appealed to God for widom at every crossroads and had even escoriated Janice for her *faithlessness*, as he called it, refusing to remember why he, his own daughter, was ever born. The wound had never healed, as had not the wound of the loss of her two brothers by enemy gunfire at Dunsmuir Bridge. The father had appeared to contend with God. That enmity alone had intruded itself into her love for her affianced one, and chilled its intimacy, its hopes and even memories that recalled from distant memories a more significant and treasured and believable past.

She forgave him, her lover, for his coolness? The distancing came only from her. Should he father a child by her he would not call the village pastor to bless the babe. He saw her independence in the quality of her love for him, asking little, reluctant to demand anything. All the time, Janice's parents remained at a distance, faces of memory that fractured and dissolved like images in troubed still waters.

"I wish we could go...back...far into the past. I would have been so...lovely back then."

"There'd have been just as many regrets and sorrows, Janice. Time never escapes them...and we cannot."

The wagon they rode atop of creaked and tilted into a deep spring-thaw rut. She fell against him and he embraced her with a kiss on her neck. When she pulled away from him, there came a moment of lostness, of distancing, of rebuke he did not understand, as though she did not love him outside the context of a past, her past, that swarmed with romantic images, moments, events and occasions and all the panopoly of faces and friendships and encounters she had once known...as the presentment, as it were, of her total being surrounded by the beauty, the engagement of her life to his. That mesmerizing vision was the condition of their anticipated union as husband and wife.

He heard her voice, her laughter like the brightntess of a child. He saw into her past with the bright clarity of a vision. Why she clung to him was not his love for her. He sorrowed for her desertion of life. She treasured up a girlhood untainted by evil, so pure it was bizzare, so protected it rebuked the shame of reality and the reason of later hardships. She did not wish to leave that past. She clothed everything in the costume and events of long ago, like a child still enamored of trunks filled with old clothing and momentos in a stale and musty attic

She grew up with the sounds of quadrille dancing, music and joy of life, the swing of singing calls of the dance caller lofting the window curtains to the social hall adjacent to her father's village church. Occasionally, she remembered, the village men had removed the tables and chairs , and the dncers had formed their squares in the big country farmhouse kitchen .

There was the dancing master from Georgia who had traveled across the country holding square dances, entertailning his countruymenin the midst of what she called "a stupid old war." It was now five years since that first shot on the Lexington-Concord Bridge. Before the arrival of the expert dancing master filled with French an English dances and inventing a few of his own, the church choirmaster had found it useful to teach the call maneuvers, good posture, the grace of rhythm, the quickened instincts for each move.

She came to admire him. He stood six feet tall, handsome in black cultivated beard, tri;m moustache, elegant cuffs and the frock of a dedicated square dance caller. ;who billed himself as a *Rhondele Caller*. He had come alone to their town. Janice was pleased to smile at him on his first night, when other girls and a few of the young men of town consented to learn dance steps under his teaching. Few diversions kept single folks in a perpetual bag of wood chips and dessicated earth, the floor covering at the grange for their youthful village pleasure. Furthermore, a wagon or buggy was not always available for junkets to the village dance, nor was there available a suitable companion to chaperone a trip into another town for trafficing with finer buggies and purchasing shoes and trinkets.

As their love grew they engaged in what prim and pious olks called
the *devil's dance*, she being the daughter of a minister and he being her suspected
seducer. It had alwlays seemed to him that folks who thought themselves most
pious exhibited the darkest thoughts toward the lighthartsed younger folk. Such
were the opinions of the town's most astute gossips. The flame of fantasy evil
was blown to a flame when her Papa got up behind his small teakwood pulpit on
Sundays to exclaim against the sin of certain pleasures, like the "High Betty
Martin" and the "Bartel's Whim", peculiar names for hoedowns amid the squares
of "Country Road" and "Summer Songs." His daughter sat not near to the front
but at the back where she might hide her blushes and observe *him* when she came
in. Few noticed this discomfiture, but all saw how he, Jonathan, was drawn
toward Janice.

Those times were lost in the dreammemories of Janice who came
from an era into the place where Jonathan could touch her and love her and know
lher. Her life went back to those days in 1770 although their village of Elkridge
had no inn as yet, nor did it boast a tavern or Ordinary. It did, however, offer a
fine Grange meetilng hall Despite the admonitions of her father, Janice went
there on the arm of another dance partner, whose name is lost to the ages--quite
some time before she had met Jonathan Whiteacre. The Inn was the scene, lavish
in simple country ways and an assembly for the dance floral and lively. Her suitor
heard and saw the splendor. Janice danced with a grace that enthralled those who
watched her.

On this particular night she had ridden to the Inn in a carriage.
Because of this venue and her dress and escort, some accused her of "swinging in
a lusty fashion, " and they were not averse to saying so openly to lneighbors and
fvriends. After all, as the preacher's daughter she was something of a celebrity.
One could see that they were simply jealousm for she danced with an admirable
grace not unbecoming a young woman of her years. Her escort on that night had
een a Major Newcome.

But Major Newcome faded from Janice's life, leaving her the
caretaker of a country store on the fringe of the early forontier America. No one
really knew how she had come into the proprietorship of the store. She was a
good taskmaster, however, and the store thrived as an enterprisw apart from her
identity as a young *enchante* to the younger men and a dutiful child of the village
man of the cloth, himself a widower. The boisterous spirit of the girl found its

outlet in the barn dance where whiskey flowed like creek water and the fiddler and dulcimer players were prodded to nip the bottle.

Janice's life had gradually assumed the dimensions of a renewed fantasy, for now she dispensed with the elaborate rich appearance of a dancing countess, and became instead the singing country maid. She met a boisterous gentleman from the Appalachian country who had come out of the hills with only his horse and belongings in saddle bags, and he had gained new wealth with the sale to the English of London of timber from land he had purchased for a song. Flint Larsen was also an expert gambler, which added to his fortune. He was, in fact, a singing troubadour. Also, he danced in a way that pleased Janice. She had grown more skilled in the dance and in making the most of her masculine company. She had become bold, always shrewed, never brash and completely self-confident, though giving the appearance of submissiveness and an irrepressible clinging.

At the country store where she waited on village folk a customer would shout *Junket! Junket!* and that very night dancers would gather in wagons for a Satsurday twilight trip to the grange hall for another heelburner. All was done within earshot. The revelers would traveled by hayrick to the dance. Janice would shut up the store, bolt the door, shutterthe windows and let the most boisterous of characters in the town escort her to the shindig. Belonging, she thought to the spirit of the dance, were the prctical jokes, which she took great delight in unraveling before their victims did . She enjoyed watching the man sprinkle pepper on ;the floor and maybe toss a pig's foot linto the wood stove. Janice loved to dance with Jonathan, paticularly the "Lady Walplole's Reel," "Morning Star," " Money Musk." And she could rattle off a good many of the most popular dance tunes and fancy-stepping music. She never forgot the old New England and scenes where she and then Major had made out so well. She loved the galloping movement of some of the dances. And--placing Jonathan Whiteacre on the back burner, she allowed herself to fall in love with Henry Wilson, a *cow wrestler*, he said. He was not just a cowpoke, however; he was also a trickster, or magician, who loved to invite himself into the parlors of the best dressed and finest ladies of the small town. When he became Janice's lover--before Jonathan's eyes of pretended indifference-- they were never seen out of the company of each other. Indeed, while she achieved a certain dark notoriety she spawned a following of young men who wanted to take over his territory but could not. For she was loyal--to one at a time--until she grew weary of his trickery and his flambuoyant jigs.

Janice Carruthers had acquired a knowledge of the dances, all of them, that she loved to dance, especially in the company of graceful gentlemen as well as the uncouth and boorish partners who clung to her like the gold they sought. She talked to her dance partners, regaled them about festivals she had attended, chancing the ngiht wsith a palm reading, a fortune telling, a toss the ring at the Ordinary. She shied clear of the tavern; she owned an instinctive distrust of the male arrogance when liquored up. Yet sought in the past those affars that drew her like a lodestone to their excitement, visual movements of the dance and the color and buoyancy, as though her spirit without these fetes would have collapsed like some distant avatar in upon itself. She used to regale folk around a bonfire with the plain talk about sugarings-off, sheepshearings and, above all else, the elegant, festive and provincial weddings in the village where she had lived before she set out upon her own voyage. In Nantucket the *Sheepsherers' Ball* lasted an entire week, yet she withstood the rigors of its excitement as if she were still a chlild.

"Oh, godoodness a mighty!..I couldn't stand their stomping their feet at first! How they clapped their hands and skipped around the floor!" Always when she mentioned those moments there came over her a shadow of sadness. There had never been any need to mention chaperones to Janice. She had grown bold, enterprising and men who saw that aspect were drawn to her, evem amidst the hayseed, hipflask activity.

She had changed, an altered pride, a retreat of the old New England posturing into a western bluster by which she continued to charm the young men at the parties. Janice not appear to count the hours, the days and years when she would no longer be wedded to this lifem to her careless and cavalier ways evident to Jonathan , by now a disappointed suitor, and to a few others who had known her for many years. In the beauty of the dance, the styling, the graceful movements she continued to find satisfaction in the rhythm of the music. Like a gay child she loved to move her feet. And any who would move with her she invited into the confines of her love and native honesty. She danced palm to palm with the men, Fiedler MacKeon, a wagoneer who had come to the town junket and though drunk, tried to pull her into his arms. A fight followed. She fled the dance...but for only an lhour. She loved to flair her skirt, Janice did, and took pleasure in seeilng that the men kept their hands at their sides for dignity and grace. Janice admired these qualities of dignity.

Always she sought excitement. That was her naure, her pursuit to calamity. She presented the Lieutenant at Fort Jackson a playing card, on the obverse side of which she wrote down the tips she was to dance. All that night, they were were dance partners. Lieutenant Talmadge, a tall, courtly man who wore the cavalry sabre and danced as if astrdie a horse, so lythe and limber and in keeping with the rhythm, yet awkward. That night at the fort the band played a jig, a reel of two, a contra dance, all of which Janice joined in with her new cavalry officer friend. She loved to dance the traditional New England quadrille. It seemed as if she never tired. The Spanish *Las Cuadrillas* charmed her most, for they had come east with cowboys and travelers to the promised New Land.

There came upon the scene one night a transit of violence, for the men at the fort, much against the orders of their commncing officer, had indulged in heavy drinking. A fight broke out, the cause of which no one could discover immediately. It seems that an especially gifted woman, in repartee, had chided the caller and he took offense whilest another lady and her officer companion took sides to protect and defend the claller.

The soldiers, as though to support the caller, began to do fancy capers, pidgeon wings, knee-to-toe brandishings, and all the small fillagree steps of the traditional dances. I saw Janice weave throughl the melee and disappear on the outer porch of the post pavillion. The call of the bugle vanished in fury of the fight; how disciplined military men, expecially the officers, could engage in such la rumpus puzzled all who simply wlooked on. This fight between the officers was barely in the rolling rhythm of Ohio flatboatmen. It was more like a *breakdown* of the barn dance, all the dancers engaged at one time in the activity. It was apparent that Janice felt confused and embarrassed. All courtesy of tradition seemed lost. All pattern was gone.

Then was heard a whistle. At that men gathered their dignity, repositioned their uniforms and bade the ladies to forgive them for their lack of civil politeness and for bad manners. A grand march ensued. Janice sort of disappeared that night, though she refused to pass up the cidre and sanwiches, turkey, venison and oysters. She did not stay until dawn when the dance ended. Most of those were at last aware of the conflit between the rough Applachian frontier manners and those of settled New England society. The country was growing and diversifying.

Iy ewa not until after a year or more was that Janice came to a dance at a country farmhouse where a dance room had been built. Ordinary the folks used the kitchen, All items of the kitchen but the stove were removed, the caller ensconcling himself atop the sinkboard, the mother bringing their babes in cradles, sometime putting them on communal beds consisting of benches pushed together. On her face Janice showed that she was greatly perplexed by the overtures of a local merchant who had engaged her attention in lthe village. It was all a far cry from the New England countryside that had been quickened and desolated by the war, the gradual loss of the younger men in particular. Janice claimed to have witnessed Gemeral Washington taking his pleasurel with "Sir Roger de Coverly," a famous and populr quadrille. She had even found pleaure in lancing with the *roundhats*, the Puritans, not as a symbol of eternal damnation and wickedness but to devlop grace and an erect carriage. Leave the lascivious dancing and wanton ditties to the pagans. The turbulence of the war had dwelt within Janice's heartall the long years of battleagainst the British. She was no lonvger the woman of the village where she had danced and played as a child-woman.

When Janice left the new country of the Ohio Valley and returned to the East, I knew some dreadful event or recognition had overtaken her, some consequential pain and delusion brought on by her idealization of men and of life generally. She had wanted a child, and she had become pregnant by the officer at the fort who, returning with her, had failed to calm her fears or change her outlook. For she was determined that he not be the father: one could never understand, such much less accept as her aspiration in life. It was sin the remembering of these lovely nights at the dance that caused her to collapse one night, almost into Jonathan's arms, he th ever flaithful, the suitlor no longer to her heart but to her charms. Her fainting had been doubtless to her pregnancy-- taken like a poison with the harsh words of the father of her child who said o her that if she did not bear him la son--for he was convinced that the child would be a boy--he shouldthat she would never see him again. Thus she was torn between the fanciful reveries of her past and the anguish of the present when she rejected the Lieutenant as beneah her. She remembered how he was engaged in the fight on that night of the dance, and that he had never shown toward her the slightest remorse or apology.

She took a drink and then another, for there was growing inside of her a life she did not want. It had come from a wanton, refined man as he looked in his soldierly appearance, but by her standards, stupid and repugant. He had never kissed her tendelry or said that he loved her. He had only commanded her and ordered her life to comform to his. This hidden anger moved her to repent before the village minster, who was to her no more than a figluehead., an icon of the local village church. She found the doctor to perform the procedure and be rid of the unwanted darkness, after which ordeal she began to repent and to visualize with great remorse that her little girl might have shared some of her gay life. Too late to recant of death, too sooin to die.

She grew more angry and strange as the days went by, so that those who she had known her younger days began to be frightened of her presence amid them. It was hardly a year that had passed, when she remembered the birthday of her little girl who did not live, for she carried this painful image of the child's death around with her like a millstone. It weighed on he . It cast its black evil chemise over her golden hair, now showing strands of gray. Never had the officer, father to the dead child, ever written to enqure about her circumstanes. This total lack of concern deepened her distress, at least he might have pretended a memory or interest. But they had not come.

Then one day a child came to her, a litle girl whom she imagined was about the same age as her dead daughter She clung to the chilld, who had been sent by the pastor on a simple errand to enquire of Janice. Momentarily distraught, the women bad claimed her and clung to her and begged her and entreated her with cookies to return the next day. This the child had done, and continued to return, some days not showing up, on which days Janice sufferfed great remorse. All the while in the ensusing months a bond grew up between them . Clarisse did not enquire who was the little girl s parents, but only that the girl filled a need. It was as if Janice had adopted her to take the place of the baby she had killed in the womb.

The relationship and words exchanged grew so bizzare that the parents found out who the new aunt was and the secret visits. They had the judge imnpose a writ upon the woman that forbade visitations, but the child did not understand the turnings of the law and continued to come until, finding out about these secret visits, the parents had Janice taken from her dwelling and put into jail for child endangerment. As if this were not enough for her poor soul to endure, the town stood aghast and against her. Not a soul vame to visit her in jail--except Jonathan. It would have turned one's heart if you could have seen a woman once considered beautiful, admirable as a potential wife for nay man, a superior dancer who loved the life of dancing soirees, the gallant men, the gay company, the lavish women--now vitually friendless.

The worst was that she did not kill herself. No, the court had the cruelty to release her for lack of evidence in the child endangerfment charge, and the last I saw of Janice , she was one of those whom society calls the *homeless,* having lost all her dignity and vital inner beauty yet hanging with a pitiful dumb temerity onto life until she should--and did-- collapse in a field of flowers, which she had always loved. There the townsmen found her, though few could recognize her as to who she really was. Jonathan, alone, identified her. He wrote the prayer. The pastor read it over her common grave. He followed the prayer with the twenty-third Psalm. As the first shovelfull of dirt fell onto the coffin lid, I looked up and at a distance there stood a little girl watching all that was going on . As to whether or not she was the spirit-child that had brought Janice to this end, I as the story teller, cannot say. Nevertheless, she was the child that was the inner Janice, and the babethat she had envisozned though dead was hers.

A BRIEF CRITIQUE ON TWO PLAYS BY AUGUST STRINDBERG (1849 - 1912) AND HIS PLAY MISS JULIE (1887)

An opening comment is of interest: by Harley Granille-Barker in his book **On Dramatic Method** (1931): "... With the actor in the ascendant the contemporary drama is generally lifeless. Remarkable plays are not written by taking the actor at his own valuation, and by giving him merely what he likes best to do. But neither are they by men who take other plays for a model and know nothing at first hand about the actor's art at all. The great periods in drama, the periods of renaissance and development, have almost invariably been dominated by dramatists who know so much about the theatre and of actors and their acting that they had no illusions left about them." (pp.31-32)

Another quote seems relevant to Strindberg: Morton Dawsen Zabel writes in **Literary Opinion in America**: "The distinction between the psychology of *information* and the psychology of *form* involves a definition of aesthetic truth." (p.675). K. Burke in his **Philosophy of Literary Form** writes that there are three levels of symbolism in a literary work of art: They are (1) biological, that is, the sensory and kinesthetic imagery, (2) personal, that is the intimate of friends, family, relationships, and (3) the abstract, that is, the part played by insignia in poetic action which allies the action with a side, or a positive persuasion. NOTE: I recommend, also, **Write That Play**, by Kenneth Thorpe Rowe, who presents problems of building technique, of style, dialogue, characterization and the best dramatic use of chosen subjects. Rowe works with short and long forms of the play and gives excellent analyses of **A Night At An Inn**, **Riders to the Sea** and **A Doll's House**.

MISS JULIE (1887); On p. 66 of his Foreward, Strindberg writes: "She is a victim of the discord which a mother's 'crime' has produced in a family, a victim too of the day's complaisance, of circumstances, of her own defective constitution, all of which are equivalent to the Fate or Universal law of former days." It is a fact that the *Hamartia*, or the tragic flaw of character in a Sophoclean tragedy, is an ill-fated flaw in an otherwise strong character, not in a degnerate one. Might not audience reactions range from pity to disgust for that reason? one may ask. Is it not an anomaly to says of Miss Julie that she is not a tragic figure, when circumstances have so cruelly shaped her life? Can the Naturalist, in other words, conceive a tragic character out of perceptions and experiences that deny to that person the use of will and a consciousness of its implications in her actions?

Miss Julie's actions are whinsical and capricious. Shaw wrote that Strindberg, whom he called one of the giants of the theatre. (Major Barbara is a far cry from Miss Julie) depicts passion in the extreme, an eccentricity, and that insofar as the playwright shows us the status of passion, he was a Romantic. The human and divine, the sensual and the sacred. Yet its difficult, if not impossible, to derive any main experience from the play about which Strindberg makes a rational statement. Furthermore, he does he lead us to any but the most scattered conclusions: that Miss Julie, having married a rotter, breaks off with him for no explicitly stated motive (although her confession to Jean after the seduction contains powerful motivation), for she realizes that Jean schemes to rise in society by using her and going to Switzerland.

On p. 55 of the forward, Strindberg further states: "Even if the father had felt impelled to take no vengeance, the daughter would have taken vengeance on herself, as she does here, from that innate or acquired sense of honor which the upper classes inherit...It is a very beautiful thing, but it has become a danger nowadays to the preservation of the race." He evidently finds evil the expression of dangerous beauty.

Is that sense of honor one of the empty ideallisms Ibsen tried to detestroy? A contemporary audience may find it impssible to discover, within the play's action, the content of that "acquired sense of honour"-- kindness toward the domestic help, orderly government of the household, sensible preparation for marriage with a dowry, cloistered tutorage, etc. Do these culture-practices and ethnic mores produce any sense honor--honor by the performance of duty, perhaps-- by Srtrindberg's reasosning?

But how shall we interpret the magnitude of Miss Julie's moral change, the realities of her degeneracy, without a character in the play who embodies the standards she falls from? That is a question relating to the craft of playwriting. Indeed, the audience is treated to an orgy of suffering , the sensuality of Strindberg's expressed self.

Although acceptable to the psychologist as material for a clinical study, the playwright's work in *Miss Julie* show that he mistakes her degenerate whimsies, her weakminded caprice, for raw realities that are both life-drama and a play. Many bits of odd action and conversation in actual life are dramatic, but they, reproduced in mime on the stage, do not constitute a play. Would Strindberg's "play," under this criticism, lead an audience to a perception of something more fundamental to human nature than the actual facts of life, givens order and balance? For example, a woman who abuses her honor, whether from a class ideal or a human ethic or religious credo, does not always suffer. In Miss Julie--and another of Strindberg's sentimentalities--she does suffer, of course, but, excepting the Naturalist's abolition of God and guilt, he's cling to the punishment conequences of sin, if only to torment his projectsed self in Miss Julie.

The ethical function of this drama is that it teaches us to understand and appreciate the responsibilities of being human; that is, the drama's "morality" and didactisicm as an end in itself, is not implied. What is the truth of the play, where is the action in the play, that conveys that ethic, that arouses in us a percep;tion of our human responsibilities? Maudlin sympathy for a woman-child is not responsible understanding , or responsible perception.

August Strindbetg would give us romantic emotionalism as reason and irrational action as free volition. There is no norm by which to compare Miss Julie with her kind. Ibsen furnishes his audience with a class model as well as his ideological norm and he shows us manners as well. Strindberg gives us no motives amenable to explicit statement for Miss Julie's caprices. The motives of Ibsen characters are always clear to the audience. We are expected to feel but not to think in a Strindberg play, a course of behavior that would lead one precisely to those symptoms of degeneracy with which, in the chaaracter of Miss Julie, Strindberg beckons our sympathies. We are expected to regard degeneracy as acceptable and if not praiseworthy at least as moral. We can discern much of modern society in a Strindberg play, for popular applause makes a hero of a calico devil.

Eric Bentley has called Strindberg's plays "the ultimate in romantic self-analysis along Freudian lines." The ultimate is the madness of unresolved dilemmas of purpose. Miss Julie is tainted with that insanity, in which amid mental chaos the mind lacks the ability to form intent. Not all self-analysis is romantic, but only where, as in the case of Miss Julie, the ability to affix reason logically, or at least rationally to external symbols breaks down. This observation is born out of Bentley's statement, farther on (p. 169): Strindberg was "always trying to discover organic and expressive shapes for chaotic experiences." For him, says the critic, "capitalism is the symbol of his own possessiveness in general." Bentley's comments: "The absolute for him (Strindberg) was relative." What he means is that Strindberg lent credence to chaotic experiences as well also to useable drama. The absolute Values of the old aristocracy were tyrannical in their influences and social applications.

THE STRONGER: The play's psychology is subtle and complex at the same time. We are given two actresses, one of whom happily admits that\ she routed the younger woman from the theatre--as a profession. A discussion of mutual intimacies follows. There is a man involved. No woman can get along without him, but one has had him first--trained him to like hot chocolate, prefer flowers, and comport himself like a domesticated French poodle. She is incensed by the younger woman's prior claim over the double lover. She denounces Miss X, with admissions that the latter has influenced the man. But in triumph she claims the bed, a throne and coffee pot by the influence of her superior love. In this play, the transitions of feeling give character to the silent Miss X who, one silenced, wilts away under her adversary's pummeling words. Like the haunting words of the dead wife of Rosmersholm, her sililoquy gives her charactera poignant reality. This ismore thqan a play about rivalry; it is a play about jealous annihilation.

EASTER: Bowed down by creditor Lindkvist, her husband in prison for embezzlement of trust funds, Mrs. Heyst frantically defends her husband's innocence, while in continual dread of the omnipresent ogre. Within the household in a provincial university town in Southern Sweden, Ells, her son, becomes schoolmaster. Shamed by dents and his father's plight, he sees his fiance Kristina tolen by a friend. Eleanora, in an institution for the insane, returns to bring light and love to their care-worn lives, while Lindkvist, inposing the condition to forgive his mother, adjures all debts to the son Ells. This is not a play about self-sacrifice so much as sit is a drsama of the power of innocence. It remlinds this critic of Dostoievsky's great novel, **The Idiot** in which Prince Myschkin rarely acts upon others in a confrontational way but, instead, moves others to act by the aura of his orthodox piety and goodness.

Note, however, that there is a duality of perception behind the drama that is both stoical and Chridstian. Eleanora comes begging others to heap their cares upon her shoulders so that she can suffer for them (the Christ-on-the-cross image). Lindkvist drops all debts upon the condtion that the son forgive his mother (salvation image). The wont of bloth Eleanora and Elais is to suffer merge in Jung's psychology of narcissism. (the image of penitence). What Jung called the "collective subconsciousness, with its homogeniety of extended world wide myth dream, might be used to point the way toward the vsision of world brotherhood. Thus the play has an encompassing aura of a world vision for the characters, a set-up for the Biblical anti-Christ..

REALISM IN THE THEATRE,
IN THE DRAMA

The *hamartia* of ancient Greek tragedy, the tragic flaw, which led to the purging of the emotions by drama, faded from theatrical fare with the advent of certain influences. The tragedy of the good man, noble in spirit, knowingly defeated by unconquerable forces, was a doctrine dashed by man's acceptance of **scientiflcly proved laws** that contolled his actions. The influence of the Greek gods was no more.

Feminine emancipation contributed to the demise of the heroine, such as **Media**, in theatre lore. The Emancipation was a movement that changed manners and dress political opinion and that gained momentum after the turn of the 19th century with its weakening of family ties and dislocations in home life in consequencs of the burgeoning of cities.

Feminism in the 1880's was very daring; in the 1910's, it was plausible yet "dangerous" as a doctrine in this country; in the 1930's the street torches were snuffed out. In England, the *Orange Woman,* the trollope and flower girl, like Lisa, knew their places. Shaw was a pioneer to encourage intelligent women to think about systems of capitalism and socialism, those who since the Middle Ages had exercised intelligence in the overseemg of household and estate. In the Europe of France and Germany, the movement never commanded much respect or loyalty.

With its attendant mass movements of people, the excesses of profit seekers, slum conditions, unfair treatment of labor--these and other realities of the **Industrial Revolution** influenced writers of protest pamphlets, novels and plays. Ideologiclly, the idea was taking shape that man could control his destiny, at least *en masse*, and that he need not remain a brute if he could enact new and human laws and could obtain better living condtions. Plays like "The Adding Machine" symbolic of robotic industrialization were becoming *passee*.

Enter next **Freudlian Psychology**. The **Id, Ego** and **Super-Ego** were Adler's psychological constructs based, in part, on Freud's theory that erotic impulses, drives, complexres are inextricably bound up, through intricate neural connnections, with nearly every activity of our conscious and unconscious mental life. The findings of these two scientists furnished material and insights for the many plays that involve treatment ot dream imagery, ego-expression, subliminal fantasies, and tragic forms of perverse psychology and psychic environmental determinism--or the fated consequences of conditioning.

Perhaps there are those who would not altogether agree with these selections. But one thing remains certain: that the subjects and the playwright choses to write about, his outlook, his style of writing and other elements of his craft and his art were and still are intrisnsicically united to the era, if not to the age, in which he continued to write. The playwrights the critic might examine in lsearch of the preceding influences consist of but are not limited to: Ibsen, Strindberg, Pirandello, Hauptman, Holman,Tschekov, Gorky and Synge. What we shall be looking for, chiefly, are *character motivations and the interplay of social mores.* The art of stagecraft will reveal many visual details about the times in the sets and details of decor. The responses of audiences will affirm many of the biases in manners of the day.   And the subtle art of play directing will give focus to what is humanly, dramaturgically--and sociologicaly --relevent to the play's theme.

A BRIEF CRITIQUE ON AUGUST STRINDBERG
(1849 - 1912) AND HIS PLAY MISS JULIE (1887)

An opening comment is of interest: by Harley Granille-Barker in his book **On Dramatic Method** (1931): "... With the actor in the ascendant the contemporary drama is generally lifeless. Remarkable plays are not written by taking the actor at his own valuation, and by giving him merely what he likes best to do. But neither are they by men who take other plays for a model and know nothing at first hand about the actor's art at all. The great periods in drama, the periods of renaissance and development, have almost invariably been dominated by dramatists who know so much about the theatre and of actors and their acting that they had no illusions left about them." (pp.31-32)

Another quote seems relevant to Strindberg: Morton Dawsen Zabel writes in **Literary Opinion in America**: "The distinction between the psychology of *information* and the psychology of *form* involves a definition of aesthetic truth." (p.675). K. Burke in his **Philosophy of Literary Form** writes that there are three levels of symbolism in a literary work of art: They are (1) biological, that is, the sensory and kinesthetic imagery, (2) personal, that is the intimate of friends, family, relationships, and (3) the abstract, that is, the part played by insignia in poetic action which allies the action with a side, or a positive persuasion. NOTE: I recommend, also, **Write That Play**, by Kenneth Thorpe Rowe, who presents problems of building technique, of style, dialogue, characterization and the best dramatic use of chosen subjects. Rowe works with short and long forms of the play and gives excellent analyses of **A Night At An Inn**, **Riders to the Sea** and **A Doll's House.**

MISS JULIE (1887)

On p. 66 of his Foreward, Strindberg writes: "She is a victim of the discord which a mother's 'crime' has produced in a family, a victim too of the day's complaisance, of circumstances, of her own defective constitution, all of which are equivalent to the Fate or Universal law of former days." It is a fact that the *Hamartia*, or the tragic flaw of character in a Sophoclean tragedy, is an ill-fated flaw in an otherwise strong character, not in a degnerate one. Might not audience reactions range from pity to disgust for that reason? one may ask. Is it not an anomaly to says of Miss Julie that she is not a tragic figure, when circumstances have so cruely shaped her life? Can the Naturalist, in other words, conceive a tragic character out of perceptions and experiences that deny to that person the use of will and a consciousness of its implications in her actions?

Miss Julie's actions are whinsical and capricious. Shaw wrote that Strindberg, whom he called one of the giants of the theatre. (Major Barbara is a far cry from Miss Julie) depicts passion in the extreme, an eccentricity, and that insofar as the playwright shows us the status of passion, he was a Romantic. The human and divine, the sensual and the sacred. Yet its difficult, if not impossible, to derive any main experience from the play about which Strindberg makes a rational statement. Furthermore, he does he lead us to any but the most scattered conclusions: that Miss Julie, having married a rotter, breaks off with him for no explicitly stated motive (although her confession to Jean after the seduction contains powerful motivation), for she realizes that Jean schemes to rise in society by using her and going to Switzerland.

On p. 55 of the forward, Strindberg further states: "Even if the father had felt impelled to take no vengeance, the daughter would have taken vengeance on herself, as she does here, from that innate or acquired sense of honor which the upper classes inherit...It is a very beautiful thing, but it has become a danger nowadays to the preservation of the race." He evidently finds evil the expression of dangerous beauty.

Is that sense of honor one of the empty ideallisms Ibsen tried to detestroy? A contemporary audience may find it impssible to discover, within the play's action, the content of that "acquired sense of honour"-- kindness toward the domestic help, orderly government of the household, sensible preparation for marriage with a dowry, cloistered tutorage, etc. Do these culture-practices and ethnic mores produce any sense honor--honor by the performance of duty, perhaps-- by Srtrindberg's reasosning?

But how shall we interpret the magnitude of Miss Julie's moral change, the realities of her degeneracy, without a character in the play who embodies the standards she falls from? That is a question relating to the craft of playwriting. Indeed, the audience is treated to an orgy of suffering , the sensuality of Strindberg's expressed self.

Although acceptable to the psychologist as material for a clinical study, the playwright's work in *Miss Julie* show that he mistakes her degenerate whimsies, her weakminded caprice, for raw realities that are both life-drama and a play. Many bits of odd action and conversation in actual life are dramatic, but they, reproduced in mime on the stage, do not constitute a play. Would Strindberg's "play," under this criticism, lead an audience to a perception of something more fundamental to human nature than the actual facts of life, givens order and balance? For example, a woman who abuses her honor, whether from a class ideal or a human ethic or religious credo, does not always suffer. In Miss Julie--and another of Strindberg's sentimentalities--she does suffer, of course, but, excepting the Naturalist's abolition of God and guilt, he's cling to the punishment conequences of sin, if only to torment his projectsed self in Miss Julie.

The ethical function of this drama is that it teaches us to understand and appreciate the responsibilities of being human; that is, the drama's "morality" and didactisicm as an end in itself, is not implied. What is the truth of the play, where is the action in the play, that conveys that ethic, that arouses in us a percep;tion of our human responsibilities? Maudlin sympathy for a woman-child is not responsible understanding , or responsible perception.

August Strindbetg would give us romantic emotionalism as reason and irrational action as free volition. There is no norm by which to compare Miss Julie with her kind. Ibsen furnishes his audience with a class model as well as his ideological norm and he shows us manners as well. Strindberg gives us no motives amenable to explicit statement for Miss Julie's caprices. The motives of Ibsen characters are always clear to the audience. We are expected to feel but not to think in a Strindberg play, a course of behavior that would lead one precisely to those symptoms of degeneracy with which, in the chaaracter of Miss Julie, Strindberg beckons our sympathies. We are expected to regard degeneracy as acceptable and if not praiseworthy at least as moral. We can discern much of modern society in a Strindberg play, for popular applause makes a hero of a calico devil.

THE FADING OF AMERICA

If you continue to believe that your material reality represents the American dream of its pioneers, your nation will never be greater than it is now. Its human constructions will constitute its greatness. If you insist on defining its spiritual strength by its material grandeur and the gold in its treasury, virtually oblivious to the spirit of its patriots and their belief in personal liberties, you will see its decline in power, influence in the world and, most deadly, its loss of the bonds of unity and spiritual strength. You will have made the mistake of civilizations before you of believing that your material things represent your liberty, your authentic strength and your destiny.

You will never know the challenges of great statesmanship; no, nor will; your generations to come. Bickering over stuff will come to represent tlhe hiatus of your dream of a city upon a hill. Your authors, your teaching intellectuals, your heroes, your men of moral and ethical wisdom, whether it is political idealism or religious faith, or from the forum of debate that once represented the pith of your universities--these ventures will carry with them the great traditions of your humble past. However, they will do so increasingly in memory instead of in practice.

In your avarice and in your spirit of things. like bright children with the toys of knowledge, you will fail to discern that there can never arise greatness from pollitical correctness but only emptiness of the spirit and, in time, the contempt of older civilizations whose people are your life blood yet whose ways you think useless. If you persist in mistaking the dream of your Washington, your Abe Lincoln, your Patrick Henry and Thomas Jefferson for today's material and technological gains, to the repudiation of the humanities of literature, philosophy, religion and the law, tomorrow will be your sorrow, for you will trample your past under foot and all that your predecessors once believed in you wlll throw out like the slag from your ore pits, the chaff from your wheatfields, the refuse from your factories. And then you will learn, as nations in the past have learned, that the strength of men rests not in their human constructions but in their faith in God, which can never be fully realized; that your freedoms were never the baubbles of tyrants to be bartered for your security, and that apologies before the world for your virtues spell the end to America's greatness.

Yet then your security, too, will crumble, for there will be nothing left of your dream of a franchised people. With each retreat you will have given away yourselves once again into the bondage of fear and submission to the envy of the world by your adoption of its faceless imported creeds. The hurricane in New Orleans, to be sure, has shown us and the world a venue of poverty, but more graphic, it has shown us that imminent death compels us to acknowldge the value of life sustained by courage and love for others.

C. E. Miller

LOVE FOR LOVE (1895), BY WILLIAM CONGREVE - A CRITIQUE

Sir Sampon Legend is the preening fool yet a hard-headed ,
practical Cit of mercantile London. It is he who, fatuously designing a *marriage
of convenience* for his younger sea-going son **Ben,** dares, by himself, to make
ridiculous overtures to the endowered beauty at the close of the play's action. A
prating and absurd fool, his vanity blinds him to the unreasonableness of matching
a sailor with a young woman of "considerable fortune," when the mutual bonds of
love and affection are left out of the cash transaction. Congreve lays the
grounwork for his attack upon the Cit's purse-proud vanity when, in Act I, Scene i,
he assigns to **Sir Sampson** the speech:

> "Odsbud you wrong me; I am not so old,
> neither to be a bare courtier, only a man
> of words; odd, I have warm blood about
> me yet, and can serve a lady any way.
> Come, come, let me tell you, you women think
> a man old too soon, faith and troth, you do! =
> come, don't despise fifty; odd, fifty, in a
> hale constitution, is no such contemptible
> age."

Angelica's money consci99ably warms the old boy's heart, she
who does not want kindness measured in gold, but instead, would try the
constancy of her lover **Valentine--Sir Sampson's** older son, now fallen under his
father's displeasure for his prodigal way of living. To win her for **Ben** is to save
the gold he would bequeath to **Valentine,** the rightful heir, under the law of
Primogeniture.   **Sir Sampson** thus stands to win twice over, financially. As for
Ben, who is "half home-bred, and half sea-bred," he would rather court the rude
country girl, the daughter of the peevish and illiterate old **Foresight,** for he end of

love without much wit or reason or a cash entanglement. Since **Sir Sampson** does not have his way with either **Angelica** or **Valentine, Ben,** in the final Act, must bear the gaff of familial leftovers--not a hard fate for a seafarer who leads a life of wandering and impecunious adventure.

Congreve's play, it can then be seen, is a comedy that deals with the *dual themes* of love without money and money without love--which were the prescribed unreasonable courses of action in the London life of Restoration England. These were codes among British Epicurean society in more'-transition and they were obviously depicted by Congreve through his plays. The advent of a new monied merchantile class, symbolized by the Cit, ushered in the sentimentality of romantic love without a monetary basis, which Congreve ridicules in this play; yet equally money without love, a Medieval concept of the marriage of covenience. Although he contradicted Jeremy Collier's argumenton *Profaneness and Immorality,* for the suppression of drunkenness, debauchery and profanity on the stage, his *Love for Love* contravenes Collier's strictures. For it is upon the excesses inherent in these two themes, drawn out in the action through the counterplay of character with character--rather than through a clever bawdy-house incident and obscene language--that the comedy turns.

In the actions of these lovers' duets in the play Congreve is adroitly pointing out that, in bending to clandestine love and legitimized marriage, men will barter a lesser foible for a greater folly. The dramatist's jest with a theatre audience is that these frail swappings do not always come off. **Ben,** for example, would trade his wanderlust for the desultory Landlubber's life of husbnd to **Miss Prue. Sir Sampson Legend,** a naval man himself, would pay off **Val's** debts, yet strip him of his inheritance and his chances with **Angelica,** whom he, Sir Sampson, covets--in exchange for, or to replace, the folly of **Val's** unstable seafarer's marriage. **Scandal,** the free-spending friend of **Val,** is duped into believing that he is slated for marriage to **Angelica**; in the end he trades his bachelor ways, his passion for etchings and strayed loves, for the auntish **Mrs. Frail.** The critic notes for the benefit of modern theatre audiences, unaccustomed to such compact social entanglements, that they can follow the action by noting the follies inherent in the names of Congreve's characters, and providing their costume and makeup and manners remain visibly distinct.

Still, another of these absured and expurgating barters concerns the superstitions and truculent **Foresight,** and his second wife, the "**Missus Positive,** superstitious, and pretending to understand Astrology, Palmistry, Psysiognony,

Omens, Dreams, etc.," Yet the bearded griffin **Foresight**, griffin of the occult, is so burie in his lore speculations that he is oblivious to the goings on of his son in his own houshold and cannot keep track of his wife. If there is one cuckold in the play, it is he. His wife has learned of **Scandal's** *parts;* malpert and a trifle shy, she is out to have her fun, too, in the pubs of London and with any a stray gentleman. Escaping a husband who dotes on his stars and elixirs, she embarks upon a love affair of convenience with the able **Scandal.** And it is this affair which, in likelihood to 17th century audiences was a fair trade--the temporary suspension of a respentable marriage yet an incompatible one for its frictions and failures, in exchange for the clandestine escapades of a novel good-wife. It was true then, as indeed it is now, that a doltish husband deserved to be duped.

Neither the wit not the barter of a lesser foible for a greater folly embue Congreve's play with the vital and human believability of these flesh and blood creatures who reveal their weaknesses, ltheir ridiculous quirks to the omniscienc audience. Of fundamental human interest are his characters' motives, which lie beneath Congreve's manipulation of outraged social codes and apparent ends to be sought in the course of the play's actions. *Love For Love* attains to high comedy because of the serousness of his principals' motives. **Valentine**, with unprobing eyes and **Angelica,** with clear-sighted vision, are willing to sacrifice their pride, as yielding and beautiful participants in an arranged marriage of convenience, for an intangible and and delusory, an almost far-fetched marriage with love. **Valentine** shows that his love is more valorous and constant a companion in wooing that than were his former back-street pub affairs, condoned by the creed for cavalier, young unmarried gentleman of the day. **Angelica**, who must chose a man of good name nd trustworthy actions so that he might father her children without blemish of scandal, pretends to a coldness that she does not feel in order that she mgiht test his devotedness. Congreve is saying that so long as two lovers doubt their love for each other, the only folly worthwhile, reasonable and common sensical is that which proves their constancy. The comedy of the play evolves from the actions of its lovers who make themselves ridiculous for no such conventionally common-sense end as a marriage withsout love.

What sets the play a-right and furnishes the audience with a norm for their ljudging, as ridiculous, the actions of the lovers is **Valenine's** odd, feigning insanity--a false sacrifice of dignity comedic in its implications, that is performed for the beauty if a young woman's love, **Angelica's.** The scene of his collapse, brought on by the relentless passion of his love--yet actually a cunning stall for time to reconcile his father with him--does not lead to any greater folly.

This is Congreve's comment upon romantic love' it is madness. The passions of the **Sir Sampson, Mrs. Foresight, Ben** and **Tattle**--the half-witted bawd--are ridiculed by the dramatist for leading for leadling to unsound bargfains. However, **Val's** love "humour" of the heart--which 17th century audiences thought a foible, out of place in a good match--nets the product of what, to Congreve's mind, is sound common sense: property, in addition to Angelic 's love. And his love, together with his stubborn self-will toward his father--strict filial obedience having been respected in earlier Restoration plays--is vindicated .

Closely related to Congreve's juxtaposition of an incongruous social code with human folly, a reasonable way of life--absurd in the eyes of pro-democratic Enland--with a ridiculous passion, is his use of *character contrasts*. Bachelor **Tattle** would be happily mrried and gone froml his crusty cronies with the shrewd and subtle, the beautiful **Angelica**. But he winds up with **Mrs. Frail**, the gentle, if fading, blossom from off Bond Street. **Ben** would surrender his jack-tar's pride, a man of the seven seas, contemptuous of landlubbers, for the provincial country maid **Prue**. **Mrs. Foresight** would show prudence, mainly decorum, in her marital life in the eyes of the town; but she scuttles her pride for a silent affair with the biggest mouth around London. Gentle **Angelica** shows us that a far-fetched hope is not so far-fetched if a person does not exchange a humn weakness--the desire for love--for a calamity marriage to an ingrate. She retstores common sense to the play and gives perspective to the actions of the others. She endures her lover's feigned madness, the advances of **Sir Sampson**, the clever designs of **Tattle**--these in order to test **Valentines** love for her. Congreve's use of his characters' contrasts to evoke laughter are resolved through the union of the two lovers, harmoniously suited to each other. In broader perspective, he also unites the marriage of convenience, as an instiution inherited from Medieval England, linked to the law of primogeniture, with a marriage of love, in another fifty years to be overworked by the feminist continental playwrights by their ode of feminist self-realization, In *Love for Love* the financial arrangement is of almost secondary importance to the match.

Congreve has spiced his play with the wit of two characters: his jocund foc'sle jack-tar, **Ben**--whose garrulous speech is interlarded wirth shipbord jargon. And--the superstitious **Foresight,** who mouths his half-articulated soothsayings. "Mercy on us! what do these lunacies sportend? --Alas, he's mad, child, stark wild!" His expostulations are couched in the lingo of quackery, funny because they lampoon the playthings of idleness and comic as pretsensions to vast visions and learnig. The coarseness in places, the *double-entendres*, the buffoonery and the richly ludicrous, vital lines in Congreve's play are all intended to illustrate that effete and bloodless marital relations, without sexual attraction and romnantic feelings, are not a part of a genuine mrriage.

Rather, as does Ethredge, he suggests that romance and the well-considered feelings of the young unmarrieds are necessary facets of courtship and of a successful arranged-marriage. These ridiculous breeches in decorum, in the crudities of speech and action, mock proprieties of the 17th century marriage of convenience. Sir **Sampson Legend**, meanwhile during the entanglements of the action, combines the paradox of the romantic fool of sentimental, neo- democratic England--the London of Whitehall, the Inner Temple and the Haymarket--with the practical Cit whose money has begun to talk but whose perceptions as a curmudgeon cruel guardian outrun his good sense and that standard of the Restoration period--*moderation*--which means compromise, a *transitional* process of thought. This play and other Restoration pieces reflected the morality figures of Medieval pageants, a fact observed in Congreve's naming of his characters.

BRIEF DISCOURSES

BRIEF DISCOURSES
by Coryphaeus

Being an argument for an ethic of creative literature on which it is hoped other interested persons wll find time for reflection. An ever so brief rebuttal—the denial response— is contained herein.

Hamlet's retribution for his father's murde by his uncle, Faust's conmpact with Mephistopholes, Rev. Dimmesdale's uncompromisnng loyalty to Hester and little Pearl, Captain Ahab's obsessed decision to pursue the Leviathan white whale Moby Dick: --each of these human actions is defineable and may be rendered meaningful in historicali larger terms than a decription of the heroe's behavior and an explanation of the psychological workings of the his mind.

In order to do so, one must grant the validity of several premises. These are *categorical imperatives*, and any argument to the contgrary is the negation of reason, which cannot be negated without the support of these admissions: --that man is capable of reasoning, of rational (1) choices, of controlling his (2) instincts, and of (3) willing. There are other faculties for the discipline of one's actions:-- pictorial imagination, innate sensibilities to rhythm, color, order, etc. intuition and apperceptive ability, but these four, I think, are the chieftest of man's supra-animal faculties.

In the absernce of thier exercises, no ethic as a law is fully comprehesible, and it must be seen that circumstances, taken with human frailites, modify and correct the judgiciousness of an ethic's application. We arfive then at the second areas of promise, that of the cfirst area being personal and inseparable from individualty. In the second and latter area of premises, the concept of ethical judgement is societal and individual that derives from a person's relations with his fellow men. This is relativism of a pragmatic meaning, i.e. that are: l man is capable of relating himself to other hunan beings, to a Diety and to nature. The communicicabl reations of the tongue and of the pen imply man's capability to articulate each instance of thouht.

If then we set the two promised areas in juxstaposition to one another, we find that there is a force operative beteween them whose produxce is action. That force is human motive. Humans willing and not God cannot be *discovered*. Remove willing and *God* cannot be disxcovered. Remove reason and the true nature of human *relationships* cannot be fathomed. Remove the power of rational choice and men cannot distinguishs between the instinctual and one of those four pricpial faculties for individual action. Therefore the strongest of his motives, the effectiveness of his actions are accorcingly altered. In the alteration there comes specialization and indilviduation as a man's energiles are channeled either toward religion and thoughts of God, or toward man and the machines and ways of his own making, or, finanly, toward conquests of nature and the aesthetic beauty it holds for him. This disciplining and directilng of the energies results from many rational choices the concentration of which causes to atropjhy the faculties of instinct-contral and of willing.

To the extent that these other facultire are neglerctged, there occurs an diminution of the power for action. The ethics of a responsible compassion, of loyalty, of social duty thereby become less meaningful. "They lose the name of action." And the young, the aged become less capable of maksing an ethical decision out of a fully comprehensible understanding of the law, the ethic, at issue. There has to be the truly ethical man who exercises, in his actions, those chief faculties, that are motivated away form specialization to the end that he attempts to relate himself to **all three realms** of human enquiry--to the people and their manners and trraditons, to abundant nature, and to a God or Divine Being. Our popularculture represents, especially in themedia,the specialization of violence, cultic personality and vacuuous entertainment.

What then do these premises sand conclusions amount to with respect to an ethic in creative literature? Not that the principal characters shall be either social-protest crusaders, or religious zealots, or fashion-mongers, or given to the animistic worlship of nature; for such liteature, and elsewhere ideas similar to these embodied by the author's characters, tends either toword bigotgry and superstition or toward affections and the gross gratification of instincts. Even in the writings of Marius, the Epicurean, where he descrines the warriors return and the houshold of Marcus Auralius, we find temperance and dessecration of the mind combined with discrimination in his selection of details, in his commentary.

It is not mandatory, futhermore, that to in order to pen a work that is ethical in intention the author and artist should assume the masks of any of these promise-specialists, the **Diest, Naturalist,** and **Humanist.** For to do so with the hope that other men will see him as a scholar or a fervent cleric or a profligate is but avanity, and few men live so long that they can afford to indulge in these luxuries.

Rather, the ethic of the natual action resides in this:--that a man increases his own understanding of his fellow man through play, poem, novel or essay; that his ideas, the thoughts embodied in his characrters, their feelings, their actions, conduce toward that end of human understandi;ng. And that any other special and insular end is but a partial fulfillment of his obligation to so show man the *loci* of moderation, the right goverment of their faculties, by inference and by direction. In this way, God be willing, the issues of the author's pen shall be an increase in human understanding and in human compassion. Follies may then be mocked and frailites countenanced. All of the wonderful complexity of human nature and the intricate labrynths of life itself may then be put into true perspetive.

The sensationalisms of contemporary literature are but the luxuries of the irrational, the nonreasoning, the undisciplined segments of our society. They are the fripperies of jaded spirits and the fruits of over-specialization. The patrons of such literature argue along this line: stark facts are what convince, violence belongs on stage; that sort of thing happens every dayl if its big ;its got to be good...whether a job, a fortune or a remance. *"Every persons is an individual and I don't think an author should try to impose his standards of morality on his readers"* This would be true were there true imposition involved, but there is not in a free society. This contention is insular, specialized and whimsical. It is often the statement of denial or avoidance. Such an assertion lacks the ethical moderation that issues from a balance in disinterested, ranginfg enquiry.

BRIEF DISCOURSES

Being brief arguments for and against Naturalism of which there is much diverse opinion concerning its validity as a religious doctrine, a tempered philosophical influence, or an empirical creed for human exploration and government.

PRO: Why have men been religious and taken the spiritualistic view of the universe? *Naturalism's* answer to this qustion is perhaps one of the more complete of arguments. It is evident in various rituals, in the literature especially, in the edifice and religious artifacts belonging to past life, that religion has played a dominant role. Why is this so? It is a truism that primitive man, at best, knew less about the entirety of the universe than we know today, and for an explanation of those fearsome phenomenon which he did not understand he invented powerful dieties. He believed that altlhough he might fear the gods they would protect him. In these ways man's early religions were pragmatically useful inventions. Today Man seeks solace for his small tragedies through artificial means of communication and an empty hope that chance will correct the inequities in his life. Mankind still dabbles in escape mechanisms mostly to obviate his fear of death.

But as the knowledge of the universe increased with the growth of the physical sciences, our philosophic outlook changed. In the light of scientific discovery of today, we see how fallacious were early man's beliefs about the universe and, for the most part, we have left off with them except to speculate on origins. That remains one of the amusements of the age. Our contemporary passion for physical violence in sophisticated-primitive form is evidene of our being intellectually in denial of proveable origins. That violence is a tribute to Naturalism's hidden *Power*, an oblation as it were.

Naturalism, furthermore, attains to a world view which is simple and unified; and while maintaining that religions have served their purpose well--that is to say, rendered men secure from harmful and threatening, inexplicable forces--Naturalism is not stuffed with ancient views about the supernatural. With this increase of concentrated strength and purpose, Naturalism has not only found religion to be a superfluous product of Man's emotions and fears, but in showing religion to be such has added *logic* to its argument. By revealing the origin and purpose of religion, Naturalism necessarily tells us of ultimate truth or falsity. Nothing is known but what it can be proved; and if it cannot be proved, then it is not known, and so does not exist. God, therefore, does not exist; and the ideological and geophysical sciences offer more tenable theories on the origin of life than do the religionists. Thus speaks the *Naturalism* philosopher.

Since Naturalism is a conception of the entirety of the universe and is not entirely of conception also, what cannot be included in its belief system? All that cannot be measured or controlled, the simple principle of Naturalism, excludes the supernatural. Precisely because we cannot measure things such things as the soul or a world hereafter, an all-seeing Power makes them super and removes them from our realm of the tangiblel Natural. They are, consequently, **supra,** and no cause obtains to prove or disprove them save what to science is unknowable. It follows then by the method of inductive, empirical logic, that the existence of an unknowable entity, or conception or **Power** cannot be proved by causes unknowable. Indeed, this is one of the major tautologies of scientific skepticism since it premises that the unknowable cannot be known, and that the limits of the knowable are immutable, its causes are absolute in that they are changeless.

Miracle and Providence by the same reasoning, are excluded from the Naturalism view because their existence as force or fact would imply an intrustion of *foreign* processes into the regular measurable and explicable processes of nature. But what about "free will," which we as conscious, reasoning creatures have, or, again, the propensity for man to be clever inventors and artistic? Are they as explicable as the Bavarian Alps formation or the snow which lies high among their crags? Consider them all as a part of the plan of nature and they fit together perfectly.

"Freedom of the will" is not actually a freedom to be separated from the laws of all nature. As we consider ourselves uncontrolled free agents, so may we feel possessed of a kind of illsional "freedom," for the very consideration of ourselves as freed from surrounding nature is an illusion. Like one stave in a barrel, we have been bound in by the all-encircling laws which control the rest of nature; so that we cannot escape even though we may imagine ourselves doing so. Every act which we commit whether it is artless or artistic, creative or non-creative, is an act which *nature has caused us to do*. Even such processes as thought and reason, which escape immediate experience by our senses, cannot escape nature's plan because we **are** a part of that plan. And as surely as we are but higher animals of the animal kingdom, a part of all life but not out of it, we cannot haughtily exclude ourselves from the rest of nature.

CON: In the view of *Positivism*, everything that is real is necessarily tied up together into a linking of a series of causes and effects.The Medievsal doctrine of Macro- and Micro-cosmic ordering of the univese encompassed this view. Nothing can happen but that it has its cause. Naturalism's logic of the physical demands that such a rule be set up to explain the universe. Can every phenomenon except creation be explained, however, by the *cause and effect* rule? The universe today must be an effect of the universe before living observers could see it, in order for the rule to be verifiable and immutably workable. Yet is it so? Physicists have shown that the mind cannot be discounted in their solutions to such problems as *time and space* calculations because it is the mind that takes into account the physical world and, one might say, instintively relates to it by a man's own cognition. If in forming our conception of the universe we are forced to consiler our relation to it, what was the conception of the universe before observing men lived in the world? Nauralism would say that this is a contradiction or at least begs the question. There bein no *mind,* there could have been no conception. Naturalism therefore cannot be positive in asserting that all things sin the universe today are effects of those things of the past; for this assertion would of necessity mean a universe of the past. And that is an illusory construct since there was no mind to know it. An oversimplified way to put this conception is to ask: Does an object exist in space when man cannot, or is not, there to observe it? Or--does Man's stating the existence of an object or phenomenon validate its existence before the proofing thereof proceeds?

It cannot be proved, therefore, that cognition or the processes of *thought* ceases to exist at the lowermost stratum of animal being, which is to say, the instincts; nor cease at the uppermost, which is to say, at an historically comprehensivle abstraction of the knowable and known by lintuition only. The unknowable cannot be disproved by the unknown; nor can the unknown by the known--since when disproved the unknown ceases to have any comprehensible existence, and, if proved, becomes known and existent. It follows by logic and by induction that the existence of the unknowable--that is, *God, the soul, a hereafter*--cannot be disproved by the known.

A chance or random thought supposes an association of ideas., whether conscious or unconscious, that gives rise to the thought. Consequently, a *prior cause* does exist. Yet can a thought rise to consciousness without a prior cause? The same truth obtains as that regardisng a universe before human concsciousness. Instincts are knowable not by prior knowledge but by cognition. Hence to assign to instincts the function of *original cause* is to attempt to prove what was not knowable before consciousness and therefore could not have been communicated as knowable. Likewise the unknown abstractions cannot be called unknowable by the argument that abstract intelligence simply fails to form a conception of an unknown which can be proved to exist. So long as the knowable is not fixed and immutable--a root principle of the sciences--cognition therefore is obligated to give credence to a thought or concept whose cause lies not beyond reason but beyond immediate scientifsic proof and the provable. The integrity of this argument for the Godhead obtains by the same *logic of continuation* that sets instincts as the lower most stratum of causes which affect cognition. Though not provable, extra-instinctual and abstract lingual causes, by which there is no humanly cognitive communication, may result in thought.

Holding that nothing lies beyond the physical, Naturalism demands a clear-cut finality to all objects existing within the universe. This demand must, of necessity, look to science as its guide in enquiries as to what the universe actually is. The reliance upon science is the *nexis* of Naturalism's philosophny.

Scientific *hypotheses* are not immutable; they are subject to new discoveries which may either cancel out the old or add to them. Science deals with truths about the physical world as it exists subject to our experiencing it. The fact that a certain hypothesis is in fact a working pragmatism in the universe is not assurance that we cannot experience wrongly and therefore reach erroneous conclusions. That is part of the task of science--to search out man's mistakes about the truth.

Upon this unstable and constantly changing of science of "facts" Naturalism waits with assurance. At one time, Nturalism's proponents believed in a distinct difference between matter (*materialism*) and energy (*energism*) and that neither one could be converted into the other nor could either be created of destroyed. Science today hs demonstrated that "radiant energy" and matter can be converted from one into the other form i.e. that light has mass in its photons and lyet cn ve ;made to vanish as heat, becoming them latlent light-enrgy, potential light as exists within the sun.

In a like manner, experimentation with the atom has revealed its internal changes--the jumping of electrons from one orbit to another orbit without intermediate positions--which phenomenon defies the Naturalistic prejudice of the ***continuity of all changes***. Science in its very experimentation has thrown doubtful light on the Naturalism view of the independence of time and space. For in working with the molecules of matter, scientists have been unble to separate the dimension of time from space. What is considered to be the separation of atoms from one another in the molecule must be defined by the character of their separation, movement, distance, relative proximity which phenomena are calculated in terms of time intervals. ***Time and space*** must go together and be codeterminants of each other. They can be explained only as they stand in relationship to the event which occurs simultaneously within each. What happens, therefor, to Naturlism's carefully-constructed prejudgements when science is compelled to write a new "law" into its books and thus to cancel out another long held truth? (Naturalism would say it does not stand on particular scientific laws but on Science's general results.)

Yet it remains true that the Naturalism view is weakened by this mutability of scientific "laws"; no law in particular can be absolute without the preclusion of the facts which extend the scope of its relative application and so redefine its inductive components. Thus does the changeability of what is known via the unknown made known, weaken Naturalism's argument; since what has been proved bears not the status of final and immutable certainty but, instead, the elusiveness of the ***Ideal***--that is to say, the unprovable ***certainty***.

There is, for example, ***no absolute zero***. It follows, therefore, that the Naturalist's ideal and unprovable certainty are unknowable. And that Science's "general results" can only be grouped into those which are unknown and those which are known. The unknowable certainties are the mysteries of the Godhead, which as ideal are elusive before and after inductive experimentation. For another example, there is ***no absolute vacuum***. The Ideal phenomenon thus cannot be proved. It is, as a consequence, taken on belief and faith, both of which are compulsory to the scientist for the above reason of the unknowability of the absolute phenomenon. For yet a third example, there is ***no total gravity, no speed in excess of light, no tem perature in excess of the sun's interior***. For these are the metes and bounds established by the Designer of the universe. The ***infinity of space*** is incomprehensible to mortal mind.

It is a constant source of annoyance to the proponent of Naturalism that any law or "fact" in the universe be considered to exist beyond the reach of science. Hence the philosophical Natural*ist*, more often than the scientist, repudiates the charge that he is an Idealist; whereas he is an idealist of the most radical sort. For in seeking to prove immutable certainty, he would deny what in the laboratory cannot be proved: the ***Ideal***. I have given examples above. The ideal can only be inferred; yet the unknowable inference, which is deductive, and the hypothesis on the unknown, which is inductive, are often confused by the Natura*list*. The **absolute,** or the **Ideal,** is never attained before a change in the form of energy or structure of mass occurs. Examples are: **velocity of electrical energy, kinetic heat and cold,** together with the absolutes noted above. {Note that someone who studies Nature is also called a Naturalist; they share the word.}

The believer in Naturalism, therefore, may set up an experiment to determine ideal maximum cold, absolute vacuum, ultimate speed of light and absolute temperature of heat as as his material "god". Yet his thinking is inductive and moves toward a hypothetical unknown-- which is mutable and imperfect and still not the unknowable certainty, inferential and elusive, of the inductive hypothesis speculated as certain, **Ideal** and **absolute**.

By revealing the origin and purpose of religion Naturalism does not tell us of ultimate truth or falsity; since the **ultimate**, future or past, is Ideal, not real. And the Ideal is non-existent in the laboratory and therefore ultimate purpose and the origin of the universe cannot be absolutely established by science. Naturalism's view is, therefore, fallible and an incomplete answer to the question of truth about the universe. **Faith and belief extend the continuum of matter from the partial Real into the absolute Ideal, the unprovable.**

The explanation of the presence of consciousness is an Achilles heel of the Naturalism. Consciousness may be roughly defined as the perception of a goal, an objective toard which to advance, and then the advancement toward the objective without accompanying resolves, experiences, emotions--such as an awareness of senations. It is the awarness of existence and movement in space.

But admitting that all life which possesses those abilities is conscious life, one might ask: At what point in evolution did the unconscious life become concious, and by what processes was the line crossed? Decartes believed that the brains of men (excluding the lower nimals) created the Pituitary body which the mind caused to vibrate and which, in turn, caused the mind to act upon a person's body. Again, however, one may ask: How is this body set into its first vibration? No explanation has been determined. The Behaviorist school proposes that the mind *is* behavior, that the function of the mind is evident in the behavior. Could not this behavior, however, be stimulated without consciousness (for we are conscious to the degree only that we are aware of the meaning of what is before and around us.)?

Behaviorism dos not explain conciouness either, because that view by itself is simply an attempt to escape, an effort to create another world for consciousness by making observed responses conform to its Ideals.

Hernert Spenser believed consciousness to be an accompaniment of changes in the brain. But, once again, what are those changes? Because the animal "mind" has developed along with the animal body, Haeskel offers the theory that "consciousness has been gradually evolved from the psychic reflex activity." The proof of his theory is incomplete with what psychology today has by way of fact to offer.

The fact that psychology is neither an exact nor a quantitative behavior science, and that although inductive in its hypothese while inferential in its particular instances, or case, conclusions, explains why its hybrid character has made of it the religion of the masses. For man accepts these tentative hypotheses as immutable certainties, the unknown for the unknowable in psychic behavior.

Now the latest concept of the Naturalism is that put forth by Lewis when he states that while the human body evolved from lower forms and thus may properly be termed resultant, the consciousness of the lmind was a unique and wholy different product coming from the same evolutionary process-- *an emergent.*

Yet, in all, no one theory proffered can today explain precisely why the presence of consciousness "emerged" with the progressive development of lower phylla animals into the higher phyla animals, dividing ultimately into families and then species .This incompleteness weakenes the Naturalism's argument supposedly embracing, with the logic of causal laws, the entire universe. Does not this incompleteness leave unfinished its major problem of the consciousness; and the central problem of philosopny: *The origin of causes?*

CONCLUSION: Although science must admit the metaphysical into its experimentation and conclusions, Science and the physical world always seem to disrupt the metaphysical theories rather than the reverse. New discoveries change both old scientific and metaphysical "truths." For this reason one may well watch Naturalism with skeptical eyes realizing that there is much reasoning of validity in its views, but also anticipating that Science may further disprove some of its long-held concepts about the universe. As Prof Wm. E. Hocking has stated, "Science will probably not discredit Science--but further thought may make clear that Science in its nature cannot cover all truth."

BRIEF DISCOURSES

BEING A BRIEF DISCUSSION ON THE SOURCES OF THE PERMANENT VALUES IN A WORK OF ART, WHOSE CHIEF INTEREST IS NOT THEIR PERMANENCE, THE WHICH CAN LEAD ONLY TO FRUITLESS TAUTOLOGICAL DEBATE AND, NOWADAYS, TO THE DESTRUCTION OF INQUIRY, SKEPTCISM, ART THEORY, FAITH AND REASON BY THE "NO EXIT" PHILOSOPH Y OF EXISTENTIONALISM; BUT THE SOURCES THEMSELVES, WHEREBY A BETTER UNDERSTANDING MAY BE GAINED OF THE WORK AS ART.

With the protection from poverty, from the police, clergy and malice by patrons of the arts; with the approval by an established church and her prelates anxious to increase the Church's symbolical magnificence; with the influence of effective and knowledgeable criticisms, the applause of newly rich merchants and the democratic masses, the arts have flourished and often despite the above intrusions and abuses. Birth and education by theselves, seem to have made little difference; talent is often not commensurate, in opulence and depth, with social station. The paradox of their human origins freuently met with in the lives of the Masters does not, however, travesty the classic creations as works of the imagination born of unworthy men. Nor, too, does their exposure to influences which might defeat both aims and work render any more
intrinsically valuable their masterpiecs--tried in the furnace ofc misery, so to speak. Furthermore, unless the fine arts--the already created works of art and the traditional forms--are to be used for politico-financial propaganda, bromides and escape, it is dubious that the writer or the painter or the sculpter or the composer will, in his lifetime, enjoy any large public recognition. There are notable exceptions, of course. And yet those are the very works that are preserved and valued when all word of mouth and written estimates contemporary to the art disappear. When the galleries and cities of their origin are destroyed, when their artists otherwise leave only a scant trace of their personal lives behind, indeed, then will the inherent aesthetic, cultural and human values, the multiple beauties of the creation, remain--or die without recogntion and are scattwered on the winds. My guess is that only some ten percent of great works of art have ever reached an audience and enjoyed preservation. God used a negative to create a positive. Nazi greed resulted in the preservation of many great art works Consider the sacking and burning of cities by the Goths, Visgoths, Vandals, Romans by which art treasures were lost forever. This is so by proof of art works created in the environs of an ancient civilizations. Obversely, it would seem, any art piece not created to please the senses and awaken the mind to fresh concepts of life, premises that morality motivated the creative act. Hogarth's series of prints "The Rakes Progress", Charles Dickens novels , both rtists accepted the dignity of human moral conduct. The Dutch Masters depicted the moral life of the family. Myriads of great art works reflect the artist's didactic intentions and yet they still it please the imagination. The Gothic lines and ornamentation of the masonry over the frongt sportal of th eChartres cathedrm on the Isle of Old Paris are pleasing to the eye, borrowed to suggest hands pointed in an atftitude of worhip; and yet religious exhaltation

and a reverent struggle for human betterment are not morally intrainsic to the style. Neither morality nor popularity insure that a work of art will remain everlastingly of value to mankind. Indeed, neither patronage nor station, nor the artists personal trials and his talents guarantee the lasting value of the work that he has created.

What, then, does give value to a Beethoven sympahony, to a fresco on the Sistine Chapel Ceiling by Michangelo, to the "Wedding Feast" by Breughal, to Williams Faulkners *Go Down Moses*, or indeed to any one of the greatest or lessor master creations born of man's prolific imagination, his disciplined mind and aesthetic sensitivity? Traditional recognition alone does not sufficiently explain the of a work's art value. Doctrines of religious and aesthetic interpretation change; the interests of an age intervene in men's judgement of a work. Canons of morality, philosophical perspectives, the comments of connoissesurs anc critiques of the literati are all mutable. Indeed, a all criteria appear to be in a constant flux.

In order to discover the *sources* of value in a work of art, I think it is essential that the reader, the patron, the connoisseur, the observer accept the work in the spirit of his receiving a *gift.* He thereby commences his appraisal with the work of art, its multiple meanings, the germinal truth of the creaton, the proportion of color, mass, line and proportion, of tonalities and instrumentation which result from the afrtists special sensivities. To start with a political credo, a religious doctrine, a moral persuasion, an ethnic description of the age that produced the work is to invite into the evaluaion of the bias of the specialist. It is for this reason that someone has said that great art is fora ll men in lall times.

Having once discarded the special doctrinal approach to evaluation and appreciation of the art work, it now becomes apparent that the didactic purpose of the artist is an unstable and moot basis upon which to rest any argument for its permanence. John Ruskin's persuasion, Panthiestic, primitive and sensual, that a painting or cathedral teaches morality by the representation of God's divine handiwork in nature is, by reason if its special bias and Hagelian-one world faith, a fallible creed of apostleship. Catholic insistence upon the sacramental character of certain Italian masterpieces created under the patronage of Papal Rome in the 15th century mistakes creed for human inspiration, artistic sensivities for systematic design, as the Holy Roman Church then and now knows it to be. The communists' use of art to propagandize their system is a crass secular example of world-view doctrine. Any one of these special credal positions--the moral, religious or plitical --has an historical integrity that that cannot be glainsaid, if one is wiling to accept the particular apostolic view as a correct, perhaps the only, interpretation.

The **sources** of value in a work of art may repose in God, nature or a temporal political hierarchy, and in some ages past the influence of all three has contributed to the creative effort. To say on the other hand, that the artist has willed a work of art into exsistence is only a description and a shallow one at that, of the psychological process of intention. What cannot be recognized by a representation of the outward forms of nature and by the laws of human conduct that transcend ethnic differences between peoples will remain hidden--as works of art, isolated and insular experiments, for the simple reason that their extreme individuality appeals chiefly to specialists. Surrealism, Expressionism, Cubism, embrace works of art that are of interest, to be sure, for their egocentric applications of aesthetics, phychology and geomentry. Recognition, not primarily by the bibliophiles, the connosseurs, academecians and curators, but by the larger masses of cultural folk has fixed the reputation of most masterpieces. And yet-- that recognition is still not a stable criterion, or else certain American advertisements would have more intrinsic value--which in some quarters they do--than Da Vinci's oil of "Madonna and Child" or a poem by Yeats.

Recognition, however, is the all eseential clue; but of what? Of the artist's unique individuality, his style, his peculiar percepion as (which he brings out by selection and emphasis), his sensitivity to form, line and color, the patterns of combinations into which his habitlually works his materials, the innovative tone tone color of Beethoven...these being but means to his end: - to communicate a particular emotional, visual, dramatic, tonal experience that was or is his. In the act of creating, he subordinates egocentricy to the disciplines of his art form and to the integrity of the truthfulness and accuracy of that experience, as a sensuous experience that must be shared in part or in its entirety with his audience. That is, then, as a **source** of greatness, this whelming desire to share a musical idea, a poetic thought, a fictitional experience, a painting vision of life. In so doing, he exerts his skill and discipline to the utmost. That is another **source** of greatness...without exception all great artists are consummate disciplinarians. Aside from any tome he may have written to explain his personal uniqueness, which he believes to be his special virtue, he has no reason other than his visible, audible art for existing as an artist. No compelling shared sensuous experience, no art, and all of his pristine "individuality"--his mode of dress, his lifestyle, his friends, his money and power-- will not add to lhis stature *as an artist*.

Radical deviations by practicing artists in any one period in history may readily discard traditional forms upon the rationalzation that they are inadequate. Most great artists are, in fact, innovative for their time. But their innovative perception begins with what is traditional. On lthe other had, "artistic rebvellion" so-called , mistakes the fervor of rebellion, political, social, artistic, for a new movement. Quite ofetn as individuals they are specialists in self-pity never having mastered the tradional forms, whilest their working credo is the environmentalism of social demand, popularity, etc. There are exceptions: Dickens was popular in his day. A great work of art however, is --as it were-- oblivious to or apart from the historical fact of war, for example, or the conquest of space or the increasisng numbers of murders .... The great work of art appeals to humanity on its most common grounds: that of the *common experiences of the human condition*

Excitement, exaltation, worship....That is, there is no theory but this, which I propose: there are universal ethnic sentiments, which derive from a people's ways, their lore, their profoundest moments in history and which confirm the emotional experiences aroused by the immediate sensuous qualities of the work of art. Those are the identifiable war and peace travail, the *universals* of the human spirit., another *source* of great art.. Providing that the artist has remained faithful to his discipline and to those insights which he cannot help but have drawn from the within himself, the life and events around him, he will have at least started in the direction of artistic production and appreciation. The recognition of Man's *commonality*, his created endowment of a unique *individuality*, the discipline and submission to an art-form craft, the application of personal integrity and aesthtic sensitivity should vbring one to the conclusion that realization that *all art is dramatically sensuous experience*: These are sources that endow a work of art with lasting value. CORYPHAEUS

BRIEF DISCOURSES

*Being an argument for an ethic in creatie literature
on which it is hoped other interestsed persons will find
time for reflection...an ever so brief rebubuttal is contained
herein.*

Hamlet's retribution for his father's murder, Faust's compact with Mephistopheles, Reverend Dimmesdale's uncompromising loyalty toward Hester and little Pearl, Captain Ahab's obsessed decision to pursue the leviathan white whale Mloby Dick: --each of these human actions is defineable and may be rendered meaningful in historically larger terms than a description of the Protagonist's behavior and an explanation of the psychological workings of his mind.

In order to create this larger meaning, one must grant the validity of several premises: there are categorical imperatives of morallity, a right action or a wrong choice. Any argument to the contrary is the negation of reason, which cannot be negated without the use of reason and cannot be sustained without the support of these admissions. Again: that man is capable of *Reasoning,* of rational *Choice,* of controlling his *Instincts,* and of responding to his *Will.* There are other faculties for the discipline of one's actions, i.e. pictorial imagination, innate sensibilities to rhythm, color, tone etc., intuition, and aperceptive ability. However, these four I think are the chief test of man's supra-animal faculties.

In the absence of their exercise, no ethic as a law is fully comprehensible, as it must needs be seen that circumstances, taken with human frailties, modify and correct the judiciousness of that ethic's application. We arrive then at the second area of premises, those of the first area being personal and inseparable from individuality. In this second and latter area of premises, the concepts are societal and indivisible from a person's relations with his fellow man. They are: that man is capable or relating himself to other human beings, to a Diety, and to Nature. The communicaion of the tongue and of the pen simply show mans concapabilty for thought in each instance. An idea is the prelude to articulation. by some means invented or natural. A choice reveals that person's value system.

If then we set the two premised areas in juxtaposition to one another, we find that there is a force operative between them whose product is *action.* That force behind that action is willed human motive. Remove *willing* and God cannot be discovered. Remove reason and the true nature of human relationships cannot be fathomed. Rmove the power of rational choice and man cannot distinguish between the instinctual and the reasonable course of action. Indeed, remove any one of these four principal faculties of individual action and the strength of his motives, the effectiveness of his actions are accordingly altered. In the alternative there comes specialization and indivduation as a man's energies are channeled either toward religion and thoughts of God, or toward man and the machines and ways of his own makling, or finally, toward conquests of nature and the aesthetic beauty it holds for him. This disciplining and directing of the energies results from many rational choices the conccentration of which causes to arophy he faculties of instinct control and of willing..

To the extent that these other faculties are neglected, there occurs a dimintion of the power for action. The ethics of responsible compassion, of loyalty, of social duty thereby become less meaningful. They "lose the name of action." And the young and the aged become less capable of making an ethical decision out of a fully comprehensible understanding of the law, the ethic, at issue. There can be no tlruly ethical man who does not exercise in his actions, these chief faculties, motivated away rom specializtion to the end that he attempts to relate himself to all three realms of human enquiry--to people and their manners and traditions, to abundant nature, and to a God or Divine Being.

What then do these premises and conclusios amount to with respect to an *ethic* in creative literature? Not that the principal characters will be ether social-protest crusaders, or religious zealots, or fashion mongers, or given to the animistic worship of nature. For such literfature tends either to ward bigotry and superstition or toward affection and the gross gratification of instincts. Even in the writings of Marius,s the epicurean, where he describes the warriors' return and the household of Marcus Aurelius, we find temperance and descretion of mind combined wirth discrimination in his selection of the details in his commentary.

It is not mandatory, moreover, that in order to pen a work that is ethical in intention the author and artist should assume the mask of any of these promised specialists, the Deist, Naturalist, the Humanist. For to do so with the hope that other men will see him as a scholar or a fervent cleric or a profligate is but a vanity, and few men live so long that they can afford to indulge in this luxury.

Rather, the ethic of the author's action resides in this: that he increase his own understanding of his fellow man through, play, poem, novel or essay; that his ideas, the thoughts of his characters, their feelings, their actions conduce toward that end, And that any other special and insular end is but a partial fulfillment of his obligation to so show men the locus, the moderation, the right government of their faculties, by inference and by direction. In this way, and if God be willing, the issue of the author's pen shall be an increase in human unerstanding and in humn compassion. Follies may then be mocked and frailties countenanced. All of the wonderful complexity of human nature and the intricate labrynths of life itself may then be put into true perspective.

The senationalisms of contemporary literature are but the luxuries of the irrational, the unreasoning, the undisciplined segments of society. They are the fripperies of jaded spirits and the fruits of over-specialization. The patrons of such literature argue along this line: that stark facts are what convince; violence belongs; that sort of thing happens every day; if its big its got to be good; controversy is the nture of the written word; shock the visitor with filty insuslt and pornographic detail. "Every person is an individual and I don't think an author should try to impose his standards of morality on his readers. "This would be true were there any imposition involved, but there is not in a free society. These contentions are insular, specialized and whimsical. They lack the ethical moderation that issues from a balance in disinterested, ranging enquiry.

BRIEF DISCOURSES

BEING A DISCOURSE ON THE NATURE OF BIGOTRY, ITS CAUSES AND ITS MANIFESTATIONS, FROM WHICH IT MAY BE SEEN, THROUGH THE DISPUTES OF THEOLOGIANS, SCHOLARS AND MORALISTS, THAT IT DOTH EXIST.

Bigotry is the wisdom of fools. Few men in their lifetime escape the effects of its insinuating drops of poison. Fewer still know how to control its inception within themselves, an ugly growth which, like a disease, doth fasten itself upon human conscience almost, as it were,unnounced, without forewarning. There it lies, a primitive substance of hatred, revenge and incipient violence until such a time as an event that begs caution and moderation in human concourse summons forth the poison to do its work against whomsoever, by whim and conjectur, doth appear to merit condemnation. Bigotry bears all the characteristics of a disease, social and psychological, that seems least harmful when it is most potent. Quiescence perforce beilng its natural state of residence within human mind, bigotry is exceedingly difficult to eradicate until some human action or event, beyond the pale of individual control, causes it to rise to the surface, from whence, even then, the manifestations are concealed by the deceit that would save its bearer from public censure or lawful trial. By this means is bigotry often apprehended and yet allowed to go unchecked because no lawful method comes to hand whereby its disseminator may be taken to task and proved to be wrong; and because the recipient of the hatred has not the power within himself to resist the anger, the contempt, the evil droplet of poison that so caustically irritates his emotions. Analgously, one may say that he is lacking the anti-bodies, in attitudes and in his thinking and in his faith of forgiveness, whereby he might throw off the poison. In this wise doth bigotry contaminate virtually all of his conflictive thinking, making of justice a bizzare comedy of human feeling given the mask of insanity. Where once there were no conflicts in his human relationships, sores then bvreak out upon his tongue, and all of life seems but a pestilence to him.

One must e careful, hower, to distinguish between bigotry, prejudice and bias. They are not the same. Although they are not unrelated emotionally, each involves a separate and distinct process of reasoning. In contradistinction to the prejudiced word and the biased deed, the bigoted speech is volatile and inflamatory, and stands in the obsessed disregard for any set of facts but those that satisfy the inner lust for revenge, the personal yearning for the safety, the sense of security and self-identification antecedent to a hunger for self- justification. Such a speech attempts neither to assess one's own values nor to judge; hence the bigotry superogates civil discipline, passing beyond ill-will and the circumstantial, the debatable, the rational argument to seize justice by force if necessary, by cunning always. Bigotry is, therefore, militant, and it becoms the more insidious to the extent that the civil, the Constitlutional and secular laws can be shaped to promote insular or doctrinal or selfish ends. For deceit then becomes a more useful weapon than violence, and the laws that *were* are made to appear in the public's eye as vicious and barren of good works. Thus doth bigotry's deceit superogate the people's will and, in a democratic society, the common good of the majority. It can then have the potency of destroying traditional law.

Bigotry often assumes the outward aspect of prejudice. And the two are confounded in the affairs of everyday life. Nevertheless the bigotry preserves its wholeness, from time to time affecting the most sensitive and innocent areas of human contact. Never scrupling to question his attitude or his conjectural assumption, the bigot, extending his premises beyond the special loci of assumptions, relies almost exclusively upon some form of absolute authority to supply him with the value judgements that best justify his very existence. And whereas his blind passions were once the means to his survival, the dicta of an absolute authority, whether of a plutocracy, an oligarchy, a monarchy, tyranny or theocracy, become that means of empowerment his survival.

The metamorphosis of bigotry into prejudice has then transpsired. there is no longer any need to hate; revenge has merged with the majority will. The volatile act has been put down in favor of the sensible under new canons of law. It is in this state of social change that men most often curry favor to win applause. For their appeals are limited and secretly appraised by the transcendent absolute authority. Ir was so under Henry VIII, under Napoleon Buonaparte, under Hitler and Stalin. And it is so under Kruschev. Corruption by devious political, financial and religious devices then makes ingress upon old institutions. And, laying by canons of decency and all the customs that inclined men toward sober equity among their fellows, the prejudiced society theruepon directs its will by State's authority. And what was in the minds of men, the freedoms and the prerogatives, must then pass the bar of censorship by malefactors who have cunningly and by ambition placed the mantle of *right authorty* upon their shoulders.

It is in this state of "evolution"-- *change* is the better word-- that the more insidious forms of moral degeneration become apparent among the body politic. For whereas men were once wont to weight their actions judiciously and in accordance with Christian-Hebraic law, or in accordance with some select secular statute, case law, local law or perceived and welcome custom, they now will violate what they once held sacrosanct and dear to them. And they do so wantonly, as though to reject the yoke of condemnation which their consciences place upon them. Too, they then train their sons in the irresponsible action, for prejudice has the destructive effect of demanding its **reward** for some untoward act, some petty crime or misdemeanor abridgiment of old custom and once accepted law, or in pragmatically valuable rules for personal behavior. Punishment of the victim has today become commonplace throughout out society.

The prejuice, whether directed against a people or against an individual, cannot jusltly then be called reasonable bias, for common to it, in its usual manifestations of ill-will, resentments, local ostracism and financial disenfranchisement, within a community, state, city and nation is one singular element--*generalized enmity*. And it is this enmity that attaches itself to whatsoever falls within the widest and narrowest circles of description, description of the *persons* and *groups* against whom the prejudice is direcrted. Like a loadstone surrounded by concentric rings of hate, dislike suspison and doubt, all resemblances and similitudes in dress, comportment, possessions and utterance are collected, as by magnetism, to the *archytypical image*, which has become the heart of the prejudice. And should the usurping and transient authority make known its will to all the people in the body politic, those individuals, groups and institutions falling within the concentric rings of generalized opprobrium, shot through by most corrosive ill-will and with little or no basis in reasonable judgement or nice assessment against previous standards, are at once marked out and set apart as undesireable. While the prejudice is then subsumed under majority will and upheld by the usurping authority, it remains viable and active in human affairs and affects the everyday relationships of neighbor to neighbor. Acts of bigotry are bound to appear wihin this environment, but they are less likely to find such vocal or vehement expresssion as is the case during the first stage, when a majority harbor violent emotions against the out-group or those who stand on the fringes of the citizenry for some important cause or reason or deviation.

We come now to the third stage, or what may rightly be called the civilized stage of society in the community, the township and , expressly, that stage wherein bias transcends prejudice in the thinking of the majority. Providing the State authority has not imposed its will by tyrannically unjust censure, abuse and corruption, and providing the chosens Government has not allowed the bigots and the prejudiced to destroy equitable law, the very sense of right justice for each and every citizen in the commonwealth, bias permits of restraint in the human emotions., It allows for disagreements, even furious and rough-shod disareemenrts such as one finds on the Americxn polical scene at election time. But that heated contention, those abiding resentments find balance after the battle, and, lessened or not, they submit to the common will under a government of laws.

In other fields, I think this transition will be found to hold true. In the arts, for example, the biased connoisseur may disapprove of an artist's technique, his subject matter, lhis treatment of his materials; but the prejudiced connoisseur will restrict that artist - his talents being roughly equal to those of competing artists - from exhibiting his painting in the local gallery. The bigot will go one step further and militantly condemn the artist for observing life as he so choses, and for painting as he wishes to paint. His censure has then passed beyond legitismate art criticism to become intimate stricture, even condemnation., It will be found, in view of these distinctions, that the biased connoisseur has submitted his artistic judgement to a set of canons governing the medium in which he works. and that prejudiced connoisseur has permitted his resentments, his ill-will to override those canons. While the bigot would have none of the painting nor of the artist, and so not only disregards the canons of the niche of art i.e realism , cubism, but like Caesar, he would impose his single will upon the public, artist, canons, all alike, and most often in the militant manner of a demigod.

We must constantly, therefore, in a free society, attempt both to express our own judgements, whether or not they agree with the majority's, and to debate what is moot.

For only thereby can we introduce the idea of difference of opinion, that we may in a small measure discourage the bigot or discriminate him from those who conscionably disagree. We must, however, be cautious at this juncture of imprisoning the thoughts and free-conscience with those of the true culprit. For as certainly as we do that, the one will contaminate the other. Nor is the imprisonment a physical act. But it is mental, psychological, ethical and spiritual, and to arrive at the maximum expression of honest bias, we must not confuse bias with prejudice, nor with bigotry, but should, if we are reasonable creatures, encourage full and responsible freedom of expression to the ends that men's sorry state of human wants and needs, and his wilderness of confusion without true leaership today maybe in a real, tangible and reassuring capacity substantially be removed, and that he may grow as an individual, utilizing those talents, in all the arts and in socializing generally, which the Creator over heaven and earth has given him.

-CORYPHAEUS

Homily of the Day

No man's folly can be so absurd that it
fails to arouse admiration from some person
who sees beyond the fiction to the reality
of intention and the vision of accomplishment.

BRIEF DISCOURSES

*BEING A SOCIO-PHILOSOPHICAL ATTEMPT TO MAKE
CLEAR FUNDAMENTAL DISTINCTIONS BETWEEN THE **REAL, REALITY**
AND **REALISM,** TERMS WHOSE MEANINGS ARE MUCH ABUSED TODAY
BY SCHOLARS, JOURNALISTS AND LITERATI*

The Real: The slick writer is interested not so much in precision of reference and the truth of an emotion as he is in arousing his audience to respond to socially-acceptable emotions, of the particular action, and commonly approved ways of looking at characer and actions. The **real is socially identifiable**. For this reason the movies, television and the masses-geared fiction slicks, appeal mainy through melodrama and farce, comedy that is sententious and flippant, and tragedy that reiterates the agonied cry, "Lets get things done!" Voila--much sex and violence nowadays! Tennessee Williams forever seems to be looking backward with a match in his hand, and Miller to be apostrophizing on the erosion of dreams. And although their work is not slick in the sense, let us say, that "The Desk Set" is slick, because *their* themes of regional and class conflicts have a certain tangential appeal to mass likes, these two writers by comparison underscore the poverty of dramatic imagination that afflicts contemporary literature for the masses. From that poverty there isssue extravagant productions and cheap innovations aimed at achieving a **novelty of effect**. In this way does the empty novelty suffice for originality, being but the dramatic embodiment and reworking of slogans, cliches, slick patterned thinking in the depicted scene . The more topicall these ingredlients, lthe more quickly the work becomes dated and obsolete. These patterns and gimmicks are the verbal masks and psychic-emotional illusions of reality which the genuinely dramatic, creative writer tries to penetrate. This is not *deconstructionism* but rather it is the display and use of a brilliant insight that is an element in originality. A writer, director and critic of my acquaintance has called these patterned responses "warehoused emotions."

The artifacts and manners of a culture, the national traits of temperament, philosophical affection, and mytho-psychological characteristics, all of which perhaps find clearest expression in a peoples folk lore, are temporal. Slick writing is, therefore, closely associated with patterned illusions of reality, immediately recognizeable by the mass audience and perforce most conducive, should the novelist, playwright or poet put them to use, to the development of his popularity. In a sense, then, every popular writer is a folklorist, a transriber of *national illusions*.

What is real in human actions is not transient or illusory or cheaply innovational. The real is that psychology and dynamic human relationship, that complex of cause and effect in human actions--in the individual as well as the trival, institutional and **group mores**-- which is universal among men. Savages, for example, may laugh at the their brother who trips on a root and falls while the tigers chases him. They may even dine that night to delebrate their friend's unseasonable and the tiger's good fortune. Yet they laugh because his danger and his death did not threaten their feelings of group security. {NOTE: Theatrical slickness in the movies and on the contemporary American stage has shifted the competition to one between media and personalities.}

If, on the other hand, the same native, a stranger, were to come into the village, because he represents an unknown force, an evil omen, a scout before war, the savages might torture him or kill him in order to protect themselves. They would kill the messenger! These two dissimilar events are the primitive origins of the psychologies of the comic and tragic perspectives. And as illustrations which empitomize those perspectives, their parallels can be found in the communicative cultures, hence the **real** dynamic relationships are **universals.**

Reality: These native recapitulations involve human dynamics of motive and action that are distinguishable from, as it were, the *statics of circumstances*. The real is narrative in character; **reality is expository**. Much of this (20th) century's protest literature treats reality almost as if it were a character in itself, a cosmic monster against which the individual or a class must battle to survive. In Hawhone's classic **The Scarlet Letter** the doctrine of New Englsand Calvinism is inseparable from the circumstances of Hester's physical and mental suffering. Thus they cannot be purged of vital ideas that arouse human character into action to the end that some universal, or real, motive is revealed. The circumstances are static until a character's actions become, at once, the demonstration and result of latent, dramatic, motivational forces inherent in the expositional reality. Perhaps its closest analgous word, in meanings, is *environment*. I'm reluctant to use the word only for the reasosn that popular usage has given it a superficial and fixed reference-value made up largely of ambiguities and half-true generaliations e.g. the cloistered **slum, refined, academic** envirnments. At all events, there may be many of such circumstantial matrices within any locality of a county, city, region or country; and so there re many realities, complexes sof circumstances charted with vital *ideational* content. The artist selects, circumscribes and redefines, from among these environment materials the characer of the particular reality which has influenced his characrters. He, in brief, makes meaningful and graphic one *reality* among many.

Realism: Whereas the real and reality are narrational and expository in character, **realism is descriptive**. Applied generally to a novel, play or painting, the term *realism* is ambiguous. The generalization, as a word of popular badinage, does not take into account the foregoing distinction. Realism is descriptive of the externals of dress, manners and dialogue. If these appearances of things are highly subjective, and yet the socio-psychology of motives is fundamentally sound and universally true in all comnmunicative cultures--that is to say, real as human truth--the resulting work of art will in all likelihood, be highly *expressionistic*.

For subjectivism does not rule out the universally valid axiom of human nature but can intensify it emsotionally. If the sensusous details are spare and/or seem not to represent the time or milieu in which the work was creatsed and yet the expossiton of a particular reality is exact, then the produced art work would in all probability be *visionary*. The point worth noting is that the three descrimiate lineaments of the real, reality and realism may be used definitively in the component analysis of, and in the *assignment of* dramatic, ethical human and aesthetic values to, the mature work of creative art. **The real is consistent with the ethical. Realism is a component of moral values. Reality is the revelation of mature perceptions.**

In the play as art form, a reality view is customarily proscribed in an opening scene, then is lent a dramtically visual, sensuous appeal by the realism of action, dialogue, costumes, lighting and set. Although an audience, however, may accept the theatrical conventions of sense appeal, contemporaries frequently find it difficult to accept the language of the past, not necessarily free-verse but poetry. "People don't talk like that?" is the usual criticism leveled at the dialogue of Fry, Lorca, Racine, Giradeux, and Shakespeare, to name a few playwrghts in whose works dialogue is not used in dialectical form for theatrical effect, as it is openly by folk dramatists. Sean O' Casey, Yeats, Dylan Thomas, Singe; Fitch, Belasco, Marc Connelly are examples who accepted and used English free-verse poetic qualities and/or provincialisms in their dialogue. Synge indeed found conteemporary realisms of dialogsue flat and pallid, the emotionsl values monotonous and unexciting, the imagery lacking in suggestive power. Styles of acting may have been partly responsible for these theatre-stage effects upon the comic Irish playrwright. Yet it cannot be gainsaid, whether for theatrical artifice or folk-lore scene painting, that realism of dialogue is based upon colloquial, vulgar usages of trhe mother tongue. Any deviations violate the fiat, and in so violating it, may at least sound exotlic, if not poetic. On that point, it is quite true nowadays that when a critic, or a player or patron, or, may the gods forbid, a director cannot fix upon any precise poetic estimates of a romantic dramatist's work, he will name what is exotic as *poetry*; and if there betrue poetry in the work, call it crude folk idiom "poetically styled"or some such nonsense. Vulgar prose, then, may strike the note of realism; it fetters creative imagination to the experiential references of the vulgar language, although the character who actually speaks the lines may be potentially a more dramatic, profounder and more fascinating character personna. The upshot is that in order to satisfy popular tastes and personal likings, the popular playwright must sound like another OL"Hernry who believed in the **phonic**, although localized, reproduction of speech.

A hard and fast adherence to realism of dialogue promises that the metaphor, or simile, as a *poetic unit of expresion* cannot be verified by the inductive method of scince or the tests of logical empiricism! A simile or metaphor, however, is a consciously intended image-analogy whose referene value is in relation to the appropriateness of the emotion it arouses, and/or any kindred quality or characterictic peculiar to both image and the reality; or to the real in the drama's action. That isthe contradiction bvretween the presumed unverifiable and the acceptably real in metaphorical speech. Sceien 13 or 'act 5 in King Lear contained an apt illustration:

> He that parts us whall bring a brand
>   from heaven
> And fire us hence like foxes. Wipe thine
>   eyes;
> The good years shall devour them, flesh and
>   fell,
> Ere they shall make us weep. Well see 'em
>   starv'd first."

This speech by the ageing, anger-wracked Lear to his youngest daughter Cordelia, reunited as luckless prisoners, expresses experiences which (those which from among many) have deep-hidden emotional and intellecltual associations. This is true generally of metaphorical language. And it is those associations that have an undeniable influence upon a person's speech and his actions. Medical science has proved that these associations are clues to inumerable reality structures in a person's past. The poet recognizes those associations in his owns terms. - *CORYPHAEUS*

EDITORIALS

EDITORIAL - (1959)

SENATE fINANCE COMMITTEE
REINFORCES ACADEMIC MEDIOCRITY

The Senate Finance Committee's rider of mandatory alternatives for the State's textbook appropriation for the 1960-61 school year contains several angles politically noteworthy. The proscription for the books, seven million readers for seven million elementary school children, will influence young minds at perhaps the most critical stage in their entire learning regimen. The rider ostensibly, by interpretation of Atty. Genl. Stanley Mosk, states that the Department of Education must either buy State-printed texts under the current allotment of 12.4 million, passed by both houses of the Legislature; or it buys no books at all. This political game is bound to affect student academic achievement in the years to come.

Such an ultimatum, rendered by the Committee on Constitutional Rights, is a piece of ethical cowardice and slipshod gerrymandering for electoral votes. No books at at all, Senators? Surely you could not espouse so haphazard an all-or-none *secessionist* educational learning scheme as that. The Educators, exclusive of AFL-CIO union members, are willing to consider an alternative as leaders in the maintenance of academic standards, rather than in sociological mass-mind political appeals.

At first glance, it would appear that the additional 2.5 million books means, acording to "a stage offlicial," the rejection of all uniformity in these elementary texts, and that the burden of the charge rests upon"the school people." That is true if the Committeee considers "School people" factionalists, which they evidently do. It is equally as true that the criteria of cheapness and uniformlity are bureaucratic and collectivistic. The State wants uniformity and cheapness first, the priority consieration. The Board of Education places the quality of the chosen readers first--not simply multi-colored inks, side-marginal page numbering and bleed-off prints, but the selection and methodology of the wrtten contents.

Texts which the Board has in mind stand "handx and shoulders" above the cheaper books, according to the Associate State Superintendant of Public Instruction, Dr. Jay Davis Connor. The pub- lishers refuse to release the plates on their books to the State, consequently there the matter stands.

One Senator has branded the modernilzed texts as "trash." However, we have yet to read a sound declarative statement that the new texts treach the fundamentals of alphabet, grammar, syntax, phonetic spelling (wihout talking syllabic picturesl), these essentials, of course, worked into the context of the reading.

This *Review* nevertheless, objects to the ultimatum tactic, and at the same time tips the balance of decision in favor of the Educators, on political principal and on faith that in the classroom Fundaments teaching will continue to involve the basics, and that, ultimately, a politician's interest and the brand a"trash" are a weaker recommendation for a textbook than are the teachers' interests and the brand of "head and shoulders" superiority for a proven teaching method, as *phonics* instead of *look-say*, *basic math* instead of *new math*, and *reading comprehension* instead of *politically-correct axsumptions*.

Uniformity guarantrees, at best, mediocrity in the reading skills of clarity, speed, accuracy and comprehension., the last pendant upon the other three, and the last spendant upon the development of experimetal imagination by "by reaching," not by repetition past the maturation point of grasp. Uniformity also fixes standards at a common denominator level determined by purpose, vote and minimal attainment. It discourages outstanding ability, more plentiful in the potential than one would suspect, by holding it to a lowerr level of learning speed and comprehension,. Uniformity subjects teachers to a curriculum scope, challenge and administrative pressure that are balsically determined by ambitionus politicians responsive to the ballots of negligent voters who cannot be botherd or who would perpetuate their personal resentments. against teachers and their superstition against teachers and their suspicions of book learning.

Asaults on teacher reputations by Representative Walters and his Committee of quixotics, alarmist tactucs by J. Edgar Hoover in his personality sketches, Hearst'sensationalist press in his broadcast to a public without case facts or clear standards of judgement or ethical discrimination--these influences have tended to flatten out academic challenges, student achievement scores and curriculum incentives into charmilng affairs of administrative wish-thinking. These pernicious political influences force teachers to preserve their political reputations through their unions while diminishing the public's acceptance of new ideas, new materials. The politicization of teaching standards thus tends to level teacher competence rather than the reverse. And that *politicization* occurs by the politicians' trifling with teacher tenure.

Uniformity encourages individlual and institutional conformity to mass standards of achievement, hence we today are experiencing a deterioration on reading skills and in the students' powers of epression, although, paradoxically, there is more matter printed than at any other time in our history. Uniformity places the contents of teacher materials under the veto survei8llance of political factionalists and favoritism, thereby involving representatives who are anything but distinterested judges of texrtbook competence amd accuracy.

In time, and with the un-Consltitlutional intrusion of Federal Goverment into the affairs of State education, not only textbooks but teacher goals will bve moulded by bureaucratic oppoortunists, trade nionism and obstructionists bent upon their missions of party politics. The academic emphasis will then shift from teaching comprehension--standards, given token respect,as they are on Civll Service examinations--to personalities, disaffiliations, and party- line slants, with the rule-of-thumb being in the book (or course) functional and utilitarian? Uniformity as an absolute can become a pernicious influence. And yet--no books, unless the "school people" accept the rider on the sentate Finance

Committee's textbook alotment.

The Commitees recidivist attitude and Governor Brown's "neuitral silence" both partake highly of the sort of power politics that invites socialistic entreprisers to control the textbook situation in the Senate. And as the competent level of student reading-ability skills is gradually razed in the more learned and articulate communities, allthough the wealth may be elsewhere, tradel unionlism, teacher hiring halls and no-payh strikes may functionalize the job of feeding human lumber througfh the school mills--which can be profitable to lthe union barons as well as to political candidates supported by union- pressurized teachers. If and when any merit pay increase does occur, the teachers, as a group, will become the press lords' fall-guys before the paying public, the purchasers of advertising space under rising newprint costs. We've already had a taste of that propaganda.

The basis tenet that seems always to escape the organizers of that classroom teaching and orfganized political bias, within the classrooms, do not mix. Successfully uniformalize all reading materials, teaching methods, academic ideologies through unions fostered by a head-and-arms stocks political control and the union narons will become the intellectual dictators--tempered, of course, by an advertising-hungry press. Authority will then become fully cenralized; and instead of a group of teachers in voluntary and free associations, we will have an army of puppet parrots girded with the ideological paraphanalia of the central bureau in Washsington. This sketched evolution, quite in line withl the Eugene Debs theory of gradualist change, can come about by a closed-mind attutude of the voters who want cheapness, uniformity and utililtarianism first and foremost. To the blazes with lthe quality and character of the content.

Two and a half million dollars is much money, it is true; that amount will buy a tail assembly on a modern long-range bomber. But to show you how lopsided values are today, note that for the billions going into national defense, the millions raised and borrowed for the construction of State schools to handle increased enrollment, into highways, farm subsidies, property and housing loans and the VA program, we have the comparative value of seven million young minds. From these minds politician Brown and the Senate Finance Committee cannot be sure of getting returns commensurate with the additional textbook costs; they may lose votes; and the Republicans in the Senate, eyeing tight money, may cause their party to suffer eclipse in the next gubernatorial election. You may be sure that the lobbyists will get their cuts. Meanwhile, textbooks said to be superior in content and make-up may well be dumped into the garbage.

These seven million minds (1960) mean cultural wealth for tomorrow, not just financial wealth. If the public of this State are so niggardly and short-sighted that the additional sum means more to them than any such "giddy and reseate" vision of the morrow, then it can be safely assumed that, to the Senators, a superior educational opportunity in a basic commodity--high-quallity textbooks-- is worthless as a means of training youth to rise above mediocrity. And that mediocrity is more easily accepted as standard the more uniformly widespread it is, down to the last State precinct.

Mediocrity, in fine, is the product of the rigid application of mass standards of conformity to individluals in the use of their God-given gifts. There is the nexus of the problem--no inalienable rights of free expression but rather State imposition of bureauctaric standards of conformity.

> *NOTE: The <u>political correctness</u> of today is a leveling mechanism that is accepted by the media and university professors of America in order to perfect achievement, a creed to cause all to think alike. It is fostered by the messianic state that would save us from ourselves, from offending others, from thinking certain thoughts and using certain words by which the users thereof are damned by the apostles of the creed. It fosters a closed system of thinking and wars with Judeo-Christian faiths. Already <u>Political Correctness</u> has expelled God, the Ten Commandments, prayer both silent and vocal and visible expressions of those faiths. Liberals are unaware that it is a sterile creed, for it outlaws excellence.*

EDITORIAL

Inasmuch as our present Democratic Congress has passed what is said to be the largest income tax in America's history, some 400 billions of dollars, I thought it approrpiate to advance the thinking a little further...into the future of our present pre-teenagers and adolescents. This editorial appeared in my little magazine *The Critics' Review* in, approximately , 1959, almost half a century ago. I think that it is worth repeating.

At election time we often hear about "future generations" from the politicians. Few challenge their mendacy. We accept the phrase, like kissing babies, as a sort of American ploy of office-runners.

But benevolent legislators in Washington, DC, know little about the existence in America of child paupers. I do not mean the half-starved children in white Appalacia, or the children in impoverished areas of Alabama and Mississippi. Nor do I allude to the children who become urchins of the homeless.

By child I mean that age when the economy most benefits by the exploitation appeals to his or her future. By pauper I mean that state of the infant and pre-adolescent citizen who is condemned to future insolvency before he can put a key to his toy bank. Such a child is politicized in a way that the year of the child twaddle does not obscure.

The cause of his pauperism is that, as a small citizen, he is made to promise against his will that he will pay the bill of our benevolent central government, benevolent to the rest of the world first. He is conpelled by his benevolent benefactors in Washington to chose a state of insolvency as a future hope. He is made to surrender all expectation that when he comes of age he may live without onerous taxes that will eat up his substance and deprive him of his new home. He becomes an accomplice to the nation's deficit spending.

In the end, this child is made to swear mute loyallty to those politicians' schemes and wire-pulling, those trickeries and compromises of the Capitol. Hill caucuses which steal from his young pockets to make grown men rich and appease their envious ambitions as well as the world's envy. Ask a child what is the value of <u>his</u> dollar.

In short, the American child is pauperized by avaracious, lazy and ambitious grownups who put him in hock for the rest of his life. Those who vote for deficit spending--squandering Congressmen--put the child on the altar of political incompetence and greed before he comes of age. By their mindless spendig to mollify the elctorate, with the pork of bribery, and his interests viz al viz lobbyists, labor and big business, politicians borrow on the stamina and labor of future Americans, the children. Mere children, by their inclusion in the national debt as negotiable entities, sanctify the destruction of excellence by men of power in statecraft. Surely deficit spending into trillions of dollars of national debt cannot be excellence by any stretch of the imagination. The strength of the children becomes the strength of Washington' planners. Pauperized children thus grow up with the vague cultural memory of their indebtedness accrued by previous generations.

What must we do about this? Keep the child from knowing his dark, debt bound future? No. Psychologists speak highly of a child's ability to solve conundrms of power plays their adults hide. Watch children at play. They accept their own selfishness. Often thus the only sensible answer to this question is--adaptation. The learn to accept their pauperization by Federal indebtednesss to the rest of the world and to their own welfare.

The child must, however, be _told_ that he is poor. The most observant parents know that children are nowadays urged to gain wealth early in life. The child must be _told_ that he is negligent. Certainly it is not wickendness in him to be negligent, the only the true reason for his natural loneliness and his excuse to do as he pleases.

The child must be _urged_ to give to a cause, such as a milk fund or school baseball equipment. In this way the most expert of parents conceal from him that if he does not receive, certainly he did not work. And that having neither worked nor received he is put to no pains to conceal his lack from others. In fact, he may trade in upon that lack, telling his peers that he is a poverty-level kid.

These devices will accustom the child to the belief that the handout. his due, is more honorable than labor, and therefore should be extended into adulthood. Without suffering trauma, he will learn that plastic credit is a substitute for labor and therefore is more honorable than labor. By this devious route, government planners can be assured that future impoverished voters in sufficient numbers will either not vote because they do not understand the _pro quid pro_ exchange of power for the investment of citizen labor, or the function of labor to create the unique welfare program of entitlement. Thus the citizen indentured to entitements rarely ever asks. _Who pays for all of this?_ It is very likely that this attitude has its roots - in the pauperization of his childhood by a megalo-spending Federal government, the which is his inheritance.

EDITORIAL

The death penalty for capital offenses is not usually associated with savage or civilized societies but with those which lie between and are Medieval in custom, institutions and laws. In such societies, control by the State rests in the hands of royalty and the clergy instead of the common people. Some of the most inhuman punishments have been meted out in the name of religious doctrine and clerical piety, endorsed by the Crown. Where that State control has shifted downward, capital punishment has changed in methods of execution, and has been rendered more legally explicit and restricted in its application to certain types of crimes, those expressly defined by the laws. Quartering, beheading, impaling, death by drowning, gibbeting and burning were a frequent occurrence in the Middle Ages, notably lin England, until the early 19th century!--long after rthe Protestant Reformation. Switzerland, for example, prohibited impaling and entombment in about 1400, and death by drownintg in 1615. In Berlin in the year 1786, the last instance of burning at the stake took place; and no similar penalty had veen imposed for seventy years before. In 1814, in England, "Romilly tried in vain to substitute simple branding for treason in place of the existing penalty of hanging, cutting down alive, disembowling, cutting off the head, and quartering the body, these butcheries performed while the criminal was alive. Though that penalty which the law provided was not actually carried out (sic) in every instance, the members of Parliament were afraid that treason would be greatly increased if the law was modified: (1)Principles of Criminology (rev.) Sutherland, pp. 334-335) We can assume that there were pleaded mitigating circumstances.

Thus it is that human enlightenment has slowly made inroads upon the barbarities of punitive justice, and where Medieval punishments have resisted the more civilized edict or legislation, it will be found that opposition is maintained chiefly for the protection of property! Yet by its imposition, society attempts to purge itrself of a sense of guilt for miscreant acts, its deficiencies in self-discipline in home, business, schools or on the streets, its imperfections of authority and human controls within the institutions of its own making. The death penalty, a dire act of vengeance, increases human blood- thirst and excites cunning, the passions of hatred and utter social contempt. "So long as capital punishment exists, neurasthenic, emotional, erotic and sadistic feelings will inevitably color the attitude of those who prosecute murderers and those who read about them." (Ibid.)

The tendency of justice is toward the substitution of a permissive for a mandatory death spenalty, a reduction in the number of defined capital crimes, and in the number of executions. In the last century twenty-four countries abolished the death penalty entirely. In the Uniited States (1939) "five states have a mandatory death penalty for certain offenses (Connecticut, Massachusetts, Vermont, North Carolina, and New Mexico), thirty-seven States have a permissive death penalty, and six States do not permit the death penalty: (2) (Ibid. pp.560-561). They are Michigan, Wisconsin, Minnesota, North Dakota, Maine and Rhode Island.

Thus the abolition of the death penalty in California would not be without numerous precedents and historically logical in the civilization of man's codes of justice, which are attendant upon enlightened laws, authorities, and the reappraisal of the criminal's exchange value--his death for a personal safer society. Homicide rates in States sanctioning the death penalty are twice those in States that have aolished it. And, in the past, lynchings have markedly decreased within the orders sof States that have eliminated capital punishment from their penal codes. Not the death penalty, therefore, but the composition of the population and the cultural incitements within any section of the country, county or city determine the homicide rate. The efficacy of the death penalty as a deterrent to capital crime is perforce negligible.

Any deterrent value at all lies in the execurtion rather than in the legal possibilities. "The evidence, such as it is, shows relatively unimportant relationsship between the murder rate and the death penalty. The argument of the advocates of the death penalty that it is the most effective deterrent is, at least, not substantiated by the data available. It is based on preconceptions rather than on data, and the preconceptions are taken from the hedonistic psychology which assumes that the psychologicl processes are much less complex tlhan they are in fact. Even premeditated murders are generally committed under e stress of a great emotion and the penalty is seldom consiered." (4) ("New Republic" editorial, Apr.

21, 1926)

On the basis then of this sociololgical data, and for the reason that no meritorious or practical end would be served by Chessman;s execution, the which might redound to the benefit of society, the laws of the State, or to the improvement of penal methods and criminal trial procedure, and in the belief that regardless of how evil or sacred men deem the life of another, to will its destruction by formal rite is savage, sub-human, Godless and contemptible. This *Review* stands opposed to the execution of the death sentence in Chessman's case. Further , it requests that the Senate before the espiration of the 60 day grace period, enact a law that will abolish completely the sentence of death for capital offenses in the Sovereign State of Calfornia.

_____*Note: My position with regard to the death penalty is now compleltely reversed. While the death penalty tends to popularize exoneration of the murderer, it is much more enlightened to retain the penalty but reassure society that by DNA tests, they got the right man. Therefore, it is necessary that that Damocles Sword of lethal execution hang over the heads of the criminal, the prosecuror and the jury in our justice system. For not to do so is to enfeeble the penalty for heinous crimes and, in order to accord with popular judgement, acquit the truly guilty--which means no penalty whatsoever. Trial by popular consensus belongs to the Middle Ages: the more who affirmed or denied the accused's guilt, the more certain the verdict--the extension of modern political polling to comtemporary jury verdicts., the corruption aided and abetted by television.*

AN EDITORIAL

Appeared in The Critics' Review, 1960

An orchestra is "a band of perormers on various instruments, including especially those of the viol class, adapted for rendering symponies, overetures, etc." That is the definition of the Hon. and most respected Noah Webster, the American lexicographer. One is constrained, however, to lend a certain piquant stress, within the context of so apt a definition, to the phrase "band of performers." For, indeed, and if we but look sharply, we will see, in I'm sure, that the symymphony orchestra in this city of San Francisco does not stand alone under so singular a banner.

Furthemore, I make so bold as to say, that it is precisely for this reason our orchestra now finds itself so lamentably short of requisite funds for operation, the which pay the salaries of the members, the costs of auditions, guest artists, music and publicity; auditorium rental ...and a handsome rebate for the city fathers...travel and maintenance expenses <u>en voyage</u>, the salaries of publicity, personal and booking managers, to say nothing of the refurbishment of properties and pay for custodians, ticket and program printing expenses and fees for legal counsel.

These and other assuming budget items do mount up, and more especially, critical seems the present financial crisis whn we but survey those <u>bands of performers</u> who compete against the orchestra. They are numerous, but I shall attempt to ring up a few, not the least of which are die-hard philanthropists who dislike the director and/or his repertory of music; instrumentalists, and in every orchestra are a few, relices of the hiring-hall days wo feel compelled to take sides in the little gains of money-prestige and politics; a raft of chizzling added-expense markup grtifters whom the Sympohony Association takes nto its bosom an as needs requires; the tax-rebate gang who withdraw their support, vestial scions of charlty , with the Federal crackdown on company entertainment expense items; the Pope's black-frocked incense-burners whose political parish influenxce and jealous eyes would channel civic funds into the support of a religious, parochial art program; the casatatas of administrative tenure, usually joiners, for whom

424

neither membership nor contribution would be politically suspicious at this time; those belle dames of society whoce chief pleare iln life is to snub the one another and deliberately claw for higher advantage, in which tricks and poses their husbands are often the pawns, and so the taker-back of every good gift.... These foregoing are the "costs" for preserving the life of a major-city full orchstra.

Is it any wonder that in the light of these gentle amenities and rare foibles that this city's orchestra, in the year 1960, should find itself on the threshhold of liquidation and dissbanment (sic). I dare say not; nor will the orchesra's plight substantially improve—not until "lviing costs go down, but until those bands of political and financial parasites either abstain from interference or resolve their dilemmas of personal special interest wilthout any appreciative cost to the orchestra as a "band of musicians."

EDITORIAL

-in remembrance of-

On Federal Art Criticism As Censorship

Congressman Francis E. Walter, Chairman of the House of Un-American activities Committee, while in the process of seeking information toward the control and outlawing of communist activities in this Country, now demands that the State Departmen ban 34 out of the 67 paintings scheduled to be shown at the Moscow exhiition. His premise is that the canvasses are unrepresenentative of American life and, as such, they constitute ideological propaganda that, by distorting the true character of our people and our native ways, encourages the enemy against us. That is to say, that the 33 paintings in question constitute pictorial acts of *treason.*

Also, classified as once officially passed upon, the public may construe them, without evidence and with improper and inadequate Committee guarantees, to be ideologically in violaion of the Federal Constitution.

If these limplications are true, then the paintings, acceptable or not, serve the same ends as diplomatic correspondence, in which case not only the 34 but the remaining 33 have already passed through the censorship of one arbiter who, upon political grounds solely, has voted yea or nay on each work of art.

This being so, and without laws to support his aritrary

and oppressive action, Congressman Walter has delegated to himself extraordinary powers superseding the bounds established by law: namely, that the Congress shall "provide for the common Defense and general Welfare of the United States." If the paintings Walter demands be "purged" from exhibit in Moscow distort the picture of American life, then would impose a party-line philosophy and doctrinaire subjects upon all artists who could calll themselves loyal citizens. If there is _A_ picture of American life, then the man is either a fool or a charlatan, for there are a thousand perspectives from which one may regard every town and hamlet. If the paintings inflame men's passions, then Congressman Walter will be constrained to prohibit publishers, who will, from reproducing them in full color.

He must further propose the establishsment of a system of weights and measures that will calculate the passions which ought not to be inflamed. At that point, we shall need a National Board of Censorship for the Arts and Letters by which to adjudicate the harmful and dangerous political content of works that shall be exported abroad, published at public expense in State textbooks, and hung in non-private galleries, from which the hateful imposition of a tax in the form of a Federl license to paint, write and compose will inevitably follow.

Every implication that issues from Walter's action spells a travesty upon our funadamental freedoms, and in doing so, compels this little publication to denounce him and his Committee of misguided Quixotics as the ingenuous perpetrators of an action that is arbitrary, despotic and totally repugnant to an enlightened citizenry.

Neither members of the Departmet of State nor Conressmen may unjustly impugn the reputation of a citizen, slander his character or destroy the fruits of his lalbors--**under any circumstances**. Our laws do not license these forms of lawlessness. By Walter's demand that the 34 paintings be withdrawn, and by his

Committee's hearings for the purpose of censorship, they commit these acts of lawlessness, failing, in the event, to show just cause as to why the particular evidence, each canvas, is expressly treasonable. Thus they set themselves up, above all else, as art critics.

Other implications of Congressman Walter's tyrannical action are equally as odious. For not only are the interpretive experiences in a work of art confused with the *political communique*, since official political censorship so classifies the product of sensuous imagination; but the aesthetics of the artist must, pass bureaucratic political muster in future shows in order that the artist may obtain token liberty from despicable servitude, promote the political persuasions and personal biases of the censor(s) or be ruled out. The gross effect will be to regiment the thinking and aesthetics of future artists and, in the breech, to misrepresent officilly, or cause to be misrepresented, the peculiar facet of American life which the work of art purports to reveal.

Walter's action establishes an ominous precedent which, furthermore, if pursued, will endanger, intimidate, and cripple the efforts of those practicing artists who cannot, excepting by the use of force, be denied the right to circulate, have printed or in any way made public their writings, paintings and compositions that, knowingly if they are to come under the scrutiny of an alien government, do not and will not represent the current enmities, the opinions, the credulities and the fashions of an individual or of a Committee in Washsington. American life and character are far too complex to allow us to countenance, by our silence, the House Un-American Activities Committee's suppression of freedom of mind and the liberty of conscience that are ours under God above..
Charles E. Miller- FRONT AND CENTER 10-30-05

NOTE; We are well along that way today with the aversion to innovative ideas and original thinking promoted in our *universities by the impositon of the **Politically Correct** credo for judgement. We only lack a similar Committee under the **Patriot Act** to judge seditious literature and **political posters** for display on government property or in global art shows. The blunting of the Americn conscience--it's coming. **"The price of liberty is eternal vigilance."***

EDITORIAL

Charles E. Miller

There are times when the most momentous enterprize is wisely undertaken if its claims are least pretentious. For *The Critics' Review*--we prefer the modest and collctive reference o ourselves-- this is a commendable and most virtuous attitude. We do now entertain it to venture in our endeavors and to step further in the direction of a finer literary perspective and taste, wherever they may be found and pleassingly cultivated.

Over a year and a half ago, this organ embarked on a course primarily marked out along the lines of theatrical reviews, critiques, original plays, and any and all other writings of literary merit which *The Critics' Review* felt would add to your enjoyment of plays staged by our local player tlroupes. We had hoped, too, in the nature of events, that these writings would, in their own measure, enhance the literature of the theatre from whence there springs the diversion and inspiration of the players and audiences alike. We felt--that is *The Critics' Review* felt--that our efforts thus far have met with a response equal to the spirit of this enterprise, and we meditate scant doubt that they will do so in the future.

The time is now pendant, however, when it seems imperative that if *The Critics' Review* is to survive as an unassuming contribution to contmporary literature, this without the blessings of four-color photos and special features requiring enormous outlays of money and admirable credit resources, we must expand the scope of the Journal.

This means that hence forth, *The Critics' Review* shall endeavsor to include in its monthly issue brief but knowledgeable critical papers in the disciplines of fiction and philosophy. The plan will, of couse include the excellent book notes and reviews by our learned *R. A. Hornbook*, of reputable parts, who has recently joined the staff. In addition, *Coryphaeus,* a gentleman of erudition and said to be related by blood to the ancient House of Atreus, will render in clear translation some of his more dour points of view for your reflection. Meanwhile, we trust that you will continue to read and to enjoy *The Critics' Review*; for we feel that it stands in a great way toward becoming one of the finest little literary journals on the West Coast.